BELLAMY AND CHILD
EUROPEAN COMMUNITY
LAW OF COMPETITION

BELLAMY AND CHILD

EUROPEAN COMMUNITY LAW OF COMPETITION

SUPPLEMENT TO SIXTH EDITION

by

VIVIEN ROSE

Chairman of the Competition Appeal Tribunal

PETER ROTH

EDITOR (OVERSEAS CASE REPORTS)

Justice of the High Court and Chairman of the Competition Appeal Tribunal

OXFORD

UNIVERSITY PRESS

OXFORD

UNIVERSITY PRESS

Great Clarendon Street, Oxford ox2 6DP

Oxford University Press is a department of the University of Oxford.
It furthers the University's objective of excellence in research, scholarship,
and education by publishing worldwide in

Oxford New York

Auckland Cape Town Dar es Salaam Hong Kong Karachi
Kuala Lumpur Madrid Melbourne Mexico City Nairobi
New Delhi Shanghai Taipei Toronto

With offices in

Argentina Austria Brazil Chile Czech Republic France Greece
Guatemala Hungary Italy Japan Poland Portugal Singapore
South Korea Switzerland Thailand Turkey Ukraine Vietnam

Oxford is a registered trade mark of Oxford University Press
in the UK and in certain other countries

Published in the United States
by Oxford University Press Inc., New York

British Library Cataloguing in Publication Data

Data available

Library of Congress Cataloging in Publication Data

Data available

Typeset by Cepha Imaging Private Ltd, Bangalore, India
Printed in Great Britain
on acid-free paper by
Ashford Colour Press Ltd, Gosport, Hampshire

ISBN 978–0–19–958667–7

1 3 5 7 9 10 8 6 4 2

CONTENTS

PREFACE AND HIGHLIGHTS
OF THE SUPPLEMENT TO THE 6TH EDITION

This first supplement to the 6th edition of *Bellamy & Child*, combined with the 2010 edition of the Materials Volume, covers the substantial changes that have occurred in the two years since the main work was published. Those two years have seen seismic shifts in the economies of the Member States and competition law has had to respond to those shifts, particularly in the field of State aid. The content of this Supplement also reflects the steady ongoing work of the European Commission in analysing and reformulating the rules. The consequences of the Modernisation package introduced in May 2004 are clearly manifested in the dearth of material to be included in Chapter 7 relating to Joint Ventures and Similar Collaborative Arrangements. No doubt practitioners have been busy across Europe applying the competition provisions to these kinds of transactions. But they now pass below the radar of the enforcement institutions.

I am grateful to my co-editor Peter Roth, now Mr Justice Roth, for coordinating and editing the contributions from our Correspondent Editors who have been supplying us with information about significant decisions in their home states. The decisions of the competition authorities and courts in the other Member States are a valuable addition to the corpus of law and practice in this area as the decentralisation of enforcement becomes a reality post Modernisation. We are both very grateful to the Correspondent Editors for providing material for this Supplement.

Many thanks go too to John Boyce and Marzena Rembowski at the Brussels office of Slaughter and May for providing the updates for the tables in the Mergers chapter and for helping me to identify the decisions under the Merger Regulation which need to be included.

Thanks also to Andrew Macnab for his excellent work in ensuring that the Materials volume continues to be a comprehensive and user-friendly source book in this area.

Some of the issues which were 'unfinished business' at the time of the 6th edition have now been resolved. Most important is that just as the text of this Supplement was being finalised, the Lisbon Treaty was ratified and came into force. For competition specialists, another important development has been the judgments of the Court of Justice in both sets of proceedings concerning GlaxoSmithKline's response to the continuing parallel trade in the pharmaceuticals sector. Other matters still remain open at the time of writing, in particular the Commission's plans to provide guidance on actions for damages in the national courts. The following paragraphs refer to the principal changes that have occurred in respect of the topics covered.

Chapter 1. The Treaty and its Territorial Reach

The Reform Treaty – which became known as the Lisbon Treaty – finally overcame all obstacles, was ratified by the 27 Member States and came into effect on 1 December 2009. This brings about various changes to the nomenclature with which we are familiar including the replacement of the EC Treaty with the Treaty on the Functioning of the European Union; the renumbering of the Treaty articles; the disappearance of the term 'European Community' in favour of 'European Union'; and the renaming of the Court of First Instance as the General Court.

There have been further cases working out the effect of the expiry of the ECSC Treaty on the Commission's jurisdiction over antitrust infringements in the sectors formerly covered by that Treaty (Cases T-27/03, etc, *SP v Commission* [2007] ECR II-4331, [2008] 4 CMLR 176; Case T-405/06 *Arcelor Mittal v Commission*, judgment of 31 March 2009; Case T-25/04 *González y Díez v Commission*, judgment of 12 September 2007; and Case C-119/05 *Lucchini Siderurgia* [2007] ECR I-6199).

Chapter 2. Article 81(1)

The fundamental concepts of Article 81 [now Article 101 TFEU] continue to develop with clarification of the circumstances in which a shareholder is to be treated as part of the undertaking in which the shares are held: Case C-222/04 *Ministero dell'Economia e delle Finanze v Cassa di Risparmio di Firenze SpA* [2006] ECR I-289, [2008] 1 CMLR 705. The vexed question of when a State entity is carrying on economic activity which is caught by the competition rules was the subject of an important judgment of the Court of Justice in Case C-113/07 P *SELEX Sistemi Integrati SpA v Commission*, judgment of 26 March 2009 holding that the range of activities which are to be treated as connected with the exercise of public functions (and hence beyond the scope of the competition rules) is wider than the Court of First Instance had indicated in its judgment in the case. The occupation and use of publicly owned facilities was also considered in Case T-196/04 *Ryanair v Commission*, judgment of 17 December 2008, a State aid case where the Court of First Instance held that the fixing of the amount of landing charges at Charleroi airport and an indemnity granted to Ryanair by the Walloon Region was an economic activity. There have been several important cases on the elements required to establish a concerted practice: Case C-8/08 *T-Mobile*

Netherlands BV v Raad van bestuur van de Nederlandse Mededingingsautoriteit, judgment of 4 June 2009 where the Court held that the presumption of an effect on the market arising from continued presence of the undertakings on the market is an integral part of applicable Community law and therefore prevails when the national court is applying Article 101. Further, the Court held, the presumption applies even if the concerted action is the result of a meeting held by the participating undertakings on a single occasion rather than of a course of conduct. The circumstances in which a plausible alternative explanation for apparent parallel conduct is relevant to the existence of a concerted practice were considered in COMP/38.698 *CISAC*, 16 July 2008, [2009] 4 CMLR 577; and Case T-36/05 *Coats Holdings Ltd v Commission* [2007] ECR II-110, [2008] 4 CMLR 45. There have been several cases concerning when a series of meetings can be characterised as a 'single continuous infringement' with the Court of First Instance overturning part of the Commission's decision in *Choline Chloride*: see Cases T-101 & 111/05 *BASF AG and UCB SA v Commission* [2007] ECR II-4949, [2008] 4 CMLR 347.

Some of the discussion in the 6th edition of the conceptual issues surrounding competition and consumer detriment must now be read in the light of the Court of Justice's judgment in Cases C-501/06 P, etc, *GlaxoSmithKline Services Unlimited v Commission*, judgment of 6 October 2009. The Court of Justice overturned the Court of First Instance's analysis insofar as it held that it was necessary to prove that an agreement entails disadvantages for final consumers as a prerequisite for a finding of anti-competitive object. There have been other important cases on how to define the 'object' of an agreement for the purposes of Article 101(1), particularly Case C-209/07 *Beef Industry Development Society Ltd v Barry Brothers (Carrigmore) Meats Ltd* [2009] 4 CMLR 310, [2009] All ER (EC) 367; and *Bookmakers' Afternoon Greyhound Services v Amalgamated Racing Ltd* [2009] EWCA Civ 750 in the English Court of Appeal.

Chapter 3. Article 81(3)

The relationship between the two paragraphs of Article 101 in the post-Modernisation world has been considered by the Commission in some important recent decisions concerning payment card systems: COMP/37.860 *Morgan Stanley/Visa International and Visa Europe*, decn of 3 October 2007; and COMP/34.579 *MasterCard MIF charges*, decn of 19 December 2007, para 690.

Chapter 4. Market Definition

The payment card system decisions have also clarified the Commission's approach to analysing 'two-sided markets'; see also COMP/38.606 *Groupement des Cartes Bancaires*, decn of 17 October 2007; and Case M.4523 *Travelport/Worldspan* (21 August 2007). Cases under the Merger Regulation continue to provide illustrations of a wide variety of issues arising from market definition such as critical loss analysis (Case M.5141 *KLM/Martinair* (17 December 2008); and Case M.4734 *INEOS/Kerling* (30 January 2008)), shock analysis or event evidence (Case M.5046 *Friesland/Campina* (17 December 2008); and Case M.4734 *INEOS/Kerling* (30 January 2008)) and the relevance of in-house production (Case M.4731 *Google/DoubleClick* (11 March 2008); and Case M.4781 *Norddeutsche Affinerie/Cumerio* (23 January 2008)).

Chapter 5. Common Horizontal Agreements

The Commission has continued to impose substantial fines on cartels in recent years. The Court of First Instance upheld the Commission's finding that a trade association which provides administrative and secretarial assistance to a cartel can be regarded as a party to the cartel even if it is not itself a producer of the relevant product: Case T-99/04 *AC-Treuhand AG v Commission* [2008] ECR II-1501, [2008] 5 CMLR 962. Important decisions have been published in particular sectors: credit cards and payments systems (COMP/34.579 *MasterCard MIF charges*, decn of 19 December 2007; COMP/34.579 *MasterCard MIF charges*, decn of 19 December 2007; and COMP/38.606 *Groupement des Cartes Bancaires*, decn of 17 October 2007) and the collective licensing of music rights (COMP/38.698 *CISAC*, 16 July 2008, [2009] 4 CMLR 577).

The Court of First Instance continued to scrutinise closely the evidence on which findings of infringement are made, for example, quashing parts of the Commission's findings in Case T-36/05 *Coats Holdings Ltd v Commission* [2007] ECR II-110, [2008] 4 CMLR 45. The Commission's White Paper on Sport published in July 2007 indicates the kinds of rules in organised sport which are likely to comply with the competition rules.

Chapter 6. Vertical Agreements Affecting Distribution or Supply

The Commission is currently consulting on the revision of the current block exemption Regulation 2790/99 when it expires in 2010 and the proposed revised guidelines focus particularly on the development of online sales in the distribution of consumer goods. In the waste packaging recycling sector, the Court of Justice handed down an important decision in Case C-385/07 P *Der Grüne Punkt – Duales System Deutschland v Commission*, judgment of 16 July 2009 upholding the Commission's condemnation of the fees imposed for the licensing of the Green Dot logo.

Chapter 7. Joint Ventures and Similar Collaborative Arrangements

There is now little material available to indicate how the application of Article 101 to joint ventures outside the Merger Regulation is progressing after Modernisation.

Chapter 8. Merger Control

The Commission has issued a revised Notice on Remedies (OJ 2008 C267/1). The Notice provides guidance on different commitments that can be offered at any stage of the process, focusing particularly on divestiture. A new Form RM has been incorporated into the Implementing Regulation as Annex IV specifying the information and documents that undertakings should submit when offering commitments. The Commission has also issued Non-Horizontal Merger Guidelines setting out how it will analyse the competitive effects in vertical and conglomerate mergers. There have also been a number of important decisions analysing vertical mergers (Case M.5121 *News Corp/Premiere* (26 June 2008); Case M.4854 *TomTom/Tele Atlas* (14 May 2008); Case M.4942 *Nokia/Navteq* (2 July 2008); and Case M.4523 *Travelport/Worldspan* (21 August 2007)) and conglomerate mergers (Case M.4731 *Google/DoubleClick* (11 March 2008)).

The discussion in this chapter of oligopolistic markets must now be read in the light of the Court of Justice's judgment in Case C-413/06 P *Bertelsmann AG and Sony Corporation of America v Impala and Commission* [2008] ECR I-4951. The test for characterising a market as oligopolistic has been applied in a number of subsequent decisions, for example Case M.4980 *ABF/GBI Business* (23 September 2008); and Case M.5114 *Pernod Ricard/V&S Vin & Sprit* (17 August 2008). A number of decisions have discussed the role of a target company which operated as a 'maverick' constraint (Case M.4919 *Statoil/ConocoPhillips (Jet)* (21 October 2008); and Case M.4844 *Fortis/ABN Amro Assets* (3 October 2007)).

Finally, the proceedings brought against Spain under Article 21 of the Merger Regulation as a result of the impediments to a merger approved by the Commission have continued: Case C-196/07 *Commission v Spain*, judgment of 6 March 2008, [2008] ECR I-41*; and Case C-207/07 *Spain v Commission*, judgment of 17 July 2008, [2008] ECR I-111*.

Chapter 9. Intellectual Property Rights

The conflict between the Court of Justice's judgments in *Silhouette* and *Sebago* and the EFTA Court's judgment in *Mag Instrument* has now been resolved in favour of a consistent interpretation of Article 7 of Directive 89/104 and a prohibition on international exhaustion within the EEA: Cases E-9 & 10/07 *L'Oréal Norge v Per Aarskog AS*, decision of the EFTA Court 8 July 2008. The Court's judgment in C-275/06 *Promusicae* [2008] ECR I-276, [2008] All ER (EC) 809 considered the obligations imposed on an internet service provider to assist a rights holder by disclosing the identities of those using file sharing internet sites. The Court also upheld the Court of First Instance's analysis of the application of Article 82 [now Article 102] to the licensing fees set for the use of the Green Dot logo on recyclable packaging: Case C-385/07 P *Der Grüne Punkt – Duales System Deutschland v Commission*, judgment of 16 July 2009.

Chapter 10. Article 82

The Commission's Guidance on Enforcement Priorities in applying Article 82 to exclusionary conduct contains much useful guidance on how the Commission will approach issues such as defining anti-competitive foreclosure generally, and in relation to particular abuses such as exclusive dealing, tying and bundling, and predation. The Commission has also adopted the decision in COMP/37.990 *Intel*, decn of 13 May 2009 imposing substantial fines for exclusionary conduct.

The discussion of collective dominance focuses on the judgment of the Court of Justice in Case C-413/06 P *Bertelsmann AG and Sony Corporation of America v Impala and Commission* [2008] ECR I-4951. The Court describes the conditions in which collective dominance will arise. The Court emphasised the importance of avoiding a mechanical approach involving the separate verification of each of those criteria taken in isolation and emphasised that one must take account of the overall economic mechanism of a hypothetical tacit coordination.

There has been a series of decisions clarifying the law on margin squeeze: Case T-271/03 *Deutsche Telekom v Commission* [2008] ECR II-477, [2008] 5 CMLR 631; COMP/38.784 *Wanadoo España/Telefónica*, decn of 4 July 2007; and, in the English Court of Appeal *Dŵr Cymru Cyfyngedig v Albion Water Limited* [2008] EWCA Civ 536 on appeal from the Competition Appeal Tribunal. It is now clear that the correct test is 'equally efficient competitor' rather than the 'reasonably efficient competitor' and that there is no need to establish that the dominant undertaking's wholesale price was excessive.

The question of objective justification for alleged abusive behaviour was discussed by the Court of Justice in Cases C-468/06, etc, *Sot Lelos kai Sia EE v GlaxoSmithKline* [2008] ECR I-7139, [2008] 5 CMLR 1382, [2009] All ER (EC) 1 and there have been some interesting decisions on pricing issues: COMP/ 37.792 *Microsoft*, decn of 27 February 2008; and Case C-52/07 *Kanal 5 Ltd and TV 4 AB v Föreningen Svenska Tonsättares Internationella Musikbyrå (STIM) upa*, judgment of 11 December 2008.

Chapter 11. The Competition Rules and the Acts of Member States

The Commission's decision in COMP/39.562 *Slovakian postal legislation relating to hybrid mail services*, 7 October 2008, [2009] 4 CMLR 663 was an interesting application of the prohibition in Article 86(1) [now Article 106(1)] to the extension of a postal monopoly to a previously liberalised service. In two recent cases, the creation of an 'inequality of opportunity' in favour of the undertaking granted special or exclusive rights has been condemned: Case C-462/99 *Connect Austria*

[2003] ECR I-5197, [2005] 5 CMLR 302; and COMP/38.700 *Greek Lignite and Electricity generation*, decn of 5 March 2008, [2009] 4 CMLR 495.

Chapter 12. Sectoral Regimes

There have been several legislative developments in the transport sectors with a new enabling regulation (Regulation 246/2009) and a new block exemption regulation (Regulation 906/2009) for liner consortia. There is also a new Code of Conduct for airline computer reservation systems (Regulation 2299/89) and a new enabling regulation in the air transport sector (Regulation 487/2009). The Commission has also issued guidance on the application of Article 81 to maritime transport services.

New directives which will replace the Electricity and Gas Directives referred to in the section dealing with energy matters have been adopted and there have been some interesting cases on the application of the competition rules in the energy sector, notably COMP/38.700 *Greek Lignite and Electricity generation,* decn of 5 March 2008, [2009] 4 CMLR 495 concerning exclusive access to lignite deposits in Greece; and cases concerning terms in energy supply contracts that have been modified following the Commission's intervention, for example COMP/39.388 & /39.389 *E.ON German electricity markets*, decn of 26 November 2008 (commitments accepted); COMP/37.811 *Algerian gas imports* Press Release IP/07/1074 (11 July 2007) (territorial restrictions removed); and COMP/37.966 *Distrigas*, decn of 11 October 2007 (long-term supply contracts modified).

In the field of electronic communications, the new package of measures originally proposed by the Commission in November 2007 was finally approved by the Council of Ministers shortly after the cut-off date for this supplement. Brief details have been incorporated in the text. The 2003 Recommendation on relevant markets has been replaced by a new Recommendation which reduces the number of markets in which *ex ante* regulation is warranted to seven, and the Postal Directive has been amended to require Member States to abolish any remaining reserved monopolies granted to the universal service provider.

Chapter 13. Enforcement and Procedure

There have been many cases concerning procedural matters – the Commission imposed a substantial fine for the breach of a seal affixed during an investigation at an undertaking's premises (COMP/39.326 *E.ON (breach of seal)*, decn of 30 January 2008, [2009] 4 CMLR 371) and there have been several judgments concerning the content of the statement of objections (see for example Case C-413/06 P *Bertelsmann AG and Sony Corporation of America v Impala and Commission* [2008] ECR I-4951; Cases C-322/07 P, etc, *Papierfabrik August Koehler AG and Bolloré SA v Commission*, judgment of 3 September 2009; and Cases C-101 &

110/07 P *Coop de France bétail et viande and FNSEA v Commission* [2009] 4 CMLR 743).

The Commission has introduced a new settlement procedure to complement the existing Leniency Notice (see Regulation 622/2008 amending Regulation 773/2004) and has published a Notice explaining how the procedure will apply.

On fines, the Community Courts have upheld the Commission's practice of dividing cartel participants of different sizes into banded categories for the purpose of setting the starting amount of the fine (Case T-68/04 *SGL Carbon AG v Commission* [2009] 4 CMLR 7) and the Court of Justice has confirmed the presumption of parental liability for the conduct of a wholly owned subsidiary (Case C-97/08 P *Akzo Nobel NV v Commission*, judgment of 10 September 2009).

A number of cases have considered the effect on the time limit for appealing to the Court of First Instance of the Commission's practice of publishing the text of a decision on the web before or instead of publishing the full text in the Official Journal (Case T-48/04 *Qualcomm Wireless Business Solutions v Commission*, judgment of 19 June 2009; and Case T-388/02 *Kronoply and Kronotex v Commission*, judgment of 10 December 2008).

The Court of Justice has handed down its judgment concerning the liability of the Commission for loss caused by a defective decision in Case C-440/07 P *Commission v Schneider Electric*, judgment of 16 July 2009 and there have been other cases in which claims for damages have been dismissed by the Court of First Instance, such as Case T-344/04 *Bouychou v Commission*, judgment of 17 July 2007, [2007] ECR II-91*.

Chapter 14. The Enforcement of the Competition Rules in the Member States

The Court of Justice has clarified the scope of the Commission's power to intervene in proceedings in national courts under Article 15 of Regulation 1/2003, holding that the power can be exercised even if the proceedings concerned do not pertain directly to the application of Articles 101 and 102: Case C-429/07 *Inspecteur van de Belastingdienst v X BV*, judgment of 11 June 2009.

The Commission's White Paper on actions for damages published in April 2008 recommends various procedural steps that the Member States could take to facilitate follow-on claims and the English Courts have considered a number of issues arising in such claims such as the availability of restitutionary remedies: *Devenish Nutrition v Sanofi-Aventis* [2008] EWCA Civ 1086; and the point at which proceedings should be stayed in the event of a challenge to the infringement decision on which the claimant relies: *National Grid Electricity Transmission plc v ABB Ltd* [2009] EWHC 1326 (Ch).

Chapter 15. State Aids

There has been a substantial volume of legislation on State aids since the 6th edition, some of which was planned as part of the State Aid Action Plan and some of which was a response to the banking crisis and the subsequent economic downturn. As to the former category, the General Block Exemption Regulation has replaced the three previous block exemptions. The new block exemption increases the aid intensities and notification ceilings allowed by the previous exemptions and introduces additional exemptions for various kinds of aid measures. Guidance on the application of the State aid rules to environmental protection measures and to aid in the form of guarantees has also been issued. Finally, the Simplification Package has introduced a simplified procedure for the notification of certain kinds of State aid. The Commission has responded to the banking crisis by issuing guidance about aid schemes aimed at stabilising individual financial institutions and taking a large number of individual decisions approving aid. It has also introduced a temporary Community framework for measures aimed at helping the real economy to recover.

There continues to be a great deal of litigation on the different elements which make up a State aid, including the application of the *Altmark* criteria (Cases T-309/04, etc, *TV2/Danmark v Commission*, judgment of 22 October 2008; and Case T-266/02 *Deutsche Post v Commission* [2008] ECR II-1233), the 'market economy investor principle' (Case T-455/05 *Componenta v Commission*, judgment of 18 December 2008; and Case T-196/04 *Ryanair v Commission*, judgment of 17 December 2008) and the criterion of selectivity in relation to regional tax measures (Cases T-211 & T-215/04 *Gibraltar v Commission*, judgment of 18 December 2008).

Significant developments as regards the role of the Member State in recovering unlawful aids have been made in the jurisprudence of the Court of Justice. The Court has clarified the effect of the final sentence of Article 88(3) EC in national courts (Case C-199/06 *CELF v SIDE* [2008] ECR I-469, [2008] 2 CMLR 561; and Case C-384/07 *Wienstrom v Bundesminister für Wirtschaft und Arbeit*, judgment of 18 December 2008). The Court has also considered when damages ordered to be paid by a Member State to a recipient of unlawful aid can be set off against the aid that the State is bound to recover: Case C-369/07 *Commission v Greece (Olympic Airways)*, judgment of 7 July 2009. The Commission has also focused on the role of the Member State in this area of the law, issuing a new Notice on the enforcement of State aid law by national courts and a Notice towards an effective implementation of Commission decisions ordering a Member State to recover unlawful aid.

The vexed question of when an undertaking is directly and individually affected by a Commission refusal to open the formal procedure and a Commission decision on the compatibility of an aid with the common market has continued to generate much case law, see for example Cases T-254/00, etc, *Hotel Cipriani v Commission*, judgment of 28 November 2008; Case C-487/06 P *British Aggregates Association v Commission*, judgment of 22 December 2008; and Case T-388/03 *Deutsche Post et DHL International v Commission*, judgment of 10 February 2009.

I have attempted to ensure that the book is up-to-date to 31 October 2009. All remaining errors and omissions are my responsibility. Since the updating of the main work is likely to be an ongoing exercise, I would be grateful if keen readers would send me a note at the Competition Appeal Tribunal if they spot anything amiss. For the sake of good order I should again make clear on my own behalf and on behalf of Mr Justice Roth that any views expressed in this Supplement should not be taken to indicate how the High Court or the Competition Appeal Tribunal may decide any issue that falls for determination in the future.

Finally may I thank Luke Adams and the team at Oxford University Press for their continued support and patience in the evolution of this work and my friends and colleagues at the Competition Appeal Tribunal who continue to make practice in this area both fascinating and enjoyable.

Vivien Rose
1 December 2009

NOTE ON THE LISBON TREATY

The Treaty of Lisbon came into force on 1 December 2009 and replaced the Treaty on European Union and the EC Treaty with a new Treaty on European Union ('TEU') and a Treaty on the Functioning of the European Union ('TFEU'). Although the term 'European Community' has now passed into history, the title of this volume still reflects the name of the main work *European Community Law of Competition* to which it is the Supplement.

The Lisbon Treaty also resulted in a renumbering of the articles of the former EC Treaty, most of which are now incorporated into the TFEU. In the text of the Supplement the new article number is indicated alongside the EC Treaty article unless this would clutter up the text. But where a paragraph or footnote in the main work needs updating only because of the changes of the numbering, this has not merited an update paragraph in the Supplement. The wording of the chapter headings and sub-headings and the bold lead-in sentences of the paragraphs have not been changed since the aim of these is to enable the reader to orient themselves from the text of the main work to the relevant paragraphs of the Supplement. The Tables of Equivalences published in the *Official Journal* are reproduced in this Supplement for the readers' convenience.

Under the Lisbon Treaty the whole court system of the European Union will be known as the Court of Justice of the European Union, currently comprising three courts: the Court of Justice, the General Court (that is, the former Court of First Instance) and the Civil Service Tribunal. However, all the judgments referred to in this Supplement were delivered before 1 December 2009 and the abbreviations 'ECJ' and 'CFI' are used throughout.

ALPHABETICAL TABLE OF
EU CASES AND DECISIONS

TABLES OF EUROPEAN COURT OF HUMAN RIGHTS, EFTA COURT AND NATIONAL CASES

CASES PUBLISHED SINCE THE 6TH EDITION

The following cases in the Courts
of the European Communities have
been published in the law reports
since the 6th edition (the judgment
date is given when only a summary
has been published in the ECR)

AEESCAM v Commission (T-95/03) [2006] ECR-II 4739
AEPI v Commission (T-229/05) judgment of 12 July 2007, [2007] ECR II-84*
Akzo Nobel Chemicals and Akcros Chemicals v Commission (T-125 & 253/03) [2007]
    ECR II-3523, [2008] 4 CMLR 97, [2008] All ER (EC) 1
Alrosa v Commission (T-170/06) [2007] ECR II-2601, [2007] 5 CMLR 493
Annemans v Commission (T-411/05), judgment of 12 July 2007, [2007] ECR II-87*
Asklepios Kliniken v Commission (T-167/04) [2007] ECR II-2379
Au Lys de France v Commission (T-458/04) judgment of 3 July 2007, [2007] ECR II-71*
Britannia Alloys v Commission (C-76/06 P) [2007] ECR I-4405, [2007] 5 CMLR 251
British Airways v Commission (C-95/04 P) [2007] ECR-I 2331, [2007] 4 CMLR 982
Boehringer Ingelheim II (C-348/04) [2007] ECR I-3391, [2007] 2 CMLR 1445
Bolloré v Commission (T-109/02, etc) [2007] ECR-II 947, [2007] 5 CMLR 66
Bouygues v Commission (T-475/04) [2007] ECR II-2097
City Motors Groep v Citroën Belux (C-421/05) [2007] ECR I-653, [2007] 4 CMLR 455
Commission v Netherlands (C-523/04) [2007] ECR I-3267, [2007] 2 CMLR 1299
Commission v Volkswagen (C-74/04 P) [2006] ECR I-6585, [2008] 4 CMLR 1297,
    [2007] ICR 217
Dalmine v Commission (C-407/04 P) [2007] ECR I-829
Degussa v Commission (T-279/02) [2006] ECR II-897, [2008] 5 CMLR 7
Endesa v Commission (T-417/05) (judgment) [2006] ECR II-2533, [2008] 4 CMLR 1472
FNCBV and FNSEA v Commission ('French Beef') (T-217 & 245/03) [2006] ECR II-4987,
    [2008] 5 CMLR 406
France Télécom v Commission (T-340/03) [2007] ECR I-107, [2007] 4 CMLR 919, [2008]
    All ER (EC) 677
France Télécom v Commission (T-339/04) [2007] ECR II-521, [2008] 5 CMLR 502
France Télécom v Commission (T-340/04) [2007] ECR II-573
Germany v Commission (C-506/03) judgment of 24 November 2005 (unpublished)
Groupe Danone v Commission (C-3/06 P) [2007] ECR I-1331, [2007] 4 CMLR 701
Groupement des cartes bancaires (CB) v Commission (T-266/03) judgment of 12 July 2007,
    [2007] ECR II-83*
Grüne Punkt – Duales System Deutschland v Commission (T-151 & 289/01) [2007] ECR
    II-1607 (Art 82) and 1691 (Art 81), [2007] 5 CMLR 300 (Art 82) and 356 (Art 81)
Holcim (Deutschland) v Commission (C-282/05P) [2007] ECR I-2941, [2007] 4 CMLR 1090
Microsoft Corp v Commission (T-201/04) [2007] ECR II-3601, [2007] 5 CMLR 846
Ministero dell'Industria v Lucchini (C-119/05), [2007] ECR-I 6199

MyTravel v Commission (T-212/03), judgment of 11 July 2007 not yet published

Peróxidos Orgánicos v Commission (T-120/04) [2006] ECR II-4441, [2007] 4 CMLR 153

Raiffeisen Zentralbank Österreich v Commission (T-259/02) [2006] ECR II-5169, [2007]
    5 CMLR 1142

Salzgitter Mannesmann v Commission (C-411/04 P) [2007] ECR I-959, [2007] 4 CMLR 682

Schneider Electric v Commission (T-351/03) [2007] ECR II-2237, [2008] 4 CMLR 1533

SELEX Sistemi Integrati v Commission (T-155/04) [2006] ECR II-4797, [2007] 4 CMLR 372

SGL Carbon v Commission (C-328/05 P) [2007] ECR I-3921, [2007] 5 CMLR 16

Sumitomo Metal Industries v Commission ('Seamless Steel Tubes') (C-403 & 405/04 P) [2007]
    ECR I-729, [2007] 4 CMLR 650

Sun Chemical Group v Commission, (T-282/06) [2007] ECR II-2149, [2007] 5 CMLR 438

Technische Glaswerke Ilmenau v Commission (C-404/04 P) judgment of 11 January 2007,
    [2007] ECR I-1*

Ter Lembeek International v Commission (T-217/02) [2006] ECR II-4483

Tirrenia di Navigazione v Commission (T-246/99) judgment of 20 June 2007, [2007]
    ECR II-65*

Unibet (C-432/05) [2007] ECR I-2271

Westfalen Gassen Nederland v Commission (T-303/02) [2006] ECR II-4567, [2007]
    4 CMLR 334

TABLES OF EQUIVALENCES (*)
(CONDENSED)

Treaty on European Union

Old numbering of the Treaty on European Union	New numbering of the Treaty on European Union
TITLE I — COMMON PROVISIONS	TITLE I — COMMON PROVISIONS
Article 1	Article 1
	Article 2
Article 2	Article 3
Article 3 (repealed)(¹)	
	Article 4
	Article 5 (²)
Article 4 (repealed) (³)	
Article 5 (repealed) (⁴)	
Article 6	Article 6
Article 7	Article 7
	Article 8
TITLE II — PROVISIONS AMENDING THE TREATY ESTABLISHING THE EUROPEAN ECONOMIC COMMUNITY WITH A VIEW TO ESTABLISHING THE EUROPEAN COMMUNITY	TITLE II — PROVISIONS ON DEMOCRATIC PRINCIPLES
Article 8 (repealed) (⁵)	Article 9
	Article 10 (⁶)

(¹) Replaced, in substance, by Article 7 of the Treaty on the Functioning of the European Union ('TFEU') and by Articles 13(1) and 21, paragraph 3, second subparagraph of the Treaty on European Union ('TEU').
(²) Replaces Article 5 of the Treaty establishing the European Community ('TEC').
(³) Replaced, in substance, by Article 15.
(⁴) Replaced, in substance, by Article 13, paragraph 2.
(⁵) Article 8 TEU, which was in force until the entry into force of the Treaty of Lisbon (hereinafter 'current'), amended the TEC. Those amendments are incorporated into the latter Treaty and Article 8 is repealed. Its number is used to insert a new provision.
(⁶) Paragraph 4 replaces, in substance, the first subparagraph of Article 191 TEC.

(*) Tables of equivalences as referred to in Article 5 of the Treaty of Lisbon. The original centre column, which set out the intermediate numbering as used in that Treaty, has been omitted.

Old numbering of the Treaty on European Union	New numbering of the Treaty on European Union
	Article 11
	Article 12
TITLE III — PROVISIONS AMENDING THE TREATY ESTABLISHING THE EUROPEAN COAL AND STEEL COMMUNITY	TITLE III — PROVISIONS ON THE INSTITUTIONS
Article 9 (repealed) [7]	Article 13
	Article 14 [8]
	Article 15 [9]
	Article 16 [10]
	Article 17 [11]
	Article 18
	Article 19 [12]
TITLE IV — PROVISIONS AMENDING THE TREATY ESTABLISHING THE EUROPEAN ATOMIC ENERGY COMMUNITY	TITLE IV — PROVISIONS ON ENHANCED COOPERATION
Article 10 (repealed) [13] Articles 27a to 27e (replaced) Articles 40 to 40b (replaced) Articles 43 to 45 (replaced)	Article 20 [14]

[7] The current Article 9 TEU amended the Treaty establishing the European Coal and Steel Community. This latter expired on 23 July 2002. Article 9 is repealed and the number thereof is used to insert another provision.

[8] — Paragraphs 1 and 2 replace, in substance, Article 189 TEC;
— paragraphs 1 to 3 replace, in substance, paragraphs 1 to 3 of Article 190 TEC;
— paragraph 1 replaces, in substance, the first subparagraph of Article 192 TEC;
— paragraph 4 replaces, in substance, the first subparagraph of Article 197 TEC.

[9] Replaces, in substance, Article 4.

[10] — Paragraph 1 replaces, in substance, the first and second indents of Article 202 TEC;
— paragraphs 2 and 9 replace, in substance, Article 203 TEC;
— paragraphs 4 and 5 replace, in substance, paragraphs 2 and 4 of Article 205 TEC.

[11] — Paragraph 1 replaces, in substance, Article 211 TEC;
— paragraphs 3 and 7 replace, in substance, Article 214 TEC;
— paragraph 6 replaces, in substance, paragraphs 1, 3 and 4 of Article 217 TEC.

[12] — Replaces, in substance, Article 220 TEC;
— the second subparagraph of paragraph 2 replaces, in substance, the first subparagraph of Article 221 TEC.

[13] The current Article 10 TEU amended the Treaty establishing the European Atomic Energy Community. Those amendments are incorporated into the Treaty of Lisbon. Article 10 is repealed and the number thereof is used to insert another provision.

[14] Also replaces Articles 11 and 11a TEC.

Treaty on the Functioning of the European Union

Old numbering of the Treaty establishing the European Community	New numbering of the Treaty on the Functioning of the European Union
PART ONE — PRINCIPLES	PART ONE — PRINCIPLES
Article 1 (repealed)	
	Article 1
Article 2 (repealed) ([25])	
	Title I — Categories and areas of union competence
	Article 2
	Article 3
	Article 4
	Article 5
	Article 6
	Title II — Provisions having general application
	Article 7
Article 3, paragraph 1 (repealed) ([26])	
Article 3, paragraph 2	Article 8
Article 4 (moved)	Article 119
Article 5 (replaced) ([27])	
	Article 9
	Article 10
Article 6	Article 11
Article 153, paragraph 2 (moved)	Article 12
	Article 13 ([28])
Article 7 (repealed) ([29])	
Article 8 (repealed) ([30])	
Article 9 (repealed)	
Article 10 (repealed) ([31])	
Article 11 (replaced) ([32])	Articles 326 to 334

([25]) Replaced, in substance, by Article 3 TEU.
([26]) Replaced, in substance, by Articles 3 to 6 TFEU.
([27]) Replaced, in substance, by Article 5 TEU.
([28]) Insertion of the operative part of the protocol on protection and welfare of animals.
([29]) Replaced, in substance, by Article 13 TEU.
([30]) Replaced, in substance, by Article 13 TEU and Article 282, paragraph 1, TFEU.
([31]) Replaced, in substance, by Article 4, paragraph 3, TEU.
([32]) Also replaced by Article 20 TEU.

Old numbering of the Treaty establishing the European Community	New numbering of the Treaty on the Functioning of the European Union
Article 11a (replaced) ([32])	Articles 326 to 334
Article 12 (repealed)	Article 18
Article 13 (moved)	Article 19
Article 14 (moved)	Article 26
Article 15 (moved)	Article 27
Article 16	Article 14
Article 255 (moved)	Article 15
Article 286 (moved)	Article 16
	Article 17
PART TWO — CITIZENSHIP OF THE UNION	PART TWO — NON-DISCRIMINATION AND CITIZENSHIP OF THE UNION
Article 12 (moved)	Article 18
Article 13 (moved)	Article 19
Article 17	Article 20
Article 18	Article 21
Article 19	Article 22
Article 20	Article 23
Article 21	Article 24
Article 22	Article 25
PART THREE — COMMUNITY POLICIES	PART THREE — POLICIES AND INTERNAL ACTIONS OF THE UNION
	Title I — The internal market
Article 14 (moved)	Article 26
Article 15 (moved)	Article 27
Title I — Free movement of goods	Title II — Free movement of goods
Article 23	Article 28
Article 24	Article 29
Chapter 1 — The customs union	Chapter 1 — The customs union
Article 25	Article 30
Article 26	Article 31
Article 27	Article 32
Part Three, Title X, Customs cooperation (moved)	Chapter 2 — Customs cooperation
Article 135 (moved)	Article 33
Chapter 2 — Prohibition of quantitative restrictions between Member States	Chapter 3 — Prohibition of quantitative restrictions between Member States

Old numbering of the Treaty establishing the European Community	New numbering of the Treaty on the Functioning of the European Union
Article 28	Article 34
Article 29	Article 35
Article 30	Article 36
Article 31	Article 37
Title II — Agriculture	Title III — Agriculture and fisheries
Article 32	Article 38
Article 33	Article 39
Article 34	Article 40
Article 35	Article 41
Article 36	Article 42
Article 37	Article 43
Article 38	Article 44
Title III — Free movement of persons, services and capital	Title IV — Free movement of persons, services and capital
Chapter 1 — Workers	Chapter 1 — Workers
Article 39	Article 45
Article 40	Article 46
Article 41	Article 47
Article 42	Article 48
Chapter 2 — Right of establishment	Chapter 2 — Right of establishment
Article 43	Article 49
Article 44	Article 50
Article 45	Article 51
Article 46	Article 52
Article 47	Article 53
Article 48	Article 54
Article 294 (moved)	Article 55
Chapter 3 — Services	Chapter 3 — Services
Article 49	Article 56
Article 50	Article 57
Article 51	Article 58
Article 52	Article 59
Article 53	Article 60
Article 54	Article 61
Article 55	Article 62
Chapter 4 — Capital and payments	Chapter 4 — Capital and payments

Old numbering of the Treaty establishing the European Community	New numbering of the Treaty on the Functioning of the European Union
Article 56	Article 63
Article 57	Article 64
Article 58	Article 65
Article 59	Article 66
Article 60 (moved)	Article 75
Title IV — Visas, asylum, immigration and other policies related to free movement of persons	Title V — Area of freedom, security and justice
	Chapter 1 — General provisions
Article 61	Article 67 (³³)
	Article 68
	Article 69
	Article 70
	Article 71 (³⁴)
Article 64, paragraph 1 (replaced)	Article 72 (³⁵)
	Article 73
Article 66 (replaced)	Article 74
Article 60 (moved)	Article 75
	Article 76
	Chapter 2 — Policies on border checks, asylum and immigration
Article 62	Article 77
Article 63, points 1 et 2, and Article 64, paragraph 2 (³⁶)	Article 78
Article 63, points 3 and 4	Article 79
	Article 80
Article 64, paragraph 1 (replaced)	Article 72
	Chapter 3 — Judicial cooperation in civil matters
Article 65	Article 81
Article 66 (replaced)	Article 74

(³³) Also replaces the current Article 29 TEU.
(³⁴) Also replaces the current Article 36 TEU.
(³⁵) lso replaces the current Article 33 TEU.
(³⁶) Points 1 and 2 of Article 63 EC are replaced by paragraphs 1 and 2 of Article 78 TFEU, and paragraph 2 of Article 64 is replaced by paragraph 3 of Article 78 TFEU.

Old numbering of the Treaty establishing the European Community	New numbering of the Treaty on the Functioning of the European Union
Article 67 (repealed)	
Article 68 (repealed)	
Article 69 (repealed)	
	Chapter 4 — Judicial cooperation in criminal matters
	Article 82 ([37])
	Article 83 ([37])
	Article 84
	Article 85 ([37])
	Article 86
	Chapter 5 — Police cooperation
	Article 87 ([38])
	Article 88 ([38])
	Article 89 ([39])
Title V — Transport	Title VI — Transport
Article 70	Article 90
Article 71	Article 91
Article 72	Article 92
Article 73	Article 93
Article 74	Article 94
Article 75	Article 95
Article 76	Article 96
Article 77	Article 97
Article 78	Article 98
Article 79	Article 99
Article 80	Article 100
Title VI — Common rules on competition, taxation and approximation of laws	Title VII — Common rules on competition, taxation and approximation of laws
Chapter 1 — Rules on competition	Chapter 1 — Rules on competition
Section 1 — Rules applying to undertakings	Section 1 — Rules applying to undertakings
Article 81	Article 101
Article 83	Article 103

([37]) Replaces the current Article 31 TEU.
([38]) Replaces the current Article 30 TEU.
([39]) Replaces the current Article 32 TEU.

Old numbering of the Treaty establishing the European Community	New numbering of the Treaty on the Functioning of the European Union
Article 84	Article 104
Article 85	Article 105
Article 86	Article 106
Section 2 — Aids granted by States	Section 2 — Aids granted by States
Article 87	Article 107
Article 88	Article 108
Article 89	Article 109
Chapter 2 — Tax provisions	Chapter 2 — Tax provisions
Article 90	Article 110
Article 91	Article 111
Article 92	Article 112
Article 93	Article 113
Chapter 3 — Approximation of laws	Chapter 3 — Approximation of laws
Article 95 (moved)	Article 114
Article 94 (moved)	Article 115
Article 96	Article 116
Article 97	Article 117
	Article 118
Title VII — Economic and monetary policy	Title VIII — Economic and monetary policy
Article 4 (moved)	Article 119
Chapter 1 — Economic policy	Chapter 1 — Economic policy
Article 98	Article 120
Article 99	Article 121
Article 100	Article 122
Article 101	Article 123
Article 102	Article 124
Article 103	Article 125
Article 104	Article 126
Chapter 2 — monetary policy	Chapter 2 — monetary policy
Article 105	Article 127
Article 106	Article 128
Article 107	Article 129

Old numbering of the Treaty establishing the European Community	New numbering of the Treaty on the Functioning of the European Union
Article 108	Article 130
Article 109	Article 131
Article 110	Article 132
Article 111, paragraphs 1 to 3 and 5 (moved)	Article 219
Article 111, paragraph 4 (moved)	Article 138
	Article 133
Chapter 3 — Institutional provisions	Chapter 3 — Institutional provisions
Article 112 (moved)	Article 283
Article 113 (moved)	Article 284
Article 114	Article 134
Article 115	Article 135
	Chapter 4 — Provisions specific to Member States whose currency is the euro
	Article 136
	Article 137
Article 111, paragraph 4 (moved)	Article 138
Chapter 4 — Transitional provisions	Chapter 5 — Transitional provisions
Article 116 (repealed)	
	Article 139
Article 117, paragraphs 1, 2, sixth indent, and 3 to 9 (repealed)	
Article 117, paragraph 2, first five indents (moved)	Article 141, paragraph 2
Article 121, paragraph 1 (moved) Article 122, paragraph 2, second sentence (moved) Article 123, paragraph 5 (moved)	Article 140 (^{40})
Article 118 (repealed)	
Article 123, paragraph 3 (moved) Article 117, paragraph 2, first five indents (moved)	Article 141 (^{41})
Article 124, paragraph 1 (moved)	Article 142
Article 119	Article 143

(^{40}) — Article 140, paragraph 1 takes over the wording of paragraph 1 of Article 121.
    — Article 140, paragraph 2 takes over the second sentence of paragraph 2 of Article 122.
    — Article 140, paragraph 3 takes over paragraph 5 of Article 123.
(^{41}) — Article 141, paragraph 1 takes over paragraph 3 of Article 123.
    — Article 141, paragraph 2 takes over the first five indents of paragraph 2 of Article 117.

Old numbering of the Treaty establishing the European Community	New numbering of the Treaty on the Functioning of the European Union
Article 120	Article 144
Article 121, paragraph 1 (moved)	Article 140, paragraph 1
Article 121, paragraphs 2 to 4 (repealed)	
Article 122, paragraphs 1, 2, first sentence, 3, 4, 5 and 6 (repealed)	
Article 122, paragraph 2, second sentence (moved)	Article 140, paragraph 2, first subparagraph
Article 123, paragraphs 1, 2 and 4 (repealed)	
Article 123, paragraph 3 (moved)	Article 141, paragraph 1
Article 123, paragraph 5 (moved)	Article 140, paragraph 3
Article 124, paragraph 1 (moved)	Article 142
Article 124, paragraph 2 (repealed)	
Title VIII — Employment	Title IX — Employment
Article 125	Article 145
Article 126	Article 146
Article 127	Article 147
Article 128	Article 148
Article 129	Article 149
Article 130	Article 150
Title IX — Common commercial policy (moved)	Part Five, Title II, common commercial policy
Article 131 (moved)	Article 206
Article 132 (repealed)	
Article 133 (moved)	Article 207
Article 134 (repealed)	
Title X — Customs cooperation (moved)	Part Three, Title II, Chapter 2, Customs cooperation
Article 135 (moved)	Article 33
Title XI — Social policy, education, vocational training and youth	Title X — Social policy
Chapter 1 — social provisions (repealed)	
Article 136	Article 151
	Article 152
Article 137	Article 153
Article 138	Article 154
Article 139	Article 155
Article 140	Article 156
Article 141	Article 157
Article 142	Article 158

Old numbering of the Treaty establishing the European Community	New numbering of the Treaty on the Functioning of the European Union
Article 143	Article 159
Article 144	Article 160
Article 145	Article 161
Chapter 2 — The European Social Fund	Title XI — The European Social Fund
Article 146	Article 162
Article 147	Article 163
Article 148	Article 164
Chapter 3 — Education, vocational training and youth	Title XII — Education, vocational training, youth and sport
Article 149	Article 165
Article 150	Article 166
Title XII — Culture	Title XIII — Culture
Article 151	Article 167
Title XIII — Public health	Title XIV — Public health
Article 152	Article 168
Title XIV — Consumer protection	Title XV — Consumer protection
Article 153, paragraphs 1, 3, 4 and 5	Article 169
Article 153, paragraph 2 (moved)	Article 12
Title XV — Trans-European networks	Title XVI — Trans-European networks
Article 154	Article 170
Article 155	Article 171
Article 156	Article 172
Title XVI — Industry	Title XVII — Industry
Article 157	Article 173
Title XVII — Economic and social cohesion	Title XVIII — Economic, social and territorial cohesion
Article 158	Article 174
Article 159	Article 175
Article 160	Article 176
Article 161	Article 177
Article 162	Article 178
Title XVIII — Research and technological development	Title XIX — Research and technological development and space
Article 163	Article 179
Article 164	Article 180
Article 165	Article 181

Old numbering of the Treaty establishing the European Community	New numbering of the Treaty on the Functioning of the European Union
Article 166	Article 182
Article 167	Article 183
Article 168	Article 184
Article 169	Article 185
Article 170	Article 186
Article 171	Article 187
Article 172	Article 188
	Article 189
Article 173	Article 190
Title XIX — Environment	Title XX — Environment
Article 174	Article 191
Article 175	Article 192
Article 176	Article 193
	Titre XXI — Energy
	Article 194
	Title XXII — Tourism
	Article 195
	Title XXIII — Civil protection
	Article 196
	Title XXIV — Administrative cooperation
	Article 197
Title XX — Development cooperation (moved)	Part Five, Title III, Chapter 1, Development cooperation
Article 177 (moved)	Article 208
Article 178 (repealed) ([42])	
Article 179 (moved)	Article 209
Article 180 (moved)	Article 210
Article 181 (moved)	Article 211
Title XXI — Economic, financial and technical cooperation with third countries (moved)	Part Five, Title III, Chapter 2, Economic, financial and technical cooperation with third countries
Article 181a (moved)	Article 212

([42]) Replaced, in substance, by the second sentence of the second subparagraph of paragraph 1 of Article 208 TFEU.

Old numbering of the Treaty establishing the European Community	New numbering of the Treaty on the Functioning of the European Union
PART FOUR — ASSOCIATION OF THE OVERSEAS COUNTRIES AND TERRITORIES	PART FOUR — ASSOCIATION OF THE OVERSEAS COUNTRIES AND TERRITORIES
Article 182	Article 198
Article 183	Article 199
Article 184	Article 200
Article 185	Article 201
Article 186	Article 202
Article 187	Article 203
Article 188	Article 204
	PART FIVE — EXTERNAL ACTION BY THE UNION
	Title I — General provisions on the union's external action
	Article 205
Part Three, Title IX, Common commercial policy (moved)	Title II — Common commercial policy
Article 131 (moved)	Article 206
Article 133 (moved)	Article 207
	Title III — Cooperation with third countries and humanitarian aid
Part Three, Title XX, Development cooperation (moved)	Chapter 1 — development cooperation
Article 177 (moved)	Article 208 ([43])
Article 179 (moved)	Article 209
Article 180 (moved)	Article 210
Article 181 (moved)	Article 211
Part Three, Title XXI, Economic, financial and technical cooperation with third countries (moved)	Chapter 2 — Economic, financial and technical cooperation with third countries
Article 181a (moved)	Article 212
	Article 213
	Chapter 3 — Humanitarian aid
	Article 214
	Title IV — Restrictive measures
Article 301 (replaced)	Article 215

([43])   The second sentence of the second subparagraph of paragraph 1 replaces, in substance, Article 178 TEC.

Old numbering of the Treaty establishing the European Community	New numbering of the Treaty on the Functioning of the European Union
	Title V — International agreements
	Article 216
Article 310 (moved)	Article 217
Article 300 (replaced)	Article 218
Article 111, paragraphs 1 to 3 and 5 (moved)	Article 219
	Title VI — The Union's relations with international organisations and third countries and the Union delegations
Articles 302 to 304 (replaced)	Article 220
	Article 221
	Title VII — Solidarity clause
	Article 222
PART FIVE — INSTITUTIONS OF THE COMMUNITY	PART SIX — INSTITUTIONAL AND FINANCIAL PROVISIONS
Title I — Institutional provisions	Title I — Institutional provisions
Chapter 1 — The institutions	Chapter 1 — The institutions
Section 1 — The European Parliament	Section 1 — The European Parliament
Article 189 (repealed) [44]	
Article 190, paragraphs 1 to 3 (repealed) [45]	
Article 190, paragraphs 4 and 5	Article 223
Article 191, first paragraph (repealed) [46]	
Article 191, second paragraph	Article 224
Article 192, first paragraph (repealed) [47]	
Article 192, second paragraph	Article 225
Article 193	Article 226
Article 194	Article 227
Article 195	Article 228
Article 196	Article 229
Article 197, first paragraph (repealed) [48]	

[44] Replaced, in substance, by Article 14, paragraphs 1 and 2, TEU.
[45] Replaced, in substance, by Article 14, paragraphs 1 to 3, TEU.
[46] Replaced, in substance, by Article 11, paragraph 4, TEU.
[47] Replaced, in substance, by Article 14, paragraph 1, TEU.
[48] Replaced, in substance, by Article 14, paragraph 4, TEU.

Old numbering of the Treaty establishing the European Community	New numbering of the Treaty on the Functioning of the European Union
Article 197, second, third and fourth paragraphs	Article 230
Article 198	Article 231
Article 199	Article 232
Article 200	Article 233
Article 201	Article 234
	Section 2 — The European Council
	Article 235
	Article 236
Section 2 — The Council	Section 3 — The Council
Article 202 (repealed) (^{49})	
Article 203 (repealed) (^{50})	
Article 204	Article 237
Article 205, paragraphs 2 and 4 (repealed) (^{51})	
Article 205, paragraphs 1 and 3	Article 238
Article 206	Article 239
Article 207	Article 240
Article 208	Article 241
Article 209	Article 242
Article 210	Article 243
Section 3 — The Commission	Section 4 — The Commission
Article 211 (repealed) (^{53})	
	Article 244
Article 212 (moved)	Article 249, paragraph 2
Article 213	Article 245
Article 214 (repealed) (^{55})	
Article 215	Article 246
Article 216	Article 247
Article 217, paragraphs 1, 3 and 4 (repealed) (^{56})	
Article 217, paragraph 2	Article 248
Article 218, paragraph 1 (repealed) (^{57})	

(^{49}) Replaced, in substance, by Article 16, paragraph 1, TEU and by Articles 290 and 291 TFEU.
(^{50}) Replaced, in substance, by Article 16, paragraphs 2 and 9 TEU.
(^{51}) Replaced, in substance, by Article 16, paragraphs 4 and 5 TEU.
(^{53}) Replaced, in substance, by Article 17, paragraph 1 TEU.
(^{55}) Replaced, in substance, by Article 17, paragraphs 3 and 7 TEU.
(^{56}) Replaced, in substance, by Article 17, paragraph 6, TEU.
(^{57}) Replaced, in substance, by Article 295 TFEU.

Old numbering of the Treaty establishing the European Community	New numbering of the Treaty on the Functioning of the European Union
Article 218, paragraph 2	Article 249
Article 219	Article 250
Section 4 — The Court of Justice	Section 5 — The Court of Justice of the European Union
Article 220 (repealed) ([58])	
Article 221, first paragraph (repealed) ([59])	
Article 221, second and third paragraphs	Article 251
Article 222	Article 252
Article 223	Article 253
Article 224 ([60])	Article 254
	Article 255
Article 225	Article 256
Article 225a	Article 257
Article 226	Article 258
Article 227	Article 259
Article 228	Article 260
Article 229	Article 261
Article 229a	Article 262
Article 230	Article 263
Article 231	Article 264
Article 232	Article 265
Article 233	Article 266
Article 234	Article 267
Article 235	Article 268
	Article 269
Article 236	Article 270
Article 237	Article 271
Article 238	Article 272
Article 239	Article 273
Article 240	Article 274
	Article 275
	Article 276

([58]) Replaced, in substance, by Article 19 TEU.
([59]) Replaced, in substance, by Article 19, paragraph 2, first subparagraph, of the TEU.
([60]) The first sentence of the first subparagraph is replaced, in substance, by Article 19, paragraph 2, second subparagraph of the TEU.

Old numbering of the Treaty establishing the European Community	New numbering of the Treaty on the Functioning of the European Union
Article 241	Article 277
Article 242	Article 278
Article 243	Article 279
Article 244	Article 280
Article 245	Article 281
	Section 6 — The European Central Bank
	Article 282
Article 112 (moved)	Article 283
Article 113 (moved)	Article 284
Section 5 — The Court of Auditors	Section 7 — The Court of Auditors
Article 246	Article 285
Article 247	Article 286
Article 248	Article 287
Chapter 2 — Provisions common to several institutions	Chapter 2 — Legal acts of the Union, adoption procedures and other provisions
	Section 1 — The legal acts of the Union
Article 249	Article 288
	Article 289
	Article 290 (^{61})
	Article 291 (^{61})
	Article 292
	Section 2 — Procedures for the adoption of acts and other provisions
Article 250	Article 293
Article 251	Article 294
Article 252 (repealed)	
	Article 295
Article 253	Article 296
Article 254	Article 297
	Article 298
Article 255 (moved)	Article 15
Article 256	Article 299

(^{61}) Replaces, in substance, the third indent of Article 202 TEC.

Old numbering of the Treaty establishing the European Community	New numbering of the Treaty on the Functioning of the European Union
	Chapter 3 — The Union's advisory bodies
	Article 300
Chapter 3 — The Economic and Social Committee	Section 1 — The Economic and Social Committee
Article 257 (repealed) ([62])	
Article 258, first, second and fourth paragraphs	Article 301
Article 258, third paragraph (repealed) ([63])	
Article 259	Article 302
Article 260	Article 303
Article 261 (repealed)	
Article 262	Article 304
Chapter 4 — The Committee of the Regions	Section 2 — The Committee of the Regions
Article 263, first and fifth paragraphs (repealed) ([64])	
Article 263, second to fourth paragraphs	Article 305
Article 264	Article 306
Article 265	Article 307
Chapter 5 — The European Investment Bank	Chapter 4 — The European Investment Bank
Article 266	Article 308
Article 267	Article 309
Title II — Financial provisions	Title II — Financial provisions
Article 268	Article 310
	Chapter 1 — The Union's own resources
Article 269	Article 311
Article 270 (repealed) ([65])	
	Chapter 2 — The multiannual financial framework
	Article 312
	Chapter 3 — The Union's annual budget
Article 272, paragraph 1 (moved)	Article 313
Article 271 (moved)	Article 316
Article 272, paragraph 1 (moved)	Article 313
Article 272, paragraphs 2 to 10	Article 314

([62]) Replaced, in substance, by Article 300, paragraph 2 of the TFEU.
([63]) Replaced, in substance, by Article 300, paragraph 4 of the TFEU.
([64]) Replaced, in substance, by Article 300, paragraphs 3 and 4, TFEU.
([65]) Replaced, in substance, by Article 310, paragraph 4, TFEU.

Old numbering of the Treaty establishing the European Community	New numbering of the Treaty on the Functioning of the European Union
Article 273	Article 315
Article 271 (moved)	Article 316
	Chapter 4 — Implementation of the budget and discharge
Article 274	Article 317
Article 275	Article 318
Article 276	Article 319
	Chapter 5 — Common provisions
Article 277	Article 320
Article 278	Article 321
Article 279	Article 322
	Article 323
	Article 324
	Chapter 6 — Combating fraud
Article 280	Article 325
	Title III — Enhanced cooperation
Articles 11 and 11a (replaced)	Article 326 [66]
Articles 11 and 11a (replaced)	Article 327 [66]
Articles 11 and 11a (replaced)	Article 328 [66]
Articles 11 and 11a (replaced)	Article 329 [66]
Articles 11 and 11a (replaced)	Article 330 [66]
Articles 11 and 11a (replaced)	Article 331 [66]
Articles 11 and 11a (replaced)	Article 332 [66]
Articles 11 and 11a (replaced)	Article 333 [66]
Articles 11 and 11a (replaced)	Article 334 [66]
PART SIX — GENERAL AND FINAL PROVISIONS	PART SEVEN — GENERAL AND FINAL PROVISIONS
Article 281 (repealed) [67]	
Article 282	Article 335
Article 283	Article 336
Article 284	Article 337
Article 285	Article 338
Article 286 (replaced)	Article 16
Article 287	Article 339
Article 288	Article 340
Article 289	Article 341

[66]   Also replaces the current Articles 27a to 27e, 40 to 40b, and 43 to 45 TEU.
[67]   Replaced, in substance, by Article 47 TEU.

Old numbering of the Treaty establishing the European Community	New numbering of the Treaty on the Functioning of the European Union
Article 290	Article 342
Article 291	Article 343
Article 292	Article 344
Article 293 (repealed)	
Article 294 (moved)	Article 55
Article 295	Article 345
Article 296	Article 346
Article 297	Article 347
Article 298	Article 348
Article 299, paragraph 1 (repealed) ([68])	
Article 299, paragraph 2, second, third and fourth subparagraphs	Article 349
Article 299, paragraph 2, first subparagraph, and paragraphs 3 to 6 (moved)	Article 355
Article 300 (replaced)	Article 218
Article 301 (replaced)	Article 215
Article 302 (replaced)	Article 220
Article 303 (replaced)	Article 220
Article 304 (replaced)	Article 220
Article 305 (repealed)	
Article 306	Article 350
Article 307	Article 351
Article 308	Article 352
	Article 353
Article 309	Article 354
Article 310 (moved)	Article 217
Article 311 (repealed) ([69])	
Article 299, paragraph 2, first subparagraph, and paragraphs 3 to 6 (moved)	Article 355
Article 312	Article 356
Final Provisions	
Article 313	Article 357
	Article 358
Article 314 (repealed) ([70])	

([68]) Replaced, in substance by Article 52 TEU.
([69]) Replaced, in substance by Article 51 TEU.
([70]) Replaced, in substance by Article 55 TEU.

1

THE TREATY AND ITS
TERRITORIAL REACH

2. The Community Treaties

The ECSC Treaty.   The CFI considered the effect of the expiry of this Treaty on   **1.004**
the Commission's jurisdiction in Cases T-27/03, etc, *SP v Commission* [2007]
ECR II-4331, [2008] 4 CMLR 176. These were the appeals from *Concrete
Reinforcing Bars* in which the Commission had purported to adopt a decision
establishing a breach of Article 65(1) ECSC after the expiry of that Treaty. The
CFI stated that, on expiry of the ECSC Treaty, the sectors which had previously
come under the *lex specialis* of that Treaty came within the scope of the *lex generalis*
of the EC Treaty. In order to ensure observance of the principles of legal certainty
and legitimate expectations, the substantive rules applicable to the alleged conduct were those set out in the ECSC Treaty. But this did not confer competence
on the Commission to take a decision under the expired provisions. The CFI
therefore annulled the decision. The CFI distinguished the position of an appel-
late court which could still apply the ECSC Treaty when reviewing the legality of
measures adopted by the Commission before the Treaty expired. The CFI delivered one judgment on 25 October 2007 in Cases T-27/03, T-46/03, T-58/03,
T-79/03, T-80/03, T-97/03 and T-98/03 and separate judgments on the same day
and to the same effect in Cases T-45/03, T-77/03 and T-94/03. The Commission
has since readopted the decision using Regulation 1/2003 as the legal base: decn
of 30 September 2009. See to similar effect Case T-405/06 *Arcelor Mittal v
Commission*, judgment of 31 March 2009 (on further appeal Case C-201/09 P,
not yet decided).

As to the application of the State aid rules to the sectors previously covered by
the ECSC Treaty see Case T-25/04 *González y Díez v Commission*, judgment of
12 September 2007. The CFI held that the Commission had been correct to apply
Article 88(2) EC [now Article 108(2) TFEU] and the State Aids Procedural

Regulation in its decision adopted after the ECSC Treaty expired relating to an aid granted before that expiry. But the Commission erred in deciding that a State aid put into effect without its prior approval would be subject to the provisions of Regulation 1407/2002 which was adopted after the aid was put into effect. (Note that this conclusion may need to be reconsidered in the light of Case C-334/07 P *Commission v Freistaat Sachsen*, judgment of 11 December 2008). However, since the relevant provisions of Regulation 1407/2002 were identical to earlier provisions which were in force at the relevant time, the CFI in *González y Díez* found that the error did not affect the validity of the decision.

In Case T-27/04 *ThyssenKrupp Stainless AG v Commission*, judgment of 1 July 2009 the CFI applied the principles established in judgments in *SP v Commission* and *González y Díez v Commission* and held that the Commission was right to use Regulation 1/2003 to adopt a decision applying Article 65 ECSC to conduct which took place before the expiry of that Treaty (on further appeal Case C-352/09 P *ThyssenKrupp Nirosta v Commission*, not yet decided).

In Case T-122/04 *Outokumpu Oyj v Commission* [2009] 5 CMLR 1553 the CFI held that the Commission was entitled to increase a fine imposed for a cartel infringement under the EC Treaty because of an earlier cartel infringement decision taken under the ECSC Treaty competition provisions.

The ECJ still has jurisdiction to answer preliminary references on the interpretation of the ECSC Treaty even after its expiry: Case C-119/05 *Lucchini Siderurgia* [2007] ECR I-6199.

1.007 **The single currency.**   Cyprus and Malta adopted the euro on 1 January 2008. Slovakia adopted the euro on 1 January 2009.

1.010 **Charter of Fundamental Rights.**   Article 6 of the new TEU states that the Union recognises the rights, freedoms and principles set out in the Charter of Fundamental Rights and states that they have the 'same legal value' as the Treaties. However, the article also makes clear that the provisions of the Charter do not extend the Union's competence. Note also that the Charter cannot be invoked against the United Kingdom or Poland: Protocol 30 to the TFEU.

1.012 **The Reform Treaty.**   The Reform Treaty fared somewhat better than the Constitutional Treaty. The Treaty was signed by EU leaders on 13 December 2007 in Lisbon but the people of Ireland rejected the Treaty in a referendum in June 2008. A challenge to the decision of the United Kingdom Government not to hold a referendum before ratifying the Treaty was dismissed by the English High Court: *Wheeler v The Office of the Prime Minister* [2008] EWHC 1409 (Admin), [2008] 2 CMLR 1583. Ireland held a further referendum in October 2009 and the Lisbon Treaty was approved. Following the signature of the Czech President on 4 November 2009, the Treaty came into force on 1 December 2009.

As indicated in the text the term 'European Union' has now replaced the term 'European Community' and there are now two treaties of equal status – the Treaty on European Union (TEU) and the Treaty on the Functioning of the European Union (TFEU). The TEU contains many of the provisions previously found in the old TEU (signed in Maastricht) but many provisions have been repealed or replaced. Some of the provisions that were previously in the early articles of the old EC Treaty have been replaced by provisions in the new TEU. Thus, contrary to what is stated in the text, Article 3(1) of the EC Treaty is repealed by the Lisbon Treaty but reappears in modified form as Article 3(1)(b) of the Treaty on the Functioning of the European Union. This provides that the Union has exclusive competence in 'the establishing of the competition rules necessary for the functioning of the internal market'. Note also, as referred to in fn 37, that although the proposed reference to free and undistorted competition was not included in the final version of Article 3 of the new TEU, Protocol 27 to the Treaty states that the Member States 'considering that the internal market as set out in Article 3 of the Treaty on European Union includes a system ensuring that competition is not distorted' have agreed that the Union shall, if necessary, take action under the provisions of the Treaties to that end. What effect these changes will have in future years remains to be seen.

3. The EC Treaty

(a) Generally

The structure of the EC Treaty.   The structure of the new treaties, the Treaty on   **1.014**
the European Union (TEU) and the Treaty on the Functioning of the European Union (TFEU), has overtaken the content of this paragraph as from 1 December 2009 when the Lisbon Treaty came into force. The European Union now has legal personality.

Fundamental human rights.   In Case T-99/04 *AC-Treuhand AG v Commission*   **1.016**
[2008] ECR II-1501, [2008] 5 CMLR 962, the CFI commented that 'fundamental rights are an integral part of the general principles of law whose observance the Community judicature ensures by taking account, in particular, of the ECHR as a source of inspiration': para 138.

See also Case T-69/04 *Schunk GmbH v Commission* [2009] 4 CMLR 2 where the CFI considered the case law of the Court of Human Rights on Article 7 ECHR in relation to an assertion that the wide discretion given to the Commission when imposing a fine infringed the principle of legal certainty: paras 28–50.

Article 6 of the new TEU provides that the Union shall accede to the European Convention on Human Rights but that such accession shall not affect the Union's competences as defined in the Treaties. Further, Article 6 provides that fundamental rights, as guaranteed by the Convention and as they result from the constitutional traditions common to the Member States, shall constitute general principles of the Union's law.

1.017 **A presumption of compliance: *Bosphorus Airways*.**   The Court's decision in this case was distinguished in Application No. 71412/01 *Behrami v France*, judgment of 2 May 2007, see esp para 145.

(b) The main competition provisions

1.018 **Generally.**   When the Treaty on the Functioning of the European Union came into effect on 1 December 2009 the Treaty provisions were renumbered in accordance with Article 5 of the Treaty of Lisbon. That Treaty has an annex containing a table of equivalences between the old and new treaties. Articles 81–89 of the EC Treaty are now Articles 101–109 of the TFEU.

(c) Other provisions of the Treaty

Note that the numbers of the Articles of the EC Treaty referred to in the paragraphs in this section have changed on the coming into force of the Treaty on the Functioning of the European Union and, in some instances, the provisions themselves have been revised.

1.026 **Article 3: the activities of the Community.**   The term European Community has now been replaced by the term European Union. Article 3(1) EC which listed the activities of the Community has been repealed and replaced in substance by paragraphs 3–6 TFEU. The new Article 3 TFEU list the areas in which the Union has exclusive competence, including establishing the competition rules necessary for the functioning of the internal market. Article 4 TFEU lists those areas where the Union shares competence with the Member States including the internal market, consumer protection, transport, and energy. Article 3(3) of the new TEU provides that the Union shall establish an internal market and work for the sustainable development of Europe based on, among other things 'a highly competitive social market economy . . .'.

1.027 **Article 3(1)(g).**   Article 3(1) of the EC Treaty is repealed by the Lisbon Treaty but reappears in modified form as Article 3(1)(b) of the Treaty on the Functioning of the European Union. This provides that the Union has exclusive competence in 'the establishing of the competition rules necessary for the functioning of the internal market'. Note also Protocol 27 to the Treaty states that the Member States 'considering that the internal market as set out in Article 3 of the Treaty on European Union includes a system ensuring that competition is not distorted' have agreed that the Union shall, if necessary, take action under the provisions of the Treaties to that end.

Article 5: subsidiarity.   Article 5 EC was repealed by the Lisbon Treaty and has   **1.028**
been replaced by Article 5 of the new TEU. This provides that the use of Union
competences is governed by the principles of subsidiarity and proportionality and
describes those principles using similar wording to that in Article 5 EC.

Subsidiarity and decentralisation of competition law.   **Fn 80.** Both appeals   **1.029**
referred to have now been decided: Cases C-501/06 P, etc, *GlaxoSmithKline*
Services Unlimited v Commission, judgment of 6 October 2009 and Cases C-125/
07 P, etc, *Erste Bank der österreichischen Sparkassen v Commission*, judgment of
24 September 2009. The point discussed in this paragraph is not affected.

Article 10: duties of Member States.   The substance of what was Article 10 EC   **1.030**
has been incorporated into Article 4 of the new TEU. In Case C-441/06
Commission v France [2007] ECR I-8887, the ECJ held that France was in breach
of its obligations under Article 10 because of its failure to cooperate with the
Commission in the implementation of a State aid decision.

Article 12: non-discrimination.   **Fn 88.** Article 12 EC is now Article 18 TFEU.   **1.031**
As to national disparities in the regulation of the pharmaceuticals market see
also Cases C-468/06, etc, *Sot Lelos kai Sia EE v GlaxoSmithKline* [2008] ECR
I-7139, [2008] 5 CMLR 1382, [2009] All ER (EC) 1 (extent to which a dominant undertaking can refuse to fulfil orders by a wholesaler who engages in parallel
trading).

The *Cassis de Dijon* principle and the *Keck* distinction.   Articles 28, 29 and 30   **1.033**
EC are now Articles 34, 35 and 36 TFEU. For a recent decision on *Keck* see Case
C-141/07 *Re Supply of Medicines by Pharmacies to nearby Hospitals: Commission v*
Germany [2008] ECR I-6935, [2008] 3 CMLR 1479 (national law the effect of
which was that only local pharmacies could supply medicinal products to hospitals
was a selling arrangement within the meaning of *Keck*). Cf Case C-531/07 *Fachver-*
band der Buch- und Medienwirtschaft v LIBRO Handelsgesellschaft mbH, judgment
of 30 April 2009 where the ECJ held that Austrian legislation which prevented an
importer of German books from selling those books at a price lower than the minimum fixed under Austrian legislation was not a selling arrangement within the
Keck distinction and was contrary to Article 28 EC [now Article 34 TFEU].

Other relevant Treaty provisions.   Following the renumbering of the Treaty   **1.037**
articles on 1 December 2009:

- Articles 32–38 EC dealing with common agricultural policy are now Articles
  38–44 TFEU;
- Articles 70–80 EC dealing with a common transport policy are now Articles
  90–100 TFEU;
- Article 151 EC concerning the cultural aspects of the Union is now Article 167
  TFEU;

- Article 174 EC concerning environmental policy is now Article 191 TFEU;
- Article 296 EC concerning national security is now Article 346 TFEU;
- Articles 90–93 EC concerning taxation are now Articles 110–113 TFEU;
- Article 133 EC concerning the common commercial policy and anti-dumping is now Article 207;
- Articles 133(3) EC concerning treaties with third countries is now Article 207(3) TFEU; Article 300 has been replaced by Article 218 TFEU;
- Article 134 EC has been repealed;
- Articles 136–145 EC concerning social policy are now Articles 151–161 TFEU; and
- Articles 39–42 EC concerning free movement are now Articles 45–48 TFEU.

As to Article 151(4) (cultural aspects) [now Article 167(4) TFEU] see the discussion in COMP/38.698 *CISAC*, decn of 16 July 2008, [2009] 4 CMLR 577, para 95 where the Commission rejected a submission that its condemnation of certain territorial delineation terms in the model contract recommended by a collecting society was likely to harm cultural diversity. The case is on appeal Cases T-398, 410, 411, 413–422, 425, 432, 434, 442, 451/08, not yet decided.

Further on the application of Article 151(4) [now Article 167(4) TFEU] see Case C-531/07 *Fachverband der Buch- und Medienwirtschaft v LIBRO Handelsgesellschaft mbH*, judgment of 30 April 2009 where the ECJ noted that the protection of books as cultural objects can be considered as an overriding requirement in the public interest capable of justifying measures restricting the free movement of goods, on condition that those measures are appropriate for achieving the objective fixed and do not go beyond what is necessary to achieve it. However, the Court held in that case that the objective of the protection of books as cultural objects could be achieved by measures less restrictive than the legislation being challenged under Article 28 EC [now Article 34 TFEU].

4. The Institutional Structure of the Community

(a) The Community institutions

1.038 **The institutions of the Community.** The Lisbon Treaty made some important changes to the institutions mentioned in this paragraph, in particular creating the new post of President of the Council. The Treaty also created the role of High Representative concerned with foreign affairs and security policy. This office is supported by a new diplomatic service called the European External Action Service.

1.039 **The official languages of the Community.** In Case C-161/06 *Skoma-Lux sro v Celiní Editelství Olomouc* [2007] ECR I-10841, [2008] 1 CMLR 1336, the ECJ was asked on a reference for a preliminary ruling whether Community law provisions were binding on the citizens of a new Member State before the provisions had been published in that State's official language in the *Official Journal*. The Court held that the provisions were not binding, even though electronic versions were available in Czech. However, the Court stated that the requirements of legal certainty dictate that this did not affect the validity of national decisions taken pursuant to those provisions, with the exception of decisions which were the subject of administrative or judicial proceedings at the date of the Court's judgment. The Member States concerned were not, under Community law, obliged to call in question the administrative or judicial decisions taken on the basis of such rules where those decisions have become definitive under the applicable national rules.

The fact that a hearing in a Dutch case is conducted in English is not a breach of the rights of the defence unless the parties can show that they were prejudiced by this: Case T-151/05 *Nederlandse Vakbond Varkenshouders (NVV) v Commission* [2009] 5 CMLR 1613, para 211.

The European Parliament.   Under the Lisbon Treaty, the number of MEPs is   **1.040** limited to 751 and each Member State will have between six and 96 members. The Treaty expands the role of the Parliament by increasing the number of legislative measures that are adopted using the co-decision procedure.

The Council.   The Council is now headed by a permanent President of the   **1.041** Council in accordance with Article 15(6) TEU.

(b) The Community and EFTA Courts

The Community Courts.   The coming into force of the Lisbon Treaty on   **1.045** 1 December 2009 brought about a restructuring of the Community Courts. From that date the whole court system of the European Union is to be known as the Court of Justice of the European Union and will comprise three courts: the Court of Justice, the General Court (previously the Court of First Instance) and the specialised courts, currently the Civil Service Tribunal.

References under Article 234.   Article 234 EC is now Article 267 TFEU. For   **1.049** the nature of the proceedings under Article 267 see Case C-2/06 *Kempter v Haupzollamt Hamburg-Jonas* [2008] ECR I-411, [2008] 2 CMLR 586: 'the system of references for a preliminary ruling is based on a dialogue between one court and another, the initiation of which depends entirely on the national court's assessment as to whether a reference is appropriate and necessary' (para 42).

(c) The Directorate-General for Competition

(iii) Enforcement through legislation and guidance

General Notices and Guidance.   In February 2009 the Commission issued its   **1.066** Guidance on the Commission's enforcement priorities in applying Article 82 to abusive exclusionary conduct by dominant undertakings: OJ 2009 C45/7: Vol II, App C19. The Guidance is not intended to be a statement of the law but aims to provide greater clarity and predictability as regards the general framework of analysis that the Commission will employ when determining whether to pursue cases (para 2). The Guidance is considered in more detail in Chapter 10.

1.068 **The DG Competition website.**   The CFI has held that putting a non-confidential version of a decision on the website constitutes a continuing publication of that decision so that the Commission can be ordered to remove confidential information which it has wrongly included in the decision: Case T-474/04 *Pergan Hilfsstoffe für industrielle Prozesse GmbH v Commission* [2007] ECR II-4225, [2008] 4 CMLR 148, para 41.

Publication of a decision on the website may not of itself start the time for lodging an appeal; but where a notification is published in the *Official Journal* that the decision can be found on the website, the time for appealing runs from that time: Case T-274/06 *Estaser El Mareny v Commission* [2007] ECR II-143*. See further the update to paragraph 13.232, below.

5. The Aims of the Community Rules on Competition

1.072 **A competitive market economy.**   Fn 207. The ECJ overturned the CFI's analysis on this point in Cases C-501/06 P, etc, *GlaxoSmithKline Services Unlimited v Commission*, judgment of 6 October 2009. The ECJ held that neither the wording of Article 81(1) [now Article 101(1) TFEU] nor the case law supports the contention that agreements limiting parallel trade only have the object of restricting competition if they disadvantage final consumers: para 62.

1.074 **Market integration.**   The final sentence of this paragraph must now be read in the light of the ECJ's rejection of the CFI's analysis on this point: Cases C-501/06 P, etc, *GlaxoSmithKline Services Unlimited v Commission*, judgment of 6 October 2009.

1.075 **Importance of parallel trading.**   See also Cases C-468/06, etc, *Sot Lelos kai Sia EE v GlaxoSmithKline* [2008] ECR I-7139, [2008] 5 CMLR 1382, [2009] All ER (EC) 1 (application of Article 82 [now Article 102 TFEU] to dominant undertaking refusing to fulfil orders by a wholesaler who engages in parallel trading); Cases C-501/06 P, etc, *GlaxoSmithKline Services Unlimited v Commission*, judgment of 6 October 2009.

1.076 **Liberalisation of markets.**   Fn 217. The appeal by Deutsche Telekom was dismissed by the CFI: Case T-271/03 *Deutsche Telekom AG v Commission* [2008] ECR II-477, [2008] 5 CMLR 631. The CFI's judgment is on appeal: Case C-280/08 P, not yet decided.

6. Territorial Ambit of EC Competition Rules

(a) The Member States: enlargement

Becoming 27. For the retrospective effect of the Protocol relating to the Polish **1.082**
steel industry see Cases T-273 & 297/06 *ISD Polska v Commission*, judgment of
1 July 2009.

(c) EFTA and the EEA

The EEA Agreement. Note that according to Article 8(3) (a) and (b) of the **1.086**
EEA Agreement, the provisions of the EEA Agreement only apply to products
falling within Chapters 25–97 of the Harmonized Commodity Description and
Coding System and to products specified in Protocol 3 of the EEA Agreement.
Thus, for example, the Commission did not have jurisdiction to apply Article 53
EEA to bananas: COMP/39.188 *Bananas*, decn of 15 October 2008, para 210.

Homogeneity objective in the application of EC jurisprudence in the EEA. For **1.089**
an interesting case in which the EFTA Court considered whether the principle of
homogeneity was overridden by compelling reasons for a divergent interpretation
as regards international exhaustion of trade mark rights: see Cases E-9 & 10/07
L'Oréal Norge v Per Aarskog AS, judgment of 8 July 2008.

Allocation of jurisdiction under the EEA Agreement. For a case where the **1.091**
Commission had jurisdiction to apply Article 82 EC [now Article 102 TFEU]
and Article 54 EEA where an undertaking whose parent company was Norwegian
was held to be dominant in national markets in the EU and in the EEA see
COMP/38.113 *Prokent-Tomra*, decn of 29 March 2006, [2009] 4 CMLR 101
(on appeal Case T-155/06 *Tomra Systems*, not yet decided).

For a case concerning an international body with members in both the EU and the
EEA see COMP/38.698 *CISAC*, decn of 16 July 2008, [2009] 4 CMLR 577
(paras 84–86) (on appeal Cases T-398, 410, 411, 413–422, 425, 432, 434, 442,
451/08, not yet decided).

Fn 275. The appeals in *Video Games, Nintendo Distribution* have now been
decided by a series of judgments issued on 30 April 2009. The CFI did not consider the issue discussed in this paragraph. The appeal in Case T-99/04 *AC Treuhand*
was dismissed on other grounds: [2008] ECR II-1501, [2008] 5 CMLR 962.

(d) Agreements between the Community and third countries

Croatia, the FYR of Macedonia, and Albania. On the progress of the candidate **1.098**
countries (Croatia, FYR of Macedonia and Turkey) see COM(2008) 674 final
(5 November 2008) Communication from the Commission to the Council and

the European Parliament '*Enlargement Strategy and Main Challenges 2008-2009*'. Of the other Western Balkan countries, the SAA with Albania entered into force on 1 April 2009; Montenegro, Serbia, and Bosnia and Herzegovina have each signed an SAA with the EU (in October 2007, April 2008 and June 2008, respectively) but these are not yet in force.

Fn 303. The SAA with the former Yugoslav Republic of Macedonia entered into force on 1 April 2004 not 1 May 2004 as cited in the footnote.

7. The Territorial Jurisdiction of the Community Institutions

(c) Jurisdiction over undertakings outside the Community

1.110 **The issue.** In COMP/39.181 *Candle Waxes*, decn of 1 October 2008, [2009] 5 CMLR 2441 the Commission rejected a challenge to its jurisdiction by a Hungarian company in respect of cartel activity before Hungary joined the Community. The Commission stated that under the effects doctrine, jurisdiction can be established on the basis of economic effects within a territory, and MOL, as well as the other cartel participants, had sales in several Member States: para 190.

8. Effect on Trade between Member States

(a) Generally

1.115 **Rule of jurisdiction.** **Fn 377.** Both appeals referred to have now been decided: Cases C-501/06 P, etc, *GlaxoSmithKline Services Unlimited v Commission*, judgment of 6 October 2009 and Cases C-125/07 P, etc, *Erste Bank der österreichischen Sparkassen v Commission*, judgment of 24 September 2009. The point discussed in this paragraph is not affected.

1.117 **Trade.** **Fn 401.** See also COMP/38.700 *Greek Lignite and Electricity generation*, decn of 5 March 2008, [2009] 4 CMLR 495 where the Commission held, in a case under Article 86(1) EC [now Article 106(1) TFEU], that the State measures challenged discouraged potential entrants from investing in electricity generation and supply in Greece, including those who had applied for and obtained electricity generation and electricity supply licences. These operators were not using these licences yet, and were thus not using their right of establishment in Greece. This constituted an effect on trade for the purposes of Article 86 in conjunction with Article 82: para 244. The case is on appeal: Case T-169/08 *DEI v Commission*, not yet decided.

(b) Particular aspects

Particular kinds of domestic agreements.   **Fn 491.** A further appeal in *Der*   **1.131**
Grüne Punkt was dismissed: Case C-385/07 P *Der Grüne Punkt – Duales System
Deutschland v Commission*, judgment of 16 July 2009, [2009] 5 CMLR 2215.

Particular kinds of domestic abuse.   **Fn 499.** Note that the ECJ in the appeal   **1.132**
from Case T-229/05 *AEPI v Commission* referred to in the footnote held that the
CFI had confused two separate concepts – the concept of the effect on trade
between Member States and the concept of whether there is a serious impediment
to intra-Community trade. The latter concept was relevant to the Commission's
assessment of whether there was a sufficient Community interest in investigating
a complaint. The ECJ held therefore that the Commission had rejected the complaint not because of an absence of effect on trade but because there was no serious
impediment to intra-Community trade: see Case C-425/07 P *AEPI v Commission*,
judgment of 23 April 2009.

Fn 499. A further appeal in *Der Grüne Punkt* was dismissed: Case C-385/07 P *Der
Grüne Punkt – Duales System Deutschland v Commission*, judgment of 16 July
2009, [2009] 5 CMLR 2215.

2

ARTICLE 81(1)

2. Undertakings

(a) Generally

Note: Article 81(1) EC has now become Article 101(1) TFEU

Undertakings.   In Case C-113/07 P *SELEX Sistemi Integrati SpA v Commission,*   **2.003**
judgment of 26 March 2009, Eurocontrol's argument that, as an international
organisation, it was immune from investigation by the Commission was rejected,
though primarily for procedural reasons: paras 55 *et seq.*

Fn 12. See also Case C-49/07 *Motosykletistiki Omospondia Ellados NPID (MOTOE) v
Elliniko Dimosio* [2008] ECR I-4863, [2008] 5 CMLR 790, [2009] All ER (EC)
150, paras 27 and 28 (a non-profit making entity may be competing with profit
making entities or with other non-profit making entities).

Individuals as undertakings.   **Fn 17.** The proper citation for the *CNSD* case   **2.004**
referred to in line 4 is OJ 1993 L203/27, [1995] 5 CMLR 495 (appeal dismissed,
Case T-513/93 *CNSD v Commission* [2000] ECR II-1807, [2000] 5 CMLR 614).

Shareholders as undertakings.   The question whether a legal entity which holds   **2.004A**
shares in an undertaking which carries on commercial activity is itself an undertaking was considered by the ECJ in Case C-222/04 *Ministero dell'Economia
e delle Finanze v Cassa di Risparmio di Firenze SpA* [2006] ECR I-289, [2008]
1 CMLR 705. The ECJ held that the mere fact of holding shares, even controlling shareholdings, is insufficient to characterise as economic an activity of the
entity holding those shares, when it gives rise only to the exercise of the rights
attached to the status of shareholder or member, as well as, if appropriate, the
receipt of dividends. On the other hand, an entity which, owning controlling
shareholdings in a company, actually exercises that control by involving itself
directly or indirectly in the management thereof must be regarded as taking part

13

in the economic activity carried on by the controlled undertaking. It was for the national court to determine whether the entity concerned not only held controlling shareholdings, but also actually exercised that control by involving itself directly or indirectly in the management of the latter.

2.005 **Economic or commercial activity.** Fn 23. In Case C-113/07 P *SELEX Sistemi Integrati SpA v Commission*, judgment of 26 March 2009 the ECJ overturned much of the CFI's analysis of what does and does not constitute economic activity although it ultimately upheld the CFI's decision that the Commission had been right to reject the complaint: see update to paragraph 2.007, below.

(b) The State as an undertaking

2.007 **Member States and the essential functions of the State.** See now Case C-113/07 P *SELEX Sistemi Integrati SpA v Commission*, judgment of 26 March 2009. The judgment makes clear first, the importance of the constitution of the entity in establishing the scope of its functions and secondly, that the range of activities which are to be treated as connected with the exercise of public functions (and hence beyond the scope of the competition rules) is wider than the CFI indicated in its judgment. Having examined the instrument setting up Eurocontrol, in particular its objectives, the ECJ held that the provision of advice by Eurocontrol in connection with tendering procedures carried out by the Contracting States when buying equipment and systems for air traffic management was not an economic activity. It was closely linked to the task of technical standardisation entrusted to Eurocontrol in the context of the States' cooperation in maintaining and developing the safety of air navigation. It was thus connected with the exercise of public powers: para 76. The fact that the assistance provided by Eurocontrol was optional and that only certain States have had recourse to it did not alter the nature of the activity. Moreover, in order for there to be a connection with the exercise of public powers, it was not necessary for the activity concerned to be essential or indispensable for ensuring the safety of air navigation: para 79. The Court also held that the CFI had erred in drawing a distinction between Eurocontrol's function of adopting technical standards (which the CFI agreed was a legislative, sovereign function) and the function of preparing and producing those standards (which the CFI held was an economic activity). Again, examining the Convention establishing Eurocontrol, the Court held that the Contracting States entrusted Eurocontrol with both the preparation and production of standards and with their adoption, without separating those functions. Moreover, the production of technical standards was an integral part of, and directly connected to, the task of technical standardisation entrusted to Eurocontrol in the context of cooperation among States with a view to maintaining and developing the safety of air navigation, which constitute public powers. See also the rejection of the damages claim: C-481/07 P *SELEX Sistemi Integrati SpA v Commission*, judgment of 16 July 2009.

In COMP/38.469 *Athens International Airport*, decn of 2 May 2005, the Commission rejected a complaint against the level of charges imposed for passenger security checks at the airport. The main ground for rejecting the complaint was lack of Community interest but the Commission stated that when carrying out such checks, the airport, or any other entity carrying out the checks on behalf of the Greek state, was not exercising an economic activity for the purposes of Article 82 [now Article 102 TFEU] (para 49). On appeal, the CFI did not address this issue: Case T-306/05 *Scippacercola and Terezakis v Commission* [2008] ECR II-4*, [2008] 4 CMLR 1418, para 145 (further appeal dismissed Case C-159/08 P, Order of 25 March 2009).

The Commission has also commented on this issue in its Communication on services of general interest: Vol II, App F7 and in the Staff Working Document answering frequently asked questions about Decn 2005/842: Vol II, App F8.

Activities of State body to be considered individually. Fn 42. See also Case **2.009** C-49/07 *Motosykletistiki Omospondia Ellados NPID (MOTOE) v Elliniko Dimosio* [2008] ECR I-4863, [2008] 5 CMLR 790, [2009] All ER (EC) 150 (the power to authorise the organisation by others of motorcycling events stems from an act of public authority and cannot be classified as an economic activity but can be separated from the economic activity of organising and commercially exploiting motorcycling events).

Occupation and use of publicly owned facilities. See also Case T-196/04 **2.010** *Ryanair v Commission*, judgment of 17 December 2008, a State aid case concerning advantages granted to Ryanair by the Walloon Region when Ryanair established its services at Charleroi airport. The CFI held that the fixing of the amount of landing charges and the indemnity granted to Ryanair was in this case an activity directly connected with the management of airport infrastructure, which is an economic activity. It did not follow from the fact that an activity represents in legal terms an exemption from a tariff scale laid down in a regulation that that activity must be described as non-economic.

Insurance and social security schemes. The earlier case law was reviewed and **2.012** the principles applied in Case C-350/07 *Kattner Stahlbau GmbH v Maschinenbau-und Metall-Berufsgenossenschaft*, judgment of 5 March 2009.

Similar arguments were relied on by the applicant in a State aid context where the EFTA Court held that municipal kindergartens in Norway were not undertakings: Case E-5/07 *Private Barnehagers Landsforbund v EFTA Surveillance Authority*, decn of 8 February 2008, [2008] 2 CMLR 818. The fact that 80 per cent of the costs of the kindergartens was borne by the public purse and that the fee paid by the parents was not connected to the cost of providing the service indicated that the Norwegian state was not seeking to engage in gainful activity but was fulfilling its duties towards its own population in the social, cultural and educational fields.

2.014 **Activities ancillary to exercise of public functions.** See Case C-113/07 P *SELEX Sistemi Integrati SpA v Commission*, judgment of 26 March 2009, discussed in the update to paragraph 2.007, above. In that judgment, the ECJ also upheld the CFI's application of *FENIN* as regards purchasing activity: the fact that technical standardisation was not an economic activity meant that the acquisition of prototypes in connection with that standardisation was not an economic activity either: para 102.

(c) Treatment of economically linked legal entities

2.018 **Subsidiary companies and branches.** Fn 77. The appeal in Case T-112/05 *Akzo Nobel* and a further appeal to the ECJ have now been decided: Case C-97/08 P *Akzo Nobel NV v Commission*, judgment of 10 September 2009. The ECJ reaffirmed the presumption of decisive influence arising from 100 per cent ownership, see the update to paragraph 13.205, below.

2.020 **Agents.** Fn 90. See similarly Case C-279/06 *CEPSA v Tobar* [2008] ECR I-6681, paras 38–39.

3. Agreements, Decisions and Concerted Practices

(a) Agreements

2.023 **Agreements may be informal.** As to gentlemen's agreements see Case T-53/03 *BPB plc v Commission* [2008] ECR II-1333, [2008] 5 CMLR 1201, para 82.

2.024 **Unilateral action.** Note also that the fact that one party to an agreement concedes that the agreement existed does not preclude the other alleged party from disputing the existence of the agreement: Case T-18/03 *CD-Contact Data v Commission*, judgment of 30 April 2009, para 51.

2.026 **Cases applying *ADALAT*.** Fn 121. The point made here was not affected by the ECJ's judgment in Cases C-501/06 P, etc, *GlaxoSmithKline Services Unlimited v Commission*, judgment of 6 October 2009.

2.027 **Incorporation of terms in an agreement.** Fn 123. See also COMP/38.698 *CISAC*, decn of 16 July 2008, [2009] 4 CMLR 577 where the Commission held that the membership clause under consideration had the object of allocating authors according to their nationality. It was therefore not necessary to show that the clause was applied or enforced: 'The mere existence of the clause creates a "visual and psychological" background which deters collecting societies from attracting authors who are currently either members of other collecting societies or who are not nationals of their domestic territory': para 130 (on appeal Cases T-398, 410, 411, 413–422, 425, 432, 434, 442, 451/08, not yet decided).

Fn 124. The appeals in *Video Games, Nintendo Distribution* have now been decided by a series of judgments issued on 30 April 2009. As regards the point made in this paragraph, the CFI upheld the finding that the agreement underlying the written agreement existed: Case T-18/03 *CD-Contact Data v Commission*, judgment of 30 April 2009 (on further appeal Case C-260/09P *Activision Blizzard Germany*, not yet decided).

Terminated or 'spent' agreements.   For a case where an infringing exclusivity   **2.032** term was removed from a recommended model contract issued by a collecting society but where the members continued to include the term in their bilateral contracts, see COMP/38.698 *CISAC*, decn of 16 July 2008, [2009] 4 CMLR 577, para 144. The case is on appeal Cases T-398, 410, 411, 413–422, 425, 432, 434, 442, 451/08, not yet decided.

Collective labour relations agreements.   The fact that collective agreements   **2.034** fall outside the scope of Article 101 TFEU does not mean that they also fall out-side the scope of the Treaty provisions on free movement of persons or services: Case C-438/05 *International Transport Workers Federation v Viking Line ABP* [2007] ECR I-10779, [2008] 1 CMLR 1372. Further, a trade union may still rely on the impact on it of an alleged State aid in order to establish standing to challenge the Commission's rejection of a complaint under Article 88(2) [now Article 108(2) TFEU]: Case C-319/07 P *3F v Commission*, judgment of 9 July 2009.

(b) Concerted practices

In general.   Many of the principles set out in this paragraph were restated by the   **2.038** ECJ in Case C-8/08 *T-Mobile Netherlands BV v Raad van bestuur van de Nederlandse Mededingingsautoriteit*, judgment of 4 June 2009, an Article 267 reference con-cerning a concerted practice by mobile phone companies.

Polypropylene: **presumption as regards effect on particpants' conduct.**   Note   **2.042** that in this paragraph, the text immediately below the quotation refers to the judgment of the ECJ on the further appeal.

In Case C-8/08 *T-Mobile Netherlands BV v Raad van bestuur van de Nederlandse Mededingingsautoriteit*, judgment of 4 June 2009 the ECJ stated that this pre-sumption is an integral part of applicable Community law and not merely a pro-cedural point concerning the burden of proof. The presumption therefore prevails when the national court is applying Article 81 [now Article 101 TFEU] (para 53). Further, the Court held, the presumption applies even if the concerted action is the result of a meeting held by the participating undertakings on a single occasion rather than of a course of conduct: para 62.

2.045 **Concerted practices: the requisite elements.** Note that a concerted practice can be proved even if the participating undertakings meet on a single occasion: Case C-8/08 *T-Mobile Netherlands BV v Raad van bestuur van de Nederlandse Mededingingsautoriteit*, judgment of 4 June 2009, para 62 (an Article 267 TFEU reference concerning a concerted practice by mobile phone companies). See also Case T-53/03 *BPB plc v Commission* [2008] ECR II-1333, [2008] 5 CMLR 1201, para 183 (Commission was right to hold that in a highly concentrated market, the mere disclosure by an undertaking of the fact that it does not want a larger market share is sufficient to inform competitors of an essential element of its strategy).

2.046 **Alternative explanations for parallel behaviour.** In COMP/38.698 *CISAC*, decn of 16 July 2008, [2009] 4 CMLR 577, the Commission analysed whether the inclusion of a territorial delineation clause in a series of bilateral reciprocal copyright licences entered into by collecting societies who were members of CISAC was the result of autonomous business decisions on the part of those collecting societies or the result of coordination among them. The Commission found that the practice of granting exclusivity could not be explained by the market conditions but was the result of a coordinated approach to territorial restrictions. Thus each participating collecting society had a degree of certainty that national territorial delineation will not only be reciprocally accepted by its contracting counterparty but will also be implemented in all the bilateral reciprocal representation agreements signed by the EEA CISAC members (para 157). The Commission also found that even in cases where no exclusivity clauses were inserted into the bilateral representation agreements; where such clauses had allegedly not been applied; or where they had been removed, the practice had continued whereby collecting societies limited the licences they granted to the exploitation in domestic territories only (para 170). The decision is on appeal on the issue of whether the Commission was correct to find the existence of a concerted practice as regards the limitation of the licences to the domestic territory of the licensee: see Cases T-398, 410, 411, 413–422, 425, 432, 434, 442, 451/08, not yet decided. The CFI rejected an application for interim measures to suspend parts of the Commission's order Case T-411/08R *Artijus Magyar v Commission* [2009] 4 CMLR 353 and this judgment is itself under appeal: Case C-32/09 P(R), not yet decided.

Fn 201. In Case T-36/05 *Coats Holdings Ltd v Commission* [2007] ECR II-110, [2008] 4 CMLR 45 the CFI repeated that the question of whether there is another 'plausible explanation' for coordinated behaviour only arises where the Commission's case is not based on documentary evidence of collusion (para 72). But the CFI went on to find that the documentary evidence relied on by the Commission was ambiguous and since that evidence was 'documentary evidence' only if the Commission's, rather than the applicants', interpretation of it was accepted, it followed that there was no documentary evidence within the meaning of the case law. As far as certain alleged aspects of agreement were concerned, the applicants were thus free to put forward a 'plausible explanation' of the facts as an alternative to the one adopted by the Commission. The CFI found that only some of the elements on which the Commission had relied to fix Coats with participation in the cartel stood up to scrutiny and so reduced the fine. Coats' appeal against this decision was dismissed: Case C-468/07 P [2009] 4 CMLR 301.

(c) Agreements and concerted practices: other issues

Single overall infringement.   The appeal in the *Choline Chloride* case mentioned   **2.052** in fn 225 has now been decided: Cases T-101 & 111/05 *BASF AG and UCB SA v Commission* [2007] ECR II-4949, [2008] 4 CMLR 347. In the decision the Commission held that there had been a single continuous infringement comprising a global cartel operating between October 1992 and April 1994 and a European wide cartel operating between March 1994 and October 1998. Could these be characterised as a single continuous infringement even though they overlapped only for a short period? The CFI noted that the case law envisages the existence of a common objective consisting in distorting the normal development of prices as providing a basis for treating the various agreements and concerted practices as the constituent elements of a single infringement: see paras 158 *et seq*. It is not enough to say that all the conduct concerned distorts competition in a general sense. To determine whether the conduct shared a common objective it is necessary to take into account any circumstance capable of establishing or casting doubt on that link, such as the period of application and the content (including the methods used). On examination of the facts the CFI held that the Commission had not shown that these two cartels were a single infringement (paras 208 *et seq*). The result of this was that the global cartel was time barred and the fine that had been imposed for the years covered only by the global cartel was quashed. Unfortunately for BASF, the reduction in fine it had been given because of its cooperation with the investigation of the global cartel was also quashed so that BASF's fine in fact increased as a result of its success on this ground of appeal: para 222.

In Case T-53/03 *BPB plc v Commission* [2008] ECR II-1333, [2008] 5 CMLR 1201 the CFI upheld the Commission's finding of a single continuous infringement, holding that the appellant's participation in meetings was 'characterised by the sole purpose of putting an end to the price war and stabilising the four plasterboard markets' (para 253). The CFI held that it would be artificial to split up such continuous conduct when what was involved was a single infringement which progressively manifested itself in both agreements and concerted practices. The fact that not all participants took part in all aspects of the cartel did not undermine this finding. Interestingly, the Court expressly transposed the *Aalborg Portland* reference to inferring agreement from 'a number of coincidences and indicia' to the concept of a single and continuous infringement: '[w]here there is a complex, single and continuous infringement, each manifestation corroborates the actual occurrence of such an infringement': para 249.

See also COMP/38.638 *Butadiene Rubber and Emulsion Styrene Butadiene Rubber*, decn of 29 November 2006, [2009] 4 CMLR 421 where the Commission treated agreements relating to two kinds of rubber as part of a single infringement so that companies which produced only one kind were nevertheless held to be responsible for the whole infringement (para 297). See similarly Case T-73/04 *Le Carbone-Lorraine v Commission*, judgment of 8 October 2008 (further appeal dismissed, Case C-554/08 P, judgment of 12 November 2009).

In COMP/39.188 *Bananas*, decn of 15 October 2008, the Commission found bilateral discussions had taken place between various banana importers. These bilateral contacts constituted a single continuous concerted practice because the discussions followed a common pattern and involved the same personnel. There was no need to demonstrate that the parties were aware of all details concerning communications between the other parties (para 252) but it was established that each was aware of the bilateral discussions between the others, or at least foresaw such discussions and took the risk that there was a common objective. The decision is under appeal: Cases T-587 & 588/08, not yet decided.

Fn 222. Substantial parts of the Commission's decision in *Needles* were overturned as regards Coats' involvement: Case T-36/05 *Coats Holdings Ltd v Commission* [2007] ECR II-110, [2008] 4 CMLR 45, discussed in the update to paragraph 5.062, below. Prym's appeal to the CFI against the same decision was also dismissed save for a small reduction in the fine: Case T-30/05 *Prym v Commission* [2007] ECR II-107* (further appeal dismissed: Case C-534/07, judgment of 3 September 2009, [2009] 5 CMLR 2377).

Fn 223. In Case T-68/04 *SGL Carbon AG v Commission* [2009] 4 CMLR 7, the appellant complained that by finding four separate infringements and adopting four separate decisions imposing fines in relation to cartel activity involving graphite products, the Commission had circumvented the 10 per cent of turnover ceiling on fines. The CFI rejected this and upheld the fine: paras 131 *et seq.* A further appeal was dismissed: Case C-564/08 P, judgment of 12 November 2009.

Fn 225. The appeal in Case T-112/05 *Akzo Nobel* and a further appeal to the ECJ have now been decided: Case C-97/08 P *Akzo Nobel NV v Commission*, judgment of 10 September 2009.

2.053 **Parties to the agreement/concerted practice.**   The appeal by the trade association fined in the *Organic Peroxides* decision for providing administrative and secretarial services to the cartel was dismissed by the CFI: Case T-99/04 *AC-Treuhand AG v Commission* [2008] ECR II-1501, [2008] 5 CMLR 962. See update to paragraph 5.014, below.

Proof of participation.   The judgment in Case T-36/05 *Coats Holdings Ltd v*   **2.055** *Commission* [2007] ECR II-110, [2008] 4 CMLR 45 provides a useful example of the CFI examining each of the planks on which the Commission's decision was based and finding many of them had not been established to the necessary legal standard. In particular the CFI found that the mere fact that Coats had been informed about an anti-competitive agreement between two producers, Prym and Entaco, cannot give rise to liability for the infringement (para 105). But the CFI found that in the circumstances of the case, the fact that Coats had, by the sale of its needles business, triggered the mechanism of the Prym/Entaco cartel did implicate Coats in that cartel, because the sale was part of a common plan. The fact that Coats' suppliers, Entaco and Prym, had discussed confidential issues (such as the creation of a cartel) with Coats showed, the CFI found, that Coats' intentions must have been of an anti-competitive nature. Note also the CFI's comments on the unreliability of one of the witnesses to whose evidence the Commission had referred: paras 165–167. Coats' fine was reduced to reflect the more limited nature of its involvement. Coats' appeal against this decision was dismissed: Case C-468/07 P [2009] 4 CMLR 301. Prym's appeal to the CFI against the same decision was also dismissed save for a small reduction in the fine: Case T-30/05 *Prym v Commission* [2007] ECR II-107* (further appeal dismissed: Case C-534/07, judgment of 3 September 2009, [2009] 5 CMLR 2377).

The fact that one party to an agreement concedes that the agreement existed does not preclude the other alleged party from disputing the existence of the agreement: Case T-18/03 *CD-Contact Data v Commission*, judgment of 30 April 2009, para 51.

For the use by the Commission of statements made by one cartel member incriminating others see Case T-54/03 *Lafarge v Commission* [2008] ECR II-120*, paras 57 *et seq* (on appeal Case C-413/08 P, not yet decided).

In COMP/39.181 *Candle Waxes*, decn of 1 October 2008, [2009] 5 CMLR 2441, the Commission rejected the suggestion that corporate statements submitted by one party under the Leniency Notice might contain a distorted version of events and said, to the contrary, that such evidence is particularly reliable. The Commission also noted that 'recollection of facts does not need to be perfect in order to be credible': para 217. The decision is on appeal, Cases T-540, 541, 543, 544, 548, 550, 551, 558, 562/08, not yet decided.

For the approach of the English courts to this issue see *Bookmakers' Afternoon Greyhound Services v Amalgamated Racing Ltd* [2008] EWHC 2688 (Ch), paras 15–18. The judge held that the evidence of collusion relied on by the claimants was 'nowhere near strong enough' to justify him in rejecting the sworn evidence to the contrary of the defendants' witnesses: para 140.

2.058 **Authority to enter into agreements.** The fact that the director attending meetings was acting contrary to instructions does not affect the undertaking's liability: see Case T-53/03 *BPB plc v Commission* [2008] ECR II-1333, [2008] 5 CMLR 1201, paras 360 and 431: 'Thus, even if Mr [D] did in actual fact disobey the instructions of BPB's Board of Directors and continue the information exchanges without the latter's knowledge, the Commission was entitled to impose a fine on the undertaking, whilst BPB and/or its owners were free to pursue any action deemed appropriate against Mr [D]'.

(d) Decisions by associations of undertakings

2.059 **Associations of undertakings.** In COMP/34.579 *MasterCard MIF charges*, decn of 19 December 2007 the Commission held that the rules of the MasterCard organisation were still decisions of an association of undertakings after MasterCard was listed on the New York Stock Exchange. The Commission held that the bank members of the organisation had agreed to the IPO and the ensuing changes in the organisation's governance 'in order to perpetuate the MIF as part of the business model in a form which they perceived to be less exposed to antitrust scrutiny' (paras 3, 99 and 338 *et seq*). The case is on appeal: Case T-111/08, not yet decided.

Fn 265. The appeal in the *French Beef* case was dismissed: Cases C-101 & 110/07 P *Coop de France bétail et viande and FNSEA v Commission*, judgment of 18 December 2008, [2009] 4 CMLR 743.

2.060 **Decisions.** For there to be a decision it is not necessary that the members unanimously approve it or that each of them agrees on all aspects of a decision. It is sufficient that a decision is taken by the competent body within the association: COMP/34.579 *MasterCard MIF charges*, decn of 19 December 2007, para 384. The case is on appeal: Case T-111/08, not yet decided.

As to recommendations being regarded as decisions see COMP/38.698 *CISAC*, decn of 16 July 2008, [2009] 4 CMLR 577, paras 91 and 92: model contract terms adopted by the collecting society were not binding but members were encouraged to use them and did use them. Note, however, that the finding of infringement was addressed to the members and not to the collecting society itself (on appeal Cases T-398, 410, 411, 413–422, 425, 432, 434, 442, 451/08, not yet decided).

As to when non-binding acts of an association can fall within the prohibition, in *AUV v NMA*, judgment of 3 July 2008 the Dutch Trade and Industry Appeal Tribunal held that in deciding to refuse to supply veterinary medicines to members

who did not comply with its rules prohibiting onward supply other than to existing clients, the Dutch cooperative association of veterinarians was acting in its
capacity as an association of undertakings within the Dutch equivalent of Article
81(1) [now Article 101(1) TFEU] and not as an individual undertaking: the
impugned conduct was carried out at the request of some members and was
intended to coordinate members' conduct on the market.

4. Restriction of Competition

(a) Some conceptual issues

The competition rules and consumer detriment.   The ECJ overturned the   **2.064**
CFI's analysis insofar as it held that it was necessary to prove that an agreement
entails disadvantages for final consumers as a prerequisite for a finding of anti-
competitive object: Cases C-501/06 P, etc, *GlaxoSmithKline Services Unlimited v
Commission*, judgment of 6 October 2009. But the ECJ upheld the CFI's decision that the Commission had failed properly to examine GSK's arguments for
exemption under Article 81(3) [now Article 101(3) TFEU]: para 104. See also
Cases C-468/06, etc, *Sot Lelos kai Sia EE v GlaxoSmithKline* [2008] ECR I-7139,
[2008] 5 CMLR 1382, [2009] All ER (EC) 1 (State regulation of prices does
not mean that benefits of parallel trading for consumers are minimal).

Inter-brand and intra-brand competition.   This distinction was important in   **2.067**
the Commission's analysis in COMP/37.860 *Morgan Stanley/Visa International
and Visa Europe*, decn of 3 October 2007. The case is on appeal: Case T-461/07
Visa Europe and Visa International Service Association v Commission, not yet
decided. See similarly, COMP/38.606 *Groupement des Cartes Bancaires*, decn of
17 October 2007 where the Commission stated (also as regards payment card
networks) that '[t]he weakness of intersystem competition in France increases the
need for robust intrasystem competition. In other words, the stronger the position of a system in intersystem competition, the more serious is any weakening
of competition inside it': para 170. In *Groupement des Cartes Bancaires* the Commission described the free-rider argument as 'confused' because Groupement's
argument was really that the new entrants to the payment system were benefiting
from the investment made in the past over a period of many years by the traditional members. This was not a free-riding argument since there was no evidence
to show how much investment had been made, whether that investment had
already been recouped or whether the traditional members would have been discouraged from making that investment if they had known that later banks would
have been able to benefit from it: para 382. The case is on appeal Case T-491/07
CB v Commission, not yet decided.

(b) The main decisions

(i) The two seminal cases

2.077 **The interpretation of *Consten and Grundig* in *GlaxoSmithKline*.**   This paragraph must now be read in the light of the ECJ's judgment in the appeal: Cases C-501/06 P, etc, *GlaxoSmithKline Services Unlimited v Commission*, judgment of 6 October 2009. The ECJ firmly rejected the CFI's analysis and held that neither the wording of Article 81(1) [now Article 101(1) TFEU] nor the case law lends support to the CFI's statement that an agreement limiting parallel trade only has the object of restricting competition if it disadvantages final consumers: para 62. The Court cited both very early case law and its recent decisions in Cases C-468/06, etc, *Sot Lelos kai Sia EE v GlaxoSmithKline* and Case C-8/08 *T-Mobile Netherlands BV* to conclude that by requiring proof that the agreement entails disadvantages for final consumers and by not finding that GSK's agreement had such an object the CFI had committed an error of law. But the ECJ upheld the CFI's decision that the Commission had failed properly to examine GSK's arguments for exemption of the notified agreement under Article 81(3) [now Article 101(3) TFEU]: para 104.

(ii) Market analysis

2.087 ***European Night Services*: comment.**   See the application of *European Night Services* and subsequent case law in COMP/37.860 *Morgan Stanley/Visa International and Visa Europe*, decn of 3 October 2007: para 136.

(iii) Consideration of pro- and anti-competitive effects

2.091 **'Rule of reason' in Community law?**   The Commission applied the *Gøttrup-Klim, Métropole Télévision* line of cases in examining the objective justification of a rule of the Visa payment card network which refused membership to a competitor: COMP/37.860 *Morgan Stanley/Visa International and Visa Europe*, decn of 3 October 2007. Having found, on an analysis of the market, that the rule as applied to Morgan Stanley had appreciable restrictive effects on competition (para 201) the Commission considered that, nonetheless, the rule would not fall under Article 81(1) EC [now Article 101(1) TFEU] if it was directly related to and necessary (proportionate and non-discriminatory) for the proper functioning of Visa's network. On the facts the Commission held that this was not the case, and the rule did not fulfil the conditions of Article 81(3) either. The case is on appeal: Case T-461/07 *Visa Europe and Visa International Service Association v Commission*, not yet decided.

2.092 ***Wouters* and *Meca-Medina*.**   Fn 371. See also the Belgian Cour de Cassation in *CT v Orde de Architecten* (D.06.0010.N), judgment of 27 April 2007: decision of the Belgian Association of Architects that requires architects' fees to be determined on the basis of the nature and dimensions of the assignment has the purpose of ensuring the proper practice of the profession and accordingly does not fall within the prohibition of Belgian competition law. Cf *L'Orde des Pharmaciens* (2007/ MR/5), Brussels Court of Appeal, judgment of 7 April 2009: although the requirements on pharmacists for on-call duty served the general interest, the rule of the Belgian Pharmacists Association regarding opening hours was not proportionate in support of those requirements and therefore did not satisfy the criteria of *Wouters* so as to escape condemnation under Belgian competition law.

Article 81(1) and Article 81(3) relationship illustrated.   In COMP/34.579 **2.093** *MasterCard MIF charges*, decn of 19 December 2007, paras 524 *et seq*, the Commission set out the case law from *Pronuptia* and *Metropole* to *Gøttrup-Klim* and *Wouters* when considering whether a payment card system could operate without a multilateral exchange fee such that the fee fell outside Article 81(1) [now Article 101(1) TFEU]. The Commission accepted that the Article 81(1) test covered the question whether there was an alternative to the fee which was 'feasible' but held that the secondary question – whether that alternative was better than the MIF – was a question to be addressed under Article 81(3) not Article 81(1): para 542. To hold otherwise would be to reverse the burden of proof under Article 81(3) [now Article 101(3) TFEU]. In the event, the Commission held that it was feasible to operate the system without an MIF: para 549. The case is on appeal: Case T-111/08, not yet decided.

See also *Bookmakers' Afternoon Greyhound Services v Amalgamated Racing Ltd* [2009] EWCA Civ 750 where the English Court of Appeal applied the principles in *Métropole Télévision (M6)* and *Wouters* in finding that an agreement among racecourses to grant exclusive media rights to a joint venture which they had set up to compete with a former monopsony owned by the bookmakers did not have the object or effect of restricting competition and so did not fall within Article 81(1) [now Article 101(1) TFEU]. The Court discussed the O_2 *(Germany)* case and the opinion of the Advocate General in C-209/07 *Beef Industry Development Society Ltd v Barry Brothers (Carrigmore) Meats Ltd* [2009] 4 CMLR 310, [2009] All ER (EC) 367 and rejected the argument that pro-competitive aspects of the agreement fell to be considered only under Article 81(3) [now Article 101(3) TFEU].

(c) **The present law**

In general.   Fn 373. Note that the ECJ overturned the CFI's analysis insofar as **2.094** it held that it was necessary to prove that an agreement entails disadvantages for final consumers as a prerequisite for a finding of anti-competitive object: Cases C-501/06 P, etc, *GlaxoSmithKline Services Unlimited v Commission*, judgment of 6 October 2009.

2.095 **The main considerations.**   Note that the restriction of competition may arise in a market where the infringer is not itself active: for example in COMP/38.606 *Groupement des Cartes Bancaires*, decn of 17 October 2007 the Commission found that the bankers' association's decisions restricted competition in the market for issuing payment cards, even though the Groupement did not itself issue such cards: 'it does not follow from the fact that the Groupement is not itself an issuer (it being the banks members of the Groupement that are the issuers) that the measures cannot be examined in the context of the issuance market. Community competition law is applicable to the conduct of an undertaking or association of undertakings restricting competition in a market other than that in which it provides its services and for the benefit of undertakings other than itself': para 179.

2.096 **The object.**   In Case C-209/07 *Beef Industry Development Society Ltd v Barry Brothers (Carrigmore) Meats Ltd* [2009] 4 CMLR 310, [2009] All ER (EC) 367, the ECJ described the object of the agreement as 'the precise purpose of the agreement, in the economic context in which it is to be applied' (para 15). Even if the parties acted without any subjective intention of restricting competition, but with the object of remedying the effects of an overcapacity crisis in their sector, such considerations are irrelevant for the purposes of applying Article 81(1) [now Article 101(1) TFEU] and are only relevant for the purposes of Article 81(3) [now Article 101(3) TFEU]. An agreement may be regarded as having a restrictive object even if it does not have the restriction of competition as its sole aim but also pursues other legitimate objectives. The arrangements which had been notified to the Irish competition authority were intended to enable undertakings in the beef and veal processing market to implement a common policy which encouraged some of them to withdraw from the market and thereby bring about a reduction of overcapacity. The ECJ held that the agreement patently conflicted with the competition rules because it was intended to dissuade the undertakings which remained in the market from increasing their market share and also discouraged new entry. The ECJ did not rule out the application of Article 81(3) but this was not part of the questions referred by the Irish court for the preliminary ruling. On 3 November 2009 the Irish Supreme Court referred the matter back to the trial judge to reconsider the application of Article 81(3), Kearns J commenting that 'the initiative giving rise to the BIDS scheme was as far removed as one could imagine from objectionable cartel practises': [2009] IESC 72. See similarly, Case C-8/08 *T-Mobile Netherlands BV v Raad van bestuur van de Nederlandse Mededingingsautoriteit*, judgment of 4 June 2009, paras 28 and 30; Cases C-501/06 P, etc, *GlaxoSmithKline Services Unlimited v Commission*, judgment of 6 October 2009, para 55. In COMP/38.606 *Groupement des Cartes Bancaires*, decn of 17 October 2007 the Commission rejected the submissions made by the parties when they notified the rules under Regulation 17 and found that the real object of the agreement was to hinder market entry: para 251.

In *Bookmakers' Afternoon Greyhound Services v Amalgamated Racing Ltd* [2009] EWCA Civ 750 the English Court of Appeal distinguished the ECJ's judgment in *Irish Beef* in relation to an agreement among racecourses to grant exclusive rights to broadcast horse races to bookmakers' premises to a joint venture which they had set up to compete with a former monopsony owned by the bookmakers. The Court rejected the allegation that the agreement had the object of restricting competition as not 'reflecting in any realistic way either the economic context in which the arrangements were made, or the object of the arrangements, ascertained objectively by reference to their nature and terms in the relevant context': para 83.

Fn 388. See also Cases C-501/06 P, etc, *GlaxoSmithKline Services Unlimited v Commission*, judgment of 6 October 2009, para 58 where the ECJ noted that although the parties' intention is not a necessary factor in determining whether an agreement is restrictive, there is nothing prohibiting the Commission from taking that aspect into account.

'Hard-core' restrictions: objects restrictive *per se*.   The qualification introduced **2.097** by the CFI in *GlaxoSmithKline* was firmly rejected by the ECJ's judgment in the appeal: Cases C-501/06 P, etc, *GlaxoSmithKline Services Unlimited v Commission*, judgment of 6 October 2009. The Court cited both very early case law and its recent decisions in Cases C-468/06, etc, *Sot Lelos kai Sia EE v GlaxoSmithKline* and Case C-8/08 *T-Mobile Netherlands BV* to conclude that by requiring proof that the agreement entails disadvantages for final consumers as a prerequisite for a finding of anti-competitive object and by not finding that GSK's agreement had such an object the CFI had committed an error of law. But the ECJ upheld the CFI's decision that the Commission had failed properly to examine GSK's arguments for exemption under Article 81(3) [now Article 101(3) TFEU]: para 104.

As regards the penultimate sentence of this paragraph see Case T-53/03 *BPB plc v Commission* [2008] ECR II-1333, [2008] 5 CMLR 1201, para 90 where the CFI said that '[u]ndertakings which conclude an agreement whose purpose is to restrict competition cannot, in principle, avoid the application of Article 81(1) EC by claiming that their agreement was not intended to have an appreciable effect on competition'.

The effects on competition: the whole economic context.   As to the use of **2.099** expert economic evidence see the comments of Morgan J in *Bookmakers' Afternoon Greyhound Services v Amalgamated Racing Ltd* [2008] EWHC 1978 (Ch), paras 287 and 288 that the expert witnesses did not confine themselves to matters of microeconomics on which they could give admissible opinion evidence for the assistance of the court but also summarised their understanding of the legal principles which fell to be applied and then offered their conclusions as to the result of applying those legal principles to this case. Although the parties did not distinguish between parts of their statements which were truly admissible expert evidence on matters of microeconomics and those parts which went beyond the proper bounds of expert evidence, the learned judge considered it important to do so.

2.105 **Markets where scope for competition is limited.** **Fn 442.** In the appeal Cases C-501/06 P, etc, *GlaxoSmithKline Services Unlimited v Commission*, judgment of 6 October 2009 the ECJ held that the agreement did have an anti-competitive object so that there was no need to consider the effect of the agreement in the context of Article 81(1) [now Article 101(1) TFEU].

2.110 **Vertical restrictions affecting exports or imports.** The qualification introduced by the CFI in *GlaxoSmithKline* was firmly rejected by the ECJ's judgment in the appeal: Cases C-501/06 P, etc, *GlaxoSmithKline Services Unlimited v Commission*, judgment of 6 October 2009. The Court concluded that by requiring proof that the agreement entails disadvantages for final consumers as a prerequisite for a finding of anti-competitive object and by not finding that GSK's agreement had such an object the CFI had committed an error of law. Since the agreement did have an anti-competitive object, there was no need to consider the effect of the agreement in the context of Article 81(1) [now Article 101(1) TFEU]. See now also Cases C-468/06, etc, *Sot Lelos kai Sia EE v GlaxoSmithKline* [2008] ECR I-7139, [2008] 5 CMLR 1382, [2009] All ER (EC) 1 (reference for a preliminary ruling concerning the application of Article 102 TFEU to GlaxoSmithKline's refusal to fulfil orders from a wholesaler who engages in parallel trading).

Fn 447. The appeals in *Video Games, Nintendo Distribution* have now been decided: Case T-18/03 *CD-Contact Data v Commission*, judgment of 30 April 2009 (fine reduced) (on further appeal Case C-260/09P *Activision Blizzard Germany*, not yet decided); Case T-12/03 *Itochu* [2009] 5 CMLR 1375 (appeal dismissed); Case T-13/03 *Nintendo* [2009] 5 CMLR 1421 (fine reduced); Case T-398/02 *Linea Gig* (removed from register 2 May 2005).

2.112 **Ancillary restrictions not within Article 81(1).** See *Bookmakers' Afternoon Greyhound Services v Amalgamated Racing Ltd* [2009] EWCA Civ 750 where the English Court of Appeal upheld the first instance judge's decision ([2008] EWHC 1978 (Ch)) that the exclusive grant of media rights was an ancillary restriction within the principles established in Case T-112/99 *Métropole Télévision (M6) v Commission* [2001] ECR II-2459 and Case C-309/99 *Wouters* [2002] ECR I-1577: para 121.

2.116 **Restrictions necessary and proportionate to legitimate objective.** See also *Bookmakers' Afternoon Greyhound Services v Amalgamated Racing Ltd* [2009] EWCA Civ 750.

5. Appreciable Effect on Competition

In general. As regards the application of the *de minimis* threshold to agreements **2.121** which have the object of restricting competition see Case T-53/03 *BPB plc v Commission* [2008] ECR II-1333, [2008] 5 CMLR 1201, para 90 where the CFI said that '[u]ndertakings which conclude an agreement whose purpose is to restrict competition cannot, in principle, avoid the application of Article 81(1) EC by claiming that their agreement was not intended to have an appreciable effect on competition'.

See Case C-506/07 *Lubricarga v Petrogal Española*, not yet decided, where the ECJ has been asked whether a contract which fixes resale prices can still fall outside Article 101(1) TFEU if it is *de minimis*.

3

ARTICLE 81(3)

1. Introduction

Note: Article 81(3) EC has now become Article 101(3) TFEU

Lapse of extant notifications for exemption. In COMP/37.860 *Morgan*   **3.009**
Stanley/Visa International and Visa Europe, decn of 3 October 2007 the Commission found that a rule applied by Visa to exclude its competitor Morgan Stanley
from the Visa payment card network infringed Article 81 [now Article 101
TFEU]. The Rule had been notified to the Commission in 1990. The Commission
noted that the immunity from fines conferred by notification lapsed once
Regulation 1/2003 came into force. Further, Visa could not sustain a claim of
legitimate expectation of immunity from fines for the period after the statement
of objections was delivered since that statement clearly indicated that the
Commission was envisaging imposing a fine (para 341). A fine was imposed for
the period starting with the date on which the statement of objections was issued
until the infringing conduct ceased. The case is on appeal: Case T-461/07 *Visa
Europe and Visa International Service Association v Commission*, not yet decided.

Fn 18. In the appeal Cases C-501/06 P, etc, *GlaxoSmithKline Services Unlimited v
Commission*, judgment of 6 October 2009 the ECJ found that the agreement had
an anti-competitive object but still upheld the CFI's decision that the Commission
had failed properly to examine GSK's arguments for exemption under Article 81(3)
[now Article 101(3) TFEU]: para 104.

Relationship between Article 81(1) and 81(3). See how the Commission   **3.011**
approached this in COMP/37.860 *Morgan Stanley/Visa International and Visa
Europe*, decn of 3 October 2007. The Commission found, on an analysis of the
market, that a rule of the Visa payment network, as applied to exclude Morgan
Stanley, had appreciable restrictive effects on competition (para 201). Referring to
the *Gøttrup-Klim*, *Métropole Télévision* line of cases, the Commission considered
that, nonetheless, the rule would not fall under Article 81(1) [now Article 101(1)

TFEU] if it was directly related to and necessary (proportionate and non-discriminatory) for the proper functioning of Visa's network. On the facts the Commission held that this was not the case. The Commission then went on to consider whether the conditions of Article 81(3) [now Article 101(3) TFEU] were fulfilled. Visa had not expressly relied on the points raised in relation to objective justification as also being relevant to the application of Article 81(3). But the Commission considered that such arguments needed to be taken into account in considering whether the exclusion of Morgan Stanley from the network was necessary to generate efficiencies that outweigh and thereby justify the restriction of competition caused by such exclusion: para 317. The Commission held that the conditions of Article 81(3) were not fulfilled. The case is on appeal: Case T-461/07 *Visa Europe and Visa International Service Association v Commission*, not yet decided.

2. Application in Individual Cases

(a) Generally

3.013 **Unlimited theoretical application of Article 81(3).** Note *Competition Authority v Beef Industry Development Society Ltd* [2009] IESC 72, where after the ECJ's ruled on a reference under Article 234 [now Article 267 TFEU] that the arrangements for reducing overcapacity in the beef slaughtering industry gave rise to an infringement by object, the Irish Supreme Court referred the case back to the High Court to determine whether the conditions of Article 81(3) [now Article 101(3) TFEU] were satisfied. However, the case concerned an open and transparent rationalisation scheme, not a secret cartel. (For the ECJ judgment, see further the update to paragraph 2.096, above).

3.015 **Burden of proof.** The burden and standard of proof for Article 81(3) [now Article 101(3) TFEU] was considered by the ECJ in Cases C-501/06 P, etc, *GlaxoSmithKline Services Unlimited v Commission*, judgment of 6 October 2009. First, the Court rejected an argument that attempted to draw an analogy between the appraisal of the competitive effects of a concentration with the appraisal needed under Article 81(3): para 78. Thus the ECJ confirmed that it is for the undertakings concerned to demonstrate by means of convincing arguments and evidence that the conditions are fulfilled. However, the facts relied on by that undertaking 'may be such as to oblige the other party to provide an explanation or justification, failing which it is permissible to conclude that the burden of proof has been discharged': para 83. The ECJ upheld the CFI's finding that the Commission had failed to take into account certain aspects of the market which had been highlighted by GSK in its request for exemption: para 104. See also the

Advocate General's comments on the standard of proof required: para 193 of her opinion, approved by the Court at para 93 of the judgment.

(b) The first condition: economic and other benefits

(i) Generally

Benefits must be objective. See also Cases C-501/06 P, etc, *GlaxoSmithKline* **3.020** *Services Unlimited v Commission*, judgment of 6 October 2009, para 102.

Efficiencies and other benefits. The Commission has stressed that the existence **3.021** of efficiencies cannot be determined in a general manner by economic theory alone, 'as theories always rely on assumptions that may not sufficiently reflect market reality'. Claims that restrictions create efficiencies 'must be founded on detailed, robust and compelling analysis that relies in its assumptions and deductions on empirical data and facts': COMP/34.579 *MasterCard MIF charges*, decn of 19 December 2007, para 690. The Commission held that MasterCard had not established that the first condition of Article 81(3) [now Article 101(3) TFEU] was met. The case is on appeal: Case T-111/08, not yet decided.

On appeal in the *GlaxoSmithKline* case mentioned towards the end of the paragraph, the ECJ upheld the CFI's analysis as regards the application of Article 81(3) [now Article 101(3) TFEU]: Cases C-501/06 P, etc, *GlaxoSmithKline Services Unlimited v Commission*, judgment of 6 October 2009. The Advocate General noted at para 193 of her opinion that Article 81(3) required a prospective analysis of the likely occurrence of the advantages said to arise from the agreement. The first condition of Article 81(3) would therefore be satisfied if the Commission was able, on the basis of the arguments and evidence submitted, to arrive at the conviction that the occurrence of the appreciable objective advantage is sufficiently likely in the light of actual experience. In her opinion, a high degree of probability must be required since the existence of losses in efficiency in the form of a restriction of competition must *ex hypothesi* exist. The Court approved this passage: see para 93 of the judgment.

Commission's current approach. However, in *Competition Authority v Beef* **3.028** *Industry Development Society Ltd* [2009] IESC 72, the Irish Supreme Court, commenting on the Article 81(3) Guidelines, held that it was not necessary to establish with precision what the exact value or magnitude of the benefits resulting from the arrangements would be. Per Kearns P: 'It will suffice if BIDS can demonstrate positive gains or at least a state of neutrality from the point of view of the consumer'. These observations were expressly made in the context of the facts of the case, which concerned a rationalisation scheme in an industry facing chronic overcapacity.

(d) The third condition: indispensability of restrictions

3.060 **Establishing indispensability.** Fn 195. As to the last sentence see now *Competition Authority v Beef Industry Development Society Ltd* [2009] IESC 72. The Irish Supreme Court first referred questions to the ECJ under Article 234 [now Article 267 TFEU] and, following the preliminary ruling (Case C-209/07 [2009] 4 CMLR 310), referred the case back to the Irish High Court to assess the application of Article 81(3) [now Article 101(3) TFEU]. In his judgment the President of the Irish Supreme Court, Kearns P, indicated that the imposition of non-compete covenants on those paid to leave the market may be indispensable conditions of an industry rationalisation scheme if the objective of reducing capacity came within Article 81(3).

Fn 196. A further appeal in *Der Grüne Punkt* was dismissed: Case C-385/07 P *Der Grüne Punkt – Duales System Deutschland v Commission*, judgment of 16 July 2009, [2009] 5 CMLR 2215.

3. Block Exemption

(a) Generally

3.075 **Council enabling regulations.** Regulation 3976/87 relating to air transport and the regulations amending it have been repealed and replaced as from the end of June 2009 by a consolidating instrument: Regulation 487/2009 on the application of Article 81(3) of the Treaty to certain categories of agreements and concerted practices in the air transport sector, OJ 2009 L148/1: Vol II, App E9A.

Regulation 479/92 relating to liner consortia has been replaced as from March 2009 by Regulation 246/2009 on the application of Article 81(3) of the Treaty to certain categories of agreements, decisions and concerted practices between liner shipping companies (consortia), OJ 2009 L79/1: Vol II, App E7A.

(b) Current block exemption regulations

3.078 **Vertical restraints.** The Commission has consulted on a revised block exemption to come into effect when Regulation 2790/99 expires on 1 June 2010: see Press Release IP/09/1197 (28 July 2009) which includes links to the draft regulation and draft new guidelines, see further the update to paragraph 6.010, below.

3.081 **Insurance.** The Commission is consulting on a revised regulation which would renew two of the four categories of agreements currently exempted, namely information exchange and insurance pools, with certain amendments: see Press Release IP/09/1413 (5 October 2009).

Liner consortia. The Commission has adopted a new block exemption for liner **3.084** consortia, pursuant to the new enabling regulation: Regulation 906/2009, OJ 2009 L256/31: Vol II, App E7B. The Regulation will enter into force on 26 April 2010 when Regulation 823/2000 expires. The Regulation applies only to consortia insofar as they provide international liner shipping services from or to one or more Community ports. But the new Regulation extends to all liner shipping cargo services, whether containerised or not. The list of exempted activities has been revised in order to reflect current market practices and hard-core restrictions such as price-fixing and market- or customer-sharing will still deprive the agreement of the benefit of the exemption. The market share threshold has been reduced from 35 per cent to 30 per cent and the method of its calculation has been clarified. The permissible restrictions on a member withdrawing from the consortium have also been revised.

4

MARKET DEFINITION

1. Introduction and Overview

(a) The concept of the relevant market

Risk of error in defining markets. For an example of the difficulty of conclusive **4.004** definition of the relevant market see COMP/38.113 *Prokent-Tomra* [2009] 4 CMLR 101, para 46 where the Commission took a wider market definition as the basis for the decision since this favoured the undertaking alleged to be dominant (on appeal Case T-155/06 *Tomra Systems*, not yet decided).

(b) Relevance of market definition in EC competition law

Merger cases. See, eg Case M.4691 *Schering-Plough/Organon Biosciences* **4.012** (11 October 2007) where the Commission examined the competitive impact of the merger on over 200 relevant markets, noting that many animal health markets have quite a small size, sometimes as small as €10,000 (for example the market for monovalent tetanus vaccine for horses in Denmark) (para 50).

(c) Methodology for determining market definition

(i) Jurisprudence and guidelines

Reconciling the various approaches to market definition. Fn 57. The appeal **4.018** referred to in the footnote was dismissed by the ECJ: Case C-202/07 P *France Télécom v Commission*, judgment of 2 April 2009. The ECJ judgment did not consider issues concerning market definition. In Case M.5141 *KLM/Martinair* (17 December 2008) the Commission described the market survey carried out among passengers flying from Schiphol airport to the Caribbean: see paras 105 *et seq.*

(ii) Factors relevant to defining markets

Market definitions are contextual. In COMP/39.181 *Candle Waxes*, decn of **4.021** 1 October 2008, [2009] 5 CMLR 2441 the Commission stated that it is not obliged to engage in any market definition when conducting cartel investigations. Instead, it is the subject of the contacts between the companies involved in a cartel which defines the products to which the infringement relates. It was therefore not surprising that such a definition may be different from a market definition used in a merger control procedure. That the Commission may have defined a market in a certain way in a merger decision has no relevance for a cartel decision: para 279. The decision is on appeal, Cases T-540, 541, 543, 544, 548, 550, 551, 558, 562/08, not yet decided.

4.022A **Analysis of two-sided demand markets.** In COMP/34.579 *MasterCard MIF charges*, decn of 19 December 2007 the Commission considered how to define markets in a case under Article 81 [now Article 101 TFEU] where there is a two-sided demand; in that case, a demand on the part of merchants who honour the cards at their point of sale and a demand on the part of cardholders who use the cards to make payments. There were also 'network' effects in the sense that both merchants and cardholders saw a benefit in having a larger network of users of the system. MasterCard argued that in these circumstances there was in fact 'joint demand' on the part of merchants and cardholders matched by a 'joint service' by acquiring and issuing banks so that the product was in fact the whole card payment system. They argued that the SSNIP test should thus be applied to the aggregate of the charges set for merchants and cardholders to see how far that payment system competed with other card payment systems, with cash and other payment methods. The Commission rejected this analysis holding that such an approach was not appropriate for assessing the potential effect of the charge in question on competition *within* the payment scheme and as between acquiring banks because it ignores the different levels of interaction and supply and demand within such a scheme (para 265). Instead the Commission identified an upstream 'network market' where card scheme owners compete to persuade financial institutions to join their scheme and on which they provide services to such institutions. There were also the downstream markets for acquiring merchants and issuing cards to cardholders. The downstream acquirers market did not compete with cash or other payment methods (paras 285 and 307). On the issuing market, cash and cheques were held not to be sufficiently substitutable on the demand side (paras 310 *et seq*). The Commission concluded that the relevant market for assessing the MIF fees was the market for acquiring payment cards: para 329. The case is on appeal: Case T-111/08, not yet decided. See also COMP/37.860 *Morgan Stanley/Visa International and Visa Europe*, decn of 3 October 2007 where the Commission identified three relevant markets in a case under Article 81(1) about a rule excluding competitors from Visa network membership: (i) a market for network services, in which card networks (such as Visa or MasterCard) provide services to individual financial institutions; (ii) an 'issuing market' in which card issuers compete with each other to issue cards and provide card-related services to individuals; and (iii) an 'acquiring market' in which acquirers sign merchants for all of the services necessary for the merchant to accept cards: para 41. The case is on appeal: Case T-461/07 *Visa Europe and Visa International Service Association v Commission*, not yet decided. See similarly, COMP/38.606 *Groupement des Cartes Bancaires*, decn of 17 October 2007, 'the "two-sided" nature of an economic activity by no means signifies that the system concerned constitutes a single market': para 180 (on appeal Case T-491/07 *CB v Commission*, not yet decided).

On two-sided markets see also Case M.4523 *Travelport/Worldspan* (21 August 2007) (global distribution systems for travel services provide a service to airlines, hotels and other travel services providers on one side and to travel agents on the other). This case, and the theory of harm for two-sided markets are discussed in Vannini, 'Bargaining and two-sided markets: the case of Global Distribution Systems (GDS) in Travelport's acquisition of Worldspan' (2008) 2 Competition Policy Newsletter 43.

(iv) Limitations on the SSNIP test

Circumstances where the SSNIP test cannot be applied. See, eg the analysis of **4.029** bidding data in Case M.4662 *Syniverse/BSG Wireless Business* (4 December 2007) (analysis of the participation of the data clearing houses in tenders and on the ranking data provided by customers was carried out on two datasets: one based on information received from the customers and the other one based on data received mainly from the parties) and Case M.4647 *AEE/Lentjes* (5 December 2007).

The 'cellophane fallacy'. In COMP/34.579 *MasterCard MIF charges*, decn of **4.030** 19 December 2007 the Commission found that the SSNIP test was not a reliable indicator of what products should be included in the relevant market because there was a significant risk of the 'cellophane fallacy' applying in relation to charges imposed by acquirers on merchants in the MasterCard payment scheme: paras 286–287. The case is on appeal: Case T-111/08, not yet decided.

See also *Soda-Club*, WuW DE-R 2268, judgment of German Federal Supreme Court of 4 March 2008 in a case under Article 81 [now Article 101 TFEU], holding that the SSNIP test there was only a guide and could not determine the market definition, in part because the prices charged by Soda-Club, a dominant company, could not be regarded as competitive market prices.

2. Product Market

(a) Demand-side substitution

Product characteristics and functional interchangeability. In *Bookmakers'* **4.034** *Afternoon Greyhound Services v Amalgamated Racing Ltd* [2009] EWCA Civ 750 the English Court of Appeal held that racecourses are not in competition with each other for the sale of rights to broadcast horse races to bookmakers' premises. The Court took into account the fact that races held at British racecourses are deliberately scheduled by the British Horseracing Authority so as to take place at different times and not to coincide. Secondly, bookmakers have an incentive to show live coverage of as many British races as possible and to screen a succession of races throughout the day in order to maximise their betting turnover: paras 58 *et seq*. The case was therefore distinguishable from *UEFA Champions League* [2004] 4 CMLR 9.

4.035 **Switching data.**   See the detailed analysis of switching in Case M.4731 *Google/ DoubleClick* (11 March 2008) where the Commission identified three major steps that a customer would need to take before switching between ad serving providers and noted that perception of the switching process in terms of time and cost varied significantly among market players (para 138). The Commission found evidence that a large number of publishers and advertisers had switched from DoubleClick to other service providers (and vice versa) in the previous few years.

4.037 **Consumer preferences and perceptions.**   The segmentation of spirits into markets for different spirit types has been confirmed by the Commission in a number of merger cases: see, eg Case M.5114 *Pernod Ricard/V&S Vin & Sprit* (17 August 2008) and the cases cited there. In that case the Commission also considered whether vodka should be further segmented according to price. The notifying party disputed this arguing that vodkas form a price continuum, meaning that there is a continuous distribution of prices with no clear break. They did acknowledge however that a limited number of brands that are sold at significantly higher prices but in limited quantities may not form part of the price continuum. The Commission found that the econometric analysis available was inconclusive and left the question open.

See the description of 'conjoint analysis' in COMP/34.579 *MasterCard MIF charges*, decn of 19 December 2007, para 292. Where a product has a range of attributes, conjoint analysis is used to determine which combinations of attributes the customer most values. The case is on appeal: Case T-111/08, not yet decided.

4.040 **Shock analysis or event evidence.**   See, eg Case M.5141 *KLM/Martinair* (17 December 2008) where the Commission considered the effect on leisure travel of the introduction of a Dutch ticket tax at Schiphol airport: para 182.

4.042 **Different absolute price levels.**   In its decision of 27 February 2008 (COMP/ 37.792) fixing the periodic penalty payment for Microsoft's failure to offer non-patented interoperability information on reasonable terms, the Commission stressed that it was necessary to exclude from the assessment of the value of the technology the 'strategic value' stemming from Microsoft's market power in the client PC and work group server operating system markets: see paras 107 *et seq.* The decision is under appeal: Case T-167/08, not yet decided.

Critical loss analysis.   The Commission considered a critical loss analysis put   **4.044** forward by the parties in Case M.5141 *KLM/Martinair* (17 December 2008) and concluded that 'it appears more likely than not that any significant non transitory price increase on the part of the merged entity would be unprofitable': paras 296 *et seq.*

See also the analysis in Case M.4734 *INEOS/Kerling* (30 January 2008), paras 95 *et seq.* Having found that the results derived from econometric analysis were inconclusive, the Commission focused on other quantitative and qualitative evidence gathered during the market investigation to assess whether the estimated volumes needed to defeat a potential price increase by the merging parties could be provided by the Continental suppliers. The Commission therefore looked at the current level of imports, the role of importers, Continental suppliers' ability to expand their sales in the United Kingdom, transport costs and the future expansion of capacities: para 105. For an explanation of the Commission's methodology in conducting a critical loss analysis in this case see Amelio et al, 'Ineos/Kerling merger: an example of quantitative analysis in support of a clearance decision' (2008) 1 Competition Policy Newsletter 65.

(b) Supply-side substitution

Use of supply-side substitution in practice.   The first step in considering supply   **4.052** substitution may be to examine the amount of spare capacity available to existing competitors. For example, in Case M.4525 *Kronospan/Constantia* (19 July 2007) (a case under the Merger Regulation) the Commission found that the main suppliers did not have significant spare capacity to increase supplies into the affected area and that expanding capacity would need considerable investment and a significant lead time (paras 60 and 61). The Commission also noted that capacity constraints are more likely to be important when goods are relatively homogeneous.

Supply-side substitutability was an important issue in Case M.4513 *Arjowiggins/ M-Real Zanders' Reflect paper mill* (4 June 2008) concerning carbonless paper reels and sheets. The notifying party referred to the fact that the Relevant Market Notice specifically mentions the paper industry as an example of supply-side substitutability. The Commission noted that it is not simply a question of whether it is technically possible for suppliers to switch – marketing and distribution issues are also relevant. Supply-side substitutability is less likely in markets for heavily branded goods. The Commission adopted two techniques for analysing the market: 'correlation analysis' which measures the extent to which price movements of one product are associated with price movements of another product;

and 'stationarity analysis' which uses sophisticated statistical tests to gauge whether the relative price of two products tends to revert to a constant value over time (that is to say, whether the relative price is 'stationary'); but ultimately the question was left open: paras 48 *et seq.*

4.057 **Supply-side substitution: shock analysis or event evidence.**   In Case M.5046 *Friesland/Campina* (17 December 2008) the parties submitted evidence about the effect of a fire which had closed one of the parties' plants for the whole of 2005, leading to a significant reduction in production. However, the Commission concluded on the facts that the supply shock analysis was of limited informative value regarding the incentives of the merged entity to raise prices: para 799.

(c) Particular issues in determining the product market

(i) Connected markets

4.059 **Connected markets.**   **Fn 167.** For another example of a 'two sided market' see Case M.4523 *Travelport/Worldspan* (21 August 2007) (global distribution systems for travel services provide a service to airlines, hotels and other travel services providers on one side and to travel agents on the other). See further new paragraph 4.022A, above.

4.059A **Potential or hypothetical markets.**   In COMP/38.700 *Greek Lignite and Electricity generation*, decn of 5 March 2008, [2009] 4 CMLR 495 the Commission considered whether PPC could be dominant in the market for the supply of lignite in Greece when no such market currently existed because PPC had the exclusive right to mine all available deposits of lignite to use in its own plants for generating electricity. The Commission referred to the statement of the ECJ in Case C-418/01 *IMS Health* [2004] ECR I-5039, [2004] 4 CMLR 1543, [2004] All ER (EC) 813 to the effect that 'it is sufficient that a potential market or even a hypothetical market can be identified'. The Commission held that since the reason why there was no market for the sale of lignite was because PPC had already monopolised this activity and vertically integrated it, PPC could be held to be dominant in the market for the supply of lignite. The case is on appeal, Case T-169/08 *DEI v Commission*, not yet decided.

4.060 **Systems markets.**   In *Soda-Club* WuW DE-R 2268, judgment of 4 March 2008, the German Federal Supreme Court held that the supply of home water carbonation systems was distinct from the market for refilling or replacing empty carbonators for such systems. Bottled sparkling water acted to constrain prices of the former systems, but once consumers had purchased a system, there was a distinct, secondary market for the carbonators.

Fn 178. See also COMP/39.391 *Printers (EFIM complaint)*, decn of 20 May 2009, where the Commission rejected a complaint adopting similar reasoning to that relied on in *Pelikan/Kyocera* and *Info-Lab/Ricoh*. The case is on appeal: Case T-296/09, not yet decided.

Market in licences or access to facilities.   In Case M.5224 *EdF/British Energy*   **4.061** (22 December 2008) the Commission held that there is a separate product market akin to a real estate market for sites considered suitable for building new nuclear power stations: para 104. Clearance of the proposed merger was conditional on divestment of one of these sites.

(ii) Branded goods

Separate markets for branded and own label products.   Note that this is a dif-   **4.064** ferent question from the question whether the market for supplying branded product to retailers is different from the market for supplying own label product to retailers: see Case M.4842 *Danone/Numico* (31 October 2007), para 32 and the cases cited therein.

Fn 186. See also Case M.4533 *SCA/ P&G (European tissue business)* (5 September 2008) where the Commission held that the markets for the supply of consumer tissue products to retailers should be divided into (a) production and supply of manufacturer brands/branded products; and (b) production and supply of private labels/retailer brands and applied those distinctions separately to the three categories of tissue products (toilet paper, kitchen towels, and handkerchiefs/facials). However, the Commission stressed that the competition at the retail level between the branded and unbranded products was crucial for the assessment of the case. Note that the Commission's market investigation established that 'toilet paper (as opposed to handkerchiefs/facials) is a "low emotion" commoditized product where brands do not play an important role': para 114.

(iii) In-house production

In-house production.   In Case M.4731 *Google/DoubleClick* (11 March 2008)   **4.065** the Commission found that the fact that major advertisers could and did opt to develop in-house technology for ad serving diminished the market position of DoubleClick substantially (para 178). The ability to develop in-house solutions imposed a constraint on the merged entity in two ways. First, publishers could develop an in-house solution for their own use in response to a price increase by third-party ad serving tool providers. Secondly, in-house solutions could ultimately also be marketed and sold to third parties as well (that is to say customers could become competitors) as had in fact occurred in the relevant market. See also Case M.4781 *Norddeutsche Affinerie/Cumerio* (23 January 2008) where the Commission found that copper shapes were produced for selling on the merchant market and also for internal processing into downstream semi-finished copper products. In fact only 17 per cent of all copper shapes produced were sold on the merchant market, the rest were used in-house (para 130). The Commission found that the ability of users to increase production of copper shapes either for their own in-house use or for sale on the merchant market acted as a constraint on the merged entity: para 152.

In *Independent Media Support Ltd v OFCOM* [2008] CAT 13, the UK Competition Appeal Tribunal considered paragraph 98 of the Commission's Guidelines on Vertical Restraints which states that in assessing market share, in-house production should be left out of account.

(v) Procurement markets

4.067 **Supply and procurement markets.** In Case M.5224 *EdF/British Energy* (22 December 2008) the Commission found that there was a market in the procurement of nuclear fuel: para 127.

Fn 199. The appeal against the *Sovion/HMG* merger clearance has been dismissed: Case T-151/05 *Nederlandse Vakbond Varkenshouders (NVV) v Commission* [2009] 5 CMLR 1613.

3. Geographic Market

(a) Overview

4.070 **Definition of the relevant product market.** For a recent case which turned on the proper definition of the geographic market see Case T-151/05 *Nederlandse Vakbond Varkenshouders (NVV) v Commission* [2009] 5 CMLR 1613, concerning the merger of two Dutch pig slaughterhouses. An association of Dutch pig farmers challenged the clearance of the merger on the basis (among other arguments) that the Commission had erred in finding that German slaughterhouses competed with Dutch slaughterhouses for the business of Dutch pig farmers within a 150 km radius of the main cities of the pig breeding areas of the Netherlands. The CFI upheld the Commission's decision, holding that 'the fundamental question for the purposes of defining the geographic market in the present case is therefore whether, if there were to be a small but sustainable reduction in the purchase price for pigs or sows in the areas concerned, the customers of the parties to the concentration and, in particular, the pig breeders, would switch to slaughterhouses located elsewhere' (para 122). The CFI upheld the findings that (i) differences in the weight of German and Dutch pigs or in their type or breed did not preclude Dutch farmers using German slaughterhouses; (ii) fluctuations in the prices paid for pig meat in the two countries had a direct effect on the scale of exports; (iii) the effect of disease outbreaks leading to temporary bans on exports did not restrict the market to a national market because after such bans were lifted, exports quickly resumed their previous levels; and (iv) transport costs are not decisive inasmuch as their impact on the price of pigs for slaughter is marginal. As regards the use of

150 km radius in defining the geographic market, the decisive question was whether suppliers of pigs for slaughter would be willing to transport their animals over a distance of 150 km to competing slaughterhouses if there were to be a small but sustainable reduction in the purchase price for pigs, with the result that such a drop in prices would not be profitable for the body which emerged from the concentration. The fact that the majority of pigs for slaughter are usually transported over distances of less than 150 km did not therefore constitute, in itself, a decisive factor for defining the relevant market.

Methodology. For an example, see Case M.4734 *INEOS/Kerling* (30 January **4.071** 2008) where the geographic market definition for a certain kind of PVC was crucial for the assessment of the merger in particular with respect to the United Kingdom, as the position of the parties was substantially different depending on whether the market was national or wider than national. The Commission noted that certain customers indicated that concerns about flexibility and reliability of supply, short lead times and precise timing of deliveries made it unlikely that they would source product from outside the United Kingdom. To determine whether these concerns were justified, the Commission carried out an assessment of the sourcing and switching patterns of these customers and a quantitative and qualitative analysis to assess to what extent Continental suppliers would be in a position to defeat a hypothetical price increase in the United Kingdom (the SSNIP test). The analysis was supported by the qualitative evidence of the current level of imports, transport costs and reported planned capacity expansions compared with demand growth, and the assessment of barriers to expansion in the United Kingdom: see paras 83 *et seq*. The Commission concluded that the evidence showed that the market was wider than just the United Kingdom.

Geographic market definition in the context of the removal of barriers to **4.072** **trade.** In COMP/38.700 *Greek Lignite and Electricity generation*, decn of 5 March 2008, [2009] 4 CMLR 495 the Commission noted that it had usually defined the geographic market for the wholesale supply of electricity as a national one. But in the case of Greece where only the part of the territory that was covered by the interconnector system had been opened up to competition so far as retail supply was concerned, the geographic market was held to be the territory of the interconnecter system: para 172. The case is on appeal: Case T-169/08 *DEI v Commission*, not yet decided.

(b) Demand-side substitution

Transport costs. Where transport costs are high relative to the value of the **4.073** product, the geographic market may be defined in terms of distance from the individual production plant: see, eg Case M.4525 *Kronospan/Constantia* (19 July 2007) (shipment data from suppliers and customers showed that the vast majority of shipments of raw particle board were within a 500 km radius of the plant regardless of national boundaries). This meant that national market shares were imperfect indicators of post-merger market power, as national boundaries did not necessarily reflect the competitive interaction between plants (paras 26 *et seq*). By contrast a significant amount of coated particle board was shipped more than 1000 km from the plant. See similarly Case T-151/05 *Nederlandse Vakbond Varkenshouders (NVV) v Commission* [2009] 5 CMLR 1613, where the territory within 150 km radius of the main pig breeding areas of the Netherlands was found to be the relevant geographic market, even if the radius covered territory across the border in Germany.

4.074 **Pricing data.** In Case M.4980 *ABF/GBI Business* (23 September 2008) the Commission found that there was a striking difference between trends in the average price of compressed yeast in Portugal compared with trends in neighbouring Spain, in particular that a large price level drop which occurred in Portugal did not seem to have had any influence on the Spanish prices. This indicated that the dynamics of the market were different in these two Member States and that the competitive interplay between producers and demand was to a large degree independent: para 76.

4.076 **National preferences and cultural features.** See also COMP/38.113 *Prokent-Tomra* [2009] 4 CMLR 101, paras 47–55 where the Commission considered the geographic market for reverse vending machines for recycling empty containers. The Commission found that the existence and volume of demand in any country was very dependent on the existence of national legislation relating to waste management in general and deposit systems for used drink containers in particular. Further, the prevalence and volumes of particular drink containers in the individual countries, as they result from regulatory requirements, from the choices made by the beverage industry, or from retail sector or consumer preferences, played a decisive role. For these and other reasons the Commission concluded that the market was national in scope. The case is on appeal Case T-155/06 *Tomra Systems*, not yet decided.

See also the discussion in Case T-151/05 *Nederlandse Vakbond Varkenshouders (NVV) v Commission* [2009] 5 CMLR 1613 of the weight and genetic differences between Dutch and German pigs.

4.079 **Shock analysis or event evidence.** In Case M.4734 *INEOS/Kerling* (30 January 2008) the Commission considered a 'natural experiment' in the form of an outage in one of the parties' United Kingdom plants. The Commission noted that this type of natural experiment, although it does not in itself provide sufficiently conclusive evidence with respect to the geographic market definition, provides for a picture of the flows of the product between regions during an unexpected event, namely the extent to which a shortage in supply is counterbalanced by local and external producers. This in turn can constitute an indication of the patterns of supply and demand within a national market, should production output in that market be restricted or the price for the product be increased on a longer term basis: para 140. The Commission concluded that the assessment of Ineos' outage in mid 2004 therefore suggested that, apart from Kerling, importers were in a position to react swiftly to any attempts of Ineos to reduce output so as to increase prices. This provided evidence that both Ineos and Kerling were constrained by importers, even in the event of an output shortage, which in turn suggested that the market was wider than the United Kingdom: para 149.

4. Temporal Market

Existence of temporal dimension. For a case in which the temporal dimension **4.089** of market demand was expressly addressed see COMP/38.113 *Prokent-Tomra* [2009] 4 CMLR 101, paras 56, 287, 343 and 344, concerning the market for reverse vending machines for recycling empty containers. The Commission noted that the volume of sales increased considerably during 'key years' which occurred when national legislation mandating recycling of, or deposit systems for, used drinks containers was introduced. In one Member State a key year also occurred on the introduction of the euro when many customers chose to renew their equipment. The case is on appeal Case T-155/06 *Tomra Systems*, not yet decided.

5. Market Definitions in Particular Sectors

Introduction. In relation to the segmentation of the market in IT services see, **4.091** eg Case M.5301 *Cap Gemini/BAS* (13 October 2008) where the Commission referred to a report produced by the Gartner Group, an independent industry analyst company which specialised in the IT industry: paras 9 and 10 and the other cases cited therein.

Pharmaceuticals. In Case M.5253 *Sanofi-Aventis/Zentiva* (4 February 2009) **4.092** the Commission noted that competition at the more detailed molecule level was particularly relevant in a case where the producer of an originator drug acquires an important, or even the sole, producer of its generic equivalent on the market. The role of the molecule level in the market analysis is important in those cases where (i) doctors may, or are even required to, prescribe medicines using the international non-proprietary name (INN) of the molecule rather than by brand name; (ii) reimbursement is based on the price of a generic version of the originator medicine; and (iii) pharmacies may, or are required to, offer the patient the opportunity to substitute an originator medicine with a generic equivalent. The Commission also distinguished in this case between OTC and prescription-only medicines. In Case M.5295 *Teva/Barr* (19 December 2008) the Commission considered a merger between two companies which specialised in producing generic pharmaceuticals. Due to the greater importance of competition between drugs based on the same molecule in markets where generics were available – in particular for drugs aimed at serious illnesses and procured by hospitals – the Commission analysed the markets affected by the notified operation not only at the ATC3 level but also at molecule level: para 18. The merger was approved conditional upon certain divestments.

For market definition in the animal health sector see Case M.4691 *Schering-Plough/Organon Biosciences* (11 October 2007) where the Commission referred to three core areas, namely (i) biological (vaccines); (ii) pharmaceuticals; and (iii) medicinal feed additives, each containing hundreds of relevant markets; also Case M.5476 *Pfizer/Wyeth* (17 July 2009).

Fn 269. The issue of market definition was not raised in the appeal Cases C-501/06 P, etc, *GlaxoSmithKline Services Unlimited v Commission*, judgment of 6 October 2009.

4.094 **Telecommunications: the Commission's Recommendation on Relevant Markets.** The 2003 Recommendation referred to in this paragraph has been replaced by the 2007 Recommendation, 2007 OJ L344/65. This Recommendation sets out the three cumulative criteria to be applied in determining whether a market is one in which *ex ante* regulation may be warranted, namely (a) the presence of high and non-transitory barriers to entry which may be of a structural, legal or regulatory nature; (b) a market structure which does not tend towards effective competition within the relevant time horizon; and (c) the insufficiency of competition law alone adequately to address the market failure(s) concerned. The Annex to the Recommendation now lists only seven such markets identified by the Commission on the basis of those criteria. When considering whether SMP exists in markets not included in the Annex to the Recommendation, the Member States must apply those three criteria.

For the application of this Recommendation in the merger context see, eg Case M.5148 *Deutsche Telekom/OTE* (2 October 2008) and the cases cited therein.

4.096 **Broadcasting and television.** In COMP/38.698 *CISAC*, decn of 16 July 2008, [2009] 4 CMLR 577, the Commission identified a number of separate relevant product markets in a case concerning bilateral reciprocal licensing arrangements between collecting societies licensing music performance rights. The Commission noted that collective management of copyright covers different activities corresponding to many different relevant product markets: paras 48 *et seq*. The case is on appeal Cases T-398, 410, 411, 413–422, 425, 432, 434, 442, 451/08, not yet decided.

The Commission analysed the various markets in broadcasting and programme acquisition in Case M.5121 *News Corp/Premiere* (26 June 2008). However, many aspects of market definition, such as whether there were separate markets for feature films and other TV content did not need to be decided since the merger did not raise any competition concerns.

Transport routes.   In Case M.5403 *Lufthansa/British Midland* (14 May 2009)   **4.097** the Commission treated air and rail services between London and Brussels as operating in the same market: paras 63 and 64. In considering this concentration, the Commission adopted the 'point of origin/point of destination' approach to market definition and then considered in relation to each city pair which airports or other services were substitutable and whether indirect flights were substitutable for direct flights for long-haul pairs. See similarly, Case M.5141 *KLM/Martinair* (17 December 2008), paras 122 *et seq*.

Air transport: business and leisure passengers; cargo.   In Case M.5403   **4.098** *Lufthansa/British Midland* (14 May 2009) the Commission confirmed that point of origin/point of destination analysis is not appropriate for air cargo markets (paras 18 *et seq*). As concerns intercontinental routes, the corresponding catchment areas broadly correspond to continents, at least for those continents where local infrastructure is adequate to allow for onward connections. For continents (eg Africa) where local infrastructure is less developed, the catchment area corresponds to the countries of destination. Market definition must also take account of the fact that cargo air transport is by nature unidirectional as the demand on each end of the route differs substantially. On air cargo markets see also Case M.5141 *KLM/Martinair* (17 December 2008), paras 28 *et seq*. That case also considered the separate markets for the wholesale supply of seats to tour operators. The distinction between business and leisure may extend to the market for the vessels themselves: see Case M.4956 *STX/Aker Yards* (5 May 2008) and the discussion of the distinction between ferries, cruise ships, and other commercial ships.

5

COMMON HORIZONTAL AGREEMENTS

2. Cartels and other Covert Conduct

(a) The Commission's approach to cartel activity

Increasing focus of law enforcement.   The Commission has established a settle-   **5.006**
ment procedure intended to enable it to handle cartel cases more quickly and
efficiently. Regulation 773/2004 has been amended by Regulation 622/2008,
OJ 2008 L171/3, [2008] 5 CMLR 1032 to incorporate this procedure as Article 10a of Regulation 773/2004. The Commission has also issued a Notice on
the Conduct of Settlement Procedures in cartel cases, explaining how the procedure will operate: see OJ 2008 C167/1, [2008] 5 CMLR 1055. The new settlement procedure introduced by Regulation 622/2008 is discussed in new
paragraphs 13.113A–13.113D, below.

In 2007 the Commission took eight decisions condemning cartels and imposed
fines totalling €3.3 billion and in 2008 it took seven decisions and imposed fines
totalling €2.3 billion.

(b) Anatomy of a classic cartel

How and why cartels form: *Choline Chloride*.   The appeal in the *Choline Chloride*   **5.008**
case mentioned in fn 18 has now been decided: Cases T-101 & 111/05 *BASF AG
and UCB SA v Commission* [2007] ECR II-4949, [2008] 4 CMLR 347. The CFI
quashed the Commission's finding that the global and European aspects of the
cartel were a single continuous infringement (paras 208 *et seq*). The result of
this was that the global cartel was time barred and the fine that had been imposed
for the years covered only by the global cartel was quashed. Unfortunately for
BASF, the reduction in fine it had been given because of its cooperation with the
investigation of the global cartel was also quashed so that BASF's fine in fact
increased as a result of its success on this ground of appeal: para 222.

5.009 *Choline Chloride*: **the global aspect of the cartel.**   **Fn 20.** The pending appeal mentioned has now been decided: Case C-511/06 P *Archer Daniels Midland v Commission (citric acid)*, judgment of 9 July 2009 and related solely to the fine imposed.

5.011 *Choline Chloride*: **the Commission's findings.**   The appeal in the *Choline Chloride* case mentioned in fn 21 has now been decided: Cases T-101 & 111/05 *BASF AG and UCB SA v Commission* [2007] ECR II-4949, [2008] 4 CMLR 347. The CFI quashed the Commission's finding that the global and European aspects of the cartel were a single continuous infringement.

(c) **Ancillary restrictions supporting cartel activity**

5.012 **Restrictions ancillary to the main anti-competitive restrictions.**   For a recent example of information exchange and customer allocation in support of a price-fixing cartel see COMP/38.638 *Butadiene Rubber and Emulsion Styrene Butadiene Rubber*, decn of 29 November 2006, [2009] 4 CMLR 421.

5.013 **Restrictions on advertising.**   **Fn 30.** The appeal in Case T-68/04 *SGL Carbon AG v Commission* has been decided: [2009] 4 CMLR 7 but related to fine only. A further appeal was dismissed: Case C-564/08 P, judgment of 12 November 2009.

5.014 **Cartel 'consultancy'.**   The appeal by the trade association fined in *Organic Peroxides* for providing administrative and secretarial services to the cartel was dismissed by the CFI: Case T-99/04 *AC-Treuhand AG v Commission* [2008] ECR II-1501, [2008] 5 CMLR 962. The CFI noted that the Community Courts had given a broad meaning to the term 'agreement between undertakings' and that a contextual and teleological approach to interpreting Article 81 [now Article 101 TFEU] confirmed that the notions of a cartel and of an undertaking which is the perpetrator of an infringement are conceptually independent of any distinction based on the sector or the market on which the undertakings concerned are active. The principle of *nullum crimen, nulla poena sine lege* did not preclude the gradual clarification, through the development of case law, of legislative provisions. Further, the CFI held that it had been reasonably foreseeable that a consultancy firm would infringe Article 81 where it contributed actively and intentionally to a cartel between producers active on a market other than that on which the consultancy firm itself operates. On the facts, the CFI upheld the Commission's finding of liability.

See also COMP/39.181 *Candle Waxes*, decn of 1 October 2008, [2009] 5 CMLR 2441 where the Commission rejected, on the evidence, a claim by one company that it had only attended the legitimate, technical part of the meetings: paras 222 *et seq.* The decision is on appeal, Cases T-540, 541, 543, 544, 548, 550, 551, 558, 562/08, not yet decided.

3. Agreements on Prices and Trading Conditions

(a) Price-fixing

(i) Generally

Price-fixing prohibited.   For a recent example of a straightforward horizontal, **5.015**
price-fixing agreement see COMP/38.432 *Professional Videotape* [2008] 5 CMLR
122 (price increases agreed and, when market circumstances would not allow
further price increases, the parties agreed to maintain prices unchanged at the
previously agreed level, or at least to prevent them 'from tumbling down uncon-
trollably' (para 127)).

Fn 37. The appeals in *Industrial copper tubes* (all relating to fine only) were
dismissed by the CFI in three judgments given on 6 May 2009: Case T-127/04
KM Europa Metal [2009] 5 CMLR 1574 (on further appeal C-272/09 P, not yet
decided); Case T-122/04 *Outokumpu* [2009] 5 CMLR 1553; Case T-116/04
Wieland-Werke AG [2009] 5 CMLR 1517.

What constitutes price-fixing.   In Case C-8/08 *T-Mobile Netherlands BV v Raad* **5.016**
van bestuur van de Nederlandse Mededingingsautoriteit, judgment of 4 June 2009,
the ECJ confirmed that a concerted practice can have the object of price-fixing
even if it does not relate to consumer end prices. Thus where the concerted practice concerned the payments made by mobile phone operators to phone dealers it
could be an 'object' infringement even though there might not be a direct link
between the practice and consumer prices. Article 81 [now Article 101 TFEU] is
designed not only to protect the immediate interests of individual competitors
or consumers but also to protect the structure of the market and thus competition
as such: para 38.

See also COMP/39.188 *Bananas*, decn of 15 October 2008 where the Commission
found that regular bilateral phone calls between importers of bananas took place
in which they discussed price setting factors, that is factors relevant for setting of
quotation prices for the upcoming week and/or discussed or disclosed their views
about price trends and/or indications of quotation prices for the upcoming week
for the Northern European region. Such conduct, which was monitored by subsequent disclosure of quoted prices, led to coordination of their quotation prices.
Note that the Commission also held that even if the parties did not discuss their
particular prices, discussions or disclosure of expectations as to the 'development'
or 'evolution' of prices were liable to reveal to competitors their intentions concerning future pricing decisions for setting of quotation prices. Viewed in their
context, the discussions and disclosures on either 'price trends' or specifically on
quotation prices had the object of coordinating the setting of quotation prices by

the parties: para 262. This led the Commission to find 'a concerted practice which concerned the fixing of prices': para 289. The decision is under appeal: Cases T-587 & 588/08, not yet decided.

Fn 41. The appeal in Case T-68/04 *SGL Carbon AG v Commission* has been decided: [2009] 4 CMLR 7 but related to fine only. A further appeal was dismissed: Case C-564/08 P, judgment of 12 November 2009.

5.019 **Price agreements among distributors.**   **Fn 69.** The appeal in the *French Beef* case was dismissed: Cases C-101 & 110/07 P *Coop de France bétail et viande and FNSEA v Commission* [2009] 4 CMLR 743.

(iii) Resale and purchase prices

5.025 **Resale price maintenance for books.**   Following on from the commitments given to settle the *Sammelrevers* case see now Case C-531/07 *Fachverband der Buch- und Medienwirtschaft v LIBRO Handelsgesellschaft mbH*, judgment of 30 April 2009. The Austrian court requested a preliminary ruling in the course of proceedings brought by an Austrian publishers trade association to enforce a minimum price set for retail books in Austria. That price was set pursuant to Austrian legislation allowing the association to fix minimum prices for books. The defendant was a book retailer which was importing books from Germany and selling them in Austria at the minimum retail price fixed for the book under the corresponding German law, that price being lower than the minimum price fixed in Austria. The ECJ held that the legislation fell within Article 28 EC and was not justified under Article 30 [now Articles 34 and 36 TFEU]. Referring to Article 151 EC [now Article 167 TFEU] the ECJ noted that the protection of books as cultural objects can be considered as an overriding requirement in the public interest capable of justifying measures restricting the free movement of goods, on condition that those measures are appropriate for achieving the objective fixed and do not go beyond what is necessary to achieve it. However, the Court held that the objective of the protection of books as cultural objects can be achieved by measures less restrictive for the importer, for example by allowing the latter or the foreign publisher to fix a retail price for the Austrian market which takes the conditions of that market into account.

Fn 92. Following the Council Resolution referred to in the footnote see also Council Resolution on the application of national fixed book-price systems, OJ 2001 C73/5.

5.027 **Fixing of purchase prices.**   **Fn 98.** The appeal in the *French Beef* case was dismissed: Cases C-101 & 110/07 P *Coop de France bétail et viande and FNSEA v Commission* [2009] 4 CMLR 743.

(iv) Application of Article 81(3)

Relevance of state of the industry.   A further appeal in the *French Beef* case was   **5.028**
dismissed: Cases C-101 & 110/07 P *Coop de France bétail et viande and FNSEA v
Commission* [2009] 4 CMLR 743.

Fn 107. The appeal against the readoption of the decision condemning the steel
beams cartel has been decided: Case T-405/06 *Arcelor Mittal v Commission*, judgment of 31 March 2009. The decision was annulled as against two of the addressees on the basis that the decision was adopted outside the limitation period
(on further appeal Case C-201/09 P, not yet decided).

(c) Professional services

Professional services: current practice.   The ECJ has recently reiterated that in   **5.040**
the absence of an agreement between undertakings, the competition rules do
not apply to legislation adopted by a Member States prohibiting advertising:
Case C-446/05 *Doulamis* [2008] ECR I-1377.

The recommendation of a fee scale by a professional association, although detailed
and followed by the members, may not be a restriction by object when there
would not in any event be appreciable price-related competition between those
professionals. The Dutch Trade and Industry Appeals Tribunal thus upheld the
quashing of a decision by the Dutch Competition Authority concerning the
annual recommendations published jointly by the three Dutch associations of
psychologists and psychotherapists concerning fees that were not covered by
standard health insurance. The Authority had failed to consider whether the
recommendations were likely to have an adverse impact on competition, in particular since the choice of psychologist was often made by the patient's general
practitioner and based on the professional qualifications and experience of the
psychologist, his or her availability and the urgency of treatment, and not on the
level of fee; and even where patients approached a psychologist directly for treatment, the associations argued that fees were not relevant to the selection of
specialist. This particular economic context meant that there was insufficient
basis to condemn the recommendations as restrictions by object. *NMa v NIP,
NVVP and LVE* (LJN: BF8820) judgment of 6 October 2008.

Fn 142. In the Hungarian Bar Association case, the Budapest Metropolitan
District Court modified the GVH's decision, holding that the rules did not impose
a complete ban on advertising and that some of the restrictions were proportionate to the need to preserve ethical standards in the profession (eg the prohibition of all internet advertising could not be justified but the prohibition on
reference to names of clients was upheld): Case No. 2.K.30.863/2009, judgment
of 29 October 2009; a further appeal to the Court of Appeal is likely.

(d) Banking and payment services

5.045 Credit cards and payment systems. See also the analysis of the different kinds of credit and debit cards available and the definition of relevant product markets in the merger case Case M.5384 *BNP Paribas/Fortis* (3 December 2008).

> **Fn 162.** For a discussion of the Dutch case *Interpay* see also COMP/34.579 *MasterCard MIF charges*, decn of 19 December 2007, para 304. The Commission also refers to later decisions of the Polish competition authority prohibiting MIF charges (para 305). See also the judgments of the Austrian Courts in *Europay*, holding that a JV of Austrian commercial banks that offered payment card acquiring services to merchants infringed the domestic equivalents of Article 81 [now Article 101 TFEU] (in fixing the fees that the parent banks would charge competitors to the Europay system for processing transactions) and of Article 82 [now Article 102 TFEU] (by charging excessive fees both to competitors and by way of merchant service charges to small retailers): GZ 27 Kt 20, 24, 27/06, judgment of the Cartel Court of 22 December 2006; on appeal, 16 Ok 4/07, judgment of the Supreme Court of 12 September 2007.

5.046 Multilateral interchange fees. The Commission adopted a prohibition decision under Article 81 [now Article 101 TFEU] in relation to the MasterCard MIF charges referred to in fn 164: COMP/34.579 *MasterCard MIF charges*, decn of 19 December 2007. The Commission decided it was not necessary to reach a definite conclusion as to whether the MIF was a restriction by object since the effect of the fee clearly restricted competition: paras 401–407. The Commission held that the MIF restricted competition by inflating the base on which acquiring banks set charges for merchants. Prices set by acquiring banks would be lower in the absence of the rule. The MIF created an artificial cost base that was common for all acquirers and the merchant fee typically reflected the costs of the MIF: para 410. The Commission rejected an argument based on *Wouters* that banks could not operate a card payment system without MIFs. Turning to the application of Article 81(3) [now Article 101(3) TFEU], the Commission acknowledged, referring to the earlier *Visa MIF* decision, that in principle in a payment card system characterised by indirect network externalities, interchange fees can help optimise the utility of the network to its users. But both the existence and the level of the fee had to be justified by empirical evidence showing that the fee enhanced the output of the payment scheme. MasterCard had not provided any such analysis and hence the first condition of Article 81(3) was not shown to be fulfilled: paras 729–733. The Commission went on to find that the other conditions were also not fulfilled. MasterCard was allowed six months in which to amend its rules and ordered to publicise the effect of the Commission's decision on its website in each country: para 766. No fine was imposed since the agreement had been notified under Regulation 17, but periodic penalty payments were imposed in the event that MasterCard failed to comply with the order to terminate the infringement: paras 773 *et seq*. The case is on appeal: Case T-111/08, not yet decided. MasterCard has temporarily withdrawn the MIF: see MEMO/08/397, 12 June 2008.

For a discussion of this case see Repa et al, 'Commission prohibits MasterCard's multilateral interchange fees for cross-border card payments in the EEA' (2008) 1 Competition Policy Newsletter 1. Also compare the judgment of the Polish Court for Competition and Consumer Protection, annulling the decision of the Polish Competition Authority that the setting by the member banks of the domestic MIF in, separately, the Visa and MasterCard networks was contrary to Article 81(1) and the Polish domestic equivalent: *Visa – MasterCard*, Case No. XVII AmA 109/07, judgment of 12 November 2008. The Court held that the Authority was wrong to find that MIF distorted the market for acquiring services and that it could not substitute a new evaluation of the effect on the market for card issuing services. The judgment is on appeal.

The exemption granted in 2002 to Visa expired at the end of 2007: the Commission has sent a statement of objections to Visa alleging that the agreements for the payment of the MIF contravene Article 81 [now Article 101 TFEU], for reasons similar to those relied on in the *MasterCard* case: see COMP/39.398 *Visa Europe MIF fees*.

Sectoral inquiry and payment cards.   The Commission's analysis of this market **5.047** was confirmed in its decision in COMP/37.860 *Morgan Stanley/Visa International and Visa Europe*, decn of 3 October 2007 in which it imposed a fine on Visa for applying a rule which excluded competitors from the network to refuse membership to Morgan Stanley. The Commission found that barriers to entry made it unrealistic to expect Morgan Stanley to enter the European market to engage in inter-brand competition by expanding the card network it operates in the USA. But there was scope for it to contribute to intra-brand competition if it joined the Visa network as a card provider and merchant acquirer. The exclusion of Morgan Stanley therefore had appreciable restrictive effects on competition: para 201. The Commission considered that, nonetheless, the application of the Rule to Morgan Stanley would not fall under Article 81(1) [now Article 101(1) TFEU] if it was directly related to and necessary (proportionate and non-discriminatory) for the proper functioning of Visa's network. On the facts the Commission held that this was not the case, and the rule did not fulfil the conditions of Article 81(3) [now Article 101(3) TFEU] either. A fine of €10.2 million was imposed in relation to the application of the rule (which had been notified to the Commission under Regulation 17) during the period starting with the issue of the statement of objections (in which the Commission made it clear it was contemplating imposing a fine) and ending with the admission of Morgan Stanley to the network in 2006.

The case is on appeal: Case T-461/07 *Visa Europe and Visa International Service Association v Commission*, not yet decided. See similarly, COMP/38.606 *Groupement des Cartes Bancaires*, decn of 17 October 2007 (on appeal Case T-491/07 *CB v Commission*, not yet decided).

4. Output Restrictions

5.054 **Domestic restructuring of a national industry:** *Dutch Bricks.* Restructuring arrangements must now be considered in the light of the ECJ's judgment in Case C-209/07 *Beef Industry Development Society Ltd v Barry Brothers (Carrigmore) Meats Ltd* [2009] 4 CMLR 310, [2009] All ER (EC) 367 (mentioned in fn 177). There the ECJ considered arrangements for the restructuring of the Irish beef and veal processing industry. Under the arrangements, total capacity would be reduced by 25 per cent by some processors leaving the market with each 'stayer' paying a levy in accordance with its share of the market. The Court held that this agreement had as its object the restriction of competition contrary to Article 81(1) [now Article 101(1) TFEU]. The application of Article 81(3) [now Article 101(3) TFEU] was not raised in the request for a preliminary ruling. Following the ECJ ruling, the Irish Supreme Court remitted the case back to the judge of first instance to determine whether the conditions of Article 81(3) were satisfied on the facts, referring expressly to *Synthetic Fibres* and *Dutch Bricks*: *Competition Authority v Beef Industry Development Society Ltd* [2009] IESC 72.

5. Market-sharing and Customer Allocation

(a) Generally

5.059 **Market-sharing.** Another common mechanism by which markets and customers are allocated is by bid-rigging in relation to sales of products which are usually the subject of tenders by purchasers: for two recent examples see COMP/39.406 *Marine Hoses*, decn of 28 January 2009 and COMP/39.125 *Car glass*, decn of 12 November 2008. Both decisions are on appeal: *Marine Hoses*: Cases T-146, 147, 148, 154/09, not yet decided and *Car glass*: Cases T-56, 68, 72, 73/09, not yet decided.

5.062 **Market-sharing in product and geographic markets.** Substantial parts of the Commission's decision in *Needles* was overturned as regards Coats' involvement: Case T-36/05 *Coats Holdings Ltd v Commission* [2007] ECR II-110, [2008] 4 CMLR 45. The CFI found that the mere fact that Coats had been informed about an anti-competitive agreement between two producers, Prym and Entaco, cannot give rise to liability for the infringement (para 105). Further, the CFI found on the facts that Coats had not influenced the drafting of the anti-competitive Heads of Agreement between Prym and Entaco. The CFI then considered the fact that the terms of the anti-competitive agreement between Prym and Entaco provided that its coming into effect would be triggered when Coats sold its business. The CFI held that Coats' decision to proceed with the sale of its business was not capable by itself of proving that its purpose was to contribute to the objectives of the Prym/Entaco cartel. The fact that Prym and Entaco decided to make that event the date on which their cartel would come into force could not, at first sight, be attributed to Coats. However, in the circumstances of the case, the fact that Coats triggered the mechanism of the Prym/Entaco cartel could implicate Coats in that cartel, if that act was part of a common plan. The CFI found that Coats' anti-competitive intentions were demonstrated by the fact that the Heads of Agreement were disclosed to it. In that regard, the Commission had rightly observed that suppliers do not generally inform their customers about the cartels of which they are members and this highly unusual step showed that, contrary to Coats' claim, it was not the 'victim' of a cartel. The very fact that Entaco and Prym discussed confidential issues (such as the creation of a cartel) showed, the CFI found, that Coats' intentions must have been of an anti-competitive nature. By facilitating the entry into force of the Heads of Agreement between Prym and Entaco, Coats became liable until that agreement came to an end on 13 March 1997. The CFI went on to overturn the Commission's finding of a trilateral arrangement arising from the several bilateral arrangements between Coats, Prym and Entaco. The Court examined the wording of the relevant clause, the structure and context of the clause, the intended objective and history of the clause. It found that Coats' alternative explanation of the clause was plausible and convincing and that there was no tripartite agreement established. Coats' fine was reduced to reflect the more limited nature of its involvement. Coats' appeal against this decision was dismissed: Case C-468/07 P [2009] 4 CMLR 301. Prym's appeal to the CFI against the same decision was also dismissed save for a small reduction in the fine: Case T-30/05 *Prym v Commission* [2007] ECR II-107* (further appeal dismissed: Case C-534/07, judgment of 3 September 2009, [2009] 5 CMLR 2377).

Control over imports and exports.   See also COMP/39.401 *E.On - GdF collusion*, decn of 8 July 2009 where the Commission imposed substantial fines on the joint owners of a pipeline importing Russian gas into Germany and France. The parties had agreed not to supply gas into each other's markets: see Press Release IP/09/1099 (8 July 2009).   **5.065**

(f) Customer allocation

Customer allocation.   **Fn 240.** The appeal in the *Choline Chloride* case has now been decided: Cases T-101 & 111/05 *BASF AG and UCB SA v Commission* [2007] ECR II-4949, [2008] 4 CMLR 347. The CFI quashed the Commission's finding   **5.083**

that the global and European aspects of the cartel were a single continuous infringement (paras 208 *et seq*). The appeal in Case T-112/05 *Akzo Nobel* and a further appeal to the ECJ have also now been decided: Case C-97/08 P *Akzo Nobel NV v Commission*, judgment of 10 September 2009.

6. Information Exchange

5.085 **Information exchange ancillary to a cartel.** See also the discussion of COMP/39.188 *Bananas*, decn of 15 October 2008 in the update to paragraph 5.016, above. The Commission stated that the cartel in that case was distinguished from an information exchange of the kind discussed in *United Kingdom Agricultural Tractor Registration Exchange* because it concerned pre-pricing communications and not *ex post* exchanges of information about transactions already completed. The decision is under appeal: Cases T-587 & 588/08, not yet decided.

Fn 244. The appeals in *Industrial copper tubes* (all relating to fine only) were dismissed by the CFI in three judgments given on 6 May 2009: Case T-127/04 *KM Europa Metal* [2009] 5 CMLR 1574 (on further appeal C-272/09 P, not yet decided); Case T-122/04 *Outokumpu* [2009] 5 CMLR 1553; Case T-116/04 *Wieland-Werke AG* [2009] 5 CMLR 1517.

5.087 *The United Kingdom Agricultural Tractor Registration Exchange.* The principles here were confirmed by the ECJ in Case C-8/08 *T-Mobile Netherlands BV v Raad van bestuur van de Nederlandse Mededingingsautoriteit*, judgment of 4 June 2009: 'An exchange of information between competitors is tainted with an anticompetitive object if the exchange is capable of removing uncertainties concerning the intended conduct of the participating undertakings': para 43.

5.088 *Wirtschaftsvereiningung Stahl.* In Case T-53/03 *BPB plc v Commission* [2008] ECR II-1333, [2008] 5 CMLR 1201 the CFI emphasised the different effect of information exchange in different market structures. In a truly competitive market, an information exchange system is not likely to reduce or remove uncertainty about the foreseeable nature of competitors' conduct. However, on a highly concentrated oligopolistic market, the exchange of information does enable operators to know the market positions and strategies of their competitors and thus impairs competition appreciably: paras 107 *et seq*.

5.089 **Artificial market transparency.** In Case T-53/03 *BPB plc v Commission* [2008] ECR II-1333, [2008] 5 CMLR 1201 the CFI confirmed that the mere fact of receiving information concerning competitors, which an independent operator preserves as business secrets, is sufficient to demonstrate the existence of an anticompetitive intention. The fact that price information was known by customers before it was transmitted to the competitors and, therefore, could be collected on the market did not negate the existence of an anti-competitive agreement. It did not make the prices readily accessible. The fact that price lists were sent directly from one competitor to another allowed the competitors to become aware of that information more simply, rapidly and directly than they would via the market. Further, that prior notification allowed them to create a climate of mutual certainty as to their future pricing policies: paras 235–236.

Information on output and sales.   Similarly, where a trade association publishes **5.090** cost forecasts to its members, this is likely to affect their pricing decisions for the future and thus restrict competition. In separate decisions, the Danish Competition Council found that the two Danish Freight Transport Associations violated the domestic equivalent of Article 81 [now Article 101 TFEU] by issuing such forecasts to their members, along with cost calculation models that they can use to calculate their freight rates by applying their own costs according to a uniform programme: *Dansk Transport og Logistik (DTL)*, decn of 17 December 2008; *International Transport Danmark (ITD)*, decn of 25 February 2009 (taken also under Article 81). The decision in *DTL* is under appeal.

A disclosure by one undertaking in a highly concentrated and oligopolistic market of the fact that it does not want a larger market share than the one it already holds is sufficient to inform competitors of an essential element of its strategy and therefore to restrict competition: see Case T-53/03 *BPB plc v Commission* [2008] ECR II-1333, [2008] 5 CMLR 1201, para 183.

Fn 269. In the *Bouygues Télécom* case, on reference back from the Cour de Cassation (now reported in translation at [2008] ECC 439), the Paris Court of Appeal rejected the appeals brought by the three French mobile network operators, Bouygues, Orange and SFR. The court held that the information exchanged was confidential and, having regard to its detail and the frequency of exchange, was of considerable value to the commercial strategy of the individual companies since it enabled them to adapt to the evolution of the commercial policies of each other. Accordingly, the requisite anti-competitive effect was demonstrated: *Bouygues Télécom, SFR, Orange*, judgment of 11 March 2009, BOCCRF No. 7 of 17 July 2009. A further appeal to the Cour de Cassation is pending.

7. Collective Trading Arrangements

(a) Boycotts and collective exclusive dealing

Collective refusal to deal.   See also *Lottoblock*, WuW DE-R 2408, judgment of **5.100** the German Federal Supreme Court of 14 August 2008 (resolution by Association of German Lottery Companies advising its members not to accept business generated by commercial brokers through certain channels of distribution, which threatened their regional monopolies, was a decision by an association of under-takings that infringed Article 81).

(c) Collective selling of intellectual property and media rights

5.111 **Joint selling of rights.** In COMP/38.698 *CISAC*, decn of 16 July 2008, [2009] 4 CMLR 577, the Commission noted that individual management of rights is often not feasible: para 42. See also the Commission's market analysis in Case M.5533 *Bertelsmann/KRR/JV* (8 September 2009) (a case under the Merger Regulation).

5.112 **Collective selling of rights: music and films.** The Commission's increasingly interventionist approach to the licensing of music rights by collecting societies is demonstrated by COMP/38.698 *CISAC*, decn of 16 July 2008, [2009] 4 CMLR 577. The Commission examined the provisions of the bilateral reciprocal licens-ing agreements between the EEA members of CISAC relating to the use of music in satellite, cable and internet transmission modes. Those agreements were based in part on the model clauses adopted by CISAC. Some of the clauses complained of had been deleted from those model clauses but were still found in the bilateral contracts. The Commission held that a membership clause whereby the collecting societies agreed that neither of them would, without the consent of the other, accept as member any member of the other society or any person having the nationality of one of the countries in which the other society operates infringed Article 81 [now Article 101 TFEU]. The clause restricted competition between collecting societies on the market for the provision of services to rights holders and, indirectly, may also affect competition between collecting societies on the market for the licensing of rights to commercial users: para 126. In line with the *Simulcasting* decision, the Commission held that the concerted practice among the societies whereby the territory licensed was limited to the domestic territory of the licensee society led to national monopolies for the multi-repertoire licens-ing of public performance rights and had the effect of segmenting the EEA into national markets (paras 204 *et seq*). The Commission was careful to make clear that it was only the coordination aspect of the grant of a limited territory that was condemned in the decision; 'in isolation, the granting of a licence limited to a certain territory, even to the domestic territory, is not automatically restrictive of competition' (para 201). The Commission also left open whether, as regards exploitation of performing rights in offline applications (bars, restaurants, discos, etc) the territorial delineation of licences along national borders might be justified on the basis that duplication of copyright usage monitoring structures in all territories would lack economic rationale. But that could not justify such limita-tions for the applications covered by the decision namely satellite, cable and internet transmission modes: para 184. The decision also contains an interesting analysis of the relevant product markets for the exploitation of rights for satellite, cable and internet transmission modes (paras 48 *et seq*). Note that the finding of infringement was addressed to the members and not to the collecting society itself. The decision is on appeal on the issue of whether the Commission was correct to find the existence of a concerted practice as regards the limitation of the licences to the domestic territory of the licensee: see Cases T-398, 410, 411, 413–422, 425, 432, 434, 442, 451/08, not yet decided. The CFI rejected an application for interim measures to suspend parts of the Commission's order Case T-411/08R *Artijus Magyar v Commission* [2009] 4 CMLR 353 and this judgment is itself under appeal: Case C-32/09 P(R), not yet decided.

Licensing use of rights on the internet. In COMP/38.698 *CISAC*, decn of 16 **5.113** July 2008, [2009] 4 CMLR 577, discussed above, the Commission applied the principles laid down in the *Simulcasting* decision. As regards the definition of the relevant product market, the Commission noted that technical and legal distinctions could point in favour of separate product markets for each of the satellite, cable and internet transmission modes. However, in view of the increasing convergence between television and internet services, this might change: para 57. The Commission relied on the particular characteristics of these applications as contrasted with offline applications (broadcast in bars, restaurants and discos, etc) in finding that there was no need for local monitoring and enforcement and hence no economic rationale for territorial limitations: para 184. The case is on appeal Cases T-398, 410, 411, 413–422, 425, 432, 434, 442, 451/08, not yet decided.

In April 2007 the Commission issued a statement of objections alleging an agreement among Apple and the major record companies to the effect that consumers can only buy music from the iTunes' online store in their country of residence and are thereby restricted in the choice of where to buy music and at what price. The Commission later closed the case having ascertained that the organisation of the iTunes store in Europe is not determined by agreements between Apple and the major record companies. Apple nonetheless agreed to equalise prices for downloads of songs from its iTunes online store in Europe within six months. This put an end to the different treatment of UK consumers who previously paid higher prices for downloads: see COMP/39.154 *Apple and iTunes* Press Release IP/08/22 (9 January 2008).

Licensing of music rights: further steps. See the discussion of the Commission **5.114** Recommendation 2005/737/EC in COMP/38.698 *CISAC*, decn of 16 July 2008, [2009] 4 CMLR 577, paras 106–110. The case is on appeal Cases T-398, 410, 411, 413–422, 425, 432, 434, 442, 451/08, not yet decided.

Collective selling of rights: sporting events. In July 2007, the Commission **5.115** adopted a White Paper on Sport (COM(2007)391 final) which was accompanied by a Staff Working Document 'The EU and Sport: Background and Context' (SEC(2007) 935). Annex I to that Staff Working Document entitled 'Sport and the EU Competition Rules' provides an overview of the principal case law on the application of Articles 81 and 82 [now Articles 101 and 102 TFEU] to the sports sector, dealing both with the organisational aspects of sport (notably sporting rules) and with the revenue-generating aspects of sport (in particular the sale of sport media rights). The White Paper discusses product market definition, particularly the distinction between upstream markets where rights owners sell rights to media companies and downstream markets in which those media companies operate. It analyses the *UEFA Champions League, German Bundeliga* and *FA Premier League* decisions and lists the remedies that the Commission has used to redress the restrictive effects of collective selling such as limiting the duration of exclusive vertical contracts and imposing a 'no single buyer' obligation. See further new paragraphs 5.156A and 5.156B, below.

5.116 **Commission policy: sports content rights and broadcasting.**   **Fn 330.** The appeal in the *Infront* case has been decided: Case C-125/06 P *Commission v Infront WM* [2008] ECR I-1451, [2008] 2 CMLR 785. The ECJ upheld the CFI's judgment that Infront, which was the holder, for the countries of Europe for the years 2002 and 2006, of the exclusive broadcasting rights in respect of the football World Cup finals organised by FIFA, was directly and individually concerned by the Commission's decision approving the designation by the United Kingdom of those events as listed events and so could challenge that decision.

Fn 332. The decision in the *Polish Football Association* case was upheld on further appeal by the Polish Supreme Court: case III SK 16/08, judgment of 7 January 2009.

5.116A **Sponsoring of competing joint selling vehicle.**   Where particular rights have been sold through a monopoly acquirer, an arrangement among sellers under which they grant exclusive rights to a competing joint venture will not fall within Article 101(1) where the exclusivity is necessary to enable the joint venture to compete with the incumbent. In *Bookmakers' Afternoon Greyhound Services v Amalgamated Racing Ltd* [2009] EWCA Civ 750 the English Court of Appeal upheld a decision that a joint venture to which a group of racecourses sold the exclusive right to broadcast horse races to licensed bookmakers' premises had neither the object nor the effect of restricting competition since it challenged the existing monopsony of an organisation owned by the bookmakers. Lloyd LJ stated: 'Given that the incumbent operator was dominated by the interests of the purchasers in the downstream market, given the high cost of entry, and given the very long period in which no other operator had shown any interest in entry to these markets, it seems to me that it was obviously necessary that the new entrant would have to be promoted by or in association with a number of racecourses, and that it would need to be protected, at the stage of its establishment, from competition from the incumbent, since otherwise it would never get off the ground': para 85. The Court of Appeal considered the Commission's decisions in *UEFA Champions League* and *FA Premier League* on the question of whether the racecourses could be regarded as being in competition with each other, given that the races were organised so as not to coincide with each other. The Court held that they were not in competition with each other. The Court upheld the first instance judge's decision ([2008] EWHC 1978 (Ch)) on the basis that the exclusivity was an ancillary restriction within the principles established in Case T-112/99 *Métropole Télévision (M6) v Commission* [2001] ECR II-2459 and Case C-309/99 *Wouters* [2002] ECR I-1577.

(d) Joint tendering

Bidders' reciprocal sub-contracting arrangements.   The decision of the **5.123** Hungarian Competition Office was upheld on appeal, finally by the Supreme Court of Hungary: Case Kfv.II.39162/2008, judgment of 17 June 2009.

8. Trade Associations, Cooperatives and Exhibitions

(b) Common standards

Agreements on technical standards.   See also Piesiewicz and Schellingerhout, **5.139** 'Intellectual property rights in standard setting from a competition law perspective' (2007) 3 Competition Policy Newsletter 36.

Use of standard forms, etc.   As regards the final sentence of this paragraph, on **5.143** 25 September 2007, the Commission published the Final Report of the sector inquiry into business insurance. The Final Report focuses in substance on two main issues. The first is competition in the wholesale subscription market, that is where an ad hoc syndication arrangement is set up by a broker or client to cover a given risk. The Report considers the use of 'Best Terms and Conditions' clauses whereby an insurer makes an offer to subscribe conditional on no other participant receiving better terms in respect of either a higher price or a more advantageous policy. The Commission notes that this may lead to an upward alignment of premiums and/or contract uncertainty. The second issue is broker conflicts of interest and the Commission has undertaken to look at these issues in the framework of the review of the Insurance Mediation Directive.

(d) Trade exhibitions and auctions

Application of Article 81(1).   **Fn 426.** See now *FBIAC v WEX* (2006/AR/2392), **5.153** [2008] ECC 9, judgment of the Brussels Court of Appeal of 15 June 2007, to the same effect as the judgment of 2005 cited in the footnote, which was a preliminary ruling on a reference from the Brussels Commercial Court. (The subsequent decision of the Commercial Court determining the case was in turn appealed, giving rise to the 2007 judgment which is final.)

5.155 **Auctions.**   Fn 433. The decision of the Dutch Competition Authority in *Dutch shrimp producers and wholesalers agreement* was upheld by the Trade and Industry Appeals Tribunal: Cases AWB 06/599, etc, judgment of 19 January 2009, LJN: BD0436.

9. Sporting Bodies and Competitions

5.156 **Introduction.**   For a case concerning the organisation of motorcycle racing events see Case C-49/07 *Motosykletistiki Omospondia Ellados NPID (MOTOE) v Elliniko Dimosio* [2008] ECR I-4863, [2008] 5 CMLR 790, [2009] All ER (EC) 150, esp para 22.

5.156A **Commission White Paper on Sport.**   In July 2007, the Commission adopted a White Paper on Sport (COM(2007)391 final) which was accompanied by a Staff Working Document 'The EU and Sport: Background and Context' (SEC(2007) 935). Annex I to that Staff Working Document entitled 'Sport and the EU Competition Rules' provides an overview of the principal case law on the application of Articles 81 and 82 [now Articles 101 and 102 TFEU] to the sports sector, dealing with both the organisational aspects of sport, notably sporting rules and revenue-generating aspects of sport, in particular the sale of sport media rights.

5.156B **The White Paper: application of competition law to sporting rules.**   The White Paper confirms the importance of *Meca Medina* in establishing that there is no category of purely sporting rules excluded from the scope of competition law. Rather it is necessary, once it has been established that the various elements in Article 101(1) are satisfied, to consider first, the overall context in which the rule was adopted or in which it has its effect; secondly whether the restriction of competition arising from the rule is inherent in the pursuit of the objective of the rule; and thirdly whether the rule is proportionate in the light of the objective pursued. It is also necessary to consider whether Article 101(3) applies or whether the rule can be objectively justified for the purposes of Article 102. The White Paper sets out an indicative list of rules that are more likely to comply with the competition rules, namely selection criteria for sport competitions, 'at home and away' rules, transfer periods, nationality clauses for national teams, rules prohibiting the multiple ownership of clubs, anti-doping rules and the rules of the game. Sporting rules that are less likely to comply include rules prohibiting clubs or athletes from participating in competitions organised by a rival sporting body, rules regulating professions ancillary to sport such as football players' agents, and rules excluding legal challenges of decisions by sports associations before the ordinary courts. In addition, rules limiting the number of foreign players or requiring transfer payments for players whose contracts have expired may fall to be assessed under competition rules as well as under free movement provisions.

Proportionality under Article 81 in the sporting context. In *ADIPAV*, Case **5.162**
640/08, decn of 29 December 2008 the Spanish Competition Commission held
that the provision in the technical regulations of the International Association of
Patin Sailing Boats that wood is the only permitted material for manufacturing
such boats was proportionate and legitimate for the objective of ensuring a neutral
sporting competition; whereas the rule which limited the price of such boats
was not so justified and infringed the Spanish domestic equivalent of Article 81
EC [now Article 101 TFEU].

6

VERTICAL AGREEMENTS AFFECTING DISTRIBUTION OR SUPPLY

2. Regulation 2790/99

In general.   The Commission has consulted on a revised block exemption to **6.010** come into effect when Regulation 2790/99 expires on 1 June 2010: see Press Release IP/09/1197 (28 July 2009) which includes links to the draft regulation and guidelines. The draft regulation broadly continues the current exemption in effect but reflects what the Commission sees as the two main market developments since Regulation 2790/99. The first of these is the increase in the market power of major retailers. The draft therefore requires that for a vertical agreement to benefit from the block exemption, not only the supplier's market share (as is currently the case) but also the buyer's market share should not exceed 30 per cent 'on any of the relevant markets affected by the agreement'. Note that paragraph 83 of the draft guidelines refers to the buyer's share of the market where it (re)sells the contract products. The second development is the growth of sales over the internet. In this regard the draft new Guidelines explain, in the online context, the distinction between sales made as a result of active marketing and sales made as a result of the consumer taking the initiative (ie between active and passive sales). It lists the restrictions that the Commission would regard as hard-core restrictions of passive selling, including requiring a (exclusive) distributor to prevent customers located in another (exclusive) territory from viewing its website; requiring a (exclusive) distributor to terminate consumers' transactions over the internet once their credit card data reveal an address that is not within the distributor's (exclusive) territory; or requiring a distributor to pay a higher price for products intended to be resold by the distributor online than for products intended to be resold offline (para 52). As a general rule, a website is not considered a form of active selling to certain customers unless it is specifically targeted at those customers. The Guidelines also explain how the revised Regulation would deal with conditions imposed in relation to internet sales, such as a requirement imposed by a supplier that the distributor should have a 'bricks and mortar' shop before engaging in online sales.

(d) Withdrawal and disapplication

6.026 **Withdrawal by a national authority.** Where the effects result from a network of similar agreements, the national authority will need to consider whether withdrawal of the benefit of the block exemption as regards only one supplier would be discriminatory and thus itself distort competition. Thus the Hungarian Competition Authority decided not to withdraw the application of Regulation 2790/99 in respect of the beer-tie agreements of the supplier under investigation (Borsodi) when two other suppliers had equal shares of the market and it was the cumulative effect of all their agreements that restricted competition under the *Delimitis* test: see decision of 16 May 2008, Case No. Vj-28/20007/42.

3. Agency Agreements

6.030 **Financial or commercial risk.** Fn 105. See similarly Case C-279/06 *CEPSA v Tobar* [2008] ECR I-6681, para 40.

4. Exclusive Distribution and Supply Agreements

(b) Application of Article 81(1)

(i) The hard-core restrictions

6.050 **Resale price maintenance.** See Case C-506/07 *Lubricarga v Petrogal Española*, not yet decided, where the ECJ has been asked whether a contract which fixes resale prices and which contains other hard-core clauses taking it outside Regulation 1984/83 can still fall outside Article 101(1) if it is *de minimis*.

6.052 **Maximum retail prices.** Fn 173. The appeal referred to in the footnote was found to be inadmissible: Case T-274/06 *Estaser El Mareny v Commission* [2007] ECR II-143*.

6.053 **Measures obstructing parallel imports.** Fn 175. The discussion of export restrictions in the pharmaceutical market must be read in the light of the ECJ's judgment in Cases C-501/06 P, etc, *GlaxoSmithKline Services Unlimited v Commission*, judgment of 6 October 2009. The ECJ did not regard the pharmaceuticals market as a special case and rejected the argument that an agreement limiting parallel trade only has the object of restricting competition if it disadvantages final consumers: para 62. The ECJ held that the agreement setting different prices for product depending on whether it would be resold domestically or exported had as its object the restriction of competition so that there was no need to examine its effect on the market. But the ECJ upheld the CFI's decision that the Commission had failed properly to examine GSK's arguments for the application of Article 81(3) [now Article 101(3) TFEU]: para 104. See also Cases C-468/06, etc, *Sot Lelos kai Sia EE v GlaxoSmithKline* [2008] ECR I-7139, [2008] 5 CMLR 1382, [2009] All ER (EC) 1 (State regulation of prices does not mean that benefits of parallel trading for consumers are minimal).

Fn 177. The appeals in *Video Games, Nintendo Distribution* have now been decided: Case T-18/03 *CD-Contact Data v Commission*, judgment of 30 April 2009 (fine reduced) (on further appeal Case C-260/09 P *Activision Blizzard Germany*, not yet decided); Case T-12/03 *Itochu* [2009] 5 CMLR 1375 (appeal dismissed); Case T-13/03 *Nintendo* [2009] 5 CMLR 1421 (fine reduced); Case T-398/02 *Linea Gig* (removed from register 2 May 2005).

'Active' and 'passive' sales and absolute territorial protection. The sentence **6.054** ending with the marker for fn 184 should refer to the contract being limited to banning active sales not passive sales.

The Commission is consulting on a revised block exemption to come into effect when Regulation 2790/99 expires on 1 June 2010: see Press Release IP/09/1197 (28 July 2009) which includes links to the draft regulation and guidelines. The draft new Guidelines explain the distinction between active and passive sales in the online context. See further update to paragraph 6.010, above.

Financial disincentives for dealers who export. See also COMP/37.811 *Algerian* **6.056** *gas imports* Press Release IP/07/1074 (11 July 2007) concerning a profit sharing mechanism under which the buyer/importer of gas from Algeria was obliged to share part of the profit with the supplier/producer if the gas was sold on by the importer to a customer outside the agreed territory or to a customer using the gas for a purpose other than the one agreed upon. A common understanding was reached between the Commission and Algeria that the conditions would be deleted.

Other indirect measures preventing parallel imports. Fn 207. In Cases **6.058** C-501/06 P, etc, *GlaxoSmithKline Services Unlimited v Commission*, judgment of 6 October 2009 the ECJ held that the agreement setting different prices for a product depending on whether it would be resold domestically or exported had as its object the restriction of competition so that there was no need to examine its effect on the market. See also Cases C-468/06, etc, *Sot Lelos kai Sia EE v GlaxoSmithKline* [2008] ECR I-7139, [2008] 5 CMLR 1382, [2009] All ER (EC) 1 (State regulation of prices does not mean that benefits of parallel trading for consumers are minimal).

6.061 **Measures aimed at monitoring and identifying the source of parallel imports.** **Fn 217.** The appeals in *Video Games, Nintendo Distribution* have now been decided: Case T-18/03 *CD-Contact Data v Commission*, judgment of 30 April 2009 (fine reduced) (on further appeal Case C-260/09P *Activision Blizzard Germany*, not yet decided); Case T-12/03 *Itochu* [2009] 5 CMLR 1375 (appeal dismissed); Case T-13/03 *Nintendo* [2009] 5 CMLR 1421 (fine reduced); Case T-398/02 *Linea Gig* (removed from register 2 May 2005). Nothing was stated in those appeals to detract from the points made in this paragraph.

(c) **Application of Article 81(3) to individual agreements**

6.081 **Application of Article 81(3) to exclusive distribution agreements.** The need to protect investments incurred in the launch of a new product was held by the Paris Court of Appeal not to be established as justification for restrictions in the agreement between Apple and Orange making the latter the exclusive network operator and wholesaler of the iPhone in France. Examining the investments relied on and the profits being made, the Court upheld the decision of the competition authority that the five-year exclusive contract was out of proportion to the investment risk. The judgment was on appeal from the authority's decision taking interim measures that prohibited Apple from refusing to distribute through other network operators: *Apple Sales International v Bouygues Télécom*, judgment of 4 February 2009, BOCCRF No. 4 of 8 April 2009; on appeal to the Cour de Cassation, not yet decided. The Court also held that the restrictions in the agreement took it outside the scope of Regulation 2790/99. In November 2009, Apple and Orange announced that they were abandoning their exclusivity arrangement.

5. Selective Distribution Systems

(b) **Article 81(1)**

6.093 **Luxury and prestige products.** As to when trade mark rights can be enforced in respect of luxury goods sold by a licensee to a discount store outside the network see Case C-59/08 *Copad SA v Christian Dior couture SA and SIL*, judgment of 23 April 2009 where the ECJ interpreted the reference in Article 8(2) of Directive 80/104 to the 'quality' of goods as including 'the allure and prestigious image which bestows on the goods an aura of luxury'.

6.095 **Restrictions on sales over the internet.** See also draft new Guidelines (Press Release IP/09/1197 (28 July 2009)) which explain the distinction between active and passive sales in the online context. The Guidelines also explain how the revised Regulation would deal with conditions imposed in relation to internet sales, such as a requirement imposed by a supplier that the distributor should have a 'bricks and mortar' shop before engaging in online sales.

Territorial and other restrictions on resale. See also Case T-427/08 *CEAHR v* **6.101**
Commission, not yet decided (appeal against rejection of complaint alleging breach
of Article 82 [now Article 102 TFEU] by watch manufacturer refusing to sell
spare parts outside the distribution system).

Fn 380. See also *re the Léonidas Network* [2008] ECC 190 (Decn No 07-D-24)
where the French Competition Council found that the distribution arrangements operated by the Belgian chocolate manufacturer infringed Article 81 [now
Article 101 TFEU] and the equivalent provision in the French Commercial
Code. The network comprised 13 resellers who were authorised to import products to sell in their own shops and also to sell to other authorised retailers who
countersigned the reseller's contract with Léonidas. Each retailer could only buy
supplies from the reseller who had introduced him to the network or from a
subsequent replacement reseller but they could not buy from more than one specified supplier at any given time. Further, the retailers were required only to supply
end-users. The Council held that these terms fell within Article 4(b) of Regulation
2790/1999 so that the block exemption did not apply. A fine of €120,000 was
imposed.

(d) Motor vehicle distribution and servicing

Regulation 1400/2002. The Commission has published an evaluation report **6.109**
of the operation of Regulation 1400/2002: Press Release IP/08/810 (28 May 2008).
It has also issued a Communication 'The Future Competition Law Framework
applicable to the motor vehicle sector' (COM/2009/0388 final (22 July 2009))
setting out the key elements of the competition regime which will apply to the
motor vehicle sector after the expiry of the current block exemption.

Other conditions for the application of the exemption. Fn 467. See also the **6.123**
judgment of the Higher Regional Court of Frankfurt, *Secondary Car Dealer*,
13 May 2008, WuW DE-R 2444 (one-year notice period economically justified).

Active and passive sales. See also para 52 of the proposed new Guidelines on the **6.128**
draft new Vertical Restraints block exemption as to the distinction between active
and passive sales in the online context: Press Release IP/09/1197 (28 July 2009)
which includes links to the draft regulation and guidelines.

Hard-core restrictions concerning access to information. The Commission **6.131**
opened proceedings against four car manufacturers alleging a breach of Article 81
EC [now Article 101 TFEU] in that the agreements between the manufacturer
and its dealer network restricted the disclosure of information to independent
repairers. The Commission accepted commitments under which (i) the manufacturers would ensure that all information provided to authorised repairers was
also made available to independent repairers on a non-discriminatory basis;
(ii) although manufacturers may withhold information relating to anti-theft or

performance limiting functions of on-board electronics, they have to ensure that this does not prevent independent repairers from performing repairs not directly related to these functions; and (iii) the information made available to repairers must be unbundled and priced in a way which takes account of the extent to which they use it (eg by hourly charges for access to the website). All four manufacturers also agreed to accept arbitration or mediation mechanisms for disputes. The commitments expire at the same time as Regulation 1400/2002 expires: COMP/39.140-143 *DaimlerChrysler and others* Press Release IP/07/1332 (14 September 2007).

6. Exclusive Purchasing, Single Branding and Tying

(b) Application of Article 81(1)

6.152 **Resale from supplier's premises.** Fn 566. See Case C-260/07 *Pedro IV Servicios v Total España* [2009] 5 CMLR 1291 where a long-term exclusive purchasing obligation on the lessor of a service station qualified for exemption under Regulation 1984/83 but not under Regulation 2790/99.

Fn 568. The appeal referred to in the footnote was found to be inadmissible: Case T-274/06 *Estaser El Mareny v Commission* [2007] ECR II-143*.

6.157 **Quantity forcing.** That quantity forcing can be achieved in various ways is illustrated by the arrangements between motor vehicle insurers and car dealers that were condemned by the Hungarian Competition Authority, under the domestic equivalent of Article 101, in a decision upheld by the Budapest Court of Appeal. The two major motor vehicle insurers in Hungary (who together accounted for about 80 per cent of the market) each had agreements with car dealers under which the rate of remuneration for repair work was significantly increased each year in return for the dealers selling a certain amount of policies for that insurer to customers purchasing cars. This provided an incentive to dealers to sell an even greater proportion of new policies on behalf of those insurers and thus operated to foreclose smaller, competing insurers (although they then had no choice but to offer the same, higher rates). The agreements between insurers and dealers were held to have the object of restricting competition: *Allianz Hungária, Generali-Providencia and ors*, 2.Kf.27.129/2009, judgment of the Budapest Court of Appeal of 23 September 2009.

6.159 **'English clause'.** Fn 595. The decision in the *Polish Football Association* case was upheld on further appeal by the Polish Supreme Court: case III SK 16/08, judgment of 7 January 2009.

9. Waste Packaging Recycling Arrangements

Generally. In COMP/38.113 *Prokent-Tomra* [2009] 4 CMLR 101 the Com- **6.196**
mission condemned a series of exclusivity arrangements and loyalty rebate schemes
entered into by Tomra which was dominant in the supply of reverse vending
machines for recycling empty containers in a number of EU and EEA Member
States. The Commission noted that the volume of sales increased considerably
during 'key years' which occurred when national legislation mandating recycling
of, or deposit systems for, used drinks containers was introduced. The case is on
appeal Case T-155/06 *Tomra Systems*, not yet decided.

Relationship between the system operator and the producers and distributors **6.198**
of packaged goods. The appeal to the ECJ in *DSD* was dismissed: Case
C-385/07 P *Der Grüne Punkt – Duales System Deutschland v Commission*, judgment of 16 July 2009, [2009] 5 CMLR 2215. The CFI analysed the case under
Article 82(a) [now Article 102(a) TFEU], referring to settled case law according
to which an undertaking abuses its dominant position where it charges fees which
are disproportionate to the economic value of the service provided. The conduct
objected to here, namely requiring payment of a fee for all packaging bearing the
DGP logo and put into circulation in Germany, even where customers of the
company show that they do not use the DGP system for some or all of that packaging, constituted an abuse of a dominant position within that case law. The ECJ
upheld this analysis, emphasising that the remedies imposed by the decision did
not amount to an obligation to grant a licence to use the DGP logo. There was
nothing in the decision which affects DSD's freedom of choice as to the grant of
licences – the decision at issue merely obliges DSD not to claim payment from its
contractual partners for take-back and recovery services which it has not provided. Note that the CFI stated that the decision did not stop DSD levying
an adequate fee for merely using the DGP mark even where it is shown that the
packaging bearing the DGP logo has been taken back and recovered by another
system. The green dot affixed to the packaging may have economic value as such,
since it can inform the consumer that the packaging at issue may be brought to the
DSD system: paras 193 and 194.

7

JOINT VENTURES AND SIMILAR COLLABORATIVE ARRANGEMENTS

7. Joint Ventures in Practice

(f) Airline alliances

Collaborative arrangements.   **Fn 380.** The Commission market tested commit- **7.133** ments in COMP/37.984 *SkyTeam* (making slots available to new competitors; sharing Frequent Flyer Programmes with new entrant; interlining, etc) but no final decision has been published: [2008] 4 CMLR 228.

In Case M.5403 *Lufthansa/British Midland* (14 May 2009) the Commission considered the implications for assessing a merger of the two airlines of the fact that (a) Lufthansa was a member of the Star Alliance; and (b) the merging entities already operated a code-sharing arrangement. The Commission found that the issue of the treatment of the parties' alliance partners could be left open, as the proposed concentration did not raise serious doubts under the Merger Regulation, whether or not Lufthansa's alliance partners should be considered as competitors of Lufthansa (para 35) (see also on this point Case M.5141 *KLM/Martinair* (17 December 2008), para 23). The Commission held that pre-merger cooperation that was not contrary to Article 81 [now Article 101 TFEU] could form the relevant counterfactual for assessing the competitive effect of the merger. In such a case the proposed concentration could raise serious doubts only if (i) despite the code-share agreements, the operating carrier and the marketing carrier exert a significant constraint on each other as actual competitors (with respect to sales of seats on the operating carrier's flights); or (ii) if, in the presence of the code-share agreement, the marketing carrier were to be likely to enter the respective route as an operating carrier. In this case, the Commission found that there was no such significant constraint prior to the merger.

8

MERGER CONTROL

1. Introduction

(a) Summary

Merger Regulation.   The Commission has adopted a report on the operation **8.001**
of the Merger Regulation as required by Article 1(4) of the Merger Regulation.
The report concludes that overall, the jurisdictional and referral mechanisms
have provided the appropriate legal framework for a flexible allocation and
reallocation of cases by effectively distinguishing in most cases mergers that have
an EU relevance from those which are primarily national. During the consultation, concerns were raised regarding cumbersome and lengthy referral procedures
and it was suggested that efforts towards further convergence of national rules
governing merger control and their relation to EU rules could reduce difficulties
with regard to multiple filings: see Press Release IP/09/963 (18 June 2009) which
contains a link to the Report.

(b) Commission guidance

Implementing Regulation and Notices   **8.008**

(b) *Jurisdictional Notice*. The Consolidated Jurisdictional Notice has now been
published: OJ 2008 C95/1.
(f) *Remedies Notice*. The revised Notice on Remedies has now been adopted:
Notice on remedies acceptable under the EC Merger Regulation and under
Commission Regulation (EC) No 802/2004, OJ 2008 C267/1: Vol II,
App D15, see update to paragraph 8.162, below. The new Form RM was also
incorporated into the Implementing Regulation as Annex IV by Commission
Regulation 1033/2008, OJ 2008 L279/3: see Vol II, App D2.
(g) *Horizontal Merger Guidelines*. The proposed Non-horizontal merger guide-
lines mentioned in sub-para (g) have now been adopted: OJ 2008 C265/6:
Vol II, App D14.

(c) Case law and statistics

8.011 **Statistics.** Table (c) fn (i). The *Schneider Electric* case referred to in the footnote was partly overturned on appeal: see Case C-440/07 P *Commission v Schneider Electric*, judgment of 16 July 2009 (Commission's liability confirmed in principle but appeal allowed in part on issue of causation of loss).

The tables can be updated as follows:

(a) Total number of notifications and referrals by year

Year	Notifications to Commission	Referrals from Member States to Commission		Referrals from Commission to Member States	
		Pre-notification (Art 4(5))	Post-notification (Art 22)	Pre-notification (Art 4(4))	Post-notification (Art 9)
2007	402	50	3	5	2
2008	347	22	2	9	4
Total	4,015	151	21	40	71

(b) Different Phase I outcomes by year

Year	Clearance decisions				No jurisdiction	Referred to Phase II decisions		Notifications withdrawn during Phase I	
	Unconditional		Conditional						
2007	368	(91%)	18	(4%)	-	15	(4%)	5	(1%)
2008	307	(89%)	19	(5%)	-	10	(3%)	10	(3%)
Total	3,472	(87%)	177	(4%)	52 (1%)	186	(5%)	90	(2%)

(c) Different Phase II outcomes by year

Year	Clearance decisions				Prohibition decisions		Notifications withdrawn during Phase II	
	Unconditional		Conditional					
2007	5	(42%)	4	(33%)	1	(8%)	2	(17%)
2008	9	(60%)	5	(33%)	-	-	1	(7%)
Total	46	(25%)	88	(47%)	20	(11%)	32	(17%)

2. Jurisdictional Scope of the Merger Regulation

(b) Concentrations

(iii) Acquisitions

Definition of control.   Fn 62. The appeal in *Cementbouw* was dismissed: Case   **8.024**
C-202/06 P *Cementbouw Handel & Industrie BV v Commission* [2007] ECR
I-12129, [2008] 4 CMLR 1324. The ECJ confirmed that control of a company
is obtained by the power to block strategic decisions, including the appointment
of the company's management or board.

(iv) Sole control

Sole control through minority shareholding.   Fn 76. See also Case M.4956   **8.029**
STX/Aker Yards (5 May 2008). In Case M.5121 *News Corp/Premiere* (26 June
2008) the target company's most recent AGM had occurred after News Corp had
acquired its interest in the company but before it was able to exercise the voting
rights attached to the shares. The Commission considered that the unusually high
attendance of shareholders was atypical and that the shareholders wanted 'to be
able to influence the course of the company for one last time before News Corp
would take control'. Attendance was likely to return to its earlier lower levels,
giving News Corp *de facto* control: para 8. In Case M.5518 *Fiat/Chrysler* (24 July
2009) the Commission held that Fiat had obtained *de jure* control over Chrysler
even though it held only a minority interest because it had extensive governance
rights that no other shareholder enjoyed: para 7.

Other factors leading to *de facto* control.   See also Case M.5148 *Deutsche*   **8.032**
Telekom/OTE (2 October 2008) (DT to hold 25 per cent plus 12 shares; but the
shareholder agreement gave DT rights to nominate the senior officers of the company who had a casting vote on decisions so DT acquired sole control). See also
Case M.5545 *ArcelorMittal/Noble Eruopean Holding* (17 July 2009) where the
Commission left open the question whether control was acquired in March 2008
when ArcelorMittal acquired 49.9 per cent of the shares and the right to nominate
the majority of board members or in May 2009 when it acquired 100 per cent of
the shares: para 7.

(v) Joint control

Concept of joint control.   In Case M.5533 *Bertelsmann/KRR/JV* (8 September   **8.033**
2009) the Commission considered a joint venture between a private equity company (which would own 51 per cent of the joint venture) and one of the main
music industry companies (which would own 49 per cent). The Commission
examined the factors that gave each partner influence and concluded that in light
of the terms of the proposed transaction and in view of the overall context of the

planned operation, the private equity partner would need to cooperate with Bertelsmann in order to determine the strategic behaviour of the proposed JV; and Bertelsmann can be reasonably expected to be in a position to block important strategic decisions in the proposed JV which are not in its interest. The Commission therefore concluded that the parties held joint control over the JV.

8.036 **Focus on strategic business policy.**   **Fn 88.** An appeal against the CFI's judgment in *Cementbouw* was dismissed: Case C-202/06 P *Cementbouw Handel & Industrie BV v Commission* [2007] ECR I-12129, [2008] 4 CMLR 1324.

(vi) Changes in quality of control

8.041 **Changes from joint to sole control.**   **Fn 100.** See also Case M.5141 *KLM/ Martinair* (17 December 2008) (move from 50 per cent to 100 per cent holding was a concentration). The Commission considered the question whether the effect of the concentration should be assessed taking into account the pre-existing joint control (which the parties argued meant that very little would change as a result of the acquisition). The Commission stated that it is first necessary to analyse the extent to which the parties have constrained each other pre-merger. This involves considering the organisation and corporate governance of the target company as well as the extent and nature of the competitive interaction between the parties on the markets where their activities overlap. In this case, the Commission found, the parties were, in principle, to be treated as competitors though the fact that KLM already had control of Martinair pre-merger clearly reduced the likely anti-competitive effects of the merger.

(vii) Interrelated transactions

8.044 **Transactions involving different steps.**   The appeal against the CFI's judgment in *Cementbouw* was dismissed: Case C-202/06 P *Cementbouw Handel & Industrie BV v Commission* [2007] ECR I-12129, [2008] 4 CMLR 1324.

Fn 113. See also Case M.5296 *Deutsche Bank /ABN AMRO Assets* (1 October 2008). In Case M.4980 *ABF/GBI Business* (23 September 2008) the Commission found that the acquisition by ABF of GBI Holding's yeast operations in various Member States as well as shares in other undertakings and assets in yet others (including employees, customer contracts and intellectual property rights) constituted a single concentration. The Commission referred to the 'clear business rationale' which was to gain sole control of what it called 'the GBI business'. In Case M.5533 *Bertelsmann/KRR/JV* (8 September 2009) the proposed concentration consisted of two transactions, one of which was *de facto* dependent on the other and one of which was *de jure* dependent on the other. The Commission noted that under the Jurisdictional Notice, even if several transactions are linked by condition upon one another, they can only be treated as a single concentration if control is acquired ultimately by the same undertakings. It held that the transactions did result in a single concentration.

Break-up bids and other operations with on-sale arrangements.   Fn 117. See, **8.046** eg Case M.4844 *Fortis ABN Amro Assets* (3 October 2007), paras 6–8; Case M.4963 *Rexel/Hagemeyer* (22 February 2008), paras 5–9. In the case of the break up of the brewer Scottish & Newcastle which was shared between Carlsberg and Heineken the Commission cleared the Carlsberg acquisition of S&N assets (Case M.4952 *Carlsberg/Scottish & Newcastle assets* (7 March 2008)) and on the same day referred the merger as regards the Irish beer markets back to the Irish competition authority under Article 9(2) and cleared the remainder of the Heineken acquisition (Case M.4999 *Heineken/Scottish & Newcastle* (3 April 2008)).

(c) Full-function joint venture undertakings

(ii) Full functionality

Key principles of full functionality.   Fn 143. See also Case M.5533 *Bertelsmann/* **8.054** *KRR/JV* (8 September 2009).

(iii) Lasting basis

Durability.   Fn 154. An appeal against the *DaimlerChrysler/Deutsche Telekom/* **8.058** *JV* decision was dismissed: Case T-48/04 *Qualcomm Wireless Business Solutions v Commission*, judgment of 19 June 2009.

(d) Community dimension

(i) Turnover thresholds

Worldwide and Community-wide turnover.   In Case C-202/06 P *Cementbouw* **8.060** *Handel & Industrie BV v Commission* [2007] ECR I-12129, [2008] 4 CMLR 1324 the ECJ held that the competence of the Commission to make findings in relation to a concentration must be established, as regards the whole of the proceedings, at a fixed time. Having regard to the importance of the obligation of pre-notification, that time must necessarily be closely related to the notification of the concentration. It was accepted by the parties that the concentration had a Community dimension on the date when the two groups of transactions which comprised the concentration were concluded and on the date of the notification made at the Commission's request. The fact that during the course of the investigation the concentration may no longer have met the thresholds did not deprive the Commission of jurisdiction. The Court did not have to rule therefore on whether the relevant time for the purpose of determining the Commission's competence is the time at which the obligation to notify arose or the time at which the notification should have been made or even the time at which it was actually made: para 44.

(e) **Pre-notification reallocation of jurisdiction**

(ii) Article 4(5) referrals to Commission

8.085 **Suitable case for Article 4(5) referral.** See, eg Case M.4942 *Nokia/Navteq* (2 July 2008) (proposed transaction could have been reviewed in 11 Member States); Case M.4513 *Arjowiggins/M-Real Zanders' Reflect paper mill* (4 June 2008) (seven Member States); Case M.4854 *Tom Tom/Tele Atlas* (14 May 2008) (four Member States); Case M.4731 *Google/DoubleClick* (11 March 2008) (at least three Member States).

(f) **Post-notification reallocation of jurisdiction**

(i) Article 9 referrals from Commission to NCAs

8.091 **Legal requirements under Article 9.** In Case M.5112 *Rewe/Plus Discount* (3 July 2008) the Commission considered a request by the Czech authorities for a reference back to them of the acquisition by the Rewe group of a chain of Czech discount stores engaged in the retail sale of daily consumer goods. The request was made under both Article 9(2)(a) and 9(2)(b). So far as the application of Article 9(2)(b) was concerned, the Commission concluded that there were strong indications that the criteria were fulfilled so far as the retail level of the relevant market was concerned but that they were not fulfilled as regards the procurement markets, that is the market for sales by producers to wholesalers and retailers. However, the Commission found that the criteria in Article 9(2)(a) were fulfilled in respect of both retail and procurement markets and exercised its discretion to refer the whole merger to the Czech authorities: an assessment of the procurement markets without the assessment of the retail markets was not appropriate. In Case M.4999 *Heineken/Scottish & Newcastle* (3 April 2008) the Commission decided that the relevant markets for beer in Ireland presented the characteristics of a distinct market and the Irish aspect of the merger was referred back under Article 9(2)(a). The rest of the merger (other than the Irish beer markets) was cleared under Article 6(1)(b) on the same day.

(g) **National investigations on grounds other than competition**

(i) Legitimate interests under Article 21(4)

8.104 **Other legitimate public interest grounds.** Fn 292. The appeal in Case T-41/06 *Republic of Poland v Commission* was withdrawn, 10 April 2008.

Fn 293. The proceedings concerning the Article 21 decisions against Spain in Case M.4197 continue. The Commission brought an infringement action under Article 226 EC [now Article 258 TFEU]: Case C-196/07 *Commission v Spain*, judgment of 6 March 2008, [2008] ECR I-41*, in which the ECJ found that Spain had violated EC law by failing to comply with the Article 21 decisions.

The ECJ confirmed that, before adopting the contested measures, Spain should have communicated to the Commission the legitimate interests that those measures were intended to protect (namely, the guarantee of the supply of energy). The ECJ also stated that, when a Member State disagrees with an Article 21 decision, it must challenge the legality of that decision before the Community Courts and cannot simply fail to comply with it. In the meantime, the original bid had been abandoned. The Endesa undertaking was then the subject of a subsequent public bid which was approved by the Commission on 5 July 2007: Case M.4685 *Acciona/Enel/Endesa* (2007 OJ C130/19). The Spanish authorities authorised the operation on 4 July 2007 but again subject to a number of conditions. By a decision of 5 December 2007, the Commission found that Spain had violated Article 21 ECMR, as well as the Treaty provisions on free movement of capital and goods and freedom of establishment. Spain has challenged the legality of this decision before the CFI (Case T-65/08, not yet decided). Spain's application for interim measures to suspend the implementation of the decision was rejected by the President of the CFI: Case T-65/08 R, Order of 30 April 2008, [2008] ECR II-69*. Note that the ECJ has also held that, by attributing these powers to the Energy Regulator, Spain had infringed Articles 43 and 56 EC [now Articles 49 and 63 TFEU] (see Case C-207/07 *Spain v Commission*, judgment of 17 July 2008, [2008] ECR I-111*). For a description of the rather tangled procedural history of this matter see Busa and Zaera Cuadrado, 'Application of Article 21 of the Merger Regulation in the E.ON/Endesa case' (2008) 2 Competition Policy Newsletter 1.

3. Procedure

(a) In general

(i) *Commission hierarchy for merger control proceedings*

Case teams. The Commission has now published instructions for a case team **8.108** allocation request: Vol II, App D18.

(iii) *Obligation to notify*

Timing of formal notification. The Commission has published a Merger **8.111** Notification and Procedures Template to provide a starting point for the analysis of a particular transaction: Vol II, App D17.

(iv) *Formalities*

Form CO. The Form CO has been amended by Commission Regulation **8.117** 1033/2008, OJ 2008 L279/3: see Vol II, App D2. Most of the amendments draw the parties' attention to the corresponding provisions of the EEA Agreement.

8.120 **Business secrets.** Note that the Implementing Regulation was amended in 2008 to provide that if the parties do not identify confidential information as required by Article 18(2) and (3), the Commission may assume that the documents or statements concerned do not contain confidential information: see Article 18(4) inserted by Commission Regulation 1033/2008, OJ 2008 L279/3: Vol II, App D2.

8.121 **Need for full and accurate disclosure.** The Commission has published guidance on the delivery of correspondence from the parties to the Commission, including the procedure for ensuring the security of documents: Vol II, App D16.

(v) Simplified procedure

8.124 **Short Form.** The Short Form has been amended by Commission Regulation 1033/2008, OJ 2008 L279/3: see Vol II, App D2. Most of the amendments draw the parties' attention to the corresponding provisions of the EEA Agreement.

(b) Initial Phase I investigation

(i) Phase I process

8.133 **Duration of Phase I investigation.** In Case T-151/05 *Nederlandse Vakbond Varkenshouders (NVV) v Commission* [2009] 5 CMLR 1613 the CFI stated, in relation to a merger cleared at Phase I: 'in view of the need for speed and the very tight deadlines to which the Commission is subject in the procedure for the control of concentrations, the Commission cannot be required, in the absence of evidence indicating that information provided to it is inaccurate, to verify all the information it receives. Although the diligent and impartial examination which the Commission is obliged to carry out in the context of that procedure does not permit it to base itself on facts or information which cannot be regarded as accurate, the abovementioned need for speed presupposes that it cannot itself verify down to the last detail the authenticity and reliability of all the information it receives, since the procedure for the control of concentrations is based, of necessity and to a certain extent, on trust': para 184. The CFI also referred to the fact that sanctions exist for the provision of inaccurate information and that clearance based on incorrect information can be revoked: para 185.

(ii) Possible outcomes at Phase I

8.137 **Deemed decisions.** The ECJ has rejected an argument that the existence of this deeming provision means that a Commission clearance decision cannot be annulled on the basis of inadequate reasoning: see Case C-413/06 P *Bertelsmann AG and Sony Corporation of America v Impala and Commission* [2008] ECR I-4951, para 175.

(c) In-depth Phase II investigation

(i) Phase II process

Statement of objections. In Case C-413/06 P *Bertelsmann AG and Sony* **8.145**
Corporation of America v Impala and Commission [2008] ECR I-4951 the ECJ,
drawing an analogy with proceedings under Articles 81 and 82 [now Articles 101
and 102 TFEU], stressed that the statement of objections is a provisional account
of the facts and is subject to amendment in the light of the observations submitted
by the parties and of subsequent findings of fact: paras 63 *et seq.* The ECJ held that
the CFI had erred in law in criticising inconsistencies between the facts as set out
in the statement of objections and the findings set out in the decision. The CFI
can refer to the statement of objections to interpret a decision of the Commission,
particularly as regards the examination of its factual basis. But the CFI had gone
beyond what was permissible by treating what it termed 'findings of fact made
previously' in that statement as being more reliable and more conclusive than the
findings set out in the contested decision itself: see paras 69 *et seq.*

Access to file. Note that if the Commission was precluded from relying on doc- **8.146**
uments because they had not been disclosed to the applicant, the CFI cannot rely
on them in its review of the Commission's decision: Case C-413/06 P *Bertelsmann
AG and Sony Corporation of America v Impala and Commission* [2008] ECR
I-4951, para 102.

Reply to statement of objections. The notifying parties cannot, as a rule, be **8.147**
criticised for putting forward certain – potentially decisive – arguments, facts or
evidence only in their arguments in reply to the statement of objections. It is only
with that statement that the parties to the concentration know in detail what
concerns the Commission has about the concentration and the arguments and
evidence on which it relies in that regard: see Case C-413/06 P *Bertelsmann AG
and Sony Corporation of America v Impala and Commission* [2008] ECR I-4951,
para 89. The ECJ expressly disapproved para 414 of the CFI's judgment referred
to in fn 428, holding that the arguments set out in reply to the statement of objections cannot be subject to more demanding standards as to their probative value
and their cogency than those applied to the arguments of competitors, customers
and other third parties. Further, the CFI had erred in finding that the absence of
additional market investigation after communication of the statement of objections and the adoption by the Commission of the appellants' arguments in defence
amounted to an unlawful delegation of the investigation to the parties to the concentration: paras 93 *et seq.*

(iii) Role of Member States

Advisory Committee. For the problems that can arise when the Advisory **8.155**
Committee objects to the Commission's proposed decision on a merger see Case
T-145/06 *Omya AG v Commission* [2009] 4 CMLR 827, paras 4 *et seq.*

(iv) Possible outcomes at Phase II

8.156 **Decisions following a Phase II investigation.** As to adequacy of reasoning in the decision, see Case C-413/06 P *Bertelsmann AG and Sony Corporation of America v Impala and Commission* [2008] ECR I-4951. There the ECJ confirmed that the extent of the Commission's reasoning had to take into account the need for speed and the short timescales set for the Commission under the Merger Regulation: paras 166–169 and 174–176. The CFI had erred in holding that the Commission's decision was inadequately reasoned. The ECJ rejected an argument that the deeming provision in Article 10(6) of the Merger Regulation meant that a Commission clearance decision could not be annulled for lack of reasoning: para 175.

8.160 **Dissolution of prohibited concentrations and other restorative measures.** Following the prohibition of the acquisition by Ryanair of Aer Lingus (M.4439 decn of 27 June 2007) Ryanair bought a further 4.3 per cent of the share capital of Aer Lingus bringing its total shareholding to 29.4 per cent. Aer Lingus asked the Commission to open proceedings against Ryanair under Article 8(4) of the Merger Regulation and to adopt interim measures to prevent Ryanair from exercising its voting rights in Aer Lingus. The Commission rejected Aer Lingus's request on the grounds that it did not have power to intervene in a situation where Ryanair had not taken control of Aer Lingus. Aer Lingus appealed to the CFI against this rejection (Case T-411/07, not yet decided). Ryanair had also appealed against the prohibition of the merger (Case T-342/07, not yet decided). Aer Lingus requested interim measures from the Court pending the hearing of its appeal. The CFI rejected the request for interim measures: Case T-411/07 R *Aer Lingus v Commission* [2008] ECR II-411, [2008] 5 CMLR 538. The President held (a) interim measures could only ever extend until the disposal of the appeal in Case T-411/07, and could not extend until the disposal of Case T-342/07; (b) an order could not be issued suspending the effect of a negative administration decision by the Commission because the grant of suspension could not change the applicant's position (para 46); (c) the CFI could not order the Commission to give directions under Article 8(4) and 8(5) because this would constitute an interference with the exercise of the Commission's powers; and (d) as regards the request that the CFI issue orders against Ryanair directly, the President did not rule out the exercise of such a power against Ryanair as a third party to the instant appeal, provided that procedural safeguards were put in place (para 56). However, the CFI held that Aer Lingus had failed to establish a *prima facie* case that Ryanair had 'implemented' a concentration within the meaning of Article 8(4) or 8(5) given that it was accepted that there had been no change of control by reason of the acquisition of the minority shareholding (paras 84 *et seq*). Having compared various language versions of the Merger Regulation, the President concluded that the powers in Article 8(4) and 8(5) were triggered only if there was an acquisition of control.

(d) Commitments to enable clearance

(i) Commitments at Phase I or Phase II

In general.   The revised Notice on Remedies has now been adopted: Notice on   **8.162**
remedies acceptable under the EC Merger Regulation and under Commission
Regulation (EC) No 802/2004, OJ 2008 C267/1: see Vol II, App D15. The Notice
sets out the general principles which will guide the Commission's assessment of
proposed commitments at all stages of the process. It then covers particular kinds
of commitments, primarily divestiture of a business to a suitable purchaser but
also referring to removal of links with competitors and other remedies such as
access commitments and amendments to long-term exclusive contracts. The
Notice states that whatever the kind of commitment accepted, the Commission
will require a review clause though the Commission makes clear that modification
of the commitments will not heal retroactively any breach of the commitments
which has been committed before the time of the modification. The Notice then
sets out the procedure for the submission of commitments at Phase I or Phase II
of the investigation and gives further guidance on implementation. The main
changes from the earlier notice are (a) more stringent information requirements
on the parties including the new 'Form RM'; (b) the reform clarifies and tightens
up the requirements for the sufficient scope of divestitures and for the suitability
of purchasers, in particular explaining the application of 'up-front buyer' provisions and 'fix-it-first' solutions that can address possible uncertainties in finding a
suitable purchaser; (c) the reform provides that carve-outs from the divested business may be accepted in certain circumstances provided that they are finalised
prior to the sale to a purchaser; and (d) as to non-divestiture remedies, the Notice
underlines that such remedies are only acceptable where they are equivalent in
their effects to a divestiture. Access commitments are only acceptable if there is a
sufficient likelihood that they will actually be used by competitors in practice. The
Notice further stresses that difficulties of monitoring and risks concerning effectiveness may lead to non-divestiture remedies being rejected.

Form RM.   The new Form RM referred to in fn 479 was also incorporated into   **8.162A**
the Implementing Regulation as Annex IV by Commission Regulation 1033/2008,
OJ 2008 L279/3: see Vol II, App D2. The form specifies the information and
documents to be submitted by the undertakings concerned at the same time as
offering commitments. The Form sets out in detail the information and documents required to be submitted when the commitments offered include the divestiture of a business.

Phase I commitments.   For examples of commitments accepted at Phase I see   **8.163**
Case M.5152 *Posten AB/Post Danmark A/S* (21 April 2009) (divestment of assets
and customer contracts) and Case M.5406 *IPIC/MAN Ferrostaal* (13 March
2009) (divestment of shareholding in subsidiary).

Fn 484. The new Form RM referred to has now been incorporated into the Implementing Regulation as Annex IV by Commission Regulation 1033/2008, OJ 2008 L279/3: see Vol II, App D2.

8.164 **Phase II commitments.** **Fn 487.** Note that the Implementing Regulation was amended in 2008 to provide that the undertakings must, at the same time as offering commitments, submit one original and 10 copies of the information and documents prescribed by the Form RM relating to remedies as set out in Annex IV to the Regulation: see Article 20(1a) inserted by Commission Regulation 1033/2008, OJ 2008 L279/3: see Vol II, App D2. Form RM has been incorporated as Annex IV of the Implementing Regulation, see new paragraph 8.162A, above.

8.165 **Common principles.** **Fn 492.** The appeal to the ECJ in relation to the Handel/Cementbouw concentration was dismissed: Case C-202/06 P *Cementbouw Handel & Industrie BV v Commission* [2007] ECR I-12129, [2008] 4 CMLR 1324. The ECJ held that review by the Community judicature of the exercise of the Commission's discretion as regards acceptance of commitments must take account of the discretionary margin implicit in the provisions of an economic nature. The CFI had been right to hold that the Commission was not required to accept the first draft of the commitments offered since it considered that they were insufficient to resolve the competition problem it had identified: paras 53 *et seq*.

Fn 493. The new Form RM referred to has now been incorporated into the Implementing Regulation as Annex IV by Commission Regulation 1033/2008, OJ 2008 L279/3: see Vol II, App D2, see new paragraph 8.162A, above.

(ii) Scope of commitments

8.166 **Structural and behavioural commitments.** In Case M.4842 *Danone/Numico* (31 October 2007) the commitments included the grant of a five-year exclusive licence of certain brands followed by a five-year commitment not to reintroduce the divested brands in Belgium, the transfer of product formulations and recipes and transfer of the contract with an existing supplier: paras 86 *et seq*. In Case M.4691 *Schering-Plough/Organon Biosciences* (11 October 2007) the divestiture was accompanied by technical assistance, at the option of the purchaser to help the purchaser to assume responsibility for the manufacture, sale and marketing of the divested businesses.

Fn 499. On the disposal of slots in aviation mergers see also Case M.5364 *Iberia/Clickair/Vueling* (9 January 2009) (proposed acquisition by Spanish national carrier of two low cost Spanish airlines: Phase I clearance conditional on giving up slots at Spanish and other European airports).

8.167 **Divestiture.** In Case M.5153 *Arsenal/DSP* (9 January 2009) the Commission accepted a commitment to divest in a case where it had found that the merged entity would have run the only two production plants of a particular chemical in the EEA and that imports of the product were very low.

The divestiture may also, of course, give rise to a concentration under the Merger Regulation and need to be cleared by the Commission: see, eg Case M.5220 *ENI/Distrigaz* (15 October 2008) following Case M.4180 *Gaz de France/Suez* which required GDF and Suez to divest Suez's share in the capital of Distrigaz. Following a bid process, ENI was elected as proposed purchaser and was approved by the Commission as a suitable buyer in line with the previous procedure. See similarly Case M.5519 *E.ON/Electrabel Acquired Assets* (13 September 2009).

(iii) Implementation of commitments

Role of trustees. The Implementing Regulation now provides that commit- **8.170** ments offered at either Phase I or Phase II may include, at the expense of the undertakings concerned, the appointment of an independent trustee (or trustees) assisting the Commission in overseeing the parties' compliance with the commitments or having a mandate to implement the commitments. The trustee may be appointed by the parties, after the Commission has approved its identity, or by the Commission. The trustee carries out its tasks under the supervision of the Commission. The Commission may attach such trustee-related provisions of the commitments as conditions and obligations under Articles 6(2) or 8(2) of the Merger Regulation: see Article 20a inserted by Commission Regulation 1033/2008, OJ 2008 L279/3: see Vol II, App D2.

(e) Commission's powers of investigation

(i) Means of obtaining information

Information requests. In Case T-145/06 *Omya AG v Commission* [2009] 4 CMLR **8.172** 827 the CFI interpreted the requirement in Article 11(1) that the information requested be 'necessary'. The Court held that the need for the information must be assessed by reference to the view that the Commission could reasonably have held, at the time the request in question was made, of the extent of the information necessary to examine the concentration. As to when it was necessary to ask the parties to correct information already communicated, the Court held that the Commission is entitled to request the correction of erroneous information if there is a risk that the errors identified could have a significant impact on its assessment of whether the concentration is compatible with the common market. These criteria were not to be applied strictly and the Court would have a limited role in reviewing the Commission's decisions in this regard. The Court rejected Omya's assertion that the Commission's request had been used as a pretext to suspend the time running under the Regulation in light of objections raised by the Advisory Committee to a proposed clearance of the merger.

(ii) Suspension of Phase I and Phase II timetables

8.175 **Article 11 decisions.**   The appeal in Case T-145/06 *Omya AG v Commission* was dismissed: [2009] 4 CMLR 827. The CFI held that the information requested by the Commission and the request for correction of that information was not a misuse of power and had properly suspended the running of time under the Regulation.

(f) Commission's powers of sanction

(ii) Fines and penalty payments

8.181 **Fines for substantive infringement.**   The Commission has imposed a fine of €20 million for failure to notify a concentration: Case M.4994 *Electrabel/ Compagnie Nationale du Rhône* (10 June 2009). The acquisition was cleared by the Commission on 29 April 2008 but the Commission found that Electrabel had already acquired *de facto* control of CNR in December 2003. Although Electrabel at that time had acquired less than 50 per cent of the shares, the Commission found that the widespread dispersion of the remaining shareholding and other factors meant that Electrabel had acquired control. In setting the fine the Commission had regard to the fact that Electrabel should have known that the 2003 transaction triggered the obligation to notify but also to the fact that the transaction did not give rise to any competition concerns and Electrabel had subsequently voluntarily informed the Commission of the acquisition of control: see Press Release IP/09/895 (10 June 2009). The case is on appeal: Case T-332/09, not yet decided. Cf Case M.5545 *ArcelorMittal/Noble European Holding* (17 July 2009) where the Commission left open the question whether control was acquired in March 2008 when ArcelorMittal acquired 49.9 per cent of the shares and the right to nominate the majority of board members; or in May 2009 when it acquired 100 per cent of the shares: para 7.

4. Substantive Appraisal of Concentrations

(c) SIEC test

(ii) Relationship with concept of dominance

8.196 **Dominance remains a relevant consideration.**   In Case M.4513 *Arjowiggins/ M-Real Zanders' Reflect paper mill* (4 June 2008) the Commission found that the merged entity would have more than 50 per cent of the market in carbonless paper. The merger was cleared following the acceptance of commitments.

(iii) Checks and balances

8.198 **Prospect of judicial review.**   Fn 607. The *Schneider Electric* case referred to at the end of the footnote was partly overturned on appeal: see Case C-440/07 P

Commission v Schneider Electric, judgment of 16 July 2009 (Commission's liability confirmed in principle but appeal allowed in part on issue of causation of loss).

(iv) General content of assessment

Horizontal and non-horizontal mergers and their economic effects. For a **8.202** helpful example of the application of the Horizontal Merger Guidelines and the Non-Horizontal Merger Guidelines see Case M.4731 *Google/DoubleClick* (11 March 2008). The Commission did not consider the parties to be actual competitors but analysed whether the removal of DoubleClick as a potential competitor could impede competition: paras 222 *et seq*. Further, while DoubleClick might have grown into an effective competitive force in online ad intermediation services, there were likely to be sufficient other competitors left in the market to maintain competitive pressure after the merger: para 278. An analysis of the potential conglomerate effects of the merger did not reveal any competition concerns and the merger was cleared in Phase II, see update to paragraph 8.219, below.

Fn 626. The Commission has now published its Non-Horizontal Merger Guidelines, OJ 2008 C265/6: Vol II, App D14. These are discussed in new paragraphs 8.217A (vertical mergers) and 8.219A (conglomerate mergers), below.

(d) Unilateral effects

(i) In general

Relevance of market shares and concentration levels. In Case M.4956 *STX/* **8.204** *Aker Yards* (5 May 2008) the Commission considered the implications of possible State subsidies from South Korea to the merged entity. The Commission analysed the earlier ECSC case of Case T-156/98 *RJB Mining plc v Commission* [2001] ECR II-337 and held that it was not required to make a 'pre-assessment' of alleged subsidies within a merger control procedure by conducting a *quasi* State aid investigation to identify whether subsidies were granted by a non-Member State. In principle, the Commission accepted that it must take into account any subsidies as factors potentially increasing a merged entity's financial strength, insofar as evidence supports the existence or the likelihood of such subsidies. However, if there is no clear evidence of the existence of such subsidies provided by third countries, the Commission is not obliged to investigate further. Any alleged inadequacies of the international procedures, such as the WTO procedures, are not relevant in this respect: paras 75 *et seq*.

Fn 634. See, eg Case M.4533 *SCA/ P&G (European tissue business)* (5 September 2008) where the merged entity would have an 80–90 per cent share in the supply of branded kitchen paper but would not have market power because of the strong competition from private label product at the retail level: 'high market shares did not reflect their real market power vis-à-vis retailers and, ultimately, end-consumers': para 126.

(ii) Relevant considerations

8.207 **Potentially relevant factors.** Note that the CFI has said that the Horizontal Merger Guidelines do not require an examination in every case of all the factors mentioned in the Guidelines, since the Commission enjoys a discretion enabling it to take account or not to take account of certain factors: Case T-282/06 *Sun Chemical Group v Commission* [2007] ECR II-2149, para 57.

In Case M.5141 *KLM/Martinair* (17 December 2008) the Commission found that an important element of the counterfactual was that Martinair's business was loss-making and the existing owner had no strategic interest in making the investment necessary to reverse this decline. It was likely that the competitive constraint exerted by Martinair on KLM would be eroded in the foreseeable future absent the merger: para 175. See also Case M.4647 *AEE/Lentjes* (5 December 2007) where the Commission noted that the past market position of Lentjes was likely to weaken because demand in the German market in which it had a strong reputation was likely to decline: para 101.

As to mergers between close competitors see the analysis of the Commission in Case M.4842 *Danone/Numico* (31 October 2007) as regards the Belgian market for baby meals: merged entity would have a market share of 75–80 per cent, far ahead of that of its closest rival and undertakings wishing to enter or expand would 'experience the utmost difficulties': paras 63 *et seq.* In Case M.4828 *Owens Corning/Saint Gobain Vetrotex* (26 October 2007) the Commission noted that the merger would create a market leader with significantly higher sales and capacity than any other competitors and that the parties were generally considered as the leading innovators in the industry, with high quality R&D departments capable of developing entirely new products to suit customer needs: para 71. The commitments accepted before the clearance of the merger included the divestment of a product R&D centre, including a team of 20 experienced engineers, chemists and technicians under the direction of the R&D leader and a fully equipped laboratory.

Fn 643. As to merger with a potential competitor see also Case M.5096 *RCA/MAV Cargo* (25 November 2008) where the Commission conditionally cleared a merger which led to the removal of the most likely new entrant in each of the parties' domestic rail freight markets. In Case M.4956 *STX/Aker Yards* (5 May 2008) the Commission, referring to para 60 of the Horizontal Merger Guidelines, found no plans or specific evidence indicating a likely and timely entry by STX in the relevant market in a significant way absent the merger. Other Far East shipbuilders were more advanced than STX in their steps towards entering into the cruise ship market. The Commission concluded that the merger would not have significant anti-competitive effects as a result of the elimination of STX as a potential competitor of the three current large builders of cruise ships.

Fn 653. As to pricing 'mavericks' see Case M.4919 *Statoil/ConocoPhillips (Jet)* (21 October 2008) where the Commission found that JET Sweden played a unique role in the Swedish market as a low price supplier in retail sales of motor fuels and that its removal from the market would have a greater effect than its market share would imply at first glance: paras 91 *et seq*. Similarly in Case M.4844 *Fortis/ABN Amro Assets* (3 October 2007) Fortis as a smaller competitor had the incentive to break into existing customer relations and compete on price and non-price parameters in order to increase its customer base. This incentive would disappear once it was acquired by the market leader. In Case M.4999 *Heineken/Scottish & Newcastle* (3 April 2008) the fact that S&N was regarded as a price maverick in the Irish beer market was relevant to the decision whether to refer the merger back to the Irish competition authorities under Article 9(2) of the Merger Regulation: paras 41 *et seq*. In Case M.4523 *Travelport/Worldspan* (21 August 2007) the Commission rejected arguments that Worldspan acted as a price maverick since the market investigation did not establish that Worldspan's prices were lower than its competitors' before the merger and Worldspan's market share was declining: para 104. A similar submission was also rejected in Case M.4963 *Rexel/Hagemeyer* (22 February 2008), para 71.

(e) Coordinated effects

(i) In general

Opportunities for tacit collusion.   This and the following paragraphs must now   **8.210**
be read in the light of the ECJ's judgment in Case C-413/06 P *Bertelsmann AG and Sony Corporation of America v Impala and Commission* [2008] ECR I-4951. The ECJ overturned the CFI's judgment, finding that the CFI had erred in a number of respects both procedural and substantive. The ECJ set out the test that the Commission must apply in the case of an alleged creation or strengthening of a collective dominant position: see paras 119 *et seq*. The Court emphasised that in applying the criteria, it is necessary to avoid a mechanical approach involving the separate verification of each of those criteria taken in isolation, while taking no account of the overall economic mechanism of a hypothetical tacit coordination. See further the update to paragraph 10.053, below.

(ii) Relevant considerations

Characterising a market as oligopolistic.   The test as set out by the ECJ in the   **8.211**
IMPALA judgment was applied by the Commission in granting conditional clearance at Phase II of the investigation into a merger in Case M.4980 *ABF/GBI Business* (23 September 2008) (paras 144 *et seq*). The Commission found as regards the Portuguese market: the three existing entities all had a strong presence in the market and faced virtually no threat of entry or expansion from competitors; the market was characterised by the high frequency of interaction between suppliers,

indirectly via their distributors; demand for the product was relatively inelastic; there were high barriers to entry arising from the importance of having a local distribution network and a strong reputation for quality and reliability; the product was fairly homogeneous across suppliers and thus subject to similar supply or demand shocks; there was transparency of price, sales and capacity and the technology used in the market was mature and not expected to change or improve. All these factors indicated that the market conditions were conducive to coordination. So far as mechanisms for policing the coordination were concerned, the Commission cited instances in the past where attempts by the *de facto* exclusive distributor of one supplier to expand its share of the market in an area had been disciplined by the supplier: 'This demonstrates how the system corrects itself when a distributor is trying to deviate from the paradigm imposed by the suppliers': para 219. The Commission went on to find that the other conditions set in *IMPALA* were also satisfied and that the merger, by creating a duopoly would increase the incentives for coordination. The merger was cleared on the basis of divestiture commitments.

By contrast in Case M.5114 *Pernod Ricard/V&S Vin & Sprit* (17 August 2008) the Commission found that the criteria for market coordination were not satisfied because prices were not transparent. Further, there were strong local producers present in most Member States who would be able to gain market shares in case of coordinated price increases from large, international players: paras 107 *et seq*. See also Case M.4942 *Nokia/Navteq* (2 July 2008) paras 395 *et seq*; and Case M.4854 *TomTom/Tele Atlas* (14 May 2008) paras 277 *et seq* (conditions for coordinated behaviour not met in vertical mergers); Case M.4781 *Norddeutsche Affinerie/Cumerio* (23 January 2008) paras 183 *et seq* (ability of actual and potential competitors to counteract any attempts of coordination reduced the ability and incentives for undertakings to try to coordinate their commercial behaviour); Case M.4523 *Travelport/Worldspan* (21 August 2007) paras 149 *et seq* (limited price transparency in the market for global distribution systems for travel services products). In Case M.5020 *Lesaffre/GBI UK* (11 July 2008) the merger would have created a duopoly in the relevant market aligning the merged entity with the existing market leader in terms of market shares, production capacity and geographic plant distribution. The merger was cleared subject to commitments which returned the position to the status quo.

8.212 **Reaching terms of coordination.**   The judgment of the CFI in Case T-464/04 *IMPALA v Commission* [2006] ECR II-2289, [2006] 5 CMLR 1049 was overturned by the ECJ on appeal: see Case C-413/06 P *Bertelsmann AG and Sony Corporation of America v Impala and Commission* [2008] ECR I-4951. The ECJ approved the criteria for collective dominance as expressed by the CFI in *Airtours* but held that the CFI had been wrong to conclude that the discounts offered by the record companies (which the Commission had found meant that prices were not transparent in the market) would have been apparent to a 'hypothetical industry professional': para 131. See further the update to paragraph 10.053, below.

Prospective analysis: *Impala*.   The judgment of the CFI in *IMPALA* was over- **8.214**
turned by the ECJ: see updates to paragraph 8.212, above and paragraph 10.053,
below.

(f) Vertical and conglomerate effects

(i) *Vertical effects*

Potential foreclosure effects.   In Case M.5121 *News Corp/Premiere* (26 June **8.216**
2008) the Commission considered whether the vertical aspect of the merger
would lead to 'input foreclosure', ie whether the upstream business of the merged
entity would have the ability and incentive to stop supplying competitors in
the downstream market and 'customer foreclosure', ie whether the downstream
business would acquire all its requirements internally, thereby removing it as a
potential outlet for competitors in the upstream market: paras 59 *et seq*. The
Commission's concerns about the strengthening of Premiere's dominant position
in the German pay-TV market were resolved by commitments which allowed the
merger to be cleared.

In Case M.4854 *Tom Tom/Tele Atlas* (14 May 2008) and Case M.4942 *Nokia/
Navteq* (2 July 2008) the Commission considered whether a vertical merger may
give the merged entity access to commercially sensitive information regarding the
downstream activity of rivals. For instance, by becoming a supplier to its downstream competitors, the merged entity may obtain critical information allowing it
to compete less aggressively or could put competitors at a disadvantage thereby
making entry and expansion less attractive (para 360 of *Nokia/Navteq* and para 276
of *Tom Tom/Tele Atlas*). The Commission found that this was not a problem on
the facts of the particular market. For a discussion of the Commission's approach
to vertical mergers in *Tom Tom/TeleAtlas* and *Nokia/Navteq* see de Coninck,
'Economic analysis in vertical mergers' (2008) 3 Competition Policy Newsletter
48; and Esteva Mosso et al, 'Digital maps go vertical: TomTom/TeleAtlas
and Nokia/NAVTEQ' (2008) 3 Competition Policy Newsletter 70. See similarly
Case M.4731 *Google/DoubleClick* (11 March 2008), para 257 (contractual restrictions on use of data collected on behalf of one customer to benefit other customers
meant that there were no network effect benefits).

A particular kind of vertical effect can arise in two-sided markets: see, eg Case
M.4523 *Travelport/Worldspan* (21 August 2007) where the Commission described
a theory of harm arising from concentration in the market for global distribution
systems for travel services. The Commission referred to potential 'vertical
cross market effects' whereby the merged entity would have an incentive to offer
favourable terms to attract more travel agents to join its network and recoup that

investment (and generate their margin) by extracting rents upstream from the travel service providers such as airlines, hotels, and car rental companies: para 76.

In the Non-Horizontal Merger Guidelines, OJ 2008 C265/6: Vol II, App D14 the Commission notes that the integration of complementary activities within a single firm may produce significant efficiencies and be pro-competitive. Vertical integration may provide an increased incentive to seek to decrease prices and increase output because the integrated firm can capture a larger fraction of the benefits. This is often referred to as the 'internalisation of double mark-ups'. Similarly, other efforts to increase sales at one level (eg improve service or step up innovation) may provide a greater reward for an integrated firm that will take into account the benefits accruing at other levels. Integration may also decrease transaction costs and allow for a better coordination in terms of product design, the organisation of the production process, and the way in which the products are sold: paras 13 and 14.

8.217A **Vertical mergers: the Non-Horizontal Merger Guidelines.** The Commission has now published its Non-Horizontal Merger Guidelines, OJ 2008 C265/6: Vol II, App D14. So far as vertical mergers are concerned, the Guidelines indicate that the Commission is unlikely to investigate a non-horizontal merger extensively where the market share post-merger of the new entity in each of the markets concerned is below 30 per cent and the post-merger HHI is below 2000 unless certain listed factors are present: para 26. The Guidelines discuss how the Commission will assess the likelihood of input foreclosure, that is, whether the upstream part of the entity is likely to restrict supplies or increase prices charged to undertakings in the downstream market which are now competing with the downstream arm of the merged entity. The Commission will examine first, whether the merged entity would have, post-merger, the ability to foreclose access to inputs, secondly, whether it would have the incentive to do so; and thirdly, whether a foreclosure strategy would have a significant detrimental effect on competition downstream. The Commission describes the kinds of circumstances in which input foreclosure is likely to be a problem.

The Commission notes that vertical mergers may generate efficiencies, in particular, a vertical merger allows the merged entity to internalise any pre-existing double mark-ups; it may further allow the parties better to coordinate the production and distribution process, and therefore to save on inventory costs and may align the incentives of the parties with regard to investments in new products, new production processes and in the marketing of products. So far as customer foreclosure is concerned, the Commission again describes the factors indicating whether the merged entity would have the ability and the incentive to engage in such conduct and whether this would have a significant detrimental effect on consumers in the downstream market: paras 58 *et seq*. Finally the Guidelines discuss the circumstances in which a vertical merger may lead to coordinated effects by making it easier for the firms in the upstream or downstream market to reach a common understanding on the terms of coordination.

In practice.   See also the Commission's analysis of possible vertical effects in a   **8.218** merger between a manufacturer of sensors used in textile weaving and spinning machines and a manufacturer of those machines: Case M.4874 *Itema/Barco Vision* (4 August 2008). Both the upstream market (for the sensors) and the downstream market (for the machines) were highly concentrated and competitors in the downstream market feared that they would no longer be able to buy sensors to incorporate into their machines. On analysis the Commission found that there was little risk of foreclosure and the merger was cleared. In Case M.4942 *Nokia/Navteq* (2 July 2008) the Commission considered a case of 'backward vertical integration' in the sense that a producer of a good (mobile phone handsets) acquired its main provider of an important input (navigable digital map databases). The Commission identified upstream, downstream and intermediate markets (for navigation software) affected by the merger. Competitors in the downstream market expressed concerns that the merged entity might pursue a foreclosure strategy either by increasing prices, by providing degraded map sets, by delaying access to the latest maps or attributes or by reserving innovative features to Nokia. The Commission applied three criteria: (i) whether the merged entity would have the *ability* post-merger to foreclose access to inputs; (ii) whether it would have the *incentive* to do so; and (iii) whether a foreclosure strategy would have a significant detrimental effect in the intermediary downstream market for navigation software and in the downstream markets. As to the first, the Commission concluded that the merged entity would have a significant degree of market power on the upstream market for navigable digital map databases but that it was unclear whether they would have the ability to adopt a strategy of foreclosure. The Commission cleared the merger on the basis that the merged entity would have no incentive to foreclose. When the Nokia/Navteq merger was notified, the Commission was part way through investigating a very similar vertical merger in the same markets and the analysis and reasoning in *Nokia/Navteq* drew heavily on the earlier decision in Case M.4854 *Tom Tom/Tele Atlas* (14 May 2008).

See also Case M.5585 *Centrica/Venture Production* (21 August 2009) where the Commission considered the possible vertical effects in a merger in the gas and crude oil production markets.

Fn 683. An appeal against the *DaimlerChrysler/Deutsche Telekom/JV* decision was dismissed: Case T-48/04 *Qualcomm Wireless Business Solutions v Commission*, judgment of 19 June 2009.

(ii) Conglomerate effects

8.219 **Conglomerate effects.**   In Case M.4731 *Google/DoubleClick* (11 March 2008),
para 257 the Commission investigated non-horizontal theories of harm arising
from the fact that intermediation and ad serving tools are products that publishers
and advertisers can purchase together (though not necessarily). With the acquisition of DoubleClick, Google would therefore acquire the leading supplier of
ad serving that publishers and advertisers can combine with intermediation
services such as those offered by Google's ad network (AdSense). The Commission therefore analysed (i) foreclosure scenarios based on DoubleClick's market
position in ad serving; (ii) foreclosure scenarios based on Google's market position
in search advertising and online ad intermediation services; and (iii) foreclosure
scenarios based on the combination of DoubleClick's and Google's databases
on customer online behaviour. The Commission concluded (para 310) that the
evidence reviewed did not support the view that the new entity would be able
to foreclose competitors in intermediation markets through leveraging of its leading position in ad serving. There were credible alternatives to which customers
(publishers/advertisers/ad networks) could switch and network effects (ie the
competitive advantages derived from having a large customer base) were not
strong. Any strategy to attract publishers/advertisers to AdSense through input
foreclosure or a variety of bundling/tweaking strategies was unlikely to be able to
foreclose rivals in intermediation markets. For a helpful discussion of the issues in
this rather complicated case see Brockhoff et al, 'Google/DoubleClick: The first
test for the Commission's non-horizontal merger guidelines' (2008) 2 Competition
Policy Newsletter 53.

8.219A **Conglomerate effects: Non-Horizontal Merger Guidelines.**   The Commission
has now published its Non-Horizontal Merger Guidelines, OJ 2008 C265/6:
Vol II, App D14. The Commission notes, as regards conglomerate mergers, that
in practice its focus is on mergers between companies that are active in closely
related markets (eg mergers involving suppliers of complementary products or of
products which belong to a range of products that is generally purchased by the
same set of customers for the same end use). The Guidelines indicate that the
Commission is unlikely to investigate a non-horizontal merger extensively where
the market share post-merger of the new entity in each of the markets concerned
is below 30 per cent and the post-merger HHI is below 2000 unless certain listed
factors are present: para 26. The main concern is that of foreclosure since the
combination of products in related markets may confer on the merged entity the
ability and incentive to leverage a strong market position from one market to
another by means of tying or bundling or other exclusionary practices: paras 93
et seq. The Commission will therefore first examine whether the merged entity
will have the ability to foreclose its rivals, secondly, whether it would have the

economic incentive to do so and, thirdly, whether a foreclosure strategy would have a significant detrimental effect on competition, thus causing harm to consumers. Foreclosure in this context involves conditioning sales in a way that links the products in the separate markets together, usually by tying or bundling.

Other conglomerate cases.   The Commission has now published its Non- **8.221**
Horizontal Merger Guidelines, OJ 2008 C265/6: Vol II, App D14 discussed in the preceding paragraphs.

Fn 702. The Commission also considered possible conglomerate effects in Case M.5114 *Pernod Ricard/V&S Vin & Sprit* (17 August 2008) but concluded that the merged entity would not be able to tie or bundle its brand portfolio: para 115.

(g) Other considerations relevant to substantive appraisal

(ii) Efficiencies

Proving efficiency benefits.   See the evidence that the parties submitted in Case **8.229**
M.5141 *KLM/Martinair* (17 December 2008), paras 408 *et seq*. The Commission found that the underlying assumptions in the report were too strong to allow any inference on their ultimate quantification, and no clear-cut indication could be drawn from it. In Case M.4942 *Nokia/Navteq* (2 July 2008) the Commission considered whether pricing efficiencies would arise from the removal of double mark-ups in a vertical merger, referring to para 55 of the Non-Horizontal Merger Guidelines (paras 365 *et seq*).

(iii) Failing firm defence

Failing firm defence.   See also Case M.5141 *KLM/Martinair* (17 December **8.230**
2008) where the Commission found that Martinair's business was loss-making and the existing owner had no strategic interest in making the investment necessary to reverse this decline. It was therefore likely that the competitive constraint exerted by Martinair on KLM would be eroded in the foreseeable future absent the merger: para 175.

(h) Coordinative aspects of certain full-function joint ventures

(i) In general

Spill-over effects.   In Case M.5332 *Ericsson/STM/JV* (25 November 2008) the **8.232**
Commission found that there were no likely coordinated effects because the market was characterised by differentiated products, long-term contracts, infrequent bidding and large volumes of individual tenders, asymmetry of players' market shares post joint venture, significant buyer power of customers and the importance of innovation in the market.

5. Judicial Review by the Community Courts

(a) Procedures

8.236 **Expedited procedure.** The judgment of the CFI in Case T-464/04 *IMPALA v Commission* [2006] ECR II-2289, [2006] 5 CMLR 1049 was overturned by the ECJ on appeal: see Case C-413/06 P *Bertelsmann AG and Sony Corporation of America v Impala and Commission* [2008] ECR I-4951. The case was referred back to the CFI to consider the other grounds of appeal not dealt with. Costs were reserved.

(c) Persons entitled to appeal

(ii) Third parties

8.240 **Competitors and customers.** Where a competitor has gone into liquidation and hence is no longer active in the relevant market, it does not have standing to challenge the clearance of a merger: Case T-269/03 *Socratec v Commission*, judgment of 19 June 2009. The CFI rejected the argument that Socratec's potential rights of action for damages against either the parties to the concentration or the Commission gave it standing.

Note that even if the Commission sends a copy of the approval decision to a complainant who has been involved in the investigation stage, the time for that complainant to bring an appeal against the clearance decision still runs only from the publication of the decision in the *Official Journal*: Case T-48/04 *Qualcomm Wireless Business Solutions v Commission*, judgment of 19 June 2009, para 58.

(d) Scope of judicial review

(i) Application of the law

8.246 **Jurisdictional issues.** **Fn 773.** The appeal in *Cementbouw* was dismissed: Case C-202/06 P *Cementbouw Handel & Industrie BV v Commission* [2007] ECR I-12129, [2008] 4 CMLR 1324.

8.247 **Procedural issues.** As to adequacy of reasoning in the decision, see Case C-413/06 P *Bertelsmann AG and Sony Corporation of America v Impala and Commission* [2008] ECR I-4951 where the ECJ confirmed that the extent of the Commission's reasoning had to take into account the need for speed and the short timescales set for the Commission under the Merger Regulation: paras 166–169. The ECJ rejected an argument that the deeming provision in Article 10(6) of the Merger Regulation meant that a Commission clearance decision could not be annulled for lack of reasoning: para 175.

(iii) Economic issues

Effective but restrained review.   In Case C-413/06 P *Bertelsmann AG and Sony* **8.252**
Corporation of America v Impala and Commission [2008] ECR I-4951, the ECJ
confirmed that while the CFI must not substitute its own economic assessment
for that of the Commission, that does not mean that the Community judicature
must refrain from reviewing the Commission's interpretation of information of
an economic nature. Although the CFI had carried out an in-depth examination
of the evidence underlying the contested decision, it had acted in conformity with
the requirements of the case law: paras 145–146.

In Case C-202/06 P *Cementbouw Handel & Industrie BV v Commission* [2007]
ECR I-12129, [2008] 4 CMLR 1324 the ECJ referred to 'the discretionary margin
implicit in the provisions of an economic nature which form part of the rules on
concentrations' in the context of a challenge to the Commission's refusal to accept
commitments offered by the parties to the concentration during a Phase II investigation: para 53.

(e) Standard of proof incumbent on Commission

Borderline cases.   In Case C-413/06 P *Bertelsmann AG and Sony Corporation* **8.255**
of America v Impala and Commission [2008] ECR I-4951 the ECJ confirmed that
there is no general presumption that a notified concentration is compatible with,
or incompatible with, the common market. The burden of proof is the same
whether the Commission is considering clearing or prohibiting the merger.
Further, there is no particularly high standard of proof in mergers involving allegations of collective dominance: paras 46 *et seq.*

6. Application of Articles 81 and 82 in Field of
Mergers and Acquisitions

Note that Articles 81 and 82 EC are now Articles 101 and 102 TFEU

(a) Background

Article 82 and concentrations.   See the rather cautious approach in COMP/ **8.259**
38.113 *Prokent-Tomra*, decn of 29 March 2006, [2009] 4 CMLR 101, paras 86,
107 and 345 where the Commission referred to the dominant undertaking's
exclusionary strategy as including acquisition of its competitors. The Commission
stated that the acquisitions were described in order to illustrate Tomra's overall
strategy and the means implemented to maintain its dominant position: 'This
decision does not question the legality of these practices, which are outside its
scope': para 107. The case is on appeal Case T-155/06 *Tomra Systems*, not yet
decided.

7. National Merger Control and International Cooperation

(a) National merger control regimes within EEA

(ii) Summary of national regimes

8.279 **Outline of national merger control rules in the EEA.** The following entries should be substituted at the appropriate place in the table.

Jurisdiction	Jurisdictional criteria	Notification requirements
Bulgaria	(a) combined turnover in Bulgaria of BGN 25m (c. €12.8m); and (b) either (1) at least two parties each have turnover in Bulgaria of BGN 3m (c. €1.5m); *or* (2) target has turnover in Bulgaria of BGN 3m (c. €1.5m)	Mandatory prior notification to Commission for Protection of Competition
Cyprus	(a) at least two parties each have worldwide turnover of €3.4m; and (b) at least one party carries on business in Cyprus; and (c) combined turnover in Cyprus of €3.4m	Mandatory prior notification to Commission for the Protection of Competition
France	(a) combined worldwide turnover of €150m; and (b) at least two parties each have turnover in France of €50m Special thresholds for concentrations in the retail trade sector or in the French Départements or Collectivités d'Outre-Mer	Mandatory prior notification to l'Autorité de la concurrence (Competition Authority)
Iceland	(a) combined turnover in Iceland of ISK 2,000m (c. €14m); and (b) at least two parties each have turnover in Iceland of ISK 200 m (c. €1.4m); *or* (a) combined turnover in Iceland of ISK 1,000m (c. €7m); and (b) authority believes the merger can substantially reduce effective competition	Mandatory prior notification to Samkeppnisstofnun (Competition Authority)
Italy	(a) combined turnover in Italy of €461m; or (b) target has turnover in Italy of €46m (Thresholds are revised annually to take account of inflation; above figures were revised in July 2009)	Mandatory prior notification to the Autorità Garante della Concorrenza e del Mercato (Competition Authority)

Jurisdiction	Jurisdictional criteria	Notification requirements
Latvia	(a) combined turnover (in Latvia) of LVL 25m (c. €35m); or (b) combined market share in relevant market of 40% Exception: Merger notification may not be necessary if turnover of one of the parties does not exceed LVL 1.5 million (c. €2.1m)	Mandatory prior notification to Konkurences Padome (Competition Council)
Malta	(a) combined turnover in Malta of €2,329,373,40, and (b) each of the undertakings concerned has turnover in Malta equivalent to at least 10% of parties' combined turnover	Mandatory prior notification to Director of the Office for Fair Competition
Slovakia	(a) combined worldwide turnover of €46m; and (b) at least two parties each have turnover in the Slovak Republic of €14m; *or* (a) at least one party has worldwide turnover of €46m; and (b) at least one other party has turnover in the Slovak Republic of €19m	Mandatory prior notification to Protimonopolného úrad (Antimonopoly Office)
Slovenia	(a) combined turnover in Slovenia of 35m; and (b) (i) target has turnover in Slovenia of €1m; or (ii) in cases of joint ventures of at least two parties, including affiliated companies, turnover in Slovenia of €1m NB: If thresholds are not met, but parties to the concentration, together with the affiliated companies, have more than 60 % market share in the Slovenian market, the undertakings concerned are obliged to inform the CPO of the concentration (but not submit a formal notification).	Mandatory prior notification to Urad RS za Varstvo Konkurence (Competition Protection Office)
Sweden	(a) combined turnover in Sweden of SEK 1,000m (c. €104m); and (b) at least two parties each have turnover in Sweden of SEK 200m (c. €20.8m)	Mandatory prior notification to Konkurrensverket (Swedish Competition Authority). Voluntary notification may be submitted by the parties if only the first turnover threshold (SEK 1,000m) is met.

9

INTELLECTUAL PROPERTY RIGHTS

2. Infringement Actions and the Free Movement Rules

(c) Trade marks

Specific subject-matter of the trade mark. In Case C-533/06 *O₂ Holdings v* **9.033**
Hutchison 3G UK Ltd [2008] ECR I-4231, [2008] 3 CMLR 397, the ECJ considered the essential function of the trade mark when deciding whether the use in an
advertisement by one mobile phone network operator (H3G) of a sign very similar
to the registered trade mark of a competitor (O_2) was a breach of the latter's rights
when the sign was being used to emphasise that H3G's prices were lower than
O_2's. The Court considered the relationship between Article 5(1) of Directive
89/104 and Directive 84/450 concerning misleading and comparative advertising
(1984 OJ L250/17 amended by Dir 2005/29 2005 OJ L149/22). O_2 accepted
that the comparison made in the advertisement was not misleading and further
that the advertisement did not suggest that there was any trade connection between
the two companies. The use of the O_2 sign did not therefore cause confusion or
otherwise jeopardise the essential function of O_2's mark. The ECJ held that the
use made of the O_2 mark did constitute 'use' within the meaning of Article 5(1)
and (2) of Directive 89/104. However, in order to reconcile Article 5 of Directive
89/104 with Article 3a(1) of Directive 84/450, these provisions must be interpreted as meaning that the trade mark owner is not entitled to prevent the use of
its mark in a comparative advertisement which satisfies all the criteria of Directive
84/450, under which comparative advertising is permitted.

Repackaging: recent case law. Following the judgment of the ECJ on the sec- **9.039**
ond preliminary ruling reference (Case C-348/04 [2007] ECR I-3391, [2007]
2 CMLR 1445, [2008] All ER (EC) 411) the English Court of Appeal noted that
both sides claimed to have won: *Boehringer Ingelheim v Swingward* [2008] EWCA
Civ 83, [2008] All ER (EC) 411. Jacob LJ commented 'European trade mark law
seems to have arrived at such a state of uncertainty that no one really knows
what the rules are. . . . Big brand owners want bigger rights; small players, no

change or less. The compromises which have emerged have very fuzzy lines'. The case concerned the practices of 're-boxing' (which generally involves re-affixing the original trade mark on the new information leaflet and box); 'de-branding' (using only the generic name of the drug on the box but not removing the brand name from the blister pack or the product itself); and 'co-branding' (where the packaging bears the trade mark of the drug but also the get up of the importer). Co-branding and de-branding were not in principle liable to damage a trade mark's reputation. The ECJ in the second reference (Case C-348/04) specifically held that whether or not those activities caused damage was a question of fact for the national court. The evidence in relation to co-branding did not establish any damage to the trade marks. The Court of Appeal further considered that total de-branding, where all traces of the trade mark sued upon were removed, was clearly not an infringement, because there was simply no use of the trade mark in any shape or form. A trade mark owner had no right to insist that his trade mark stayed on the goods for the aftermarket and, because that was so, it was impossible to say that partial de-branding was damaging in itself. The manner or form of partial de-branding could hurt the image or prestige of a trade mark. That would depend on how it was done. The judge's conclusion of fact at first instance, that the specific de-branding complained of by M did not damage their trade marks, was not shown to be wrong. Further, the importer had complied with the fourth condition in *Bristol Myers Squibb* and their activities by way of re-boxing and re-labelling had not caused damage to the reputation of M's trade marks. However, the Court of Appeal deferred making a final decision to await the outcome of a further reference to the ECJ in Case C-276/05 *Wellcome v Paranova* where the issue was whether the presentation of the new packaging was to be measured against the principle of minimum intervention or only against whether it was such as to damage the reputation of the trade mark and its proprietor. The ECJ gave judgment in Case C-276/05 *Wellcome v Paranova* on 22 December 2008. The ECJ held that Article 7(2) of Directive 89/104 is to be interpreted as meaning that, where it is established that repackaging of the pharmaceutical product is necessary for further marketing in the Member State of importation, the presenta-tion of the packaging should be assessed only against the condition that it should not be such as to be liable to damage the reputation of the trade mark or that of its proprietor. Further, Article 7(2) of Directive 89/104 is to be interpreted as mean-ing that it is for the parallel importer to furnish to the proprietor of the trade mark the information which is necessary and sufficient to enable the latter to determine whether the repackaging of the product under that trade mark is necessary in order to market it in the Member State of importation. The English proceedings then settled before they were reinstated in the Court of Appeal.

9.042 **Marketing in a manner that may affect reputation.**   In Case C-533/06 *O₂ Holdings v Hutchison 3G UK Ltd* [2008] ECR I-4231, [2008] 3 CMLR 397, the

ECJ held that Article 5 of Directive 89/104 does not entitle the trade mark owner to prevent the use of its mark in a comparative advertisement which satisfies all the criteria of Directive 84/450 (1984 OJ L250/17 amended by Directive 2005/29, 2005 OJ L149/22) under which comparative advertising is permitted.

No international exhaustion: *Silhouette.* The conflict between the ECJ's judg- **9.044** ments in *Silhouette* and *Sebago* and the EFTA Court's judgment in *Mag Instrument* has now been resolved in favour of a consistent interpretation of Article 7 of Directive 89/104 and a prohibition on international exhaustion within the EEA: Cases E-9 & 10/07 *L'Oréal Norge v Per Aarskog AS*, decn of the EFTA Court 8 July 2008. L'Oréal sought to prohibit the import into Norway of products bearing the 'Redken' mark which had been marketed by it in the USA but not within the EEA. Norwegian national law provided for international exhaustion so that L'Oréal's rights were exhausted by the marketing of the items in the USA. The EFTA Court held that the case law of the ECJ had made clear that it was not open to EU Member States to introduce or maintain a principle of international exhaustion in the light of Article 7. The EFTA Court found that there were no compelling grounds for a divergent interpretation in the EEA. Article 7 therefore precludes the unilateral introduction or maintenance of international exhaustion of rights. The Court appears to have left open the question whether the result would be different if the EFTA State in question had entered into a treaty with a third country providing for exhaustion of rights: para 32.

Consent: express or implied. In Case C-59/08 *Copad SA v Christian Dior* **9.045** *Couture SA and SIL*, judgment of 23 April 2009 the ECJ considered whether sales of marked goods by a licensee (SIL) to a discount store outside the selective distribution network (Copad) contrary to the terms of the licence with the trade mark owner (Dior) are an infringement of the trade mark or merely a breach of contract. The ECJ interpreted Article 8(2) of Directive 89/104 which provides that the proprietor of a trade mark may invoke the rights conferred by that trade mark against a licensee who contravenes a provision in his licensing contract if that provision relates to certain matters including the quality of the goods. The ECJ held that the list of matters in Article 8(2) was exhaustive and not illustrative; the mark owner could rely on its trade mark rights provided it was established that the breach of the licence terms damaged the allure and prestigious image which bestows on the goods an aura of luxury and hence damaged their quality. Further, Article 7(1) of the Directive meant that a licensee who puts goods bearing a trade mark on the market in disregard of a provision in a licence agreement does so *without* the consent of the proprietor of the trade mark where it is established that the provision in question is included in those listed in Article 8(2) of that Directive. In a case where a licensee puts luxury goods on the market in contravention of a provision in the licence agreement, but must nevertheless be considered to have done so *with* the consent of the proprietor of the trade mark, the proprietor of the trade mark can rely on such a provision to oppose a resale of those goods on the basis of Article 7(2) of the Directive only if it can be established that, taking into account the particular circumstances of the case, such resale damages the reputation of the trade mark. See also *Mastercigars Direct Ltd v Hunters & Frankau Ltd* [2007] EWCA Civ 176, [2007] RPC 24, paras 16–17 for a summary of the state of the law at that point.

(d) Copyright and similar rights

9.052 **The specific subject-matter of the copyright.** In Case C-275/06 *Promusicae* [2008] ECR I-276, [2008] All ER (EC) 809 the ECJ considered questions referred from a Spanish court arising in proceedings brought by Promusicae, a music publishers' trade association, against an internet service provider, seeking disclosure of the identities and physical addresses of persons who were using a file sharing internet site to download music in breach of the rights of Promusicae's members. The ECJ held that neither Directive 2001/29 nor other relevant EU legislation requires Member States to oblige ISPs to disclose this information to support a civil action for breach of copyright. But the ECJ added that Community law does require that, when transposing those directives, the Member States take care to rely on an interpretation of them which allows a fair balance to be struck between the various fundamental rights protected by the Community legal order. Further, when implementing the measures transposing those directives, the authorities and courts of the Member States must not only interpret their national law in a manner consistent with those directives but also make sure that they do not rely on an interpretation of them which would be in conflict with those fundamental rights or with the other general principles of Community law, such as the principle of proportionality.

3. Articles 81 and 82 and the Exercise of Intellectual Property Rights

Note that Articles 81 and 82 EC are now Articles 101 and 102 TFEU

9.072 **Article 82 and infringement suits.** See Case T-119/09 *Protégé International v Commission*, not yet decided (appeal against rejection of complaint alleging abuse of dominant position by Pernod Ricard in filing legal proceedings against the applicant contesting the registration of trade marks. It is alleged that the proceedings were aimed not at protecting Pernod Ricard's intellectual property rights in its own marks ('Wild Turkey') but of eliminating the applicant as a competitor of Pernod Ricard in the Irish whiskey market). See also Case T-96/08 *Global Digital Disc v Commission*, not yet decided (appeal against rejection of complaint alleging breach of Article 82 [now Article 102 TFEU] in licensing practices in the CD-R field).

In the final Report on the sectoral inquiry into the pharmaceutical industry published on 8 July 2009, the Commission described the scale of infringement litigation brought by originator pharmaceutical companies against both generic manufacturers and against competing originating companies. The Commission concluded that in certain instances originator companies 'may consider litigation not so much on its merits, but rather as a signal to deter generic entrants'. The Commission examined the scale of applications for interim injunctions and noted that there is a risk that settlements of litigation are concluded at the expense of consumers if they limit generic entry and include a value transfer from an originator company to a generic company. All stakeholders contributing to the inquiry emphasised the need for a unified and specialised patent litigation system in Europe.

Article 82 and refusal to license.　**Fn 235.** Note also that the German Federal **9.073**
Supreme Court has held that a patent user cannot resist an infringement action by alleging the right to a compulsory licence (and thus that a refusal to license is an abuse of a dominant position) unless it has made an unconditional, binding offer to the patent-holder and, if that was not accepted, paid the offered licence fees into an escrow account: *Orange-Book Standard*, judgment of 6 May 2009, WuW/E DE-R2613. However, this decision is based on the jurisprudence concerning the good faith provision of the German Civil Code (Article 242); in the absence of a ruling from the ECJ, it is unclear to what extent national law can restrict the application of EU competition law in this way.

6. Licences of other Intellectual Property Rights

(a) Trade marks

Trade mark licences generally.　As to when a breach by a licensee of a provision **9.172**
in the licence allows the mark owner to invoke his trade mark rights see Case C-59/08 *Copad SA v Christian Dior couture SA and SIL*, judgment of 23 April 2009, discussed in the update to paragraph 9.045, above.

Royalties for the use of the mark.　The appeal to the ECJ in *DSD* was dismissed: **9.178**
Case C-385/07 P *Der Grüne Punkt – Duales System Deutschland v Commission*, judgment of 16 July 2009, [2009] 5 CMLR 2215. The CFI analysed the case under Article 82(a) [now Article 102(a) TFEU], referring to settled case law, according to which an undertaking abuses its dominant position where it charges for its services fees which are disproportionate to the economic value of the service provided. The conduct objected to here, namely requiring payment of a fee for all packaging bearing the DGP logo and put into circulation in Germany, even where customers of the company show that they do not use the DGP system for some or all of that packaging, constituted an abuse of a dominant position within

that case law. The ECJ upheld this analysis, emphasising that the remedies imposed by the decision did not amount to an obligation to grant a licence to use the DGP logo. There was nothing in the decision which affects DSD's freedom of choice as to the grant of licences – the decision at issue merely obliges DSD not to claim payment from its contractual partners for take-back and recovery services which it has not provided. Note, however, that the CFI stated that the decision did not stop DSD levying an adequate fee for merely using the DGP mark even where it is shown that the packaging bearing the DGP logo has been taken back and recovered by another system. The green dot affixed to the packaging may have economic value as such, since it can inform the consumer that the packaging at issue may be brought to the DSD system: paras 193 and 194.

(b) Copyright

9.179 **Copyright licences generally.**   Fn 513. But note *Harry Potter*, WuW DE-R 2018, judgment of the Frankfurt am Main Higher Regional Court of 17 April 2007, holding that two merchandising agreements entered into regarding *Harry Potter and the Sorcerer's Stone* (one for products related to the book and the other for products related to the film) that limited the rights granted to the German-speaking States (ie Austria, Germany and Switzerland) and to certain means of supply (eg internet sales were excluded) did not infringe Article 81 [now Article 101 TFEU]. The experience of a licensee may relate only to certain markets, and the copyright holder could have decided to grant no licences and to decide itself which markets to enter.

10

ARTICLE 82

1. Introduction

Note that Article 82 EC is now Article 102 TFEU

(a) Generally

Link between dominant position and abuse.   On the basis of European juris-   **10.004**
prudence, the Paris Court of Appeal annulled the decision of the French competition authority finding that GlaxoSmithKline (GSK) had abused its dominant
position on the market for injectable acyclovir by predatory pricing on the market
for sodic cefuroxime. GSK was not dominant on the latter market and although
its prices for sodic cefuroxime were below average variable cost, the two markets
were not sufficiently closely connected for conduct on the latter market to constitute an abuse of GSK's position on the former market. The Court noted that
competitors on the non-dominated market were not potential competitors of
GSK on the dominated market so that the pricing could not have the alleged effect
of a 'message' to deter their entry into the dominated market: *Laboratoire
GlaxoSmithKline (France) v Competition Council*, judgment of 14 March 2007,
BOCCRF No. 7 of 15 September 2008; appeal dismissed by the Cour de Cassation,
Case No. E08-14.503, judgment No. 259 of 17 March 2009.

DG Comp Discussion Paper.   In February 2009 the Commission formally   **10.005**
adopted its Guidance on the Commission's enforcement priorities in applying
Article 82 to abusive exclusionary conduct by dominant undertakings: OJ 2009
C45/7: Vol II, App C19. The Guidance is not intended to be a statement of the
law but aims to provide greater clarity and predictability as regards the general
framework of analysis that the Commission will employ when determining
whether to pursue cases (para 2). It applies only to exclusionary conduct and only
to conduct of a single dominant firm, not to cases of collective dominance (para 4).
The Guidance sets out the Commission's approach to assessing market power
(paras 9–18); a general description of what is termed 'anti-competitive foreclosure'
and the factors that are relevant in assessing whether such foreclosure is likely

(paras 19–22); a description of price-based exclusionary conduct including the cost benchmarks that the Commission is likely to use (paras 23–27) and how the Commission will assess claims by dominant undertakings that the conduct is objectively justified (paras 28–31). There then follows a section dealing with specific abuses, exclusive dealing (including rebates); tying and bundling; predation and refusal to supply; and margin squeeze. The Commission issued a Question and Answer Memo responding to frequently asked questions: MEMO/08/761 (3 December 2008). As to the adoption by the Commission of a more economics-based analysis of infringements see the discussion of COMP/37.990 *Intel*, decn of 13 May 2009 in the update to paragraph 10.096, below.

3. Dominant Position

(b) The market position of the undertaking itself

10.021 **Market share as an indicator of dominance.**   In the Commission's Guidance on the enforcement of Article 82, OJ 2009 C45/7: Vol II, App C19, the Commission states that market shares 'provide a useful first indication' of the market structure and the relative importance of the different undertakings on the market. However, market shares will be interpreted in the light of the dynamics of the market and the extent to which products are differentiated: para 13.

10.022 **General caution about market shares.**   In Case M.4513 *Arjowiggins/M-Real Zanders' Reflect paper mill* (4 June 2008) the Commission recognised that 'Theoretically, a market where four competitors that are not capacity-constrained supply a more or less homogenous product can generate competitive outcomes, even if one firm has a 50% initial market share': para 363. However, the Commission's market analysis of customers' switching patterns did not allay the competition concerns arising from the merged entity's market share.

As regards 'bidding markets' see COMP/38.113 *Prokent-Tomra*, decn of 29 March 2006, [2009] 4 CMLR 101, para 90 (market in reverse vending machines not a bidding market) (on appeal Case T-155/06 *Tomra Systems*, not yet decided).

See also Case M.4533 *SCA/ P&G (European tissue business)* (5 September 2008) where the merged entity would have an 80–90 per cent share in the supply of branded kitchen paper but would not have market power because of the strong competition from private label product at the retail level: 'high market shares did not reflect their real market power vis-à-vis retailers and, ultimately, end-consumers': para 126.

Fn 66. See also Case M.4956 *STX/Aker Yards* (5 May 2008) where the Commission examined market shares in the cruise ship building market over a four-year period because market shares computed over a shorter period would not be a good proxy of market power, given the limited number of orders and deliveries: para 40. Similarly, in Case M.4647 *AEE/Lentjes* (5 December 2007) the Commission looked at the market position over a five-year period, supplementing this information with a detailed analysis of those tenders and projects in which both AEE and Lentjes had taken part as bidders. The Commission asked competitors and customers to furnish additional details of individual tenders, in particular those in which both parties had participated to see whether the two companies had been close competitors such that the planned merger would eliminate a significant competitive factor: paras 57 *et seq*. See similarly, Case M.4662 *Syniverse/BSG Wireless Business* (4 December 2007).

Relative market shares. In COMP/38.113 *Prokent-Tomra*, decn of 29 March **10.027** 2006, [2009] 4 CMLR 101 the Commission relied on the high market shares of Tomra and on the fact that in the relevant national markets Tomra's market share was a multiple of the market shares of its competitors: see paras 84 and 85. The case is on appeal Case T-155/06 *Tomra Systems*, not yet decided.

Stability of market shares. **Fn 87.** The appeal in *Der Grüne Punkt* was dis- **10.028** missed: Case C-385/07 P *Der Grüne Punkt – Duales System Deutschland v Commission*, judgment of 16 July 2009, [2009] 5 CMLR 2215 and did not concern the finding of dominance.

Market shares indicating dominance. In the Commission's Guidance on the **10.029** enforcement of Article 82, OJ 2009 C45/7: Vol II, App C19, the Commission states that dominance is not likely if the undertaking's market share is below 40 per cent: para 14. In COMP/37.990 *Intel*, decn of 13 May 2009 the Commission found that Intel had held very high market shares in excess of or around 80 per cent in an overall x86 CPU market and in excess of around 70 per cent in any of the sub-markets examined throughout the six-year observation period. The Commission noted that such large market shares are in themselves a clear indication of the existence of a dominant position but went on to say that this insight was subject to further verification in any given case by reference to contextual factors such as barriers to entry and expansion and buyer power: para 852.

Overall size and strength. **Fn 96.** The appeal referred to in the footnote was **10.030** dismissed by the ECJ: Case C-202/07 P *France Télécom v Commission*, judgment of 2 April 2009. The ECJ judgment did not consider issues concerning dominance.

Anti-competitive conduct as evidence of dominance. **Fn 102.** As regards the **10.031** firm's own attitude to its market position see COMP/38.113 *Prokent-Tomra*, decn of 29 March 2006, [2009] 4 CMLR 101 where the Commission relied (*inter alia*) on internal documents showing that Tomra believed that it held a dominant position: para 91. The case is on appeal Case T-155/06 *Tomra Systems*, not yet decided.

(c) Barriers to entry and expansion

10.032 **Barriers to entry: generally.**   See also the comments on barriers to entry and expansion in the Commission's Guidance on the enforcement of Article 82, OJ 2009 C45/7: paras 16 and 17.

10.034 **Scale economies.**   See, eg the Commission's analysis in COMP/37.990 *Intel*, decn of 13 May 2009, para 866. The Commission also discussed the link between high fixed costs and barriers to entry: paras 875 *et seq.*

10.036 **Ownership of intellectual property.**   In COMP/37.990 *Intel*, decn of 13 May 2009 the Commission noted that Intel's main competitor AMD manufactured its x86 CPUs on the basis of a cross licence agreement with Intel. That agreement followed on from a number of patent infringement cases brought by Intel against AMD and a global settlement between the two companies in 1995. The Commission commented that 'the extensive litigation history highlights the significant intellectual property-related barriers that any new entrant to the x86 CPU market would have to overcome': para 858.

10.038 **Advertising.**   In COMP/37.990 *Intel*, decn of 13 May 2009 the Commission noted Intel's substantial spend on marketing and concluded that its 'brand equity resulting from its investment in product differentiation and its installed base have given it "must-stock" status at the OEM level, in other words, it is an unavoidable trading partner for OEMs': para 870.

(d) Countervailing market power

10.041 **Countervailing power of buyers.**   See also the interesting analysis of countervailing buyer power in COMP/38.113 *Prokent-Tomra*, 29 decn of March 2006, [2009] 4 CMLR 101. Tomra argued that the customers for its reverse vending machines were the large supermarket retail chains who were difficult negotiating partners. But the Commission found that in some markets the customers' market shares were more fragmented and even in concentrated markets the customers' market shares did not equal Tomra's. Further the existence of buyer power requires that there are either credible alternative suppliers to which the customers could turn, or that customers are able to sponsor new entrants. In the absence of established competitors with significant and stable market shares, there was no credible threat of even the largest customers moving from Tomra. Procurement of reverse vending equipment is not part of the core activities of retail groups so they were unlikely to act in a strategic manner in order to subsidise and actively build up competing suppliers. There was therefore no countervailing buyer power: paras 88 and 89. The case is on appeal Case T-155/06 *Tomra Systems*, not yet decided.

In Case M.4662 *Syniverse/BSG Wireless Business* (4 December 2007) the Commission found that the consolidation of customers as well as a more sophisticated bidding process may give customers countervailing power. In particular, they may have a strong bargaining position by virtue of their relative financial size and the scale of their operations which they may use to influence the buying process and to sponsor new entry. Customers were also able to design sophisticated procurement processes in order to derive the best possible price and service level agreements (para 99). In Case M.4523 *Travelport/Worldspan* (21 August 2007) the Commission identified various factors in the market which were changing the bargaining interaction between GDS providers and customers on both sides of the two-sided market, resulting in increased bargaining strength of those customers relative to GDS providers. These elements (effective bargaining power of one set of customers, and ongoing or possible development of additional bargaining tools) were enough to counter the potentially detrimental effect of the reduction from four to three GDS providers (para 110).

See also the comments on countervailing buyer power in the Commission's Guidance on the enforcement of Article 82, OJ 2009 C45/7: Vol II, App C19, para 18.

The scale of countervailing buyer power was considered by the Competition Appeal Tribunal in *National Grid v The Gas and Electricity Markets Authority* [2009] CAT 10, in particular the economic effect of substantial sunk costs on the part of the allegedly dominant firm. The case is on appeal to the Court of Appeal.

Fn 127. As regards the *Hutchison 3G* case there mentioned, OFCOM held that there was insufficient buyer power to counteract Hutchison's dominance: this was upheld on appeal by the Competition Appeal Tribunal and then by the Court of Appeal: *Hutchison 3G UK Ltd v OFCOM* [2009] EWCA Civ 683.

(f) Collective or joint dominance

(i) Generally

Abuse by one or more undertakings.   In COMP/39.388 & 39.389 *E.ON* **10.048**
German electricity markets, decn of 26 November 2008, the Commission indicated, (in a decision accepting commitments) that for Article 82 [now Article 102 TFEU] to be infringed it is not necessary for all the undertakings which are considered to be collectively dominant also to be involved in the alleged abusive conduct. Thus although a collective dominant position might be held by two or three electricity companies in the German wholesale market, only E.ON was suspected of the abusive conduct: para 27.

(iii) Links arising from market structure

Market structures and coordinated policy.   This and the following paragraphs **10.053**
must now be read in the light of the ECJ's judgment in Case C-413/06 P
Bertelsmann AG and Sony Corporation of America v Impala and Commission [2008]

ECR I-4951. The ECJ overturned the CFI's decision finding that the CFI had erred in a number of respects, both procedural and substantive. The ECJ set out the test that the Commission must apply in the case of an alleged creation or strengthening of a collective dominant position: see paras 119 *et seq*. In an important passage the ECJ described the conditions in which collective dominance will arise as the relationship of interdependence existing between the parties to a tight oligopoly within which, on a market with the appropriate characteristics, in particular in terms of market concentration, transparency and product homogeneity, those parties are in a position to anticipate one another's behaviour and are therefore strongly encouraged to align their conduct on the market in such a way as to maximise their joint profits by increasing prices, reducing output, the choice or quality of goods and services, diminishing innovation, or otherwise influencing parameters of competition. In such a context, each operator is aware that highly competitive action on its part would provoke a reaction on the part of the others, so that it would derive no benefit from its initiative: para 121. The Court went on to elaborate on the conditions under which such a situation is likely to arise:

> 'Such tacit coordination is more likely to emerge if competitors can easily arrive at a common perception as to how the coordination should work, and, in particular, of the parameters that lend themselves to being a focal point of the proposed coordination. . . . Moreover, having regard to the temptation which may exist for each participant in a tacit coordination to depart from it in order to increase its short-term profit, it is necessary to determine whether such coordination is sustainable. In that regard, the coordinating undertakings must be able to monitor to a sufficient degree whether the terms of the coordination are being adhered to. There must therefore be sufficient market transparency for each undertaking concerned to be aware, sufficiently precisely and quickly, of the way in which the market conduct of each of the other participants in the coordination is evolving. Furthermore, discipline requires that there be some form of credible deterrent mechanism that can come into play if deviation is detected. In addition, the reactions of outsiders, such as current or future competitors, and also the reactions of customers, should not be such as to jeopardise the results expected from the coordination' (para 123).

The Court emphasised that in applying the criteria, it is necessary to avoid a mechanical approach involving the separate verification of each of those criteria taken in isolation, while taking no account of the overall economic mechanism of a hypothetical tacit coordination: para 125. Following the annulment of the Commission's decision, the case was re-notified to the Commission who reassessed the concentration under the current market circumstances and approved it. This decision is now under appeal: Case T-229/08 *Impala v Commission*, not yet decided.

10.054 **Collective dominance in oligopolistic markets.** In COMP/39.388 & 39.389 *E.ON German electricity markets*, decn of 26 November 2008 the Commission accepted commitments in relation to E.ON's conduct on the electricity wholesale market in Germany. The Commission considered that at least two companies were collectively dominant: they were linked by a network of agreements on production and wholesale supply; the product was homogenous and 'not evolving'; the price was transparent; decisions on capacity were transparent; the market was growing at a modest rate; and new entry was severely restricted. A common policy on pricing and production was possible because they could detect and counter any deviation and react immediately by doing the same: paras 19–22.

Three conditions for establishing collective dominance. The test as set out by **10.055** the ECJ in the *IMPALA* judgment was applied by the Commission when granting conditional clearance at Phase II of the investigation into a merger in Case M.4980 *ABF/GBI Business* (23 September 2008) (paras 144 *et seq*). The Commission found various features of the Portuguese market for compressed yeast indicated that the conditions were conducive to coordination. So far as mechanisms for policing the coordination were concerned, the Commission cited instances in the past where attempts by the *de facto* exclusive distributor of one supplier to expand its share of the market in an area had been disciplined by the supplier: 'This demonstrates how the system corrects itself when a distributor is trying to deviate from the paradigm imposed by the suppliers': para 219. The Commission went on to find that the other conditions set in *IMPALA* were also satisfied and that the merger, by creating a duopoly, would increase the incentives for coordination. By contrast, in the French market the Commission found that there was no evidence of a coordinated effect for the same product. The merger was cleared on the basis of divestiture commitments. See also the other merger cases referred to in the update to paragraph 8.211, above.

IMPALA: **retaliatory measures.** The CFI's judgment in *IMPALA* was over- **10.057** turned on appeal by the ECJ: see update to paragraph 10.053, above. The ECJ did not deal specifically with the issue of retaliatory measures.

4. Abuse of a Dominant Position

(a) Introduction

Abuse as an objective concept. See also Case T-301/04 *Clearstream Banking v* **10.060** *Commission*, judgment of 9 September 2009. The CFI emphasised that the concept of abuse is an objective one so that it was not necessary to rule on whether the Commission was right in finding that Clearstream's intention was to exclude EB from the provision of their services and, therefore, to hinder competition in the provision of cross-border secondary clearing and settlement services: para 143.

The reference to 'normal competition' in the quotation from *Hoffmann-La Roche* was considered by the Competition Appeal Tribunal in *National Grid v The Gas*

and Electricity Markets Authority [2009] CAT 10, paras 88 *et seq.* The case is on
appeal to the English Court of Appeal.

10.062 Abusive intent.   See also COMP/38.113 *Prokent-Tomra*, decn of 29 March 2006,
[2009] 4 CMLR 101 where the Commission cited some colourful extracts from
Tomra's internal documents evidencing an exclusionary intent: paras 98–105.

10.064 Comparison of objective justification with criteria in Article 81(3).   In the
Commission's Guidance on the enforcement of Article 82, OJ 2009 C45/7: Vol II,
App C19, the Commission has stated that a dominant undertaking can show
that its conduct is objectively justified either by showing that it is 'objectively
necessary' or by demonstrating that the conduct produces substantial efficiencies
which outweigh any anti-competitive effect on consumers: paras 28–31. Objective
necessity for the purposes of Article 82 [now Article 102 TFEU] can arise only
from factors external to the dominant undertaking, for example health and safety
reasons related to the nature of the product. In order to demonstrate efficiencies
the dominant undertaking must show that (i) efficiencies have been or are likely
to result from the conduct; (ii) the conduct is indispensable to the realisation of
those efficiencies; and (iii) the efficiencies outweigh any likely negative effects on
competition and consumer welfare in the affected markets.

10.065 Exclusionary and exploitative abuses.   In the Commission's Guidance on the
enforcement of Article 82, OJ 2009 C45/7: Vol II, App C19, the Commission
sets out the criteria relevant for its assessment of whether there is anti-competitive
foreclosure in a market: paras 19–22. The factors include the strength of the dominant position; whether there are economies of scale or scope and network effects
which entrench the dominant firm's position; whether there is a specific competitor which is particularly innovative or has the reputation of systematically
cutting prices; whether the conduct has been applied to selected customers; what
percentage of total sales in the market are affected by the conduct; whether there
is evidence of actual foreclosure if the conduct has been in place for a sufficient
period of time; whether there is evidence from internal documents of exclusionary
intent. However, there may be conduct which the Commission regards as raising
obstacles to competition and creating no efficiencies, in which case it is not necessary to carry out a detailed assessment before concluding that there is likely to be
consumer harm: para 22.

10.067 Efficiency and abuse.   Fn 197. The appeal by Deutsche Telekom was dismissed
by the CFI: Case T-271/03 *Deutsche Telekom AG v Commission* [2008] ECR
II-477, [2008] 5 CMLR 631. The CFI defined the margin squeeze abuse as occur-
ring '[i]f the applicant's retail prices are lower than its wholesale charges, or if the
spread between the applicant's wholesale and retail charges is insufficient to enable
an equally efficient operator to cover its product-specific costs of supplying retail
access services, a potential competitor who is just as efficient as the applicant

would not be able to enter the retail access services market without suffering losses': para 237. The CFI's judgment is on appeal: Case C-280/08 P, not yet decided.

(b) Own market abuses: exclusionary pricing practices

(i) Predatory pricing

Predatory pricing. In the Commission's Guidance on the enforcement of Article 82, OJ 2009 C45/7 the Commission states that it will normally only intervene where the conduct has already been, or is capable of, hampering competition from competitors who are as efficient as the dominant undertaking. The Commission's focus will therefore be on economic data relating to the costs of the dominant undertaking itself: paras 23–27. However, the Commission recognises that sometimes a less efficient competitor may also exert a competitive constraint which should be taken into account: para 24. See also paras 63 *et seq* of the Guidance.   **10.070**

The Court of Justice's approach. As to the last sentence of this paragraph, note that in Case C-202/07 P *France Télécom v Commission*, judgment of 2 April 2009, para 109, the ECJ said that prices below AVC 'must be considered prima facie abusive' but (at para 111) referred to the possibility of economic justification of such pricing.   **10.071**

Other measures of cost. The costs benchmarks that the Commission is likely to use are average avoidable cost (AAC) and long run incremental cost: see the Commission's Guidance on the enforcement of Article 82, OJ 2009 C45/7, paras 26, 27, 64 and 65.   **10.075**

As to the last sentence of this paragraph, the judgment of the Paris Court of Appeal in *Régie départmentale des passages d'eau de la Vendée* was annulled by the Cour de Cassation. The Cour de Cassation remitted the case for further consideration of what costs truly had to be incurred to fulfil the operator's public service obligation and thus whether any of the costs of the express ferry at issue should properly be regarded as common costs to be left out of account in a predatory pricing analysis: Cass. Com., 17 June 2008, BOCCRF No. 4 of 8 April 2009, [2009] ECC 63. In its second judgment, the Paris Court of Appeal confirmed the conclusion of the prior ruling, with additional reasoning that expressly drew on the approach of the Commission decision in *Deutsche Post* and emphasised the difference in the economic aspects of operating a mandated public service as compared to a private competitive service: judgment of 9 June 2009, BOCCRF No. 8 of 3 August 2009.

Potential for recoupment of losses: *Tetra Pak II*. The ECJ has confirmed that 'demonstrating that it is possible to recoup losses is not a necessary precondition for a finding of predatory pricing': Case C-202/07 P *France Télécom v Commission*,   **10.076**

judgment of 2 April 2009: lack of recoupment does not prevent damage to customers through the reduction in choice that results from the elimination of a competitor: paras 110–112. The ECJ noted that the possibility of recoupment may nonetheless be relevant in excluding economic justifications for pricing below AVC or in establishing a plan to eliminate a competitor under the second limb of the *AKZO* rule.

In the Commission's Guidance on the enforcement of Article 82, OJ 2009 C45/7, the Commission indicates that it is unlikely that consumers are harmed by predatory conduct unless the dominant undertaking is likely to benefit from its sacrifice. This does not mean that the dominant undertaking must be likely to be able to increase its prices; it is sufficient if, for instance, the conduct would be likely to prevent or delay a decline in prices that would otherwise have occurred: paras 70 and 71.

10.078 **Possible justifications for below-cost pricing.** The further appeal in the *Wanadoo Interactive* case was dismissed by the ECJ: Case C-202/07 P *France Télécom v Commission*, judgment of 2 April 2009. The ECJ rejected the appellant's claim that the CFI failed to state adequate reasons for rejecting arguments based on a right to align its prices on those of its competitors.

The Commission has indicated that it is unlikely that predatory conduct will create efficiencies though it will consider claims that low pricing enables the dominant firm to achieve economies of scale or efficiencies relating to expanding the market: see the Commission's Guidance on the enforcement of Article 82, OJ 2009 C45/7, para 74.

10.079 **Proof of 'intention'.** The ECJ dismissed the further appeal in the *Wanadoo Interactive* case: Case C-202/07 P *France Télécom v Commission*, judgment of 2 April 2009. The ECJ rejected arguments concerning the 'plan of predation': see paras 89 *et seq*. In the Commission's Guidance on the enforcement of Article 82, OJ 2009 C45/7 the Commission refers to 'direct evidence' of predatory strategy in documents from the dominant undertaking: see para 66.

(ii) Price discrimination or targeting

10.082 **Selective price cutting: the Courts' approach.** Fn 245. The appeal referred to in the footnote was dismissed by the CFI, Case T-276/04 *Compagnie maritime belge SA v Commission* [2008] ECR II-1277.

10.086 **Price discrimination on grounds of nationality.** As regards the penultimate sentence of this paragraph the ECJ in Cases C-501/06 P, etc, *GlaxoSmithKline Services Unlimited v Commission*, judgment of 6 October 2009 overturned the CFI's analysis insofar as it held that it was necessary to prove that an agreement entails disadvantages for final consumers as a prerequisite for a finding of anti-competitive object. The judgment did not discuss Article 82.

Objective justification for differential pricing. By contrast, heavy expenditure **10.090**
on advertising to promote special prices, above cost, that are designed to match
those of a new entrant on the market but are offered to customers generally, is not
in itself an abuse. The Spanish Supreme Court thus annulled the decision of the
Spanish competition authority which had held the massive expenditure by the
incumbent fixed line telephone operator on advertising to promote its new special
tariffs for national and international calls at the time that another company was
about to enter the market offering cheap calls with a dialling prefix constituted
an abuse: *Telefónica de España SA v Retevisión SA*, Case 9174/2003, judgment of
20 June 2006. Applying the Spanish domestic equivalent of Article 82 [now
Article 102 TFEU], the Court held that the question of abuse depended more on
objective considerations, and that intent to hinder a new entrant was not in itself
unlawful. Furthermore, the new entrant in this case also had significant financial
resources so that the incumbent's level of advertising expenditure did not constitute a barrier to entry.

In Case C-52/07 *Kanal 5 Ltd and TV 4 AB v Föreningen Svenska Tonsättares
Internationella Musikbyrå (STIM) upa*, judgment of 11 December 2008, [2009]
5 CMLR 2175 the ECJ considered whether the practice of a collecting society of
calculating royalties on different bases as between public service and commercial
broadcasters amounted to applying dissimilar conditions to equivalent transactions. In a preliminary ruling under Article 234 [now Article 267 TFEU], the ECJ
held that this could be an abuse if it placed the commercial broadcasters at a
competitive disadvantage, unless such a practice could be objectively justified.
This was for the national court to determine.

(iii) Fidelity rebates and similar practices

Fidelity rebates and similar practices. The Commission's important decision **10.091**
in COMP/38.113 *Prokent-Tomra*, decn of 29 March 2006, [2009] 4 CMLR 101
is now available on the Commission's website. The Commission condemned a
series of exclusive purchasing and rebate schemes entered into by Tomra in order
to exclude competitors: see esp paras 316 *et seq*. The Commission held that it is
not necessary that the customer explicitly accepts the respective rebate scheme: '
A unilateral granting of rebates has to be taken into account at least in so far as the
customer can have a reasonable expectation that it will be granted the discount or
rebate if it reaches the respective purchasing volume': para 318. The Commission
also relied on the division of a customer's demand into contestable and non-con-
testable parts. The Commission noted that the rebate schemes created a competitive situation where Tomra's rivals were forced to offer very low or even negative
prices in order to compete with the dominant supplier. In the relevant market, it
was unlikely that a customer would immediately buy large quantities from a new
entrant. It is normal practice for customers first to test the new machines and, subject to a satisfactory result, decide whether to purchase. These market characteristics

in conjunction with Tomra's rebate schemes had a significant impact on competitors which could only provide a small number of machines to a customer. As a result, such a new competitor would need to offer very low prices, possibly even negative prices, in order to sell in the presence of the rebate schemes employed by Tomra (para 165). The effect of this was demonstrated graphically in the decision in relation to various national markets. The Commission also emphasised that the fact that the rebate schemes were requested or welcomed by customers was no defence: paras 281 and 358 *et seq*. The Commission also roundly rejected the theoretical economic evidence that Tomra put forward attempting to show that the arrangements were 'innocuous': paras 364 *et seq*. The case is on appeal Case T-155/06 *Tomra Systems*, not yet decided.

In COMP/37.990 *Intel*, decn of 13 May 2009 the Commission fined Intel €1.6 billion for exclusionary practices. The Commission found that Intel engaged in two specific forms of illegal practice. First, Intel gave wholly or partially hidden rebates to computer manufacturers on condition that they bought all, or almost all, their x86 CPUs from Intel. Intel also made direct payments to a major retailer on condition it stock only computers with Intel x86 CPUs. Secondly, Intel made direct payments to computer manufacturers to halt or delay the launch of specific products containing competitors' x86 CPUs and to limit the sales channels available to these products. The Guidance on enforcement priorities did not apply in *Intel* but the Commission noted that the decision was in line with the orientations of that guidance: para 916. The Commission also rejected the suggestion that it was necessary to show actual foreclosure and said that the Guidance made no difference in this respect either: paras 919 and 925. The case is on appeal: Case T-286/09, not yet decided.

As to the willing acceptance by the customer of the rebate scheme, the Commission has noted that it may be in the individual interest of the customer to enter into the exclusive purchasing obligation; but this does not mean that the obligation is beneficial for customers overall or for final consumers: see the Commission's Guidance on the enforcement of Article 82, OJ 2009 C45/7, para 34. See also paras 37 *et seq* of the Guidance regarding the cases which the Commission will treat as an enforcement priority: the anti-competitive foreclosure is likely to be higher where competitors are not able to satisfy the entire demand of each individual customer and the dominant undertaking can use the 'non contestable' portion of the demand as leverage to decrease the price to be paid for the 'contestable' portion: para 39.

See also the rather unusual arrangement that was condemned as abusive by the Competition Appeal Tribunal in *National Grid v The Gas and Electricity Markets Authority* [2009] CAT 10. The case is on appeal to the Court of Appeal.

Stepped discount arrangements. See also COMP/38.113 *Prokent-Tomra*, **10.093**
decn of 29 March 2006, [2009] 4 CMLR 101, discussed in the update to paragraph 10.091, above esp paras 319 *et seq*.

On the question of objective justification for the discount scheme see the
Commission's Guidance on the enforcement of Article 82, OJ 2009 C45/7, para 46
which refers to transaction-related cost advantages and cases where relationship-
specific investment is needed by the dominant undertaking.

Discounts dependent on the dominant firm's discretion. Similarly in *Prokent-* **10.094**
Tomra, discussed in the update to paragraph 10.091, above, the Commission held
that the lack of transparency in a discount scheme was liable to strengthen its
loyalty-building character: para 324.

Across-product rebates. In the Commission's Guidance on the enforcement of **10.095**
Article 82, OJ 2009 C45/7, the Commission treats multi-product rebates as a
form of tying or bundling: paras 59 *et seq*.

Fn 308. On US antitrust law see also *Cascade Health Solutions v PeaceHealth*,
515 F.3d 883 (9th Cir, 2008): 'discount attribution' test applied instead of
approach in *LePage* to determine whether bundled rebate excludes an 'as efficient'
competitor.

Turnover related discounts: summary. See now the approach of the Commis- **10.096**
sion in COMP/37.990 *Intel*, decn of 13 May 2009. The Commission firmly
rejected Intel's argument that it was necessary to establish actual foreclosure in
order to find an infringement. Further, although the Commission asserted that
the exclusivity rebates granted by the dominant firm were in themselves enough
to establish an infringement, it went on to demonstrate that the rebates were
capable of causing or likely to cause anti-competitive foreclosure likely to result
in consumer harm: para 925. It did this by conducting an 'as efficient competitor
analysis': paras 1003 *et seq*. This analysis examines whether Intel itself, in view of
its own costs and the effect of the rebate, would be able to enter the market at a
more limited scale without incurring losses. It thereby establishes at what price a
competitor which is 'as efficient' as Intel would have to offer x86 CPUs in order to
compensate an OEM for the loss of any Intel rebate. The Commission concluded
that if Intel's rebate scheme means that in order to compensate an Intel trading
partner for the loss of the Intel rebate, an as efficient competitor has to offer its
products below a viable measure of Intel's cost, then it means that the rebate was
capable of reducing access to Intel trading partners which could offer products
from the as efficient competitor, or in other words capable of foreclosing a hypothetical as efficient competitor: paras 1154–1574.

The approach of the *Michelin II* and *British Airways* judgments has been applied by the Danish courts and competition authority. In *Schneider Electric Danmark A/S v Competition Council¸* U.2008.851/1H, the Supreme Court (judgment of 7 January 2008) upheld the finding of the Danish Competition Council that the advance order and delivery rebate system applied for the supply of electrical socket outlets infringed the domestic equivalent of Article 82 [now Article 102 TFEU]. The Court rejected the argument that since the marginal price of each unit supplied was not below the total cost of production of that unit, the price could be matched by an equally efficient competitor so that the scheme had no exclusionary effect; the Court held that the advance order rebates created loyalty effects equivalent to progressive yearly bonuses. See also *Viasat Broadcasting UK Ltd v Competition Council*, ØLR B-3926-06, judgment of the High Court of Eastern Denmark, reversing the holding of the lower court that the television advertising market had special characteristics so as to displace the finding that progressive annual rebates had a loyalty-inducing effect and thus forced competitors of the dominant commercial channel to charge lower rates. In *Post Danmark* (decn of the Danish Competition Council of 24 June 2009) the Council found the loyalty rebate scheme for direct, bulk mail delivery operated by the Danish postal operator with a share of over 90 per cent of this market violated Article 82 and its domestic equivalent even if the reduced price could be charged by an 'as efficient' competitor: the scheme involved retroactive, stepped rebates and was likely to have loyalty inducing and anti-competitive effects in a market where Post Danmark enjoyed substantial economies of scale and scope and even less efficient competitors would have a constraining effect on the dominant undertaking.

Fn 310. The description of the Swedish Market Court case in the first sentence should read: 'Swedish Market Court upheld a decision of the Swedish NCA that SAS had abused its dominant position on the market for domestic scheduled air transportation services by applying <u>on domestic routes</u> its <u>international</u> frequent flyer programme . . .'.

Further, by decision No. 324/2008 of 9 January 2009, the Swedish NCA held that the previous ruling and injunction applied to the situation as at the time of the Market Court's judgment and therefore would not apply to potential operation of the programme in current conditions on domestic routes exposed to competition. Since the NCA does not give negative clearance, it was then for SAS to decide whether conditions were sufficiently altered for it to reintroduce the scheme without committing an abuse.

(c) Own market abuses: exclusionary non-price conduct

10.097 **Discrimination on grounds of nationality.** See also COMP/39.388 & 39.389 *E.ON German electricity markets*, decn of 26 November 2008 where the Commission accepted commitments in respect of alleged discrimination by E.ON in

favour of acquiring domestic supplies of energy for balancing and against importing supplies: para 54.

Long-term exclusive dealing. In COMP/38.113 *Prokent-Tomra*, decn of **10.098**
29 March 2006, [2009] 4 CMLR 101 the Commission condemned as abusive a
wide range of exclusivity arrangements entered into by Tomra which was found to
be dominant in the market for the supply of reverse vending machines for recycling empty containers: paras 281 *et seq*. The Commission found that because
there was a peak in demand in the years when national legislation mandating
recycling or the introduction of empty container deposit schemes was introduced,
even a short-term exclusive agreement could have a significant foreclosure effect if
it covered a 'key year': para 287 and paras 303 *et seq* and para 343. The case is on
appeal Case T-155/06 *Tomra Systems*, not yet decided.

See also the Commission's Guidance on the enforcement of Article 82, OJ 2009
C45/7, paras 33–36 as regards the factors that the Commission will consider
when deciding whether to intervene.

***De facto* exclusive dealing: the 'ice cream wars'.** Van den Bergh's share of the **10.100**
market for impulse ice cream in Ireland was over 75 per cent not 40 per cent as
stated in the text.

Abusive enforcement of exclusivity provisions. Fn 332. The appeal referred to **10.101**
in the footnote was dismissed by the CFI, Case T-276/04 *Compagnie maritime
belge SA v Commission* [2008] ECR II-1277.

(d) Own market abuses: exploitative pricing

The Commission's approach: *Port of Helsingborg*. The Commission's approach **10.106**
to assessing the reasonableness of prices for the transfer of technology can be seen
in its decision in *Microsoft* of 27 February 2008 (COMP/37.792). This decision
fixed the periodic penalty payment imposed on Microsoft for setting too high a
price for the non-patented information it made available in one of the packages it
offered competitors in purported compliance with the obligations under the 2004
decision. In assessing whether the remuneration charged by Microsoft was unreasonable, the Commission referred to the 'WSPP Pricing Principles' ('WSPP'
stands for Work Group Server Protocol Program) that had been devised by
Microsoft in negotiation with the Commission during 2005 and 2006. The WSPP
Pricing Principles were based on the Commission's assertion that the upshot of the
2004 Decision was that in order for it to be reasonable, 'any remuneration charged
by Microsoft for access to or use of the Interoperability Information should be
justified by showing that it allows competitors to viably compete with Microsoft's
work group server operating system and that it represents a fair compensation for
the value of the technology that is transferred by Microsoft to recipients of the
Interoperability Information beyond the mere ability to interoperate, namely

excluding the "strategic value" stemming from Microsoft's market power in the client PC and work group server operating system markets': para 107. The WSPP Pricing Principles thus stated that the assessment of what reflects such value conferred upon a licensee to the exclusion of strategic value should in particular take into account three factors. The first was whether the protocols described in the specifications were Microsoft's own creations (as opposed to Microsoft's implementation of a publicly available standard). If Microsoft simply uses protocols that it takes from the public domain, then the only information that it is providing pursuant to the Decision is to indicate which of the protocols available in the public domain it is actually using. The Commission considered that Microsoft should not be entitled to charge any price for that information. The second factor was whether these creations by Microsoft constitute innovation. If the protocol technology currently used by Microsoft, although different from protocol technology available in the public domain, is not novel then Microsoft should not be entitled to charge for it. The third factor was to carry out a market valuation of technologies deemed comparable, excluding the strategic value that stems from the dominance of any such technologies. The Commission found that most of the information being made available in the non-patent package was not innovative and that comparable protocol technology was provided royalty-free by other undertakings. The Commission therefore found that Microsoft had charged an unreasonable fee for this information. This decision is under appeal: Case T-167/08, not yet decided.

Fn 352. The appeal in Case T-306/05 *Scippacercola and Terezakis v Commission* was dismissed, [2008] ECR II-4*, [2008] 4 CMLR 1418. The CFI upheld the Commission's rejection of the complaint on the ground of lack of Community interest and did not address the issue of excessive pricing. Further appeal dismissed Case C-159/08 P, Order of 25 March 2009.

10.107 **Benchmark comparator.** See, eg *Europay*, 16 Ok 4/07, judgment of 12 September 2007, where the Austrian Supreme Court upheld a finding of infringement of the domestic equivalent of Article 82 [now Article 102 TFEU] by a joint venture of Austrian commercial banks that offered card transaction processing systems to merchants, for the excessive charges that it was agreed would be made by the JV parent banks to competing systems. The charge was found to be excessive both on the basis of a comparison with the much lower price charged by the parent banks to Europay and by reference to the actual costs (€0.06 per transaction, for which the charge levied was €0.36–0.40). (The agreement was also found to violate the Austrian equivalent of Article 81 [now Article 101 TFEU]).

In *Iberdrola Generación*, Case 166/07, judgment of 2 July 2009, the Spanish National High Court upheld the competition tribunal's finding of infringement of the Spanish equivalent of Article 82 in the prices charged over relatively short periods when there were so-called 'technical restrictions' that prevent supply in a particular area being met from the electricity pool and enabled supplies to be required from the generator in the area at above the 'pool' price. This could give rise to a situation of temporary monopoly since there were often no other generators in the area. The Court compared the impugned prices with those charged by Iberdrola in preceding periods and also the difference between variable cost and prices charged in the daily market pool, a measure whereby Iberdrola's prices were found to be some 40 per cent higher.

Fn 361. See, eg *Canarias de Explosivos*, Case 626/07, decn of 12 February 2008, where the Spanish competition authority found the sole distributor in the Canary Islands of explosives for demolitions committed an abuse contrary to the domestic equivalent of Article 82 [now Article 102 TFEU] by charging prices that were about eight times higher than those charged in mainland Spain where the market was more competitive; transport costs could not account for this difference.

Benchmark price. When the imposition of prices which incorporate a very **10.108** high margin over costs has an exclusionary effect on the market, that may lead to the conclusion that the prices are abusive. In its first decision to find excessive pricing, the French competition authority found that France Télécom was abusing its dominant position on the fixed telephony and internet markets in the French overseas departments (DOM), which it previously monopolised, by making its competitors' entry into these markets more difficult and costly. In particular, its annual profit margin on rental of lines on the undersea connection between la Réunion and the mainland was 493 per cent in 2002 and rose to 1794 per cent in 2004. Charging such prices made it impossible for competing operators to develop in the retail market on la Réunion. Thus excessive pricing operated as an exclusionary abuse (along with other forms of exclusionary conduct): Decision No. 09-D-24 of 28 July 2009.

Fn 369. Cf the Austrian case, *Europay*, discussed in the update to paragraph 10.107, above.

Economic value. In Case C-52/07 *Kanal 5 Ltd and TV 4 AB v Föreningen Svenska* **10.109** *Tonsättares Internationella Musikbyrå (STIM) upa*, judgment of 11 December 2008, [2009] 5 CMLR 2175 the ECJ held that no abuse was committed where a copyright association set a royalty for the performing rights of its repertoire calculated as a percentage of the revenue earned by the broadcaster from television broadcasts directed at the general public and/or subscription sales. The percentage varied according to the amount of music broadcast by the TV station. The Court noted that the royalties must be analysed with respect to the value of that use in trade. Insofar as such royalties are calculated on the basis of the revenue of the television broadcasting societies, they are, in principle, reasonable in relation to the economic value of the service provided by: STIM para 37. The ECJ held that there was no abuse unless another method was available which enabled the use of those works to be identified more precisely with the audience, without a disproportionate increase in the costs incurred in the management of contracts and the supervision of the use of the copyright works.

(e) Related market abuses: exclusionary pricing

(i) Margin squeezing

10.112 **Price or margin squeezing.** There have been several important cases on margin squeeze recently: the appeal to the CFI from the Commission's decision in *Deutsche Telekom* referred to in the text: Case T-271/03 *Deutsche Telekom v Commission* [2008] ECR II-477, [2008] 5 CMLR 631; the Commission's decision in COMP/ 38.784 *Wanadoo España/Telefónica*, decn of 4 July 2007 and, in the English Court of Appeal *Albion Water Ltd v Water Services Regulation Authority (Dŵr Cymru/ Shotton Paper)* [2008] EWCA Civ 536 on appeal from the Competition Appeal Tribunal. These cases are discussed in the following paragraph updates. See also Case C-52/09 *Konkurrensverket v TeliaSonera Sverige AB*, not yet decided (reference under Article 234 [now Article 267 TFEU] concerning margin squeeze and possible objective justification).

By contrast the US Supreme Court (by a 5-4 majority) robustly rejected the concept of price squeezing as an independent form of abuse under the US antitrust laws: *Pacific Bell Telephone Co v Linkline Communications Inc* 129 S.Ct. 1109 (2009).

10.113 **The Commission's practice.** Deutsche Telekom's appeal against the Commission's decision was dismissed by the CFI: Case T-271/03, [2008] ECR II-477, [2008] 5 CMLR 631. The Court rejected arguments based on the involvement of the German telecoms regulator in the setting of DT's prices. The Court also held that it was not necessary to show that DT's retail price was unfairly high in order to establish the margin squeeze abuse: 'the abusive nature of the applicant's conduct is connected with the unfairness of the spread between its prices for wholesale access and its retail prices, which takes the form of a margin squeeze': para 167. The CFI also held that the Commission had been right to base the finding of abuse on the costs and prices of the dominant undertaking and not to examine the costs and prices of its actual or potential competitors. As well as being supported by authority (the CFI cited, among other cases, the Commission's decision in *Napier Brown/British Sugar*) this approach was consistent with the principle of legal certainty: if the lawfulness of the pricing practices of a dominant undertaking depended on the particular situation of competing undertakings, particularly their cost structure – information which is generally not known to the dominant undertaking – the latter would not be in a position to assess the lawfulness of its own activities: para 192. In response to various challenges to the way the

Commission had calculated the margin, the CFI stated that this was a matter of complex economic assessment as to which the Commission had a margin of appreciation: para 185. All DT's pleas on the detail of what revenues should or should not have been included in the calculations were rejected by the Court. Finally the CFI upheld the Commission's finding that there had been an actual effect on competition because DT's network was the only infrastructure available for competitors: 'If the applicant's retail prices are lower than its wholesale charges, or if the spread between the applicant's wholesale and retail charges is insufficient to enable an equally efficient operator to cover its product-specific costs of supplying retail access services, a potential competitor who is just as efficient as the applicant would not be able to enter the retail access services market without suffering losses': para 237. The CFI's judgment is on appeal: Case C-280/08 P, not yet decided.

In COMP/38.784 *Wanadoo España/Telefónica*, decn of 4 July 2007 the Commission imposed a fine for a margin squeeze in the Spanish broadband internet access markets. The Commission found that the incumbent, Telefónica, was the only Spanish telecommunications operator with a nationwide fixed telephone network and that it controlled the entire ADSL value chain in Spain. Alternative network operators wishing to provide retail broadband services had no other option but to contract wholesale broadband access products, all of which are built on Telefónica's local access network. From September 2001 to December 2006, the margin between Telefónica's retail prices and the price for wholesale access at regional level, on the one hand, and the margin between the retail prices and the price for wholesale access at national level, on the other hand, was insufficient to cover the costs that an operator as efficient as Telefónica would have to incur to provide retail broadband access. The methodology applied was to assess whether Telefónica's downstream arm would operate profitably on the basis of the upstream charges levied by Telefónica's upstream arm. Two profitability methods were used: the so-called period-by-period method (which assessed Telefónica's profitability every year), and the discounted cash flows method (which allowed below-cost pricing in the initial phase of an expanding market but required Telefónica to be profitable over 2001–2006) proposed by Telefónica itself. Both methods led to the same conclusion. The Commission rejected Telefónica's argument that the case should be analysed as an 'essential facilities' refusal to supply case so that the criteria laid down in *Oscar Bronner* applied. A substantial fine was imposed. The case is on appeal Cases T-336 & 398/07 *Telefónica and Telefónica de España v Commission*, not yet decided.

Note that in the Commission's Guidance on the enforcement of Article 82, OJ 2009 C45/7, the Commission treats margin squeeze as a form of refusal to supply: paras 75 *et seq*.

10.114 **Domestic cases on margin squeezing:** *Genzyme.* **Fn 393.** The case of *Albion Water Ltd v Water Services Regulation Authority (Dŵr Cymru/Shotton Paper)* went to the Court of Appeal: see the update to paragraph 10.114A, below. See also the decision on the practices of France Télécom in French overseas departments (DOM), Decision No. 09-D-24 of 28 July 2009, discussed in the update to paragraph 10.108, above, where the French Competition Authority found a margin squeeze in the pricing of broadband internet connections in la Réunion in addition to a distinct abuse of excessive pricing.

10.114A **Domestic cases on margin squeezing:** *Albion Water.* The English Court of Appeal delivered an important judgment on margin squeeze in *Albion Water Ltd v Water Services Regulation Authority (Dŵr Cymru/Shotton Paper)* [2008] EWCA Civ 536 on appeal from the decision of the Competition Appeal Tribunal [2006] CAT 23, [2007] CompAR 22 (referred to in fn 393 of the main work). The *Albion Water* judgment contains a helpful analysis of the EU and domestic case law and drew the following conclusions as to the present state of the law: paras 87 *et seq.* First, there are some features which are common to the various formulations of the test for margin squeeze in the authorities. These are the existence of two markets (upstream and downstream); a vertically integrated undertaking which is dominant on the upstream market and active (whether or not also dominant) on the downstream market; the need for access to an input from the upstream market in order to operate on the downstream market; and the setting of upstream and downstream prices by the dominant undertaking that leave an insufficient margin for an equally efficient competitor to operate profitably in the downstream market. As to the last feature, the Court of Appeal held that the earlier controversy over whether the test should refer to an 'equally efficient competitor' (in which case the analysis focuses on the costs of the dominant undertaking's own downstream operation) or a 'reasonably efficient competitor' (which focuses on the costs of an actual or potential competitor in the downstream market) was settled by the CFI in *Deutsche Telekom* in favour of the former test. The Court of Appeal rejected the arguments of the dominant water supplier Dŵr Cymru Cyfyngedig for an additional requirement, namely that the competitor must either be engaged in a 'transformative activity' (that is adding value to the product or service offered downstream by the dominant undertaking) or must displace part of the service offered by the dominant thereby enabling the dominant undertaking to avoid some of its costs. The Court referred to the fact that in *Deutsche Telekom* the Commission had found that as regards the period 1998–2001 there was a negative spread between the wholesale and retail prices (that is, the retail prices were lower than the wholesale prices) and had used that negative spread as a direct measure of the margin squeeze without any need to consider the downstream costs. This approach had been approved by the CFI, indicating that the avoidance of downstream costs is not a necessary feature of margin squeeze: para 101 of *Albion Water*.

The Court of Appeal acknowledged that it is possible for the dominant undertaking to put forward an objective justification for the squeeze and that arguments over displacement of the dominant undertaking's activity and avoided costs are relevant and important considerations when considering that: para 106. Note that the Competition Appeal Tribunal had rejected reliance by the water regulator on an approach known as the Efficient Component Pricing Rule to calculate what access price would have been appropriate, [2006] CAT 23, [2007] CompAR 22, para 875. The appellant was not given permission to appeal against that aspect of the Tribunal's reasoning: see *Albion Water*, para 40.

***Genzyme*: remedies.**   Following the finding of margin squeeze in *Albion Water*, **10.115** discussed above, the Tribunal issued a separate judgment dealing with remedies: [2009] CAT 12. For various procedural and practical reasons the Tribunal held that it was not appropriate to set a minimum retail margin in that case and the relief granted was limited to a declaration that the abuse had taken place and an order that Dŵr Cymru bring the infringement to an end and refrain from any conduct having the same or equivalent effect.

(f) Related market abuses: exclusionary non-price practices

(i) *Tying and bundling*

Introduction.   The Commission has stated that, as regards its own enforcement **10.119** priorities, it will normally take action where an undertaking is dominant in the tying market and (i) the tying and tied products are distinct products; and (ii) the tying practice is likely to lead to anti-competitive foreclosure. The risk of such foreclosure is greater where the tying or bundling strategy is a lasting one, for example in technical tying which is costly to reverse: see the Commission's Guidance on the enforcement of Article 82, OJ 2009 C45/7: Vol II, App C19, paras 47 *et seq*.

'Pure', 'technical' and 'mixed' bundling.   Fn 414. As regards US jurisprudence **10.120** see also *Cascade Health Solutions v PeaceHealth*, 515 F.3d 883 (9th Cir, 2008) for discussion as to when bundled discounts have an anti-competitive effect.

Consumables tied with machinery.   See also *Soda-Club*, WUW DE-R 2268, **10.121** judgment of the German Federal Supreme Court of 4 March 2008 in relation to the terms offered to customers by the dominant supplier of home water carbonation systems that enabled consumers to make their own soda water. The restriction imposed in the rental agreement for the gas carbonation bottles that prevented consumers from obtaining gas refills from anyone other than a Soda-Club licensed dealer was found to be an abuse.

***Microsoft*: technical bundling.**   The Commission launched further investiga **10.122** tions into Microsoft's conduct: COMP/39.294 which concerned allegations that

Microsoft had illegally refused to disclose interoperability information across a broad range of products, including information related to its Office suite and COMP/39.530 concerning allegations that a range of products have been unlawfully tied to sales of Microsoft's dominant operating system. As regards the latter investigation, Microsoft gave commitments to offer a 'consumer ballot screen' as a solution to this case whereby consumers would be shown a 'ballot screen' from which they could easily install competing browsers and disable Internet Explorer: Press Release IP/09/1941 (16 December 2009).

(ii) Refusal to supply

10.125 **Conceptual and policy difficulties relating to refusal to supply.** Interestingly, the Commission has stated that it 'starts from the position' that even a dominant firm should have the right to choose its trading partners and dispose freely of its property: see the Commission's Guidance on the enforcement priorities in applying Article 82, OJ 2009 C45/7: Vol II, App C19, para 75. The Commission also notes that (i) it is not necessary for the refused product to have been already traded provided that there is a demand from potential purchasers; and (ii) there can be a 'constructive refusal' to supply where there is undue delay or other impediments to supply (para 79).

10.127 **Discontinuing supply of services.** See also *Europe Direct AB and ors v VPC AB*, Case No. T-32799-05, judgment of the Stockholm District Court of 20 November 2008, awarding damages for breach of the Swedish equivalent of Article 82 [now Article 102 TFEU] against the operator of the central share security depository for ceasing to supply share registers in electronic form to the claimants whose businesses involved mailings to shareholders, although VPC was not itself a competitor of the claimants; on appeal to the Svea Court of Appeal, not yet decided.

10.128 **The limited scope of 'objective justification' as regards an existing customer.** The Court of Justice's decision in the reference from the Athens Court of Appeal has now been delivered: Cases C-468/06, etc, *Sot Lelos kai Sia EE v GlaxoSmithKline* [2008] ECR I-7139, [2008] 5 CMLR 1382, [2009] All ER (EC) 1. The ECJ rejected GlaxoSmithKline's argument that the pressure brought to bear on price levels by parallel trading brought only minimal benefits to consumers, since lower prices benefit patients who have to pay a proportion of the price of medicines: para 56. Referring to earlier case law condemning agreements aimed at partitioning national markets or at restricting parallel imports, the ECJ held that 'there can be no escape' from the prohibition in Article 82 [now Article 102 TFEU] for a dominant undertaking trying to avoid all parallel exports. However, the Court also noted that it was the disparities in the degree of regulation in the different Member States which created the opportunities for parallel imports by setting prices at different levels. The competition rules should not be interpreted in such a way that in order to defend its own commercial interests, the only choice left for a dominant pharmaceuticals company is not to place its medicines on the market at all in low price Member States: para 68. The ECJ therefore concluded that it would be a reasonable and proportionate measure in relation to the threat that parallel exports represent to its legitimate commercial interests for a dominant undertaking to refuse to supply a wholesaler with orders which are 'out of the ordinary' ('présentent un caractère anormal'). Thus, although a dominant pharmaceutical company cannot cease to honour the ordinary orders of an existing customer for the sole reason that the customer is exporting some of those quantities, it could refuse to supply 'significant quantities of products that are essentially destined for parallel export'. It was for the referring court to decide whether the orders at issue in the national proceedings were ordinary or not, in the light of the size of those orders in relation to the requirements of the market in the relevant Member State and the previous business relations between the dominant undertaking and the wholesalers concerned.

In *VIP Communications v OFCOM* [2009] CAT 28, the United Kingdom Competition Appeal Tribunal struck out an appeal against a rejection of a complaint which had alleged that a mobile phone operator's cessation of supply of SIM cards for use in GSM-Gateways was contrary to Article 82 [now Article 102 TFEU]. The Tribunal held that since the use proposed to be made of the SIM cards by the appellant was illegal under domestic law, the phone operator's conduct could not be abusive. This was the case even if, as the appellant alleged, the provision making that use unlawful was contrary to the European telecoms directives. Cf *SIM-Card*, WuW DE-R 2427, judgment of the Oberlandesgericht Düsseldorf of 13 March 2008 where the Court rejected arguments in a similar case that the use of SIM cards in GSM-Gateways would jeopardise the position of the plaintiff under German telecommunications law and that it could cause a technical deterioration of network connectivity.

Refusal to license intellectual property rights.   Fn 455. The appeal in *Der Grüne*   **10.129**
Punkt was dismissed: Case C-385/07 P *Der Grüne Punkt – Duales System Deutschland v Commission*, judgment of 16 July 2009, [2009] 5 CMLR 2215. The CFI analysed the case under Article 82(a) [now Article 102(a) TFEU], referring to settled case law according to which an undertaking abuses its dominant position where it charges for its services fees which are disproportionate to the economic value of the service provided. The conduct objected to here, namely requiring payment of a fee for all packaging bearing the DGP logo and put into circulation in Germany, even where customers of the company show that they do not use the DGP system for some or all of that packaging, constituted an abuse of a dominant position within that case law. The ECJ upheld this analysis, emphasising that the remedies imposed by the decision did not amount to an obligation to grant a licence to use the DGP logo. There was nothing in the decision which affected DSD's freedom of choice as the grant of licences – the decision at issue

merely obliges DSD not to claim payment from its contractual partners for take-back and recovery services which it has not provided. Note that the CFI stated that the decision did not stop DSD levying an adequate fee for merely using the DGP mark even where it is shown that the packaging bearing the DGP logo has been taken back and recovered by another system. The green dot affixed to the packaging may have economic value as such, since it can inform the consumer that the packaging may be brought to the DSD system: paras 193 and 194.

10.134 **Copyright associations.** In a dispute between a collecting society, STIM, and two commercial television broadcasters, the Swedish Market Court referred questions as to whether it was an abuse for STIM to charge royalties calculated as a percentage of the revenue earned by the broadcaster from television broadcasts directed at the general public and/or subscription sales. The percentage varied according to the amount of music broadcast by the TV station. The ECJ held that there was no abuse unless another method was available which enabled the use of those works to be identified more precisely with the audience, without a disproportionate increase in the costs incurred in the management of contracts and the supervision of the use of the copyright works. The ECJ left it to the national court to decide whether calculating royalties on different bases as between public service and commercial broadcasters amounted to applying dissimilar conditions to equivalent transactions, or whether such a practice was objectively justified: see Case C-52/07 *Kanal 5 Ltd and TV 4 AB v Föreningen Svenska Tonsättares Internationella Musikbyrå (STIM) upa*, judgment of 11 December 2008, [2009] 5 CMLR 2175.

10.135 **Refusal of access to 'essential facilities'.** Note that the Commission has said that cases will take priority as regards enforcement if (i) the refusal relates to a product or service which is objectively necessary to be able to compete effectively on a downstream market; (ii) the refusal is likely to lead to elimination of effective competition on the downstream market; and (iii) the refusal is likely to lead to consumer harm: see the Commission's Guidance on the enforcement of Article 82, OJ 2009 C45/7: Vol II, App C19, paras 81 *et seq*. These criteria apply to both cessation of existing supply and refusal of *de novo* supply: para 84.

10.138 **The criterion of 'necessity': application.** Fn 497. In the case of *MLP v NMPP*, the Cour de Cassation, judgment of 20 February 2007, rejected an appeal against the second judgment of the Paris Court of Appeal regarding the interim measures decision: BOCCRF No. 4 of 7 June 2007. NMPP then presented commitments to the French Competition Authority which were accepted, thereby concluding the proceedings.

10.141 **Essential facilities and cross-border discrimination.** The Commission's decision in *Clearstream* was upheld as regards both the refusal to supply and the discriminatory pricing infringements: Case T-301/04 *Clearstream Banking v Commission*, judgment of 9 September 2009. The CFI emphasised that the concept of abuse is an objective one so that it was not necessary to rule on whether the Commission was right in finding that Clearstream's intention was to exclude EB from the provision of their services and, therefore, to hinder competition in the provision of cross-border secondary clearing and settlement services: para 143.

(g) Other forms of abuse

Unfair trading conditions. In *CNIM v Electricité de France* [2008] ECC 208   **10.146** the French Cour de Cassation (Commercial Chamber) held that a clause limiting the electricity supplier's liability for damage caused by unexpected power cuts was not an abuse even though the supplier had a legal monopoly of supply.

Unfair trading conditions: IP licences.   **Fn 535.** The appeal in *Der Grüne Punkt*   **10.150** was dismissed: Case C-385/07 P *Der Grüne Punkt – Duales System Deutschland v Commission*, judgment of 16 July 2009, [2009] 5 CMLR 2215: see update to paragraph 10.129, above.

Limiting production, markets or technical development.   In COMP/39.388   **10.151** & 39.389 *E.ON German electricity markets*, decn of 26 November 2008 the Commission accepted commitments in a case where E.ON was suspected of having limited its own production of electricity in order to raise prices in the wholesale market.

Other examples of practices that limit the access of entrants to new markets or of access generally by competitors are found in national decisions. Hence, the requirement by the Hungarian State Railway of bank guarantees from private rail companies as a condition of securing network use agreements at the time of liberalisation of the rail network was held to be part of a strategy to hinder access to the market by new entrants and thus among the practices condemned under both Article 82 [now Article 102 TFEU] and its domestic Hungarian equivalent: *Magyar Államvasutak ('MÁV')*, case 2.Kf.27.165/2008/14, judgment of the Budapest Court of Appeal of 18 February 2009; on appeal to the Supreme Court. In Italy, the Council of State upheld the Authority's decision condemning, under the Italian equivalent of Article 82, the inadequate information provided by the dominant operator of dry docks in Naples harbour regarding the times when its docks would be available to third party ship refitters. As a result of this lack of transparency, the operator, which itself had full information as to when the docks would be available, obtained a competitive advantage for its own refitting services and secured the overwhelming majority of refitting work: *O.N.I. – Cantieri del Mediterraneo*, Case No. 7589, judgment of 3 April 2009.

In Spain, the monopoly supplier and distributor of electricity in Majorca was held to have infringed Article 82 [now Article 102 TFEU] by using the information that a new client was requesting connection to the network to make an immediate offer to carry out the related installation works, and thus obtain a competitive advantage over independent electrical installers: *ASINEM-ENDESA*, Case 606/05, decn of the Spanish Court for the Defence of Competition of 14 December 2006.

10.153   **Misconduct in acquisition of property rights:** *AstraZeneca.*   The penultimate sentence of this paragraph should read 'Moreover, it was <u>not</u> necessary to establish that the misleading representations were relied on by patent agents, patent offices and courts.'

10.154   **Impeding parallel imports and launch of competing products.**   See also the conclusions of the Commission's final report on the pharmaceutical sector published on 8 July 2009. The Commission examined the practices of the pharmaceutical companies in relation to a sample of 219 different molecules. They found that entry of generic products following the expiry of patent protection was delayed by several months and that this resulted in a substantial loss of savings by health authorities. The conduct examined included patent strategies such as filing numerous patent applications for the same medicine (forming so-called 'patent clusters' or 'patent thickets'). These strategies tended to extend the breadth and duration of their patent protection. The Commission found that the number of patent litigation cases between originator and generic companies increased by a factor of four between 2000 and 2007. In total, 698 cases of patent litigation between originator companies and generic companies were reported in relation to the medicines investigated. There were 255 applications for interim injunctions by patent originator companies. Further, patent companies regularly opposed the grant of patents to generic producers and intervened in the market authorisation process by which generic companies sought licences for their products. The inquiry also examined similar trends in litigation between originating companies. The Commission stressed the need to intensify competition scrutiny both at European level and by national authorities, The Report refers to cases at the national level such as *Napp* (discussed in paragraph 10.110); *Arrow Génériques*, judgment of the Cour de Cassation of 13 January 2009, Pourvoi No. P 08-12.510 (interim measures granted by the French competition authority to a generic company whose products were systematically criticised by a competing originator company's sales staff even after marketing authorisation) and *Glaxo-PRINCIPI ATTIVI* (Case A363), decn of Autorità Garante della Concorrenza e del Mercato of 8 February 2006, No. 15175 (refusal of an originator company to grant a licence for the production of an active ingredient, needed by producers of generic medicines to access national markets where the originator did not have any exclusive rights, infringed Article 82 EC [now Article 102 TFEU]).

11

THE COMPETITION RULES AND THE ACTS OF MEMBER STATES

1. Introduction

Undertakings granted special or exclusive rights. In COMP/38.700 *Greek* **11.001**
Lignite and Electricity generation, decn of 5 March 2008, [2009] 4 CMLR 495
the Commission held that it did not matter that the special or exclusive rights
challenged had been granted to the electricity generating company before liberalisation of the electricity market and therefore at a time when competition was not
possible. It was the maintenance of the rights (in that case the exclusive access to
the cheapest form of fuel for power generation) that distorted competition once
liberalisation had occurred: para 236. The case is on appeal, Case T-169/08
DEI v Commission, not yet decided.

2. State Compulsion

Compliance with State measures. In Case T-271/03 *Deutsche Telekom AG v* **11.004**
Commission [2008] ECR II-477, [2008] 5 CMLR 631 the CFI considered the
relevance of price regulation in the telecoms sector on an allegation of margin
squeezing by a dominant undertaking. The CFI confirmed the strictness of the
test to be applied, stating that for the national legal framework to have the effect of
making Articles 81 and 82 [now Articles 101 and 102 TFEU] inapplicable, the
restrictive effects on competition 'must originate solely in the national law': para 87.
The Court went on to examine the German legal framework in detail and found
that it allowed the applicant sufficient scope to fix its charges at a level which
would have enabled it to end or reduce the margin squeeze identified in the
contested decision: para 107. Further, the CFI rejected the argument that because
the regulator approved the charges set by the applicant, that meant that they
could not be contrary to Article 82. The regulator was not a competition authority

of the Member State and in any event, even if the regulator had decided that the charges were not contrary to Article 82, that finding did not bind the Commission: paras 113–124 and 267–271. The CFI's judgment is on appeal: Case C-280/08 P, not yet decided.

For an interesting analogous situation see Case C-431/07 P *Bouygues SA v Commission*, judgment of 2 April 2009. The ECJ upheld the finding of the CFI that the apparent advantage granted by the State when it waived part of the fees to be paid by telecoms licensees did not constitute a State aid because the waiver was necessary to avoid unequal treatment of those licensees which would be contrary to the EU telecoms regulatory scheme then in force. The waiver brought their fees in line with the fees that Bouygues had agreed to pay in a later auction of the same licences. Since the CFI had been right to hold that the principle of non-discrimination required the French authorities to align the fees due with those charged to Bouygues, there was no State aid.

Fn 7. The appeal in the *French Beef* case was dismissed: Cases C-101 & 110/07 P *Coop de France bétail et viande and FNSEA v Commission*, judgment of 18 December 2008.

11.006 Scope for residual competition. Fn 15. The appeal in *GlaxoSmithKline* has been decided: Cases C-501/06 P, etc, *GlaxoSmithKline Services Unlimited v Commission*, judgment of 6 October 2009. The judgment did not consider the point raised here.

11.008 Liability of undertakings when State compulsion is lifted. In *VIP Communications v OFCOM* [2009] CAT 28, the United Kingdom Competition Appeal Tribunal applied the principles in *CIF* in striking out an appeal against a rejection of a complaint which had alleged that a mobile phone operator's cessation of supply of SIM cards for use in GSM-Gateways was contrary to Article 82 [now Article 102 TFEU]. The Tribunal held that since the use proposed to be made of the SIM cards by the appellant was illegal under domestic law, the phone operator's conduct could not be abusive. This was the case even if, as the appellant alleged, the provision making that use unlawful was contrary to the European telecoms directives and the national telecoms regulator was under a duty to disapply the domestic provision. Unless or until a decision was taken to disapply the domestic provision as contrary to Articles 81 and 10 EC, the phone operator was shielded from sanction for any alleged abuse. Cf *SIM-Card*, WuW DE-R 2427, judgment of the Oberlandesgericht Düsseldorf of 13 March 2008 where the Court rejected arguments in a similar case that the use of SIM cards in GSM-Gateways would jeopardise the position of the plaintiff under German telecommunications law and that it could cause a technical deterioration of network connectivity.

3. The Application and Enforcement of the Prohibition in Article 86(1)

Note that Article 86 EC is now Article 106 TFEU

Application in conjunction with Treaty provisions. Fn 51. See also *Special* **11.015** *rights granted to La Banque Postale, Caisses d'Epargne and Crédit Mutuel for the distribution of the livret A and livret bleu*, decn of 10 May 2007, C(2007) 2110 final, where the Commission found that the rights granted contravened Article 86 in conjunction with Article 43 [now Articles 106 and 49 TFEU] (on appeal Cases T-279 & 289/07 *Caisse Nationale des Caisses d'Épargne et de Prévoyance v Commission*, not yet decided).

Link between the measure and the breach by the undertaking. The 'is led' **11.016** formulation was used by the ECJ in Case C-49/07 *Motosykletistiki Omospondia Ellados NPID (MOTOE) v Elliniko Dimosio* [2008] ECR I-4863, [2008] 5 CMLR 790, [2009] All ER (EC) 150, para 49. The ECJ held that 'it is not necessary that any abuse should actually occur' and that 'in any event' Articles 82 and 86(1) 'are infringed where a measure imputable to a Member State, and in particular a measure by which a Member State confers special or exclusive rights within the meaning of Article 86(1) EC, gives rise to a risk of an abuse of a dominant position'.

Inability to satisfy demand. In COMP/39.562 *Slovakian postal legislation relat-* **11.017** *ing to hybrid mail services*, decn of 7 October 2008, [2009] 4 CMLR 663 the Commission found that before the Slovakian legislation was amended to reserve a monopoly in hybrid postal services to the State-run undertaking, competitors had offered additional services such as track-and-trace which the State-run undertaking did not offer. Citing *Höfner and Elser* the Commission found that Slovakia was in breach of Article 86(1) [now Article 106(1) TFEU] in conjunction with Article 82 [now Article 102 TFEU]: by reserving the delivery of hybrid mail to Slovenská Pošta's, the Slovak Republic had limited the services available to users: paras 150 *et seq*. The decision is on appeal Case T-556/08 *Slovenská pošta v Commission*, not yet decided.

Extension of dominance into neighbouring markets. Fn 58. See also COMP/ **11.018** 39.562 *Slovakian postal legislation relating to hybrid mail services*, decn of 7 October 2008, [2009] 4 CMLR 663 (extension of postal services monopoly to hybrid electronic mail services), para 116. The decision is on appeal Case T-556/08 *Slovenská pošta v Commission*, not yet decided.

Creation of conflict of interest. In Case C-49/07 *Motosykletistiki Omospondia* **11.019** *Ellados NPID (MOTOE) v Elliniko Dimosio* [2008] ECR I-4863, [2008] 5 CMLR 790, [2009] All ER (EC) 150 the ECJ held that Article 86(1) [now Article 106(1) TFEU] in conjunction with Article 82 [now Article 102 TFEU] was infringed by a national rule which confers on a legal person which organises motorcycling events and enters into sponsorship, advertising and insurance contracts, the power to authorise such competitions, without that power being made subject to restrictions, obligations and review. The situation of unequal conditions of competition created by the power could lead the legal person entrusted with conferring authorisations to distort competition by favouring events which it organises or those in whose organisation it participates: paras 48 *et seq.*

11.020A **Creating an inequality of opportunity.** In Case C-462/99 *Connect Austria* [2003] ECR I-5197, [2005] 5 CMLR 302 the ECJ stated that a system of undistorted competition can be guaranteed only if equality of opportunity is secured as between the various economic operators. Hence if inequality of opportunity between economic operators, and therefore distorted competition, results from a State measure, such a measure constitutes an infringement of Article 86(1) [now Article 106(1) TFEU] in conjunction with Article 82 [now Article 102 TFEU] (see paras 83 and 84). The Commission applied this principle in COMP/38.700 *Greek Lignite and Electricity generation*, decn of 5 March 2008, [2009] 4 CMLR 495 where Greece had granted the former monopoly generator of electricity quasi-monopolistic rights to explore for and exploit lignite which is the cheapest source of fuel for electricity generation. Greece had thereby created inequality of opportunity between economic operators in the wholesale electricity market and distorted competition in favour of the public undertaking, reinforcing its dominance in that market. The case is on appeal: Case T-169/08 *DEI v Commission*, not yet decided.

11.023 **Commission's discretion as to enforcement.** **Fn** 77. See also Case T-60/05 *Union française de l'express (UFEX) v Commission* [2007] ECR II-3397, [2008] 5 CMLR 580, paras 189 *et seq.*

11.028 **Postal services.** Fn 91. See also COMP/39.562 *Slovakian postal legislation relating to hybrid mail services*, decn of 7 October 2008, [2009] 4 CMLR 663 (extension of postal services monopoly to hybrid electronic mail services). The decision is on appeal: Case T-556/08 *Slovenská pošta v Commission*, not yet decided.

4. Unenforceability of National Measures: Article 10

Note that the substance of Article 10 EC is now
incorporated into Article 4 TEU

11.033 **Narrow application of Articles 81, 3(1)(g) and 10.** Note that Article 3(1)(g) EC was repealed by the Lisbon Treaty and replaced in substance by Articles 3–6 TFEU. In Case C-446/05 *Doulamis* [2008] ECR I-1377 the ECJ held that these Articles do not preclude a national law which prohibits dentists from advertising their services: Case C-386/07 *Hospital Consulting v Esaote SpA*, Order of 5 May 2008.

On national legislation which may have an anti-competitive effect, see the inter-action of competition rules and the application of Article 28 EC in Case C-531/07 *Fachverband der Buch- und Medienwirtschaft v LIBRO Handelsgesellschaft mbH*, judgment of 30 April 2009.

See also Case C-393/08 *Sbarigia v Azienda USL RM/A*, not yet decided (reference for a preliminary ruling from the ECJ concerning compatibility of legislation restricting opening hours of pharmacies in Rome with Articles 81, 82 and 86 [now Articles 101, 102 and 106 TFEU]).

Direct applicability of Article 10.   Note that the substance of what was Article **11.034** 10 EC is now found in Article 4 TEU. In *Online lotteries*, WuW DE-R 2034, judgment of 8 May 2007, the German Federal Supreme Court upheld a decision of the German competition authority prohibiting as a violation of Article 10 EC, in conjunction with Article 81 EC, an agreement between the German regional states (Länder) that they would restrict the operation of licensed lottery compa-nies to the territory of the state granting the licence. This was found to have a particularly restrictive effect in the light of the development of online sales. But the Court quashed the authority's imposition of a mandatory requirement on the companies to offer internet sales beyond the State boundaries. A distinct agree-ment between the lottery companies themselves to the same effect was also pro-hibited as a clear violation of Article 81.

5. State Monopolies of a Commercial Character: Article 31

Note that Article 31 EC is now Article 27 TFEU

Monopolies for import and export.   **Fn 134.** The proceedings against Malta **11.040** were closed after Malta adopted legislative measures to create a framework for a new licensing procedure to allow companies other than the former State mon-opoly to apply for a licence to import: Press Release IP/07/1952 (18 December 2007).

6. Derogations under Articles 86(2) and 296

Note that Article 86(2) EC is now Article 106(2) TFEU and Article 296 EC is now Article 346 TFEU

(a) Article 86(2): services of general interest

Article 86(2) and State aids.   See also Case T-442/03 *SIC v Commission* [2008] **11.048** ECR II-1161 where the CFI considered the alleged grant of State aid to a public service television broadcaster.

11.049   **The task entrusted.**   **Fn 159.** The Supreme Court of Ireland allowed the appeal: see update to paragraph 11.053, below.

11.050   **Services of general economic interest.**   Member States have a wide discretion to define what they regard as SGEIs and the definition of such services by a Member State can be questioned by the Commission only in the event of manifest error: Case T-289/03 *BUPA v Commission* [2008] ECR II-81, para 166 (a State aid case). The CFI went on to hold that a private medical insurance scheme adopted by Ireland did have an SGEI mission. The CFI held that to be an SGEI, the service in question does not need to be a universal service in the strict sense of responding to a need common to the whole population or being supplied throughout a territory. The fact that the SGEI obligations in question have only a limited territorial or material application or that the services concerned are enjoyed by only a relatively limited group of users does not necessarily call in question the universal nature of an SGEI mission. Thus the CFI found that a private medical insurance scheme was an SGEI even though the complainant argued that the services represented only optional, indeed 'luxury', financial services. Further, the compulsory nature of the SGEI mission does not preclude a certain latitude being left to the operator on the market, including in relation to the content and pricing of the services which it proposes to provide. The compulsory nature of the service and, accordingly, the existence of an SGEI mission are established if the service provider is obliged to contract, on consistent conditions, without being able to reject the other contracting party. That element makes it possible to distinguish a service forming part of an SGEI mission from any other service provided on the market.

As regards public service television broadcasting see Case T-442/03 *SIC v Commission* [2008] ECR II-1161 (a State aid case) where the CFI upheld the power of the Member States to designate as a service of general economic interest, the service provided by a public broadcasting undertaking even though the undertaking broadcasts a wide range of programmes and was able to carry on commercial activities, such as the sale of advertising space. The CFI held that the Commission must satisfy itself that there is in place a mechanism for the State to monitor compliance by the undertaking of its public service remit: para 213. On the facts, the CFI found that the Commission had failed to ensure that it had reliable information available to determine what public services were actually supplied and what costs were actually incurred in supplying them. In the absence of such information, the CFI held, the Commission was unable to proceed to a meaningful verification of whether the funding under challenge was proportionate to the public service costs and was unable to make a valid finding that there had been no overcompensation of the public service costs. The Commission's decision was therefore annulled.

The Commission has published a Communication on Services of general interest, including social services of general interest, COM(2007) 725 adopted on 20 November 2007: Vol II, App F7. The Communication refers to the Protocol to be annexed by the Treaty of Lisbon to the TEU and the TFEU as part of an attempt to establish a 'transparent and reliable' EU framework which respects the principles of subsidiarity and proportionality. For the Protocol now see OJ 2007 C306/158.

Fn 166. The appeal by Deutsche Telekom was dismissed by the CFI: Case T-271/03 *Deutsche Telekom AG v Commission* [2008] ECR II-477, [2008] 5 CMLR 631, see para 314. The CFI's judgment is on appeal: Case C-280/08 P, not yet decided.

Fn 169. The appeal in Case T-490/04 was removed from the register. Note that the correct citation for the article referred to is (2005) 1 EC Competition Policy Newsletter 31.

Fn 174. See now COMP/38.698 *CISAC*, decn of 16 July 2008, [2009] 4 CMLR 577 where the Commission noted that in the *GVL* case the German legislation had not conferred the management of copyright or related rights on specific undertakings. The Commission left open whether Article 86(2) [now Article 106(2) TFEU] could apply to collecting societies in a Member State where legislation describes the function and the status of the collecting society in a way which allows the assumption that the collecting society is entrusted with the operation of services of general economic interest: para 257. The decision is on appeal: Cases T-398, 410, 411, 413–422, 425, 432, 434, 442, 451/08, not yet decided.

Fn 175. Note that the Commission has accepted that the provision of banking services to sections of the population who have difficulty accessing basic banking services can be a service of general economic interest: see *Special rights granted to La Banque Postale, Caisses d'Epargne and Crédit Mutuel for the distribution of the livret A and livret bleu*, decn of 10 May 2007, C(2007) 2110 final, where the Commission found that the rights granted contravened Article 86 in conjunction with Article 43 [now Articles 106 and 49 TFEU] (on appeal Cases T-279 & 289/07 *Caisse Nationale des Caisses d'Épargne et de Prévoyance v Commission*, not yet decided).

Obstructing the performance of the tasks.   In COMP/39.562 *Slovakian postal* **11.052** *legislation relating to hybrid mail services*, decn of 7 October 2008, [2009] 4 CMLR 663 the Commission stated that even though there is a presumption of *prima facie* justification under Article 86(2) [now Article 106(2) TFEU] for services covered by the reserved area as defined in the Postal Directive (cf Point 8.3 of the Postal Notice), that did not apply in this case because the hybrid service had at first been liberalised by Slovakia and the functioning of the public service had not been endangered: para 165. The subsequent extension of the monopoly to cover the service therefore needed specific justification. The Commission agreed with using the net avoided cost methodology to calculate the costs of providing the universal service, but did not accept the evidence as to those costs put forward by Slovakia. In particular, the Commission held that it is not permissible under the Postal Directive to finance services other than the universal postal services by maintaining or extending those reserved areas. The cost of providing other services, such as financial services, cannot be included in the cost of the universal service. The Commission therefore found that Slovakia was in breach of Article 86(1) in conjunction with Article 82. The decision is on appeal Case T-556/08 *Slovenská pošta v Commission*, not yet decided.

11.053 **The *Dutch Sectoral Pension Funds* cases.** **Fn 186.** The Supreme Court allowed the appeal in *BUPA Ireland Ltd v Health Insurance Authority* [2008] IESC 42, holding that the 'risk equalisation scheme' was *ultra vires* the Irish statute. The Supreme Court therefore did not address the Article 86(2) argument and BUPA's damages claim against the State for violation of Article 86 (in conjunction with Articles 10 and 82) is continuing in the High Court. The State argues that there was nonetheless objective justification for the anti-competitive nature of the scheme so that it did not violate competition law; and further that BUPA caused its own loss by leaving the market before its appeal was determined.

12

SECTORAL REGIMES

2. Transport

(b) Rail, road and inland waterway transport

(i) Application of Community competition rules

Article 82.   See also *Magyar Államvasutak ('MÁV')*, case 2.Kf.27.165/2008/14,   **12.014**
judgment of the Budapest Court of Appeal of 18 February 2009, discussed in the
update to paragraph 10.151, above. The Court upheld the decision of the
Hungarian Competition Authority condemning various acts engaged in by the
Hungarian State Railway company to hinder access by new entrants at the time of
rail liberalisation in Hungary (including the conclusion of long-term exclusive
agreements with major shippers of bulk products). The case is on appeal to the
Supreme Court.

(c) Maritime transport

(i) Scope of application of the competition rules

Repeal of Regulation 4056/86.   The Commission has issued guidelines con-   **12.019**
cerning the application of Article 81 [now Article 101 TFEU] to liner shipping services, cabotage and tramp services, see Guidelines on the application of
Article 81 of the EC Treaty to maritime transport services, OJ 2008 C245/2,
[2008] 5 CMLR 1037: Vol II, App E7C. The Guidelines cover the definition of
relevant product and geographic markets, indicating that containerised liner shipping services are likely to constitute a separate relevant market from other forms
of transport, because only an insufficient proportion of the goods carried by
container can easily be switched to other modes of transport, such as air transport
services. See Bermig and Ritter, 'The new Guidelines on the application of
Article 81 of the EC Treaty to the maritime sector' (2008) 3 Competition Policy
Newsletter 25.

Agreements outside Article 81(1).   See now the Commission's Guidelines   **12.020**
on the application of Article 81 of the EC Treaty to maritime transport services,

OJ 2008 C245/2, [2008] 5 CMLR 1037: Vol II, App E7C. These describe the kinds of agreements among liner shipping carriers and tramp shipping operators that generally do not come within Article 81 [now Article 101 TFEU]. These include technical agreements (such as agreements aimed at implementing technical improvements or achieving technical cooperation or relating to the implementation of environmental standards, but excluding agreements relating to price or capacity); certain kinds of information exchange agreements and pool agreements in tramp shipping where the participants are not actual or potential competitors. Conversely pool agreements between competitors limited to joint selling have as a rule the object and effect of coordinating the pricing policy of these competitors and will fall within Article 81(1). Tramp shipping pools which do not involve joint selling but nevertheless entail some degree of coordination on the parameters of competition (eg joint scheduling or joint purchasing) will be subject to Article 81(1) if the parties to the agreement have some degree of market power.

(ii) Block exemption for liner conferences

12.022 Transitional period of application. See now the Guidelines on the application of Article 81 of the EC Treaty to maritime transport services, OJ 2008 C245/2: Vol II, App E7C discussed in the updates to paragraphs 12.019 and 12.020, above.

(iii) Block exemption for consortia

12.029 Generally. The Commission has replaced Regulation 479/92 with a consolidated enabling regulation: Regulation 246/2009 on the application of Article 81(3) of the Treaty to certain categories of agreements, decisions and concerted practices between liner shipping companies (consortia), OJ 2009 L79/1: Vol II, App E7A.

12.030 Regulation 823/2000. The Commission has also adopted a new block exemption for liner consortia: Regulation 906/2009, OJ 2009 L256/31: Vol II, App E7B. The Regulation will enter into force on 26 April 2010 when Regulation 823/2000 expires. The Regulation applies only to consortia insofar as they provide international liner shipping services from or to one or more Community ports. But the new Regulation extends to all liner shipping cargo services, whether containerised or not. The definition of a consortium has been revised slightly so that it is now:

> '[A]n agreement or a set of interrelated agreements between two or more vessel-operating carriers which provide international liner shipping services exclusively for the carriage of cargo relating to one or more trades, the object of which is to bring about cooperation in the joint operation of a maritime transport service, and which improves the service that would be offered individually by each of its members in the absence of the consortium, in order to rationalise their operations by means of technical, operational and/or commercial arrangements.'

The list of exempted activities has been revised in order to reflect current market practices and hard-core restrictions such as price-fixing and market- or customer-sharing will still deprive the agreement of the benefit of the exemption. The market share threshold has been reduced from 35 per cent to 30 per cent and the method of its calculation has been clarified. The permissible restrictions on a member withdrawing from the consortium have also been revised.

(d) Air transport

(i) Scope of application of the competition rules

Developments following the '*Open Skies*' judgment.   See also Gremminger, **12.038** 'New EU–US cooperation agreement in air transport' (2007) 2 Competition Policy Newsletter 27.

(ii) The sectoral rules applicable to the air transport sector

Scope of Regulation 3976/87.   Regulation 3976/87 and the regulations amend- **12.041** ing it have been repealed and replaced by a consolidating instrument: Regulation 487/2009 on the application of Article 81(3) of the Treaty to certain categories of agreements and concerted practices in the air transport sector, OJ 2009 L148/1: Vol II, App E9A. The kinds of block exemption regulations that the Commission may adopt remain as set out in the text.

(iii) Particular issues

Computer reservation systems.   Note that in a merger case, Case M.4523 **12.048** *Travelport/Worldspan* (21 August 2007) the Commission defined global distribution systems as a separate relevant product market.

CRS code of conduct.   Regulation 2299/89 has been repealed and replaced by **12.049** Regulation 80/2009, OJ 2009 L35/47: Vol II, App E11 as from 29 March 2009. The new regulation prohibits the imposition of unfair and/or unjustified conditions by the system vendor on participating carriers. It also provides that transport providers must not discriminate against competing CRSs by refusing to provide data. Information on bus services for air transport products or rail transport products which are incorporated alongside air transport products should be included in the principal display. The Commission has also published an explanatory note with regard to the definition of 'parent carrier' in the Regulation: OJ 2009 C53/4: Vol II, App E12.

Groundhandling services.   In COMP/38.469 *Athens International Airport*, **12.050** decn of 2 May 2005, the Commission rejected a number of complaints about charges for ground services provided at Athens airport. The decision was primarily based on lack of Community interest although the Commission did carry out a comparison of the charges with those at other airports. The Commission also indicated that the carrying out of passenger security checks was not an economic activity covered by Article 82 [now Article 102 TFEU] (para 49) and that it was likely that car parking services did not form a relevant product market but competed with other means of travelling to the airport (paras 120 *et seq*). On appeal, the CFI upheld the Commission's decision that there was no Community interest: Case T-306/05 *Scippacercola and Terezakis v Commission* [2008] ECR II-4*, [2008] 4 CMLR 1418, see paras 145 *et seq* (further appeal dismissed Case C-159/08 P, Order of 25 March 2009).

3. Energy

(b) Electricity

(ii) Liberalisation

12.061 **The Electricity Directive.** Directive 2003/54 will be repealed and replaced by Directive 2009/72 concerning common rules for the internal market in electricity, OJ 2009 L211/55: Vol II, App E14A. This new directive is part of the 'Third Energy Package', intended to improve the functioning of the European Union's internal market for gas and electricity. The Directive establishes common rules for the generation, transmission, distribution and supply of electricity, together with consumer protection provisions. It lays down rules on the organisation and functioning of the electricity sector, open access to the market, calls for tender, granting of authorisations and system operation. The Directive requires Member States to ensure that electricity companies are operated so as to achieve a competitive, secure and environmentally sustainable market in electricity. It also requires Member States to ensure universal service (ie the right to be supplied with electricity of a specified quality at reasonable, easily and clearly comparable, transparent and non-discriminatory prices). Final customers must be protected, especially vulnerable customers and those in remote areas. From 3 March 2012, Member States must ensure the separation ('unbundling') of transmission systems and transmission system operators. The Directive is to be implemented by 3 March 2011, on which date all its requirements are to be applied other than Article 11. That Article, which relates to certification of transmission systems owned or operated by persons in third countries, will apply from 3 March 2013.

(iii) Long-term arrangements and exclusivity

12.066 **Length of exclusivity.** The Commission opened proceedings under Article 82 [now Article 102 TFEU] against EDF (the French electricity supplier) because of concerns over a contract concluded between EDF and Exeltium, a consortium of large industrial electricity consumers in France. Under the arrangement, EDF would supply significant volumes of electricity to the consortium on a very long term basis, subject to restrictions on resale. The Commission closed its file after substantial amendments were made to address these concerns: (i) securing an effective opt-out for the members of the consortium wishing to contract with other suppliers; (ii) removing various contractual resale restrictions; and (iii) other resale restrictions being lifted by amendments to certain provisions of the legal and regulatory framework by the French authorities: COMP/39.386 *EDF/ Exeltium*, MEMO/08/533 (31 July 2008).

Market definition in electricity supply.   So far as the geographic market is con-   **12.066A**
cerned, the Commission noted in COMP/38.700 *Greek Lignite and Electricity generation*, decn of 5 March 2008, [2009] 4 CMLR 495 that the market for wholesale electricity (generation and imports of electricity for further resale) is national or smaller in scope. A further distinction may be made between 'the interconnected system', ie mainland Greece and the interconnected islands, and 'the non-interconnected system'. Given that there is no competition possible at the wholesale level in 'the non-interconnected system', the decision addressed only the 'interconnected system'. Thus the geographical scope of the electricity wholesale market concerned was the territory of the 'interconnected system'. The case is on appeal: Case T-169/08 *DEI v Commission*, not yet decided.

See also see COMP/39.388 & /39.389 *E.ON German electricity markets*, decn of 26 November 2008 where the Commission distinguished between the wholesale electricity market in which electricity is bought for further resale and the market for balancing power needed to maintain the appropriate tension level in the grid. Because of certain technical differences and differences in demand the Commission also distinguished between secondary balancing reserves on the one hand and tertiary balancing reserves on the other. The relevant product market was therefore limited to the market for secondary balancing reserves: para 46.

Exclusivity and Article 82.   In a combined decision, the Commission accepted   **12.067**
commitments in investigations under Article 82 EC [now Article 102 TFEU] into the electricity wholesale market and the electricity balancing market in Germany: COMP/39.388 & 39.389 *E.ON German electricity markets*, decn of 26 November 2008. The Commission came to the provisional conclusion that E.ON and two other electricity companies held a collective dominant position on the wholesale market (that is generation and import of electricity for resale) and that the suspected practices of E.ON of withholding capacity and deterring investment in generation raised Article 82 concerns. Further the Commission considered that E.ON might be dominant on the market for secondary reserves and was suspected of favouring its affiliated companies as well as preventing power producers from other Member States from selling balancing energy into the balancing markets, in possible breach of Article 82.

12.067A **Other abuses in relation to electricity production.** In COMP/38.700 *Greek Lignite and Electricity generation*, decn of 5 March 2008, [2009] 4 CMLR 495 the Commission held that Greece was in breach of Article 86(1) [now Article 106(1) TFEU] by maintaining in place rights which gave the former monopoly electricity generating company exclusive access to lignite deposits; lignite being the cheapest available source of fuel for electricity generation. The case is on appeal: Case T-169/08 *DEI v Commission*, not yet decided.

12.069 **National or European markets.** **Fn 193.** The Commission has followed its previous practice in Case M.3440 *ENI/EDP/GdP* in defining relevant markets in the electricity sector: see COMP/39.388 & 39.389 *E.ON German electricity markets*, decn of 26 November 2008.

(c) **Gas**

(i) Generally

12.073 **Market structure.** In Case M.5585 *Centrica/Venture Production* (21 August 2009) the Commission considered the definition of relevant product markets at each stage of the production and supply of gas from exploration to retail supply. The Commission indicated that exploration, ie the finding of new hydrocarbon reserves, constitutes a separate product market and that there is no distinction between the exploration for oil on the one hand and exploration for natural gas on the other. However, it is appropriate to define separate product markets for the upstream production of crude oil and another relevant market for the upstream production of natural gas.

(ii) Liberalisation

12.075 **The Gas Directive.** Directive 2003/55 will be repealed and replaced by Directive 2009/73 concerning common rules for the internal market in natural gas, OJ 2009 L211/94: Vol II, App E15A. This new Directive is part of the 'Third Energy Package', intended to improve the functioning of the European Union's internal market for gas and electricity. The Directive establishes common rules for the transmission, distribution, supply and storage of natural gas. It lays down rules on the organisation and functioning of the natural gas sector, access to the market, the criteria and procedures applicable to the granting of authorisations for transmission, distribution, supply and storage of natural gas, and systems operation. The Directive also applies to biogas and to gas from biomass and other types of gas able to be injected into, and transported through, the natural gas system. Member States are required to ensure that natural gas companies are operated so as to achieve a competitive, secure and environmentally sustainable market in natural gas. Final customers must be protected, especially vulnerable customers and those in remote areas. Member States must ensure that all customers connected to the gas network are entitled to have their gas provided by a supplier from any Member State. Member States must also ensure the separation ('unbundling') of transmission systems and transmission system operators. The Directive is to be implemented by 3 March 2011, on which date all its requirements are to be applied other than Article 11. That Article, which relates to certification of transmission systems owned or operated by persons in third countries, will apply from 3 March 2013.

In Case C-347/06 *ASM Brescia v Comune de Rodengo* [2008] ECR I-5641, [2008] 3 CMLR 1024 the ECJ held, in an Article 234 [now Article 267 TFEU] reference, that Article 23(1) of Directive 2003/55 concerns the supply of natural gas not its distribution and therefore does not oblige Member States to bring to an end distribution contracts previously granted without a competitive tendering procedure. The Directive does not require existing concessions for the distribution of gas to be called into question and indeed the ECJ stated that the principle of legal certainty requires the early termination of such a concession to be coupled with a transitional period which enables the contracting parties to untie their contractual relations in a satisfactory manner.

(iii) Application of competition rules

Territorial restrictions. The Commission has negotiated the removal of territorial restrictions in gas supply contracts concluded by the Algerian gas producer Sonatrach. Algeria agreed to delete territorial restrictions and also not to include profit sharing mechanisms whereby the buyer/importer was obliged to share part of the profit with the supplier/producer if the gas was sold on by the importer to a customer outside the agreed territory or to a customer using the gas for a purpose other than the one agreed upon. These mechanisms had been used as an alternative to territorial restrictions: COMP/37.811 *Algerian gas imports* Press Release IP/07/1074 (11 July 2007).   **12.079**

In COMP/39.401 *E.On - GdF collusion*, decn of 8 July 2009 the Commission imposed substantial fines on the joint owners of a pipeline importing Russian gas into Germany and France. The parties had agreed not to supply gas into each other's markets: see Press Release IP/09/1099 (8 July 2009).

Long-term contracts and developing markets. **Fn 224.** The Commission accepted commitments from Distrigas as mentioned in the footnote: COMP/37.966 *Distrigas*, decn of 11 October 2007. The Commission calculated the proportion of the relevant market tied to Distrigas by its existing contracts and decided that the contracts concluded by Distrigas significantly foreclosed the relevant market in a way that could constitute an abuse of its dominant position. Distrigas gave commitments whereby, first, on average a minimum of 70 per cent of the gas volumes supplied by Distrigas to industrial users and electricity producers in Belgium will return to the market each year. Secondly, contracts with industrial users and electricity producers would not be for longer than five years.   **12.080**

Thirdly, Distrigas undertook not to conclude any gas supply agreements with resellers with a duration of over two years.

12.081 **Third party access.** In COMP/39.402 *RWE (gas foreclosure)*, decn of 18 March 2009, [2009] 5 CMLR 1667 the Commission has accepted a commitment from RWE to divest its entire high pressure West German gas transmission network to allay Commission concerns about access to the network. The Commission had suspected a possible refusal to supply gas transmission services to other companies and a margin squeeze aimed at lowering the margins of RWE's downstream competitors in gas supply.

4. Electronic Communications

(a) Regulatory framework

12.089 **Overview of regulatory framework.** On 20 November 2009 the Council of Ministers approved a package of measures to reform the regulation of electronic communications, following a lengthy conciliation process between the Parliament and the Council earlier that month: MEMO/09/513 (20 November 2009). The measures had first been proposed by the Commission in November 2007. The new package comprises three measures; (i) a Directive known as the Better Regulation Directive which amends the Framework Directive, the Authorisation Directive and the Access Directive; (ii) a Directive known as the Citizens' Rights Directive which amends the Universal Services Directive and the e-Privacy Directive; and (iii) a Regulation which establishes a new European Telecoms Authority 'BEREC' (Body of European Regulators for Electronic Communications) to replace the European Regulators Group.

Among the main reforms agreed are:

• an enhancement of the Commission's powers in relation to remedies proposed by national communications authorities to deal with significant market power (see update to paragraph 12.104, below);

• various measures to benefit consumers, for example setting minimum time limits for number portability; requiring more information to be provided about the services acquired, in particular minimum service quality levels; and enhancing protection against personal data breaches and spam;

• rules to strengthen the political independence of national regulators;

• introduction of functional separation as a new regulatory remedy available to all national regulators;

• measures to accelerate broadband access throughout Europe and to encourage investment in next generation access networks.

The provisions which proved most controversial were the safeguards to be put in place to restrict the rights of Member States to impose limits on an individual's access to the internet. A new Article 1(3)(a) to be inserted into the Framework Directive will provide that any measures taken by Member States regarding end-users' access to the internet shall respect the individual's human rights under the ECHR. The package is expected to come into force on publication in the *Official Journal* in December 2009, with a June 2011 deadline for implementation by the Member States.

Scope of the regulatory framework.   In Case C-262/06 *Deutsche Telekom v*   **12.090**
Bundesrepublik Deutschland [2007] ECR I-10057, [2008] 4 CMLR 240, the ECJ held, on an Article 234 [now Article 267 TFEU] reference, that the transitional provisions in Article 27 of the Framework Directive maintained in force temporarily all obligations that had been imposed on a dominant provider under the previous regulatory framework.

(i) The Framework Directive

Obligations on NRAs.   Fn 263. For the relationship between the NRA's dispute   **12.093**
resolution function and its analysis of SMP in a relevant market see *Hutchison 3G UK Ltd v OFCOM* [2009] EWCA Civ 683.

SMP requires a 'prospective' analysis.   Fn 289. As regards the *Hutchison 3G*   **12.100**
case there mentioned, OFCOM held that there was insufficient buyer power to counteract Hutchison's dominance: this was upheld on appeal by the Competition Appeal Tribunal and then by the Court of Appeal: *Hutchison 3G UK Ltd v OFCOM* [2009] EWCA Civ 683.

The Recommendation on Relevant Markets.   The 2003 Recommendation   **12.101**
referred to in this paragraph has been replaced by the 2007 Recommendation, OJ 2007 L344/65. This Recommendation sets out the three cumulative criteria to be applied in determining whether a market is one where *ex ante* regulation may be warranted, namely (a) the presence of high and non-transitory barriers to entry which may be of a structural, legal or regulatory nature; (b) a market structure which does not tend towards effective competition within the relevant time horizon; and (c) the insufficiency of competition law alone adequately to address the market failure(s) concerned. The Annex to the Recommendation now lists only seven markets identified by the Commission on the basis of those criteria. When considering whether SMP exists in markets not included in the Annex to the Recommendation, the Member States must apply those three criteria. For the application of this Recommendation in the merger context see, eg Case M.5148 *Deutsche Telekom/OTE* (2 October 2008) and the cases cited therein. For the application of the new Recommendation in two recent notifications by the Polish NRA see Szarka, 'Rolling back regulation in the telecoms sector: a practical example'

(2008) 3 Competition Policy Newsletter 21. The article describes two notifications under Article 7 of the Framework Directive where the Polish NRA had proposed *ex ante* regulation for two markets which were listed in the 2003 Recommendation but not in the new one. Applying the three criteria test the Commission issued serious doubts letters in both cases and the proposed measures were withdrawn. See also the Commission's approach to the finding of sub-national markets by OFCOM in the United Kingdom: Bringer and Schumm, 'Revolution or evolution in telecoms? Sub-national markets in sector-specific regulation when competition develops unevenly' (2008) 2 Competition Policy Newsletter 23.

12.103 **SMP Conditions.**   **Fn 314.** The Commission has issued a Recommendation on the Regulatory Treatment of Fixed and Mobile Termination Rates in the EU, OJ 2009 L124/67 giving guidance to NRAs on how to calculate costs incurred by an efficient operator for the purpose of imposing price controls and cost-accounting obligations for mobile call termination rates.

12.104 **The Commission's review of SMP designations.**   A letter sent by the Commission pursuant to Article 7(3) of the Framework Directive (stating that it does not have serious doubts about the proposed measure) is not a reviewable act for the purposes of appeal to the CFI under Article 230 EC [now Article 263 TFEU]: see Case T-109/06 *Vodafone España v Commission* [2007] ECR II-5151, [2008] 4 CMLR 1378. The CFI's order contains an interesting discussion of the consultation procedure under Article 7.

Note that under the new package of measures approved by the Council of Ministers on 20 November 2009, the scope of the Commission's review will extend to the remedies proposed by the NRA where SMP has been found. When the Commission, in cooperation with the new European Telecoms Authority BEREC, considers that a draft remedy notified by the NRA would create a barrier to the single market, the Commission may issue a recommendation that requires the NRA to amend or withdraw the planned remedy. Although the new package stops short of conferring a power of veto on the Commission as regards remedies, the Commission has a further power to adopt harmonisation measures in the form of recommendations or binding decisions if divergences in the regulatory approaches of national regulators persist across the EU in the longer term.

(iii) The Authorisation Directive

12.112 **Special provisions for radio frequencies and numbers.**   See also Case C-380/05 *Centro Europa 7 v Ministero delle Comunicazioni* [2008] ECR I-349, [2008] 2 CMLR 512 where the Italian Court requested a preliminary ruling in the context of an action for compensation brought by Centro Europa 7. The applicant had been awarded a licence to broadcast but had not been allocated any radio frequency to enable it to start up its service. The ECJ concluded that Article 49 EC [now Article 56 TFEU] in conjunction with the directives of the common regulatory framework precluded, in television broadcasting matters, national legislation which makes it impossible for an operator holding rights to broadcast in the absence of broadcasting radio frequencies granted on the basis of objective, transparent, non-discriminatory and proportionate criteria. It was for the national court to decide whether compensation was payable by reason of the breach.

(vii) Forthcoming changes

Reform.   A new package of regulatory measures was approved by the Council **12.120** of Ministers in November 2009. Further, the new Recommendation on relevant markets referred to in this paragraph has been adopted: OJ 2007 L344/65. See further the update to paragraphs 12.089 and 12.101, above.

(b) Application of competition law

(iv) Joint ventures and mergers

Mergers and full-function joint ventures.   The Commission cleared the acqui- **12.146** sition of the UK subsidiary of Tiscali SpA by the Carphone Warehouse Group: see Case M.5532 *Carphone Warehouse/Tiscali UK* (30 June 2009). The parties' activities overlap horizontally in retail and wholesale internet access provision, as well as in retail fixed line telephony services. The Commission analysed in particular the domestic sector of broadband services but found that the merged entity would continue to face competition from a number of strong players, especially BT, as well as from a number of strong alternative operators, including those based on the cable platform. Competition from other technologies, such as mobile telecommunications, was also growing: see Press Release IP/09/1054 (30 June 2009).

(v) Application of Article 82

Types of abuse.   Use of information held by the former dominant incumbent **12.151** for targeted marketing to customers of newer entrants to the market can also amount to abuse: see *Fastweb SpA v Telecom Italia SpA*, decn of Milan Court of Appeal of 16 May 2006, Giur. It. 2007, 4, 919. An interim injunction was granted to stop Telecom Italia using information from number portability requests to engage in aggressive 'win-back' strategies directed at its former customers. Since Telecom Italia subsequently discontinued the practice the case did not proceed to final judgment but a claim by Fastweb for resulting damages is pending in the Italian courts.

Similarly, in its decision on the practices of France Télécom in French overseas departments (DOM), the French Competition Authority found as an aspect of the infringement the use by France Télécom of the information which it held as administrator of the local loops to direct its marketing efforts at customers who had migrated to other providers, while also denigrating the services of those competitors: Decision No. 09-D-24 of 28 July 2009.

12.157 **Predatory behaviour.** The elements of predatory pricing were considered by the ECJ in Case C-202/07 P *France Télécom v Commission*, judgment of 2 April 2009. First, the ECJ held that the CFI's judgment under appeal had set out sufficiently clearly why the circumstances of the present case, in particular the relationship between the level of prices applied by Wanadoo and the average variable costs and average total costs borne by Wanadoo, were analogous to those in *Tetra Pak v Commission*. Many of Wanadoo's arguments concerning the calculation of costs were rejected as inadmissible or unfounded. However, the ECJ did expressly uphold the CFI's conclusion that 'demonstrating that it is possible to recoup losses is not a necessary precondition for a finding of predatory pricing': para 113.

12.162 **Imposing excessive prices.** See also the decision of the French Competition Authority regarding the practices of France Télécom in French overseas departments (DOM) (Decision No. 09-D-24 of 28 July 2009) discussed in the update to paragraph 10.108, above. As well as charging excessive prices for line rental to competitors, France Télécom refused to provide adequate security on the lines, making it impossible for them to offer services of equivalent quality.

12.164 *Deutsche Telekom.* Deutsche Telekom's appeal against the Commission's decision was dismissed by the CFI: Case T-271/03 [2008] ECR II-477, [2008] 5 CMLR 631. The Court rejected arguments based on the involvement of the German telecoms regulator in the setting of DT's prices. The Court confirmed that it was not necessary to show that DT's retail price was unfairly high in order to establish the margin squeeze abuse: 'the abusive nature of the applicant's conduct is connected with the unfairness of the spread between its prices for wholesale access and its retail prices, which takes the form of a margin squeeze': para 167. In response to various challenges to the way the Commission had calculated the margin, the CFI stated that this was a matter of complex economic assessment as to which the Commission had a margin of appreciation: para 185. All DT's pleas on the detail of what revenues should or should not have been included in the calculations were rejected by the Court. Finally, the CFI upheld the Commission's finding that there had been an actual effect on competition because DT's network was the only infrastructure available for competitors: 'If the applicant's retail prices are lower than its wholesale charges, or if the spread between the applicant's wholesale and retail charges is insufficient to enable an equally efficient operator to cover its product-specific costs of supplying retail access services, a potential competitor who is just as efficient as the applicant would not be able to enter the retail access services market without suffering losses': para 237. The CFI's judgment is on appeal: Case C-280/08 P, not yet decided.

Fn 537. In *ETNA v France Télécom and SFR*, the case was referred back to the Paris Court of Appeal which followed the position set out by the Cour de Cassation and upheld the decision of the Competition Authority: judgment of 2 April 2008, BOCCRF No. 7 of 15 September 2008. However this judgment was annulled by the Cour de Cassation for procedural reasons (judgment of 3 March 2009) so the case has been referred back to the Court of Appeal for a second time (not yet decided).

International roaming charges. The proceedings against T-Mobile and Vodafone in Germany and against O$_2$ and Vodafone in the UK were dropped following the adoption of Regulation 717/2007: Press Release IP/07/1113 (18 July 2007). The validity of the Roaming Regulation was challenged by four mobile network operators in proceedings in the High Court in England and a reference was made to the ECJ under Article 234 [now Article 267 TFEU]: Case C-58/08, not yet decided. The action challenged the legal base for the Regulation (Article 95 EC [now Article 114 TFEU]) and alleged that the Regulation was invalid on the grounds that the imposition of a price ceiling in respect of retail roaming charges infringes the principle of proportionality and/or subsidiarity. Meanwhile the Roaming Regulation has been amended by Regulation 544/2009 OJ 2009 L167/12, *inter alia*, extending the Regulation to cover SMS and data roaming charges. **12.165**

(vi) Application of Article 86

Discriminatory licensing by Member States. The disputes arising out of the Spanish operator Telefónica's refusal (i) to conclude a roaming agreement with the Gibraltar operator for mobile phone services; and (ii) to recognise the international dialling code for Gibraltar were resolved by negotiation between the UK, Spain and Gibraltar. The challenge to the Commission's rejection of the Gibtel complaint was withdrawn: Cases T-433/03, etc, *Gibtelcom v Commission*, Order of 26 June 2008, [2009] 4 CMLR 344. **12.168**

5. Insurance

Generally. The Commission investigated various markets for insurance in Case M.5075 *Vienna Insurance Group/Erste Bank* (17 June 2008) where the merger was cleared after the parties offered commitments. In September 2007, the Commission published the Final Report of the sector inquiry into business insurance. The Final Report focuses in substance on two main issues. The first is competition in the wholesale subscription market, that is where an ad hoc syndication arrangement is set up by a broker or client to cover a given risk. The Report considers the use of 'Best Terms and Conditions' clauses whereby an insurer makes an offer to subscribe conditional on no other participant receiving better terms in respect either of a higher price or a more advantageous policy. The Commission notes that this may lead to an upward alignment of premiums and/or **12.169**

contract uncertainty. The second issue is broker conflicts of interest and the Commission has undertaken to look at these issues in the framework of the review of the Insurance Mediation Directive.

12.170 **Insurance block exemption.** Regulation 358/2003 is due to expire on 31 March 2010. The Commission is consulting on a revised regulation which would renew two of the four categories of agreements currently exempted, namely information exchange and insurance pools, with certain amendments: see Press Release IP/09/1413 (5 October 2009).

12.179 **Insurance intermediaries.** Note that where the insurance broker is acting for the insured but the agreement at issue concerns arrangements between the insurer and the broker regarding the level of broker's commission, that will not be a vertical agreement within Regulation 2790/99 since the relationship between insurer and broker in that regard is not that of seller and purchaser: cf *Allianz Hungária, Generali Providencia*, 2.Kf.27.129/2009, judgment of the Budapest Court of Appeal of 23 September 2009 (re the Hungarian domestic equivalent block exemption).

6. Postal Services

(b) Liberalisation

12.183 **The Postal Directive.** The Postal Directive was amended substantially by Directive 2008/6, OJ 2008 L52/3. This took the final step of abolishing the grant of a monopoly for any part of the postal service, at the same time imposing an obligation on Member States to ensure the provision of a universal service at all points in their territory at affordable prices for at least five working days a week. Under Article 4 of the revised Directive 97/67, Member States may designate one or more undertakings as universal service providers. But instead of allowing Member States to reserve part of the service, the Directive now sets out various means by which the Member State may finance provision of the universal service. Where a Member State determines that the universal service obligations entail a net cost and 'represent an unfair financial burden' it may introduce a mechanism to compensate the provider either from public funds or by sharing the net costs between providers of services and/or users (Article 7(3)). Where the costs are to be shared among providers or users, the Member State may establish a compensation fund to which those providers or users contribute and which is administered by an independent body (Article 7(4)). For services which fall outside the scope of the universal service, Member States may introduce general authorisation to the extent necessary to guarantee compliance with the 'essential requirements' defined as non-economic issues such as the confidentiality of correspondence. But such authorisations must not be limited in number (Article 9(2)). The amendments introduced by Directive 2008/6 also laid down tariff principles for the universal service, namely that it must be affordable and cost-oriented, transparent and non-discriminatory. It also provides ancillary provisions for the financial accounts of universal service providers, for postal users' complaints procedures and, in Annex I, provides guidance on calculating the net cost, if any, of universal service. The dismantling of any remaining postal monopolies must be implemented by most Member States by 31 December 2010 though 11 Member States have a further two years in which to implement the Directive.

In Case C-162/06 *International Mail Spain SL v Administración del Estado* [2007] ECR I-9911, [2008] 4 CMLR 18 the ECJ held in an Article 234 [now Article 267 TFEU] reference that Article 7(2) of Directive 97/67 allows Member States to reserve cross-border mail to the universal provider only insofar as they establish either that, in the absence of such a reservation, that universal service could not be achieved, or that such a reservation is necessary to enable that service to be carried out under economically acceptable conditions: 'mere expediency' was not enough. The ECJ agreed with the Commission's submissions that it would be contrary to the objective of Directive 2002/39, which is to pursue the gradual and controlled opening of postal services to competition, to interpret the fourth subparagraph of Article 7(1) of Directive 97/67, as amended, as increasing the scope of discretion afforded to Member States: para 46.

Reservation of services. Article 7 of the Postal Directive was unsuccessfully **12.184** relied on by Slovakia to rebut an allegation of breach of Article 86 in conjunction with Article 82 [now Articles 106(1) and 102 TFEU]: COMP/39.562 *Slovakian postal legislation relating to hybrid mail services*, decn of 7 October 2008, [2009] 4 CMLR 663. The Commission found that Slovakia had amended its legislation to extend the monopoly of the State-owned postal service to cover 'hybrid' mail services, that is services where data are sent electronically by the client to the service provider who then prints out and delivers the individual items to the client's customers. The Commission stated that even though there is a presumption of *prima facie* justification under Article 86(2) for services covered by the reserved area as defined in the Postal Directive (cf Point 8.3 of the Postal Notice), that did not apply here because the hybrid service had at first been liberalised by Slovakia and the functioning of the public service had not been endangered: para 165. The extension of the monopoly to cover the service needed specific justification. The Commission agreed with using the net avoided cost methodology to calculate the costs of providing the universal service but did not accept the evidence as to those costs put forward by Slovakia. In particular, the Commission held that it is not permissible under the Postal Directive to finance services other than the universal postal services by maintaining or extending those reserved areas. Thus the cost of providing other services, such as financial services, cannot be included in the cost of the universal service. The decision is on appeal Case T-556/08 *Slovenská pošta v Commission*, not yet decided.

(c) **Application of competition rules**

12.188 **Jurisprudence of the Community Courts and the Commission.** In COMP/ 39.562 *Slovakian postal legislation relating to hybrid mail services*, decn of 7 October 2008, [2009] 4 CMLR 663 the Commission considered whether hybrid mail services form a separate relevant product market from traditional postal services for the purposes of applying Article 86(1) in conjunction with Article 82 [now Articles 106(1) and 102 TFEU]. The Commission found that they fulfil different business and service needs. While a part of these services is similar in that both of them ultimately concern the delivery of an item to the addressee, from the point of view of customers they are perceived as two alternative, different means of effecting the transmission of content. Further, the two services were subject to different regulatory constraints. The regulatory environment of a service is a distinguishing factor for the purposes of market definition. In Slovakia, prior to the adoption of the State measure being challenged, traditional postal services were reserved while hybrid mail services, including the delivery of hybrid mail items, were not (on this aspect see update to paragraph 12.184, above). It follows that the two categories of services were subject to different market dynamics: paras 92 *et seq*. The decision is on appeal, Case T-556/08 *Slovenská pošta v Commission*, not yet decided.

12.193 **Article 82 and consumer loyalty issues.** Similarly, in Denmark, Post Danmark was held to have abused its dominant position in the market for distribution of unaddressed items and weeklies by selectively charging lower prices to some customers of its main competitor and using progressive loyalty rebates awarded against a target agreed with the customer, which rebates did not reflect underlying cost savings: *Post Danmark v Competition Council*, ØLR (13 Afd) B 2656/05, judgment of the High Court of Eastern Denmark of 21 December 2007. The case is on appeal to the Supreme Court (Case No. 2/2008) which decided on 28 October 2009 to make a reference to the European Court of Justice. See also *Post Danmark*, decision of the Danish Competition Council of 24 June 2009 discussed in the update to paragraph 10.096, above.

7. Agriculture

Note that Article 33 EC is now Article 39 TFEU

(a) **The objectives of Article 33 of the EC Treaty**

12.196 **The agricultural sector.** In December 2008 the Commission published a Communication on Food Prices in Europe (COM(2008) 821 final (9.12.2008)) in response to the substantial increases in food commodity prices during 2007/08. The Communication lists a number of anti-competitive practices which might give rise to concerns including buying alliances and single branding obligations.

(b) Application of competition rules

The first Article 2(1) exception: national market organisations.   Fn 641. The   **12.202**
appeal in the *French Beef* case was dismissed: Cases C-101 & 110/07 P *Coop de France bétail et viande and FNSEA v Commission*, judgment of 18 December 2008, [2009] 4 CMLR 743.

The second Article 2(1) exception: necessary under Article 33.   Fn 644. The   **12.203**
appeal in the *French Beef* case was dismissed: Cases C-101 & 110/07 P *Coop de France bétail et viande and FNSEA v Commission*, judgment of 18 December 2008, [2009] 4 CMLR 743.

13

ENFORCEMENT AND PROCEDURE

2. The Former Enforcement Regime under Regulation 17

Comfort and discomfort letters.   For a case where the Commission reversed the   **13.011**
stance taken in a comfort letter because of developments in the market, in particular
the development of the internet, see COMP/38.698 *CISAC*, decn of 16 July
2008, [2009] 4 CMLR 577, paras 120–122. The case is on appeal Cases T-398,
410, 411, 413–422, 425, 432, 434, 442, 451/08, not yet decided.

4. The Commission's Powers of Investigation

(a) Fundamental rights and the Commission's powers of investigation

General principles of EC law.   See also Case T-69/04 *Schunk GmbH v Commis-*   **13.026**
sion [2009] 4 CMLR 2 where the CFI considered the case law of the Court of
Human Rights on Article 7 ECHR in relation to an assertion that the wide discretion given to the Commission when imposing a fine infringed the principle of
legal certainty: paras 28–50.

Relevant rights.   In Case T-99/04 *AC-Treuhand AG v Commission* [2008] ECR   **13.028**
II-1501, [2008] 5 CMLR 962 the CFI considered the principle of *nullum crimen,*
nulla poena sine lege which is a general principle of Union law by analogy with
Article 7 of the ECHR. This principle is described as requiring 'that any
Community legislation, in particular where it imposes or permits the imposition
of penalties, must be clear and precise so that the persons concerned may know
without ambiguity what rights and obligations flow from it and may take steps
accordingly': para 139. Although the principle allows the rules governing criminal
liability to be gradually clarified through interpretation by the courts, it may preclude the retroactive application of a new interpretation of a rule establishing an
offence. That is particularly true if the result of that interpretation was not reasonably
foreseeable at the time when the offence was committed, especially in the light of
the interpretation attributed to the provision in the case law at the material time.

The CFI held that the principle had not been infringed when the Commission imposed a fine on a trade association which had facilitated the operation of a cartel by providing administrative and secretarial support.

Fn 82. For an example of a breach of the principles of sound administration and equal treatment see Case T-410/03 *Hoechst GmbH v Commission* [2008] ECR II-881, [2008] 5 CMLR 839, paras 134–138 (Commission had assured Chisso that it would be given 'fair warning' if another undertaking looked like overtaking it in the application for leniency but had decided that it would not inform Hoechst that Chisso had applied for leniency).

13.029 **Right to a fair trial.**   A ground of appeal alleging an irregularity in the composition of the CFI involves a matter of public policy which must be raised by the Court of its own motion and can be raised at any time in the proceedings: Cases C-341 & 342/06 P *Chronopost and La Poste v UFEX* [2008] ECR I-4777, [2008] 3 CMLR 568. That case concerned an appeal against the judgment of the CFI, that CFI judgment having been delivered following the reference back of the case by the ECJ which had overturned an earlier CFI judgment in the same appeal. The duties of the Judge-Rapporteur in the Chamber which delivered the judgment under appeal were entrusted to the member who had been both President and Judge-Rapporteur in the Chamber which had delivered the earlier judgment successfully appealed against. The ECJ held, referring to jurisprudence of the Court of Human Rights, that this was not a breach of the right to a fair trial: para 60.

13.030 **'Criminal charge'.**   **Fn 95.** As to the case law of the ECtHR see also *Jussila v Finland* No. 73053/01 (2007) 45 EHRR 892.

(b) **Power to obtain information**

13.032 **Information from undertakings.**   **Fn 108.** In Case T-99/04 *AC-Treuhand AG v Commission* [2008] ECR II-1501, [2008] 5 CMLR 962 the CFI considered the scope of the Commission's obligation to inform the undertaking concerned of the subject-matter and purpose of the investigation under way. The CFI held that there had been a breach of the rights of the defence where the information request to an industry association had not made clear that the association itself, and not just its members, was considered a potential wrongdoer. But no detriment had arisen for the association from this breach, so the ground of appeal was rejected. *Quaere* whether this is correct having regard to the ECJ's judgment in Cases C-322/07 P, etc, *Papierfabrik August Koehler AG and Bolloré SA v Commission*, judgment of 3 September 2009, [2009] 5 CMLR 2301 discussed in the update to paragraph 13.084, below.

13.039 **Investigations into sectors of the economy and types of agreements.**   **Fn 145.** See, eg the Commission carried out 'dawn raids' at the outset of its inquiry into the pharmaceutical sector: Press Release IP/08/49 (16 January 2008).

(c) Powers of inspection

Powers that can be exercised during an inspection. As regards the sealing of **13.048** premises see COMP/39.326 *E.ON (breach of seal)*, decn of 30 January 2008, [2009] 4 CMLR 371 where the Commission imposed a fine of €38 million for breaking the seal. The Commission rejected various other reasons for the seal being voided including the fact that a cleaning woman may have wiped the seal with a particular brand of cleaning fluid or the possibility that frequent opening and closing of doors close by might have caused vibrations resulting in the failure of the seal. The case is under appeal: Case T-141/08, not yet decided.

Penalties in respect of inspections. Fn 213. See now COMP/39.326 *E.ON* **13.050** *(breach of seal)*, decn of 30 January 2008, [2009] 4 CMLR 371 where the Commission imposed a fine of €38 million for breaking the seal. The case is under appeal: Case T-141/08, not yet decided.

5. Complaints

Legitimate interests: the practice. Fn 282. The appeals against the decision in **13.065** *Nintendo* have now been decided: Case T-18/03 *CD-Contact Data v Commission*, judgment of 30 April 2009 (fine reduced) (on further appeal Case C-260/09P *Activision Blizzard Germany*, not yet decided); Case T-12/03 *Itochu* [2009] 5 CMLR 1375 (appeal dismissed); Case T-13/03 *Nintendo* [2009] 5 CMLR 1421 (fine reduced); Case T-398/02 *Linea Gig* (removed from register 2 May 2005). No issue arose in the appeals concerning the point made in this paragraph.

Extent of the Commission's duty to consider a complaint. The principles **13.067** described in this paragraph were applied in Case T-306/05 *Scippacercola and Terezakis v Commission* [2008] ECR II-4*, [2008] 4 CMLR 1418, paras 91 *et seq* (further appeal dismissed Case C-159/08 P, Order of 25 March 2009). The CFI also held that the decision rejecting a complaint must be based on the Commission's consideration of all relevant matters of law and of fact which exist at the time the decision is adopted not at the time the complaint was made: para 149.

Following the ECJ's judgment in Case C-119/97 P *Ufex v Commission* [1999] ECR I-1341, [2000] 4 CMLR 268, the CFI annulled the decision dismissing the complaint (Case T-77/95 *UFEX and others v Commission* [2000] ECR II-2167). The Commission re-examined the complaint but rejected it again. On appeal from that decision, the CFI upheld the Commission's rejection on the ground of lack of Community interest: see Case T-60/05 *Union française de l'express (UFEX) v Commission* [2007] ECR II-3397, [2008] 5 CMLR 580.

Lack of Community interest. In Case T-60/05 *Union française de l'express (UFEX)* **13.072** *v Commission* [2007] ECR II-3397, [2008] 5 CMLR 580 the CFI interpreted paras 93 and 95 of the earlier ECJ judgment in Case C-119/97 P *Ufex v Commission* in holding that the Commission was obliged to consider the seriousness and duration of an alleged infringement, even where the Commission found that the conduct complained of had terminated some time earlier and had no continuing anti-competitive effects. However, the CFI confirmed that it is possible for the Commission to take account of the seriousness and duration of the alleged infringement in assessing the Community interest in pursuing the complaint without determining the existence and precise characteristics of the alleged infringement: see paras 70 *et seq*. The CFI also held (a) that the Commission was entitled to assess the existence of a Community interest at the date of its decision re-examining the complaint (following the various appeals) rather than as at the time of the original complaint: para 122; and (b) that the difficulty of being able to establish an infringement to the requisite legal standard in order to adopt a decision is a matter which may be taken into account in the context of the assessment of the Community interest.

The criteria listed in (a) and (c) of para 13.072 were particularly relevant in the Commission's decision to reject a complaint about charges imposed by Athens International Airport for various groundhandling services: COMP/38.469 *Athens International Airport*, decn of 2 May 2005. The decision was upheld on appeal: Case T-306/05 *Scippacercola and Terezakis v Commission* [2008] ECR II-4*, [2008] 4 CMLR 1418 (further appeal dismissed Case C-159/08 P, Order of 25 March 2009).

Note that the question whether there is a serious impediment to intra-Community trade (which is the criterion that the Commission may apply when deciding whether there is a Community interest in investigating a particular complaint) is different from the question whether the conduct affects trade between Member States: see Case C-425/07 P *AEPI v Commission*, judgment of 23 April 2009, paras 49 *et seq* (on appeal from Case T-229/05 referred to in fn 338).

13.073 **Complainant's rights after initiation of procedure.** Conversely, even if the complaint is withdrawn, the Commission may still proceed to an infringement decision and impose a fine: see, eg COMP/37.860 *Morgan Stanley/Visa International and Visa Europe*, decn of 3 October 2007. The case is on appeal: Case T-461/07 *Visa Europe and Visa International Service Association v Commission*, not yet decided.

The complainant's right to a non-confidential copy of the statement of objections does not apply where the new settlement procedure introduced by Regulation 622/2008 applies. In such a case the Commission must inform the complainant of the nature and subject-matter of the procedure: see amended version of Article 6.1 of Regulation 773/2004 substituted by Regulation 622/2008, OJ 2008 L171/3, [2008] 5 CMLR 1032 Article 1.2. The new settlement procedure is discussed in new paragraphs 13.113A–13.113D, below. Note that the complainant does not have access to settlement submissions: Notice on the Conduct of Settlement Procedures in cartel cases: OJ 2008 C167/1: Vol II, App B17, para 34.

6. Formal Procedure Prior to an Adverse Decision

(a) The nature of Commission proceedings

An 'administrative' procedure.   In COMP/37.990 *Intel*, decn of 13 May 2009 **13.075** the Commission responded to serious allegations of malfeasance and bias levelled by Intel at the case team. The Commission stated that it was under no obligation to take minutes of meetings it held with industry participants: para 40.

Presumption of innocence and burden of proof.   See also Case T-36/05 *Coats* **13.076** *Holdings Ltd v Commission* [2007] ECR II-110, [2008] 4 CMLR 45 where the CFI stated that any doubt in the mind of the Court must operate to the advantage of the addressee of the decision finding an infringement: 'Given the nature of the infringements in question and the nature and severity of the ensuing penalties, the principle of the presumption of innocence applies in particular to the procedures relating to infringements of the competition rules applicable to undertakings that may result in the imposition of fines or periodic penalty payments': para 70. Coats' appeal against this decision was dismissed: Case C-468/07 P [2009] 4 CMLR 301. However, in Case T-53/03 *BPB plc v Commission* [2008] ECR II-1333, [2008] 5 CMLR 1201 the CFI discussed the burden of proof on the Commission and expressly rejected the appellant's assertion that the Commission must adduce proof 'beyond reasonable doubt' of the existence of the infringement in cases where it imposes heavy fines: paras 61 *et seq*.

It is contrary to the presumption of innocence for the Commission to allege in the decision that an undertaking was party to a cartel at a time subject to the limitation period where there is no finding of infringement in the operative part of the decision and where, therefore, the undertaking could not challenge the allegation on appeal: Case T-474/04 *Pergan Hilfsstoffe für industrielle Prozesse GmbH v Commission* [2007] ECR II-4225, [2008] 4 CMLR 148, para 76.

In *Bookmakers' Afternoon Greyhound Services v Amalgamated Racing Ltd* [2009] EWCA Civ 750 the English Court of Appeal was considering a case where the agreement in question was *prima facie* contrary to Article 81(1) [now Article 101(1) TFEU] but a party sought to persuade the court that the restriction on competition was justified in the particular circumstances of the case. Where this happens, the Court said, the legal burden of proving an infringement of Article 81(1) remains with the party who so asserts but the evidential burden of demonstrating that the apparent restriction on competition is justified falls upon the undertaking advancing such assertion: para 393 (citing *The Racecourse Association v Office of Fair Trading* [2005] CAT 29 at paras 132–133).

13.078 **Delay.** The principles established in Case C-105/04 P *Nederlandse Federatieve Vereniging voor de Groothandel op Elektrotechnisch Gebied ('FEG') v Commission* [2006] ECR I-8725, [2006] 5 CMLR 1223 were applied in Case T-60/05 *Union française de l'express (UFEX) v Commission* [2007] ECR II-3397, [2008] 5 CMLR 580. The CFI reiterated that it is a general principle of Community law that the administrative procedure be completed within a reasonable time but found that no prejudice to the rights of the defence had been demonstrated: see para 55. As to the effect of delay on the penalty imposed see update to paragraph 13.180, below.

Fn 377. See also the approach of the Dutch courts in *AUV v NMa, Aesculaap v NMa*, judgments of the Trade and Industry Appeals Tribunal of 3 July 2008 (Cases AWB 06/526, etc, LJN: BD6629 & 6635) (although two years for the administrative proceedings by the Dutch Competition Authority was not in itself unreasonable, the fines were reduced by 20 per cent because the process had been lengthened by periods of unjustified delay by the Authority).

13.079 **Effect of unreasonable delay.** In Case T-60/05 *Union française de l'express (UFEX) v Commission* [2007] ECR II-3397, [2008] 5 CMLR 580 the Post Office, whose conduct was the subject of a complaint that the Commission had repeatedly rejected, argued that it would not be possible for it to defend itself properly if the Commission now commenced an investigation. The CFI held that since it was impossible to know what allegations would be made by the Commission if it decided to pursue the complaint, it was also impossible to know whether the Post Office would be prejudiced: para 57. The CFI also rejected the Post Office's argument that to be under continuous investigation is seriously damaging to it, 'in the sense of its departments being deployed for unproductive ends, incurring fruitless expenses and its competitors gaining access to a large amount of commercial information'.

13.080 **The right to be heard.** Article 11(1) of Regulation 773/2004 has been substituted by Regulation 622/2008, OJ 2008 L171/3, [2008] 5 CMLR 1032 Article 1.5. That Regulation introduces the new cartel settlement procedure into Regulation 773/2004: see Vol II, App B4. The new wording of Article 11(1) is identical save that it refers to parties to whom the Commission addresses a statement of objections rather than to parties to whom the Commission has addressed a statement of objections. It is not clear what difference in substance the amendment is intended to make.

13.081 **Hearing by 'an independent and impartial tribunal'.** The principle established in *Enso Española* was reiterated in Case T-54/03 *Lafarge v Commission* [2008] ECR II-120* (on appeal Case C-413/08 P, not yet decided).

(b) Initiation of procedure and the statement of objections

Initiation of proceedings.   In Case T-99/04 *AC-Treuhand AG v Commission*   **13.082**
[2008] ECR II-1501, [2008] 5 CMLR 962 the CFI referred to the two 'distinct
and successive' stages of the Commission's investigation of an infringement, the
preliminary investigation stage and the *inter partes* stage. The issue of the statement of objections marks the move from the first to the second and it is only in the
second stage that the rights of the defence are fully engaged. However, there are
some rights of the defence relevant to the preliminary stage also: paras 47 *et seq.*

As to the possible dates which trigger the initiation of proceedings, Article 2(1) of
Regulation 773/2004 has been amended so that a request that the parties express
their interest in engaging in settlement discussions is added to the other dates listed:
see Regulation 622/2008, OJ 2008 L171/3, [2008] 5 CMLR 1032, Article 1.1.
The new settlement procedure introduced by Regulation 622/2008 is discussed
in new paragraphs 13.113A–13.113D, below.

The statement of objections: its purpose and status.   In Case C-413/06 P   **13.083**
Bertelsmann AG and Sony Corporation of America v Impala and Commission [2008]
ECR I-4951 the ECJ laid down some important principles regarding the relationship between the facts as set out in the statement of objections and the facts as
set out ultimately in the decision. Although this was in the context of a statement
of objections issued under the Merger Regulation, there is nothing to suggest that
it does not also apply to proceedings under Regulation 1/2003. The ECJ stressed
that the statement of objections is a provisional account of the facts and is subject
to amendments in the light of the observations submitted to it by the parties
and subsequent findings of fact: paras 63 *et seq.* The ECJ held that the CFI had
erred in law in criticising inconsistencies between the facts as set out in the
Commission's statement of objections and the findings in the decision. The ECJ
held that the CFI can refer to the statement of objections in order to interpret a
decision of the Commission, particularly as regards the examination of its factual
basis. But the CFI had gone beyond what was permissible by treating what it
termed 'findings of fact made previously' in that statement as being more reliable
and more conclusive than the findings set out in the contested decision itself: see
paras 69 *et seq.*

Article 10(1) of Reg 773/2004 was amended so that it now does not require the
Commission to inform the persons concerned of the objections raised against
them in writing. However, the statement of objections, once issued must be sent
in writing to each party against whom objections are raised. The purpose of the
amendment is to allow for early disclosure of the Commission's concerns and a
response to that disclosure by the parties prior to the issue of the statement of
objections as part of the settlement procedure now incorporated into Regulation
773/2004: see Regulation 622/2008, OJ 2008 L171/3, [2008] 5 CMLR 1032

Article 1.3 and Recital (2). The new settlement procedure introduced by Regulation 622/2008 is discussed in new paragraphs 13.113A–13.113D, below.

Fn 410. On appeal from the CFI's decision in Case T-351/03, the ECJ confirmed that the statement of objections is essential to the application of the principle of respect for the rights of the defence: para 163. The ECJ, however, overturned the CFI's judgment in part on the basis that there was no adequate causal link between the manifest and serious breach of the rights of the defence and the loss for which compensation had been awarded by the CFI: Case C-440/07 P *Commission v Schneider Electric*, judgment of 16 July 2009.

13.084 **Contents of the statement of objections.**   The statement of objections must also make clear whether it is alleged that the undertaking was the leader of a cartel if the Commission intends to increase the amount of the fine to be imposed on this ground: Case T-410/03 *Hoechst GmbH v Commission* [2008] ECR II-881, [2008] 5 CMLR 839, paras 423 *et seq*.

The ECJ has held that it is important that the statement of objections indicates in what capacity allegations are being made against a recipient: see Cases C-322/07 P, etc, *Papierfabrik August Koehler AG and Bolloré SA v Commission*, judgment of 3 September 2009, [2009] 5 CMLR 2301. Bolloré had been found liable in the Commission's decision both as the parent company of Copiograph and because of its own independent involvement in the *Carbonless paper* cartel. The CFI had found that the statement of objections had not made the latter allegations clear but declined to annul the decision on the grounds that Bolloré had had an opportunity to exercise its rights of defence as regards the former allegation. The ECJ held that the CFI had erred in law in failing to draw any legal conclusion from its finding that Bolloré's rights of defence had not been observed and annulled the whole of the contested decision so far as it concerned Bolloré.

As regards what must be included if the Commission intends to impose a fine: see Cases C-101 & 110/07 P *Coop de France bétail et viande and FNSEA v Commission* [2009] 4 CMLR 743, paras 47 *et seq*: it is not appropriate for the Commission to give an indication of the level of fine proposed since this anticipates the Commission's decision. But the Commission must indicate expressly that it will consider whether it is appropriate to impose fines on the undertakings concerned and must set out the principal elements of fact and of law that may give rise to a fine, such as the gravity and the duration of the alleged infringement and the fact that it has been committed 'intentionally or negligently'.

ADM's appeal referred to in fn 416 has now been decided: Case C-511/06 P *Archer Daniels Midland v Commission*, judgment of 9 July 2009. The ECJ held that it was not necessary for the statement of objections to spell out the details of why the Commission intended to classify ADM as the leader of the cartel for the purposes of the fine. But the Commission was nonetheless required, at the very least, to state those facts in the statement of objections. The CFI had held that it was sufficient that the facts on which the Commission later relied in the decision were contained in documents that had been annexed to the statement of objections even though they had not been referred to in the body of the statement of objections. The ECJ held that in the circumstances of the case, this was not sufficient to enable ADM to dispute those facts and therefore to exercise its rights of defence effectively: para 94.

Where the statement of objections follows the adoption of the settlement procedure now incorporated into Regulation 773/2004 by Regulation 622/2008, OJ 2008 L171/3, [2008] 5 CMLR 1032, it will reflect the infringement admitted by the parties.

Fn 423. This point was confirmed by the ECJ in Case C-511/06 P *Archer Daniels Midland v Commission*, judgment of 9 July 2009, para 69.

Fn 425. Following the judgment in *ARBED*, the Commission retook the decision condemning the steel beams cartel: an appeal against that decision by ARBED was dismissed but the decision was annulled as against two of the addressees on the basis that the decision was adopted outside the limitation period: Case T-405/06 *Arcelor Mittal v Commission*, judgment of 31 March 2009 (on further appeal Case C-201/09 P, not yet decided).

Reply to the statement of objections.   **Fn 440.** See also Case T-73/04 *Le Carbone-* **13.086** *Lorraine v Commission*, judgment of 8 October 2008 where the CFI held that it was open to the applicant to raise on appeal a factor in mitigation of the fine even though this had not been raised in its reply to the statement of objections: para 194. A further appeal was dismissed: Case C-554/08 P, judgment of 12 November 2009.

As to the effect of factual admissions in the reply to the statement of objections referred to in fn 440, see now Case T-69/04 *Schunk GmbH v Commission* [2009] 4 CMLR 2. Some of the points raised by Schunk in relation to the fine included various challenges to the findings of infringement. The Commission argued that these were inadmissible because Schunk had made admissions in its response to the statement of objections and should not be allowed to challenge them for the first time before the Court. The CFI agreed, holding that it is on the basis of the replies to the statement of objections that the Commission has to adopt its position regarding the future course of the administrative procedure: paras 79 *et seq*.

As to disclosure of one alleged cartel member's reply to the statement of objections to the other undertakings being investigated see Case T-53/03 *BPB plc v Commission* [2008] ECR II-1333, [2008] 5 CMLR 1201, para 41.

(c) **Access to the file**

13.088 **Access to the file.** In cases where the cartel settlement procedure in Article 10a of Regulation 773/2004 is adopted, the Commission will, on request, disclose a limited number of documents on the file to the parties involved in settlement discussions. Those parties will then confirm to the Commission in their settlement submissions that they will only require access to the file if the statement of objections does not reflect the content of their settlement submissions: see Article 15(1a) inserted by Regulation 622/2008, OJ 2008 L171/3, [2008] 5 CMLR 1032 Article 1.7. The new settlement procedure introduced by Regulation 622/2008 is discussed in new paragraphs 13.113A–13.113D, below.

Fn 448. See also Case T-53/03 *BPB plc v Commission* [2008] ECR II-1333, [2008] 5 CMLR 1201, para 31.

13.091 **Exculpatory and incriminating documents.** The principles set out in this paragraph and derived from *Aalborg Portland v Commission* were applied in Case T-410/03 *Hoechst GmbH v Commission* [2008] ECR II-881, [2008] 5 CMLR 839, paras 145–148.

In Case T-53/03 *BPB plc v Commission* [2008] ECR II-1333, [2008] 5 CMLR 1201 the CFI reiterated that 'A document can be regarded as a document that incriminates an applicant only where it is used by the Commission to support a finding of an infringement in which that party is alleged to have participated': para 32. The CFI went on to apply the principles laid down in *Aalborg Portland* as to when non-disclosure of an incriminating document affects the validity of the decision: paras 43–45.

13.093 **The documents to which access is granted.** **Fn 480.** See also Case T-410/03 *Hoechst GmbH v Commission* [2008] ECR II-881, [2008] 5 CMLR 839, para 147: 'it should be emphasised that it is not solely for the Commission, . . . to determine the documents which are of use to the defence of the undertakings concerned. However, the Commission may exclude from the administrative procedure the evidence which has no relation to the allegations of fact and of law in the statement of objections and which therefore has no relevance to the investigation. An applicant cannot properly put forward as a ground of annulment the fact that irrelevant documents were not communicated to it'.

13.094 **Internal Commission documents.** In Case T-410/03 *Hoechst GmbH v Commission* [2008] ECR II-881, [2008] 5 CMLR 839, the CFI confirmed that the Commission's internal documents can be made available only if the exceptional circumstances of the case so require 'on the basis of serious indicia which it is for the party concerned to supply': para 165. The Court found that there were no serious indicia in this case, but for the sake of completeness the Court called for the internal records of phone conversations which Hoechst had been asking for and ascertained – without disclosing them to the parties – that they were not relevant to the case. The Court returned the records to the Commission and ordered that they be removed from the file: para 170.

Business secrets and other confidential information.   The Commission cannot **13.095**
make a general reference to confidentiality to justify a total refusal to disclose documents in its file. The right of undertakings to protect their business secrets must be balanced against the safeguarding of the right of an undertaking being investigated to have access to the whole of the file: Case T-410/03 *Hoechst GmbH v Commission* [2008] ECR II-881, [2008] 5 CMLR 839, para 153. In that case where Hoechst had expressly requested sight of a particular letter sent by another alleged cartel member, the Commission had provided it with almost all the 101 pages blanked out. The CFI held that this was tantamount to not providing the letter at all and that the Commission ought to have drawn up a non-confidential version of the documents in issue or, if that proved difficult, to have prepared a list of the documents concerned and a sufficiently precise non-confidential summary of their content: para 154. The CFI adopted measures of organisation which gave Hoechst access to a better non-confidential version of the document so that they could make submissions as to how it might have affected their case.

Other confidential documents.   As regards information provided to the **13.096**
Commission on condition of anonymity see Case T-53/03 *BPB plc v Commission* [2008] ECR II-1333, [2008] 5 CMLR 1201, paras 31–38.

Provision of documents from the file to third parties.   As regards the applica- **13.100**
tion of Regulation 1049/2001 in competition cases see Case T-403/05 *My Travel Group v Commission* [2008] 3 CMLR 1517. Following the annulment of the Commission's decision in Case T-342/99 *Airtours v Commission*, the Commission established a working group of officials of DG Comp to consider whether it was appropriate to bring an appeal against that judgment and to assess the implications of that judgment on procedures for merger control. The report of the working group was presented to the Commissioner for Competition. In 2003 Airtours, now renamed MyTravel, brought an action for damages arising from the Commission's handling of the concentration. In 2005, MyTravel requested documents under Regulation 1049/2001 namely the working group report, the working papers and other internal documents. The Commission granted access to a limited number of the documents but refused to supply others relying on three exceptions: the protection of the decision-making process; the protection of inspections, investigations and audit; and the protection of court proceedings and legal advice. The CFI examined only the first and third of these exceptions and considered in respect of each document whether the Commission had committed an error of assessment in concluding that the relevant protection would be seriously undermined by disclosure and then whether it had erred in analysing the existence

of an overriding public interest. The CFI upheld the Commission's rejection of the request in relation to all but one of the documents requested. The case is on appeal: Case C-506/08 P, not yet decided. See also Case T-194/04 *Bavarian Lager Co v Commission* [2007] ECR II-4523 where the CFI considered the application of Regulation 1049/2001 in relation to personal data (on appeal Case 28/08 P, not yet decided).

The Commission has indicated that normally public disclosure of documents and written and recorded statements received in the context of the cartel settlement procedure would undermine the public interest within the meaning of Article 4 of Regulation 1049/2001: see Notice on the Conduct of Settlement Procedures in cartel cases, OJ 2008 C167/1: Vol II, App B17, para 40. For the settlement procedure generally see new paragraphs 13.113A–13.113D, below.

(d) The hearing and subsequently

13.101 **Hearings.** Article 12 of Regulation 773/2004 has been substituted by Regulation 622/2008, OJ 2008 L171/3, [2008] 5 CMLR 1032, Article. 1.6. That Regulation introduces the new cartel settlement procedure into Regulation 773/2004. The new wording of Article 12 provides that when making settlement submissions, the parties should confirm that they will only require an oral hearing if the statement of objections does not reflect the content of their settlement submissions. For the settlement procedure generally see new paragraphs 13.113A–13.113D, below.

13.102 **Hearing Officer.** The Hearing Officer may also be called upon by parties involved in the cartel settlement procedure: see Notice on the Conduct of Settlement Procedures in cartel cases, OJ 2008 C167/1: Vol II, App B17, para 18. For the settlement procedure generally see new paragraphs 13.113A–13.113D, below.

13.103 **Conduct of the hearing.** The fact that a hearing in a Dutch case is conducted in English is not a breach of the rights of the defence unless the parties can show that they were prejudiced by this: Case T-151/05 *Nederlandse Vakbond Varkenshouders (NVV) v Commission* [2009] 5 CMLR 1613, para 211.

13.109 **Rules of Procedure on adoption of decisions.** Note that in Case T-192/07 *Comité de défense de la viticulture charentaise v Commission*, not yet decided, the applicant has challenged a decision rejecting a complaint on the grounds, *inter alia* of lack of competence of the Commission member who was the signatory to the contested measure, when he signed it 'on behalf of the Commission'.

13.112 **Publication of decisions.** In Case T-474/04 *Pergan Hilfsstoffe für industrielle Prozesse GmbH v Commission* [2007] ECR II-4225, [2008] 4 CMLR 148 the applicant challenged the fact that the Commission had stated in the published decision that the applicant had been involved in the organic peroxides cartel at an early stage but that there had been insufficient evidence of their involvement in the cartel at a time not barred by the limitation period. The Court analysed the reference in Article 21 of Regulation 17 (now Article 30 of Regulation 1/2003) to the need to protect 'business secrets' and found that the obligation to redact in fact extended not only to business secrets but to other kinds of confidential information covered by Article 287 EC [now Article 339 TFEU] (see para 64 of the judgment). The applicant had not been an addressee of the decision and so any challenge to the allegation of involvement in the cartel would have been inadmissible before the CFI. The Court held that in these circumstances the allegation was contrary to the presumption of innocence and infringed the protection of professional secrecy. The Hearing Officer's decision to allow the Commission to include the allegation was annulled.

7. Commitments and Settlement

Cartel settlement.   The Commission has established a settlement procedure **13.113A** intended to enable it to handle cartel cases more quickly and efficiently. Regulation 773/2004 has been amended by Regulation 622/2008, OJ 2008 L171/3, [2008] 5 CMLR 1032 Article 1.4 to incorporate this procedure as Article 10a of Regulation 773/2004: see Vol II, App B4. The Commission has also issued a Notice on the Conduct of Settlement Procedures in cartel cases, explaining how the procedure will operate: see OJ 2008 C167/1: Vol II, App B17. See Tierno Centella, 'The new settlement procedure in selected cartel cases' (2008) 3 Competition Policy Newsletter 30.

Commencement of the settlement procedure.   After proceedings have been **13.113B** initiated, the Commission may set a time limit for the parties to indicate in writing whether they are prepared to discuss settlement (Article 10a(1)). The Notice sets out the factors that the Commission will take into account in deciding whether a case is suitable for the settlement procedure (Notice, para 5). Those then taking part in the settlement discussions may be informed by the Commission of the objections it envisages raising against them and the evidence relied on. They may also request non-confidential versions of documents on the file so far as relevant to enable the party to ascertain its position *vis-à-vis* the cartel and the range of potential fines. The parties to the proceedings may not disclose to any third party in any jurisdiction the contents of the discussions or of the documents to which they have had access.

Cartel settlement: settlement submissions and the statement of objections.   **13.113C** When progress made during the settlement discussions leads the Commission to conclude that procedural efficiencies are likely to be achieved, the Commission will set a deadline for final settlement submissions. In the submissions the parties make a formal request to settle by (i) acknowledging in clear and unequivocal terms the parties' liability for the infringement; (ii) indicating the maximum amount of the fine which the parties would accept; (iii) confirming that they have been sufficiently informed of the Commission's objections and have been given sufficient opportunity to make known their views; (iv) confirming that they do not want access to the file or an oral hearing provided that the settlement submissions are reflected in the statement of objections; and (v) agreeing to receive the statement of objections and the decision in one of the Community languages (Notice, para 20). The Commission will then issue a statement of objections which reflects the settlement submissions and the parties' reply is limited to confirming that this is the case.

13.113D **Cartel settlement: other procedural aspects.** Once the parties have confirmed that the statement of objections reflects the settlement submissions, the Commission proceeds immediately to the adoption of the final decision (Notice, para 28). If the statement of objections does not reflect the settlement submissions, the acknowledgements made by the parties are deemed to be withdrawn and cannot be used in evidence against any of the parties (Notice, para 27). Similarly, if the final decision is not going to endorse the settlement, a new statement of objections will be issued and the full rights of the defence will be granted (Notice, para 29). If the Commission decides to reward a party for settlement, the fine will be reduced by 10 per cent and this reduction will be added to the leniency reduction where the Leniency Notice also applies (Notice, paras 32 and 33). Article 17 of Regulation 773/2004 has been amended to include time limits for various stages in the settlement process: Regulation 622/2008, Article 1.8. The Notice sets out how settlement submissions will be protected from disclosure: see paras 35–40. The settlement procedure entered into force on 1 July 2008 (Regulation 622/2008, Article 2).

See also *Crest Nicholson v Office of Fair Trading* [2009] EWHC 1875 (Admin) where the application of a 'Fast Track Offer' procedure established by the Office of Fair Trading for a particular investigation into collusion in the construction industry was successfully challenged on the basis that it had not been applied fairly to the applicant.

13.114 **Article 9 of Regulation 1/2003.** The Commission has accepted commitments in the following cases:

(1) COMP/39.388 & 39.389 *E.ON German electricity markets*, decn of 26 November 2008: commitments to divest a substantial amount of electricity generation capacity and E.ON's transmission business. These commitments (the text of which runs to almost 150 pages) were described by the Commission as structural remedies to address the concerns arising from E.ON's vertically integrated business. Ancillary commitments accepted were aimed at preserving the viability of the business to be divested: hold-separate obligations,

ring fencing, non-solicitation, due diligence and reporting obligations involving the appointment of a Monitoring Trustee.

(2) COMP/39.142 *Toyota*, decn of 13 September 2007 and three other car manufacturers: commitments to make technical repair information available to independent repairers: Press Release IP/07/1332 (13 September 2007).

(3) COMP/39.402 *RWE (gas transmission services)*, decn of 18 March 2009, [2009] 5 CMLR 1667: commitment from RWE to divest its entire high pressure West German gas transmission network to allay Commission concerns about access to the network.

(4) COMP/37.966 *Distrigas*, decn of 11 October 2007: commitments to remove concerns that long-term supply agreements entered into by Distrigas significantly foreclosed the relevant market in a way that could constitute an abuse of its dominant position in the market for the supply of gas to large customers in Belgium.

Fn 607. Note that the Commission has appealed against the CFI's judgment in *Alrosa*: Case C-441/07 P *Commission v Alrosa*, not yet decided.

9. Declarations of Infringement and Orders to Terminate

Declaratory decisions.   **Fn 656.** See also COMP/37.860 *Morgan Stanley/Visa*   **13.124** *International and Visa Europe*, decn of 3 October 2007 where the infringing conduct (the exclusion of Morgan Stanley from the Visa payment card network) had ceased in 2006 and Morgan Stanley had withdrawn its complaint in accordance with its settlement agreement with Visa. The Commission held that it still had a legitimate interest in adopting a decision because (i) Visa continued to deny that their behaviour was contrary to Article 81(1) [now Article 101(1) TFEU]; (ii) it was important for the proper functioning of the single market for payments that anti-competitive practices committed by market players were not tolerated; and (iii) the Commission wished to impose a fine. The case is on appeal: Case T-461/07 *Visa Europe and Visa International Service Association v Commission*, not yet decided.

'Like effect' orders.   In Case T-410/03 *Hoechst GmbH v Commission* [2008]   **13.127** ECR II-881, [2008] 5 CMLR 839, Hoechst complained that it was wrong for the Commission to include an order prohibiting future similar conduct because Hoechst had left the sorbates market several years earlier. The CFI rejected this argument, holding that the prohibition 'is by nature preventive and does not depend on the situation of the undertakings concerned at the time of adoption of the Decision': para 200. The CFI does not appear thereby to be saying that the order would apply to similar conduct in a market other than the sorbates market.

13.128 **Power to order positive action.**   In COMP/34.579 *MasterCard MIF charges*, decn of 19 December 2007, where the Commission found that the imposition of a particular fee was unlawful, the Commission noted that the cost reduction made possible by the removal of the fee should be passed on to the customer and this was only likely to happen if the customer was aware that lower prices were now possible. The Commission therefore ordered MasterCard to publicise the Commission's decision on the front page of each of its country-specific websites: para 766. The case is on appeal: Case T-111/08, not yet decided.

A further appeal in *Der Grüne Punkt* was dismissed: Case C-385/07 P *Der Grüne Punkt – Duales System Deutschland v Commission*, judgment of 16 July 2009, [2009] 5 CMLR 2215.

10. Fines for Substantive Infringements

(b) Intentional or negligent infringement

13.138 **'Intentionally'.**   Fn 717. The appeal referred to has now been decided: Case T-85/06 *General Química v Commission*, judgment of 18 December 2008 (on further appeal Case C-90/09 P, not yet decided).

(c) The calculation of the fine

13.144 **Generally.**   In Case T-69/04 *Schunk GmbH v Commission* [2009] 4 CMLR 2 the Commission submitted that the amount of the fine imposed should be increased because the applicant had attempted to challenge facts which it had admitted during the investigation. The CFI rejected this submission holding that the amount of a fine can be determined only on the basis of the gravity and duration of the infringement. The fact that the Commission had had to prepare for the appeal on the basis that the applicant might be allowed to withdraw its previous admissions did not justify an increase of that fine. The expenses incurred by the Commission as a result of the proceedings before the Court must only be taken into account when applying the provisions of the Rules of Procedure relating to costs: para 262.

13.145 **Discretion of the Commission.**   In Case T-69/04 *Schunk GmbH v Commission* [2009] 4 CMLR 2 the CFI rejected a submission that the discretion conferred on the Commission was so wide that the power to fine infringed the principle of legal certainty. The CFI considered the jurisprudence of the Court of Human Rights on Article 7 ECHR and concluded that the fact that a law confers a discretion is not in itself inconsistent with the requirement of foreseeability, provided that the scope of the discretion and the manner of its exercise are indicated with sufficient clarity, having regard to the legitimate aim in question, to give the individual adequate protection against arbitrary interference. The Court held that the Commission's power to fine did not breach the principle: paras 28–50. See similarly, Case C-266/06 P *Degussa v Commission*, judgment of 22 May 2008.

As to the level of detail which the Commission must set out in the decision as regards the computation of the fine, the CFI has emphasised that too much detail may be counterproductive: 'it is important to ensure that fines are not easily foreseeable by economic operators. If the Commission were required to indicate in its decision the figures relating to the method of calculating the amount of fines, the deterrent effect of those fines would be undermined. If the amount of the fine were the result of a calculation which followed a simple arithmetical formula, undertakings would be able to predict the possible penalty and to compare it with the profit that they would derive from the infringement of the competition rules': see Case T-53/03 *BPB plc v Commission* [2008] ECR II-1333, [2008] 5 CMLR 1201, para 336.

A general argument that the total fine imposed on the applicant was disproportionate because it was more than five times the total value of the EEA market in the relevant product was rejected by the CFI in Case T-410/03 *Hoechst GmbH v Commission* [2008] ECR II-881, [2008] 5 CMLR 839, para 342.

Fn 755. The same point was made by the CFI in Case T-68/04 *SGL Carbon AG v Commission* [2009] 4 CMLR 7, paras 43–44. A further appeal was dismissed: Case C-564/08 P, judgment of 12 November 2009.

Retroactive application of revised Guidelines.   The retrospective application of   **13.147** the new fining Guidelines has now been confirmed several times: see, eg Case C-510/06 P *Archer Daniels Midland v Commission (sodium gluconate)* [2009] 4 CMLR 889, para 59.

(d) Basic amount

The basic amount: the 2006 Guidelines on Fines.   In Case C-510/06 P *Archer*   **13.148** *Daniels Midland v Commission (sodium gluconate)* [2009] 4 CMLR 889 (a case under the 1998 Guidelines) the ECJ held that it is permissible to take into account both the undertaking's overall turnover as an indication, however approximate and imperfect, of the size of the undertaking and its economic strength, and that part of the turnover which derives from the goods which are the subject of the infringement and which therefore is capable of giving an indication of the scale of the infringement. The Court stated that it is important not to confer on one or other of those figures an importance which is disproportionate. The Court said that there is no general principle that the penalty must be proportionate to the undertaking's turnover from sales of the product in respect of which the infringement was committed: para 75.

13.149 **Value of sales.** In Case T-127/04 *KM Europa Metal v Commission* [2009] 4 CMLR 1574 the CFI rejected an argument that because a large element of the relevant product, namely industrial copper tubes, was determined by the price of copper and that commodity price was determined on the London Metal Exchange by the buyers of the tubes, the Commission should have deducted the cost of the copper from the parties' turnover before arriving at the starting point for the fine. The CFI held that the fact that the price of copper constitutes an important part of the final price of industrial tubes or that the risk of fluctuations of copper prices is far higher than for other raw materials were irrelevant to the calculation: paras 89 *et seq*. The CFI also rejected an argument that profits rather than turnover should be used to calculate the basic amount of the fine. The CFI stated that it is undeniable that, as a factor for assessing the seriousness of the infringement, the turnover of an undertaking of a market is necessarily vague and imperfect. It does not distinguish between sectors with a high added value and those with a low added value, or between undertakings which are profitable and those which are less so. However, despite its approximate nature, turnover is an adequate criterion for assessing the size and economic power of the undertakings concerned: para 93. On further appeal: Case C-272/09 P, not yet decided.

In two recent cases the Commission has applied point 18 of the 2006 Guidelines on Fines. This provides a calculation method for assessing the value of sales for cartels that are geographically wider than the EEA: COMP/39.180 *Aluminium Fluoride*, decn of 25 June 2008 (on appeal: Case T-406/08 *ICF v Commission*, not yet decided) and COMP/39.406 *Marine Hoses*, decn of 28 January 2009, para 432 (on appeal: Cases T-146, 147, 148, 154/09, not yet decided).

Note that in COMP/39.125 *Car glass*, decn of 12 November 2008 the Commission took the unusual step of limiting, for part of the period covered by the fine, the value of sales to those sales to car manufacturers in respect of which the Commission had direct evidence of collusion. This applied both to a 'roll out phase' trial period at the start of the collusion when the Commission thought the carglass suppliers rigged the bids only within selected large accounts and to the end phase of the cartel when collusion broke down. Nonetheless, the fine imposed on St Gobain was the largest ever imposed on a single company for cartel activity. The decision is on appeal: Cases T-56, 68, 72, 73/09, not yet decided.

13.152 **Basic amount: the 1998 and 2006 Guidelines on Fines compared.** **Fn 786.** For a case where there was a considerable disparity in the size of the undertakings fined, see Case T-68/04 *SGL Carbon AG v Commission* [2009] 4 CMLR 7. A further appeal was dismissed: Case C-564/08 P, judgment of 12 November 2009.

13.153 **Hard-core cartels.** In Case T-53/03 *BPB plc v Commission* [2008] ECR II-1333, [2008] 5 CMLR 1201 (a case under the 1998 Guidelines) the CFI held that the Commission was entitled to refer to the actual impact on the market of a cartel having an anti-competitive object even though the Commission did not quantify that impact or provide any assessment in figures in this respect. The actual impact of a cartel on the market was sufficiently demonstrated if the Commission provides specific and credible evidence indicating with reasonable probability that the cartel had an impact on the market.

Basic amount: seriousness of the infringements.   **Fn 796.** See also Case T-127/   **13.154**
04 *KM Europa Metal v Commission* [2009] 4 CMLR 1574 where the CFI confirmed that the actual impact of a cartel on the market is sufficiently demonstrated if the Commission can provide specific and credible evidence indicating with reasonable probability that the cartel had an impact on the market: para 68. On further appeal: Case C-272/09 P, not yet decided. Note that under the 1998 Guidelines (para 1.A) the assessment of the gravity of the infringement could take into account its actual impact on the market 'where this can be measured'. The importance of that qualification was noted in Case C-511/06 P *Archer Daniels Midland v Commission (citric acid)*, judgment of 9 July 2009, para 125. In Case C-534/07 P *Prym and Prym Consumer v Commission*, judgment of 3 September 2009, [2009] 5 CMLR 2377 the ECJ held that the CFI had been right to reduce the fine imposed on Prym on the basis that the Commission had not given adequate reasons for concluding that the cartel had had an actual impact on the market. The ECJ held that the Commission did not have to demonstrate actual impact in order to classify the infringement as 'very serious' under the 1998 Guidelines. But if the Commission wished to increase the fine beyond the minimum then applicable to a very serious infringement, on the grounds that the cartel had an actual impact on the market, it could not simply assume that the cartel had had such an effect because it had been implemented: 'it cannot just put forward a mere presumption but . . . must provide specific, credible and adequate evidence with which to assess what actual influence the infringement may have had on competition in that market': para 82. The 2006 Guidelines do not include the 'where this can be measured' phrase.

Fn 793. The appeal referred to has now been decided: Case T-450/05 *Automobiles Peugeot SA and Peugeot Nederland NV*, judgment of 9 July 2009. The CFI reduced the fine imposed because, in finding that the restrictions had led to a reduction in exports, the Commission had not taken into account the possible effect of relative changes in price on the level of exports.

Legal considerations affecting duration.   In COMP/38.113 *Prokent-Tomra*,   **13.156**
decn of 29 March 2006, [2009] 4 CMLR 101 (a case under Article 82) the Commission treated the duration of the infringement as five years even though it was not claimed that all the abusive components identified in the decision existed throughout the entire period in question in each of the national markets investigated. The single fine imposed dealt globally with all of the infringements established,

which together covered the entire period in question. The fact that the infringement did not always cover the entire period in each of the national markets considered, and that within each national market the intensity of the infringement may have varied over time, was taken into account in establishing the basic amount of the fine (€16 million): para 418. The case is on appeal Case T-155/06 *Tomra Systems*, not yet decided.

Fn 805. In COMP/37.860 *Morgan Stanley/Visa International and Visa Europe*, decn of 3 October 2007 the Commission found that a rule applied by Visa to exclude its competitor Morgan Stanley from the Visa payment card network infringed Article 81 [now Article 101 TFEU]. The Rule had been notified to the Commission in 1990. The Commission noted that the immunity from fines conferred by notification lapsed once Regulation 1/2003 came into force. Further, Visa could not sustain a claim of legitimate expectation of immunity from fines for the period after the statement of objections was delivered since that statement clearly indicated that the Commission was envisaging imposing a fine: para 341. A fine was imposed starting with the date on which the statement of objections was issued and ending when the infringing conduct ceased. The case is on appeal: Case T-461/07 *Visa Europe and Visa International Service Association v Commission*, not yet decided.

(e) Aggravating and mitigating circumstances and deterrence

13.158 **Generally.** In Case T-127/04 *KM Europa Metal v Commission* [2009] 4 CMLR 1574 the CFI confirmed that the mere fact that the Commission has in its previous decisions granted a certain rate of reduction for specific conduct does not imply that it is required to grant the same proportionate reduction when assessing similar conduct in a subsequent administrative procedure: para 140. On further appeal: Case C-272/09 P, not yet decided.

13.160 **Repeat infringements.** In Case T-122/04 *Outokumpu Oyj v Commission* [2009] 5 CMLR 1553 the CFI held that the Commission was right to treat a decision taken under the ECSC Treaty as a previous infringement for this purpose and to do so even though no fine had been imposed in the previous case because of the unusual circumstances surrounding the earlier infringement: paras 55 *et seq*.

In COMP/38.638 *Butadiene Rubber and Emulsion Styrene Butadiene Rubber*, decn of 29 November 2006, [2009] 4 CMLR 421 the Commission stated that in order to increase a fine on the basis of an earlier infringement, it is irrelevant whether the infringement is committed in a different business sector or in respect of a different product. The requirement that the infringements must be 'similar' is satisfied by the fact that the previous decisions cited and this decision concern collusion on prices. As for the requirement that the 'person' must be the same, this requirement is satisfied when the same undertaking commits the infringements concerned. There is no requirement that the legal entities within the undertaking, products and personnel should be the same in all decisions. Internal reorganisations cannot have any effect on the assessment of the existence of this aggravating circumstance: para 488.

Fn 813. The same point was made in Cases T-101 & 111/05 *BASF AG and UCB SA v Commission* [2007] ECR II-4949, [2008] 4 CMLR 347, para 67. See also Case T-53/03 *BPB plc v Commission* [2008] ECR II-1333, [2008] 5 CMLR 1201, para 384 (a case under the 1998 Guidelines).

Fn 814. The same point was made in *BASF and UCB*, above, para 64 where the CFI said that it is sufficient if the previous infringement was under the same provision of the EC Treaty. See also Case T-410/03 *Hoechst GmbH v Commission* [2008] ECR II-881, [2008] 5 CMLR 839, para 474.

Refusal to cooperate with Commission investigation.   In COMP/38.432   **13.161**
Professional Videotape, decn of 20 November 2007, [2008] 5 CMLR 122, Sony's fine was increased by 30 per cent because of conduct during the Commission's visit (refusal to answer questions and shredding of documents). The Commission held that it was irrelevant whether the conduct had any effect on the investigation (para 221) or that the time limit for taking separate action under Article 23 of Regulation 1/2003 had expired (para 224).

Fn 818. The appeals from the *Nintendo* decision have now been decided: Case T-13/03 *Nintendo* [2009] 5 CMLR 1421 (the CFI upheld the Commission's imposition of a 25 per cent increase in the fine because Nintendo had continued with the infringement after the Commission investigation had started: para 144); Case T-18/03 *CD-Contact Data v Commission*, judgment of 30 April 2009 (fine reduced) (on further appeal: Case C-260/09P *Activision Blizzard Germany*, not yet decided); Case T-12/03 *Itochu* [2009] 5 CMLR 1375 (appeal dismissed); Case T-398/02 *Linea Gig* (removed from register 2 May 2005). No issue arose in the appeals concerning the uplift imposed on John Menzies for inaccurate answers.

'Ring leaders' of infringements and retaliatory measures.   In Case T-13/03   **13.162**
Nintendo and Nintendo Europe v Commission [2009] 5 CMLR 1421 which concerned a vertical agreement, the CFI held that in order to classify an undertaking as a 'leader', it is not necessary to prove that, in the absence of the role played by that undertaking, the infringement committed would have been less serious. The CFI also rejected Nintendo's argument that a role of leader or instigator of the infringement can be found only in restrictive horizontal agreements. The fact that, in the case of vertical agreements, the role of leader or instigator generally merges with that of the manufacturer (rather than the distributors) does not preclude an increase of the fine on this ground: para 131.

In Case T-410/03 *Hoechst GmbH v Commission* [2008] ECR II-881, [2008] 5 CMLR 839 the CFI held that the elements relied on by the Commission to establish that Hoechst had been the ring leader were not sufficiently drawn together in the statement of objections to make clear to Hoechst that this aggravating factor was alleged against it. Hoechst was thus not placed in a position to adopt an effective defence and the fine was reduced to strip out that element: paras 423 *et seq*. See also the update to paragraph 13.084, above.

Fn 819. The appeal in Case T-492/04 *Jungbunzlauer v Commission* was withdrawn on 10 July 2008.

13.163 **Mitigating circumstances.** It is open to an applicant to raise on appeal a factor in mitigation of the fine even though this has not been raised in its reply to the statement of objections: Case T-73/04 *Le Carbone-Lorraine v Commission*, judgment of 8 October 2008, para 194. A further appeal was dismissed: Case C-554/08 P, judgment of 12 November 2009.

13.164 **Prompt termination of infringement.** Conversely, a substantial increase in the fine may be imposed if the infringement continues despite the start of the Commission's investigation: Case T-13/03 *Nintendo v Commission* [2009] 5 CMLR 1421, para 144.

In recent cartel appeals the CFI has robustly confirmed that a reduction in fine is not appropriate in a cartel case: see, eg Case T-127/04 *KM Europa Metal v Commission* [2009] 4 CMLR 1574, para 121: '. . . termination constituted an appropriate and normal reaction to the Commission's intervention, and cannot be assimilated to the merits flowing from an independent initiative on the part of the applicants. Similarly, that termination merely constituted a return to lawful conduct and did not contribute to making the Commission's investigations more effective'. On further appeal: Case C-272/09 P, not yet decided. Similarly, in Case T-53/03 *BPB plc v Commission* [2008] ECR II-1333, [2008] 5 CMLR 1201, paras 437–438, the CFI held that the Commission was entitled to abandon the 'generous practice' of reducing the fine for prompt termination in cases of flagrant infringement. Thus the appropriateness of any such reduction depends on whether the applicant could reasonably doubt the illegality of its conduct. This approach has been confirmed by the ECJ: see, eg Case C-510/06 P *Archer Daniels Midland v Commission (sodium gluconate)* [2009] 4 CMLR 889 (a case under the 1998 Guidelines), para 149; and Case C-511/06 P *Archer Daniels Midland v Commission (citric acid)*, judgment of 9 July 2009, para 105.

Fn 831. A further appeal in the *French Beef* case was dismissed: Cases C-101 & 110/07 P *Coop de France bétail et viande and FNSEA v Commission*, judgment of 18 December 2008, [2009] 4 CMLR 743.

13.165 **Negligent commission of infringement.** As regards whether the existence of a compliance programme is a mitigating factor see Cases T-101 & 111/05 *BASF AG and UCB SA v Commission* [2007] ECR II-4949, [2008] 4 CMLR 347 (fine imposed under 1996 Guidelines), para 52: 'even though the measures to ensure compliance with competition law are important, they cannot affect the reality of the infringement committed'.

Limited involvement and non-implementation.   In Case T-18/03 *CD-Contact*   **13.166**
Data v Commission, judgment of 30 April 2009, the CFI granted a 50 per cent reduction to one infringer on the basis that it had played 'an exclusively passive role' in the agreement and should have been treated in the same way as another undertaking who had been granted that level of reduction: para 199.

Cooperation with Commission investigation.   See, eg *Industrial copper tubes*,   **13.167**
OJ 2004 L125/50 where one cartel member gave the Commission a memorandum showing that the cartel had operated for much longer than the Commission had previously thought. This resulted in a substantial uplift of the fine on account of its duration; an uplift which could not be mitigated under the Leniency Notice 1996 because a 50 per cent reduction was the maximum that that cartel member could earn. The Commission dealt with this by granting a *de facto* immunity under the 1998 Guidelines (ie outside the Leniency Notice) as regards the additional duration of the cartel. See also in the appeal to the CFI; Case T-127/04 *KM Europa Metal v Commission* [2009] 4 CMLR 1574, para 127 (on further appeal: Case C-272/09 P, not yet decided). A similar point arose in respect of Zeon in COMP/38.628 *Nitrile Butadiene Rubber*, decn of 23 January 2008. Since Zeon was the first to have disclosed that the cartel operated from October 2000 to May 2002, this period was not taken into consideration when considering the multiplier for duration in the calculation of the fine for Zeon.

See now also the settlement procedure for cartels: Regulation 773/2004 Article 10a as inserted by Regulation 622/2008, OJ 2008 L171/3, [2008] 5 CMLR 1032 Article 1.4 and the Commission's Notice on the Conduct of Settlement Procedures in cartel cases: OJ 2008 C167/1: Vol II, App B17. For the settlement procedure generally see new paragraphs 13.113A–13.113D, above.

Encouragement by public authorities.   In Case T-271/03 *Deutsche Telekom AG*   **13.168**
v Commission [2008] ECR II-477, [2008] 5 CMLR 631 the CFI upheld a 10 per cent reduction in the fine for margin squeeze to reflect the fact that DT's retail and wholesale charges were subject to sector-specific regulation at the national level and the fact that the national telecoms regulator had, on several occasions during the period covered by the contested decision, considered the question of the existence of a margin squeeze resulting from the applicant's tariff practices and found that there was no abuse: para 312. The CFI's judgment is on appeal: Case C-280/08 P, not yet decided.

A further appeal in the *French Beef* case was dismissed: Cases C-101 & 110/07 P *Coop de France bétail et viande and FNSEA v Commission*, judgment of 18 December 2008, [2009] 4 CMLR 743.

See also the reduction in the fine imposed on National Grid because of the regulator's involvement in the evolution of the contracts condemned as abusive: *National Grid v The Gas and Electricity Markets Authority* [2009] CAT 10. The case is on appeal to the Court of Appeal.

13.169   **Uncertainty as to the law.**   **Fn 862.** The correct citation for the *CEWAL* decision is OJ 1993 L34/20, [1995] 5 CMLR 198.

Fn 867. The appeal by Deutsche Telekom was dismissed by the CFI: Case T-271/03 *Deutsche Telekom AG v Commission* [2008] ECR II-477, [2008] 5 CMLR 631, see update to paragraph 13.168, above.

13.170   **No penalty or nominal fine.**   In Case T-271/03 *Deutsche Telekom AG v Commission* [2008] ECR II-477, [2008] 5 CMLR 631 the CFI set out the three criteria as applied by the Commission in *Deutsche Post – interception of cross border mail*, OJ 2001 L331/40, [2002] 4 CMLR 598, namely (1) the undertaking concerned had behaved in accordance with the case law of the German courts; (2) there was no Community case law relating specifically to the cross-border letter mail services concerned; and (3) the undertaking concerned had taken steps to avoid practical difficulties and facilitate the detection of future interference with free competition, should it occur. The CFI held that none of the criteria applied to Deutsche Telekom's margin squeeze abuse. The CFI's judgment is on appeal: Case C-280/08 P, not yet decided.

The appeal by AC Treuhand fined in the *Organic Peroxides* decision for providing administrative and secretarial services to the cartel was dismissed by the CFI: Case T-99/04 *AC-Treuhand AG v Commission* [2008] ECR II-1501, [2008] 5 CMLR 962.

Fn 871. The appeal in *Clearstream* was dismissed: Case T-301/04 *Clearstream Banking v Commission*, judgment of 9 September 2009.

13.171   **Other aggravating and mitigating circumstances.**   In COMP/39.188 *Bananas*, decn of 15 October 2008 a reduction of 60 per cent in the fines of all the parties to the cartel was granted to reflect the fact that during the relevant period the banana sector was subject to a very specific regulatory regime: para 467. The decision is under appeal: Cases T-587 & 588/08, not yet decided.

13.173   **Compensation paid to third parties.**   The appeals against the *Nintendo* decision have now been decided: Case T-18/03 *CD-Contact Data v Commission*, judgment of 30 April 2009 (fine reduced) (on further appeal: Case C-260/09 P *Activision Blizzard Germany*, not yet decided); Case T-12/03 *Itochu* [2009] 5 CMLR 1375 (appeal dismissed); Case T-13/03 *Nintendo* [2009] 5 CMLR 1421 (fine reduced); Case T-398/02 *Linea Gig* (removed from register 2 May 2005). In Case T-13/03 *Nintendo*, the CFI rejected the appellant's claim that a greater reduction should have been granted on this ground, holding that there had been no assurance from the Commission that the reduction in fine would exactly match the amount of compensation paid: see paras 202 *et seq.*

Fn 882. ADM's appeal referred to in fn 882 has now been decided: Case C-511/06 P *Archer Daniels Midland v Commission (citric acid)*, judgment of 9 July 2009. The question of compensation to third parties was not considered in the appeal.

Dismissal of staff responsible for the infringement. See also Case T-53/03 *BPB* **13.174**
plc v Commission [2008] ECR II-1333, [2008] 5 CMLR 1201, paras 423–424; Cases T-101 & 111/05 *BASF AG and UCB SA v Commission* [2007] ECR II-4949, [2008] 4 CMLR 347 (fine imposed under 1996 Guidelines), para 129 (dismissal not regarded as an attenuating circumstance).

Specific increase for deterrence. A substantial increase for deterrence can be **13.177**
imposed in relation to vertical infringements as well as traditional horizontal cartels: Case T-13/03 *Nintendo v Commission* [2009] 5 CMLR 1421. The CFI confirmed in that case that the Commission is not required to evaluate how likely the undertaking is to reoffend in the future before imposing an increase for deterrence: 'the pursuit of deterrent effect does not concern solely the undertakings specifically targeted by the decision imposing fines. It is also necessary to prompt undertakings of similar sizes and resources to refrain from participating in similar infringements of the competition rules': para 73.

In Case T-410/03 *Hoechst GmbH v Commission* [2008] ECR II-881, [2008] 5 CMLR 839 the fine was doubled to ensure deterrence: para 379.

In Cases T-101 & 111/05 *BASF AG and UCB SA v Commission* [2007] ECR II-4949, [2008] 4 CMLR 347 (fine imposed under 1996 Guidelines) the CFI upheld a 100 per cent increase in the fine for deterrence based on the size of BASF. The CFI confirmed that there is no need for the Commission to assess the likelihood of reoffending: para 47.

Ability to pay and performance of the sector. In COMP/38.543 *International* **13.179**
Removal Services, decn of 11 March 2008, the Commission exceptionally took into account the inability to pay and particular circumstances of Interdean and reduced its fine by 70 per cent: paras 633 *et seq.* The case is under appeal: Cases T-208/08, etc, not yet decided.

Reduction of fine for delay. In Case T-410/03 *Hoechst GmbH v Commission* **13.180**
[2008] ECR II-881, [2008] 5 CMLR 839 the CFI held that while unreasonable delay might justify annulling the decision as a whole, it cannot be relied on when only the fine is challenged by the applicant because the limitation period for imposing the fine is set by regulation: para 220.

Fn 923. This principle was applied in Case T-276/04 *Compagnie maritime belge SA v Commission* [2008] ECR II-1277 where the CFI held that Regulation 2988/74 establishes a complete system of rules covering in detail the periods within which the Commission was entitled, without undermining the fundamental requirement of legal certainty, to impose fines and that there is therefore no room for consideration of a more general duty to exercise its power to impose fines within a reasonable period.

13.181 **Maximum fine and consequential adjustment.**   In Case T-68/04 *SGL Carbon AG v Commission* [2009] 4 CMLR 7, the appellant complained that by finding four separate infringements and adopting four separate decisions imposing fines in relation to cartel activity involving graphite products, the Commission had circumvented the 10 per cent ceiling. The CFI rejected this and upheld the fine: paras 131 *et seq*. A further appeal was dismissed: Case C-564/08 P, judgment of 12 November 2009.

As regards the turnover to which the 10 per cent maximum is applied, where several companies are held jointly and severally liable for a fine on the ground that they form an undertaking for the purposes of Article 101, the cap on the fine is calculated on the basis of the total turnover of all the companies constituting the single economic entity acting as an undertaking. Only the total turnover of the component companies can constitute an indication of the size and economic power of the undertaking in question: see Case T-112/05 *Akzo Nobel NV v Commission* [2007] ECR II-5049, [2008] 4 CMLR 321, para 90 (further appeal dismissed Case C-97/08 P, judgment of 10 September 2009 not dealing with this point). The 10 per cent maximum is applied to the turnover of the parent company on whom the fine has been imposed, not of the subsidiary which was involved in the infringing conduct: Case T-12/03 *Itochu Corp v Commission* [2009] 5 CMLR 1375, para 157.

For the application of the 10 per cent maximum in the case of a trade association see: Cases T-217 & 245/03 *FNCBV and Others v Commission* [2006] ECR II-4987, paras 317 *et seq*, upheld on appeal Cases C-101 & 110/07 P *Coop de France bétail et viande and FNSEA v Commission*, judgment of 18 December 2008, [2009] 4 CMLR 743. See further update to paragraph 13.204, below.

(f) The Leniency Notice: cartel cases

13.182 **The Leniency Notice 2006.**   The leniency regime applies only to horizontal cartels and not to vertical agreements even if the vertical infringement is regarded as very serious: Case T-13/03 *Nintendo v Commission* [2009] 5 CMLR 1421, para 157 (a case under the 1996 Notice).

In addition to the Leniency Notice arrangements the Commission has introduced a procedure for settlement of cartel cases: see new paragraphs 13.113A–13.113D, above. Adoption of this procedure may lead to a reduction in the fine of 10 per cent, in addition to any reduction resulting from leniency.

Fn 933. For a case where this transitional provision was applied see Case T-410/03 *Hoechst GmbH v Commission* [2008] ECR II-881, [2008] 5 CMLR 839, paras 507–511.

Securing a marker for immunity.   In Case T-410/03 *Hoechst GmbH v Commission* [2008] ECR II-881, [2008] 5 CMLR 839 the CFI held that there had been a breach of the principle of sound administration where the Commission had assured Chisso that it would be given 'fair warning' if another undertaking looked like overtaking it in the application for leniency but had decided not to tell Hoechst that Chisso was already providing information: paras 134–138. A 10 per cent reduction in the fine was applied by the CFI: para 582.   **13.188**

Level of reduction.   In *Industrial copper tubes*, OJ 2004 L125/50 one cartel member gave the Commission a memorandum showing that the cartel had operated for much longer than the Commission had previously thought. This resulted in a substantial uplift of the fine on account of its duration; an uplift which could not be mitigated under the Leniency Notice 1996 because a 50 per cent reduction was the maximum that that cartel member could earn. The Commission dealt with this by granting a *de facto* immunity under the 1998 Guidelines (ie outside the Leniency Notice) as regards the additional duration of the cartel: see also in the appeal to the CFI; Case T-127/04 *KM Europa Metal v Commission* [2009] 4 CMLR 1574, para 127 (on further appeal: Case C-272/09 P, not yet decided).   **13.193**

Multiple leniency applications in different Member States.   **Fn 974.** If a Member State only introduces a leniency programme later, an application should be made to the NCA as soon as the national programme takes effect. Hence the Austrian Supreme Court held that an earlier leniency application to the Commission could not be accepted as an application for leniency under national competition law, although there had been no leniency programme in Austria at that time: *Elevator Cartel (I)*, 16 Ok 5/08, judgment of 18 October 2008.   **13.196**

Oral applications for leniency.   See similarly the possibility of making settlement submissions orally under the new cartel settlement procedure: Notice on the Conduct of Settlement Procedures in cartel cases, OJ 2008 C167/1: Vol II, App B17, para 38. For the settlement procedure generally see new paragraphs 13.113A–13.113D, above.   **13.197**

Fn 981. ADM's appeal referred to in fn 882 has now been decided: Case C-511/06 P *Archer Daniels Midland v Commission (citric acid)*, judgment of 9 July 2009. The application of the Leniency Notice was not considered in the appeal.

Protection of corporate statements from disclosure.   Note that the Commission's White Paper on Damages Actions for Breach of the EC Antitrust Rules COM(2008) 165 (2 April 2008) also envisages that corporate statements will be exempt from disclosure in national courts.   **13.198**

(g) Periodic penalty payments

13.201 **Periodic penalty payments.** Note that in COMP/34.579 *MasterCard MIF charges*, decn of 19 December 2007, the Commission imposed a periodic penalty payment at the same time as it held that there was an infringement, in view of the risk that MasterCard would not comply with the six-month time limit for terminating the infringement: see paras 773 *et seq*. The case is on appeal: Case T-111/08, not yet decided.

13.202 **Periodic penalty payments: *Microsoft*.** On 27 February 2008 the Commission took a further decision in COMP/37.792, following on from the findings of non-compliance in November 2005. The February 2008 decision concerned the finding that Microsoft had charged an unreasonable fee for the information that it had made available as at 15 December 2005. The decision was limited to examining the fees charged by Microsoft in only one of the packages that it made available, namely the remuneration schemes for *non-patented* Interoperability Information. The decision did not assess whether the remuneration rates requested by Microsoft for patent licences prior to 22 October 2007 were reasonable and did not establish non-compliance in this respect: see para 297. In the earlier decision dealing with the first element of non-compliance (decision of 12 July 2006) the Commission had left open the possibility of imposing a periodic penalty for the second failure to cover the period covered by its 12 July 2006 decision. But in fact the February 2008 decision fixed the fine for the second failure only for the period after the period covered by the 12 July 2006 decision until Microsoft was regarded as having complied with both requirements; namely from 21 June 2006 to 22 October 2007. The amount set was €899 million: see paras 281 *et seq*. This decision is under appeal: Case T-167/08, not yet decided. Various parties have been granted permission to intervene in the appeal: see Case T-167/08 R order of 20 November 2008, [2009] 4 CMLR 775.

(h) Ancillary matters of law and practice

13.203 **Allocation of fines between infringing parties.** In Case T-68/04 *SGL Carbon AG v Commission* [2009] 4 CMLR 7 the CFI rejected an appeal against a fine in respect of a cartel where there had been a substantial disparity in the size of the undertakings involved. The Commission had grouped the undertakings concerned into three categories on the basis of the EEA-wide turnover of each of them in relation to the goods concerned. The Commission then grouped the undertakings into bands, each band representing a 10 per cent increment of market share. The CFI rejected the argument that the undertakings should have been differentiated by grouping into 5 per cent bands. The CFI held that a division of the undertakings in three categories, namely large, medium and small operators, was not an unreasonable way of taking account of their relative importance on the market in order to set the starting amount, as long as it did not lead to a grossly inaccurate representation of the market concerned (para 70). A further appeal was dismissed: Case C-564/08 P, judgment of 12 November 2009. See similarly *Nintendo Video games distribution*, OJ 2003 L255/33 where the undertakings concerned were divided into three groups according to the relative importance of each undertaking with regard to Nintendo, as distributor of the relevant products in the EEA. This decision was approved by the CFI: see, eg Case T-12/03 *Itochu Corp v Commission* [2009] 5 CMLR 1375, paras 73–84; and Case T-18/03 *CD-Contact Data v Commission*, judgment of 30 April 2009, para 109. The CFI held that even if the effect of the division into groups is that certain undertakings are allocated the same basic amount even though they differ in size, the difference in treatment is objectively justified by the greater importance attached to the nature of the infringement than to the size of the undertakings in the assessment of the gravity of the infringement. There was no breach of the principle of equal treatment. However, in Case T-13/03 *Nintendo v Commission* [2009] 5 CMLR 1421 the CFI reduced the fine imposed on Nintendo on the basis that the Commission had granted a larger reduction for cooperation to John Menzies and the degree of cooperation of the two undertakings was the same: paras 169 *et seq*.

In Case T-127/04 *KM Europa Metal v Commission* [2009] 4 CMLR 1574 the CFI confirmed that even without proof of actual impact of the infringement on the market, the Commission is entitled to carry out differentiated treatment of the cartel participants by reference to the shares held in the market concerned; market share constitutes an objective factor which gives a fair measure of the responsibility of each of them as regards the potential harm to competition: paras 61 and 62. On further appeal: Case C-272/09 P, not yet decided.

Trade associations. The question whether the 10 per cent maximum for fines **13.204** should be calculated on the basis of the turnover of the members of the association was considered by the CFI in Cases T-217 & 245/03 *FNCBV and others v Commission* [2006] ECR II-4987, paras 317 *et seq*. The CFI held that the earlier case law, particularly Case C-298/98 P *Finnboard v Commission* [2000] ECR I-10157, did not restrict the ability of the Commission to consider the turnover of the members to those cases where the association had power, under its rules, to bind its members. The 10 per cent maximum could be based on the turnover of the members in particular where an infringement by an association involves its members' activities and where the anti-competitive practices at issue are engaged in by the association directly for the benefit of its members and in cooperation with them. This was upheld on appeal Cases C-101 & 110/07 P *Coop de France bétail et viande and FNSEA v Commission*, judgment of 18 December 2008, [2009] 4 CMLR 743, paras 93 *et seq*. Further the ECJ upheld the CFI's finding that the principle of *ne bis in idem* was not infringed by the Commission imposing penalties on three associations and on a fourth association of which the first three were members: para 130 of ECJ judgment.

Fn 1032. Following the ECJ's judgment in Cases C-395 & 396/96 P, the Commission retook the decision and reimposed fines on the members of the liner conference. An appeal against that decision was dismissed: Case T-276/04 *Compagnie maritime belge SA v Commission* [2008] ECR II-1277.

13.205 **Fines on parents and subsidiaries.** In COMP/38.638 *Butadiene Rubber and Emulsion Styrene Butadiene Rubber*, decn of 29 November 2006, [2009] 4 CMLR 421 the Commission imposed a fine on Kaucuk which had participated in the cartel through its agent Tavorex where it was clear that Tavorex participated in meetings on the basis of an agency contract with Kaucuk; that Kaucuk was kept informed of developments; and that the final responsibility for price policy was with Kaucuk: paras 415 *et seq*. However, there was not enough evidence to show that another participant, Stomil, had been acting as agent for Dowry so no liability was imposed on Stomil: para 440.

In COMP/39.188 *Bananas*, decn of 15 October 2008 the Commission held Del Monte jointly and severally liable with Weichert for the latter's infringement. Weichert was a partnership between Del Monte and the Weichert family. The Commission analysed the partnership and distribution agreements between them and concluded that Del Monte exercised decisive influence: paras 382 *et seq*. The decision is under appeal: Cases T-587 & 588/08, not yet decided.

A fine may be imposed on the ultimate parent which indirectly owns the entity which was involved in the infringement: see, eg COMP/38.432 *Professional Videotape* [2008] 5 CMLR 122, para 169 and the cases cited therein.

There have been a number of appeals in which the CFI has had to interpret paras 28 and 29 of the ECJ's judgment in Case C-286/98 P *Stora Kopparbergs v Commission* where the ECJ seemed to cast doubt on the presumption of decisive influence over a subsidiary arising from the mere fact of 100 per cent ownership without the need to establish any additional factors. The CFI consistently held that such a presumption did arise: see, eg Case T-12/03 *Itochu* [2009] 5 CMLR 1375, paras 47 *et seq*; Case T-69/04 *Schunk GmbH v Commission* [2009] 4 CMLR 2, para 57. This was ultimately confirmed by the ECJ in Case C-97/08 P in *Akzo Nobel NV v Commission*, judgment of 10 September 2009 where the ECJ stated that 'it is sufficient for the Commission to prove that the subsidiary is wholly owned by the parent company in order to presume that the parent exercises a decisive influence over the commercial policy of the subsidiary. The Commission will be able to regard the parent company as jointly and severally liable for the payment of the fine imposed on its subsidiary, unless the parent company, which has the burden of rebutting that presumption, adduces sufficient evidence to show that its subsidiary acts independently on the market': para 61. Note that in Case T-69/04, Schunk also argued that the fact that the subsidiary was a holding company meant that it operated independently from the parent but the CFI held that this was not established.

The principles discussed in this paragraph were applied in Case T-85/06 *General Química v Commission*, judgment of 18 December 2008 (on further appeal: Case C-90/09 P, not yet decided) and in Case T-175/05 *Akzo Nobel (monochloroacetic acid)*, judgment of 30 September 2009.

Note that the Commission must make clear in the statement of objections if it intends to find a company liable both for its own conduct and for that of its subsidiary: see Cases C-322/07 P, etc, *Papierfabrik August Koehler AG and Bolloré SA v Commission*, judgment of 3 September 2009, [2009] 5 CMLR 2301. Bolloré had been found liable in the Commission's decision both as the parent company of Copiograph and because of its own independent involvement in the *Carbonless paper* cartel. The CFI held that the statement of objections had not made the latter allegations clear but declined to annul the decision on the grounds that Bolloré had had an opportunity to exercise its rights of defence as regards the former allegation. The ECJ held that the CFI had erred in law in failing to draw any legal conclusion from its finding that Bolloré's rights of defence had not been observed and annulled the whole of the contested decision so far as it concerned Bolloré.

Liability of successor undertaking.   These principles were applied in COMP/ **13.206**
38.432 *Professional Videotape*, decn of 20 November 2007, [2008] 5 CMLR 122, paras 158, 183. See also COMP/38.638 *Butadiene Rubber and Emulsion Styrene Butadiene Rubber*, decn of 29 November 2006, [2009] 4 CMLR 421, paras 337 and 338. In that case the Dow Chemical Company in the US was held jointly and severally liable for the conduct of three Dow subsidiaries which had been involved in the cartel at different times. The parent's liability was therefore of a longer duration than any of the subsidiaries' looked at individually.

Double jeopardy.   The principle of *ne bis in idem* was not infringed by the Com- **13.207**
mission imposing penalties on three associations and on a fourth association of which the first three were members: Cases T-217 & 245/03 *FNCBV and others v Commission* [2006] ECR II-4987, para 344; upheld on appeal Cases C-101 & 110/07 P *Coop de France bétail et viande and FNSEA v Commission*, judgment of 18 December 2008, [2009] 4 CMLR 743, para 130.

On the relevance of fines imposed in the USA see also Case T-410/03 *Hoechst GmbH v Commission* [2008] ECR II-881, [2008] 5 CMLR 839, paras 599 *et seq*.

Limitation period for imposition of fines.   For the proper interpretation of the **13.208**
requirement in Article 25(3) that in order to interrupt the limitation period the Commission's action must be notified to an undertaking 'which has participated in the infringement', see Case T-405/06 *Arcelor Mittal v Commission*, judgment of 31 March 2009 where the Commission's decision was annulled as against two of the addressees (on further appeal: Case C-201/09 P, not yet decided).

For the application of the limitation period in a case where the CFI and ECJ upheld the Commission's finding of infringement but annulled some of the fines on procedural grounds see Case T-276/04 *Compagnie maritime belge SA v Commission* [2008] ECR II-1277. First the CFI held that such a decision should not be treated as a decision finding an infringement since the fact of infringement was definitively established by the Commission in the parts of the earlier decision that were not annulled. The CFI then held that both the five-year limit under Article 25(1)(b) and the ten-year limit under Article 25(5) had been complied with, having regard to the various interruptions and suspensions arising from the earlier investigation and the appeals from the earlier decision. The CFI further applied the principle in Case T-213/00 *CMA CGM and others v Commission (FETTCSA)* [2003] ECR II-913, [2003] 5 CMLR 268 that Regulation 2988/74 establishes a complete system of rules covering in detail the periods within which the Commission was entitled to impose fines and that there is therefore no more general duty to exercise its power to impose fines within a reasonable period.

Fn 1053. The fact that the limitation period for imposing a fine in respect of obstruction of an investigation may have expired does not prevent the Commission from treating the conduct as an aggravating factor when imposing a fine for the substantive infringement: COMP/38.432 *Professional Videotape*, decn of 20 November 2007, [2008] 5 CMLR 122, para 224.

13.209 **Payment of the fine.** In Case T-68/04 *SGL Carbon AG v Commission* [2009] 4 CMLR 7 the CFI rejected an appeal against the rate of default interest set for non-payment of the fine, holding that the Commission is entitled to adopt a point of reference higher than the applicable market rate offered to the average borrower, to an extent necessary to discourage dilatory behaviour. Interest rates of 5.5 per cent and 3.5 per cent could not be regarded as disproportionate. A further appeal was dismissed: Case C-564/08 P, judgment of 12 November 2009.

The costs of providing a bank guarantee pending an appeal are generally not recoverable if the appeal succeeds: Case T-113/04 *Atlantic Container Line AB v Commission* [2007] ECR II-171*, [2008] 4 CMLR 1357.

The ECJ has hinted strongly that fines are not tax deductible: Case C-429/07 *Inspecteur van de Belastingdienst v X BV*, judgment of 11 June 2009, para 39: 'The effectiveness of the Commission's decision by which it imposed a fine on a company might be significantly reduced if the company concerned, or at least a company linked to that company, were allowed to deduct fully or in part the amount of that fine from the amount of its taxable profits, since such a possibility would have the effect of offsetting the burden of that fine with a reduction of the tax burden'.

11. Review by the Court of First Instance

The Court of First Instance.   The Court of First Instance has been renamed the   **13.212**
General Court following the coming into effect of the Lisbon Treaty. Article 229
EC is now Article 261 TFEU and Article 230 EC is now Article 263 TFEU.

(a) Review under Articles 229 and 230

(i) The scope of review

Increase in fines.   As to the power to increase fines when admissions are with-   **13.215**
drawn on appeal, see now Case T-69/04 *Schunk GmbH v Commission* [2009]
4 CMLR 2. The CFI held that the amount of a fine can be determined only on the
basis of the gravity and duration of the infringement. The fact that the Commission
had had to prepare for the appeal on the basis that the applicant might be allowed
to withdraw its previous admissions did not justify an increase of that fine. In
other words, the expenses incurred by the Commission as a result of the proceedings before the Court are not a criterion for determining the amount of the
fine and must only be taken into account when applying the provisions of the
Rules of Procedure relating to costs: para 262.

Adjustment of fines in cases of unequal treatment.   The *Hoek Loos* approach   **13.216**
was referred to in Case T-68/04 *SGL Carbon AG v Commission* [2009] 4 CMLR 7,
though the CFI did not find that there had been an error in the calculation
of another undertaking's fine: paras 136–137. A further appeal was dismissed:
Case C-564/08 P, judgment of 12 November 2009.

Fn 1087. See also Case T-410/03 *Hoechst GmbH v Commission* [2008] ECR
II-881, [2008] 5 CMLR 839, para 371.

Non-reviewable 'acts' of the Commission.   Note that the Court should exam-   **13.220**
ine the substance of the alleged act, not just the form in which the Commission
has communicated to the applicant: in Case C-521/06 P *Athinaïki Teckniki v
Commission* [2008] ECR I-5829, [2008] 3 CMLR 979 the ECJ held that a letter
in which the Commission informed the complainant that it was closing the file
because on the basis of information available there were no grounds to justify an
investigation, was in fact a statement by the Commission that the review initiated
had not enabled it to establish the existence of State aid within the meaning of
Article 87 [now Article 107 TFEU]. It had thereby implicitly refused to initiate
the formal investigation procedure provided for in Article 88(2) [now Article
108(2) TFEU]. The informal nature of the decision and the fact that it left it open
for the complainant to provide more information did not change its nature and it
was a reviewable act.

13.221 Standing to bring appeal.   Where one applicant challenging the rejection of a complaint undoubtedly has standing, there is no need to examine the standing of the other applicant: see Case T-306/05 *Scippacercola and Terezakis v Commission* [2008] ECR II-4*, [2008] 4 CMLR 1418, paras 71 and 72 (appeal dismissed Case C-159/08 P, Order of 25 March 2009); Case C-313/90 *CIRFS and others v Commission* [1993] ECR I-1125, para 31; Case T-282/06 *Sun Chemical Group v Commission* [2007] ECR II-2149, para 50. But where two appeals are joined, one appellant in each appeal must have standing to bring an appeal: see, eg Cases T-273 & 297/06 *ISD Polska v Commission*, judgment of 1 July 2009.

The rights conferred on Member States to bring proceedings before the Court are not conferred on regional authorities within the State: Case C-461/07 P(I) *Provincia di Ascoli Piceno and Comune di Monte Urano v Sun Sang Kong Yuen Shoes Factory* [2008] ECR I-11*, [2008] 2 CMLR 425.

As regards the last sentence of this paragraph, see Case C-506/08 P *Sweden v MyTravel and Commission*, not yet decided, where Sweden has brought an appeal against the CFI's judgment in Case T-403/05 *MyTravel Group v Commission*, judgment of 9 September 2008, [2008] 3 CMLR 1517 (access to documents under Regulation 1049/2001).

(ii) The grounds of annulment

13.223 Procedural irregularities.   Fn 1117. Following the judgment in *ARBED* the Commission retook the decision condemning the steel beams cartel: an appeal against that by ARBED was dismissed but the decision was annulled as against two of the addressees on the basis that the decision was adopted outside the limitation period: Case T-405/06 *Arcelor Mittal v Commission*, judgment of 31 March 2009 (on further appeal: Case C-201/09 P, not yet decided).

13.225 Inadequacy of reasoning.   For a recent exposition of the test of adequacy of reasons see Case T-151/05 *Nederlandse Vakbond Varkenshouders (NVV) v Commission* [2009] 5 CMLR 1613, paras 191 *et seq* in the context of a merger Phase I clearance.

Fn 1142. The appeal in *SELEX Sistemi* was dismissed: Case C-113/07 P *SELEX Sistemi Integrati SpA v Commission*, judgment of 26 March 2009.

13.226 Lack of adequate proof.   As regards evidence from anonymous informants, in Case T-53/03 *BPB plc v Commission* [2008] ECR II-1333, [2008] 5 CMLR 1201 the CFI considered whether the right of access to the file included access to information provided by an anonymous informant. In that case, the CFI noted that although the Commission accepted that the information was a factor in triggering the investigations, the information was ultimately not referred to in the contested decision and the Commission's objections were proved by other evidence. In any event, where information was supplied on a purely voluntary basis, accompanied by a request for confidentiality in order to protect the informant's anonymity, the Commission if it accepts such information is bound to comply with such a condition. The CFI held that proceedings initiated on the basis of information from an undisclosed source are lawful, provided that this does not affect the ability of the person concerned to make known his views on the truth or implication of the facts, on the documents communicated or on the conclusions drawn by the Commission from them.

Scope of review by the Court of First Instance. In the appeal, the ECJ upheld **13.227** the CFI's approach to reviewing the Commission's analysis: Cases C-501/06 P, etc, *GlaxoSmithKline Services Unlimited v Commission*, judgment of 6 October 2009.

Fn 1173. Note that the Commission has appealed against the CFI's judgment in *Alrosa*: Case C-441/07 P *Commission v Alrosa*, not yet decided.

Misuse of powers. In Case T-145/06 *Omya AG v Commission* [2009] 4 CMLR **13.230** 827 Omya asserted that the Commission's request for the correction of certain information previously supplied was simply a pretext to suspend the time running under the Merger Regulation. The Advisory Committee had objected to the Commission's proposed clearance of the merger and Omya had refused an extension of time prior to the request being made. The CFI stated (para 99) that a decision may amount to a misuse of powers only if it appears, on the basis of objective, relevant and consistent factors, to have been taken for a purpose other than the purpose for which the relevant powers were conferred. Where more than one aim is pursued, even if the grounds of a decision include, in addition to proper grounds, an improper one, that would not make the decision invalid for misuse of powers, since it does not nullify the main aim.

(iii) Procedural aspects

Time limits for bringing actions. As to the uncertainty referred to in the last **13.232** sentence of fn 1196, see Case T-48/04 *Qualcomm Wireless Business Solutions v Commission*, judgment of 19 June 2009 where the CFI held that time starts to run only once the decision is published in the *Official Journal* even if the Commission had sent a copy of the merger approval decision to the appellant before that: para 56. See similarly Cases T-273 & 297/06 *ISD Polska v Commission*, judgment of 1 July 2009: although publication of the decision in that case (concerning State aid) was not a precondition for the decision to come into effect, it was consistent practice for Commission decisions closing a State aid investigation to be published in the *Official Journal*. Therefore, the applicants could legitimately expect the decision to be published and time started to run only from that publication (para 57). See similarly, Case T-354/05 *TF1 v Commission*, judgment of 11 March 2009, para 34.

As regards what constitutes publication in the *Official Journal* see Case T-388/02 *Kronoply and Kronotex v Commission*, judgment of 10 December 2008 where the CFI held that publication of a notification of a decision in the C series of the *Official Journal* with a hyperlink to the full text of the decision on the Commission's website is sufficient publication of the decision to start time running for an appeal. See also Case T-274/06 *Estaser El Mareny v Commission* [2007] ECR II-143* (publication of a decision on the DG Competition website may not of itself start the time for lodging an appeal; but where a notification is published in the *Official Journal* that the decision can be found on the website, the time for appealing runs from that notification).

See also Case C-36/09 P *Transportes Evaristo Molina SA v Commission*, not yet decided (appeal against Case T-45/08 *Transportes Evaristo Molina SA v Commission*, Order of 14 November 2008 where the CFI held that the application was brought out of time).

13.234 **Whether decisions can be supported by new material.** If the Commission was precluded from relying on documents because they had not been disclosed to the applicant, the CFI cannot rely on them in its review of the Commission's decision: Case C-413/06 P *Bertelsmann AG and Sony Corporation of America v Impala and Commission* [2008] ECR I-4951, para 102.

13.238 **Powers of partial annulment.** In Case T-276/04 *Compagnie maritime belge SA v Commission* [2008] ECR II-1277 the CFI held that those parts of a Commission decision which are not annulled on appeal 'definitively form part of the Community legal structure and produce all their legal effects'. In that case the annulment of a fine for purely procedural reasons did not in any way affect the legality of the finding of infringement. The Commission was entitled to rely on the parts of the decision that were not annulled for the purpose of adopting a later decision imposing a fine on the applicant for the abuses established in that earlier decision.

13.240 **Consequences of total annulment.** The Commission's obligation to take measures to comply with the CFI's judgment includes, where a fine imposed is annulled or reduced, repaying that fine or that part of it. That obligation applies not only to the principal amount of the fine overpaid but also to default interest on that amount: Case T-48/00 *Corus UK v Commission* [2004] ECR II-2325, para 223; and Case T-53/03 *BPB plc v Commission* [2008] ECR II-1333, [2008] 5 CMLR 1201, para 487. There is no need, therefore, for the CFI to order this on disposing of the appeal.

Fn 1232. On the ability of the Commission to pick up the investigation when a decision is annulled because the investigation was incomplete see Case T-301/01 *Alitalia v Commission* [2008] ECR II-1753, paras 97 *et seq*. The CFI confirmed that where the obligation under Article 233 [now Article 266 TFEU] to comply with the Court's judgment calls for the adoption of a number of administrative measures, the institution is allowed a reasonable period within which to comply with a judgment annulling one of its decisions. The question whether or not the period was reasonable depends on the nature of the measures to be taken and the attendant circumstances (para 155).

Powers of the Court of First Instance following annulment of decision. The **13.241** judgment of the CFI in *Schneider Electric* was appealed to the ECJ: Case C-440/ 07 P *Commission v Schneider Electric*, judgment of 16 July 2009. The ECJ upheld the CFI's finding that the Commission's decision to prohibit the merger based on an objection that had not been raised in the statement of objections was a sufficiently grave and manifest breach of the rights of the defence to trigger the Commission's liability to pay damages. But the ECJ held on the facts that there was no sufficient causal link between that breach and the loss that Schneider Electric had incurred as a result of the reduction in the transfer price of Legrand conceded in consideration for the deferral of completion of the sale. The ECJ therefore ordered that the compensation payable to Schneider Electric was limited to the costs they incurred as a result of the reopened investigation of the merger following the annulment of the original decision.

A claim for damages against the Commission in a State aid case was dismissed by the CFI on the grounds that there was insufficient causal link between the invalidity of the decision annulled and the loss alleged. The CFI did not consider whether the defects in the decision were sufficiently serious to give rise to a cause of action: Case T-344/04 *Bouychou v Commission*, judgment of 17 July 2007, [2007] ECR II-91*. See also Cases T-362 & 363/05 *Nuova Agricast v Commission*, judgment of 2 December 2008 (Commission's errors not sufficiently serious to give rise to liability: on appeal Case C-67/09, not yet decided). See also the dismissal by the CFI of a damages claim for alleged loss arising out of the Commission's rejection of a complaint: Case T-186/05 *SELEX Sistemi Integrati SpA v Commission*, Order of 29 August 2007 (appeal dismissed Case C-481/07 P, judgment of 16 July 2009).

Fn 1238. See also Case T-145/06 *Omya AG v Commission* [2009] 4 CMLR 827, para 23.

Costs and other orders. For an example of a costs order where the applicant **13.242** won the battle but lost the war, see Case C-113/07 P *SELEX Sistemi Integrati SpA v Commission*, judgment of 26 March 2009 where the ECJ found significant legal errors in the CFI's reasoning but upheld the overall result (the rejection of the applicant's complaint by the Commission). The applicant was ordered to pay the Commission's costs but only half of Eurocontrol's costs.

The CFI does not have power under Article 288 EC [now Article 340 TFEU] to order the Commission to compensate a successful appellant for the costs of providing a bank guarantee in lieu of paying the fine pending appeal, because there is an insufficient causal link between the expense and the Commission's error: Case T-113/04 *Atlantic Container Line AB v Commission* [2007] ECR II-171*, [2008] 4 CMLR 1357. The applicants' claim that the Commission's failure to pay for the bank guarantee was a breach of its obligation under Article 233 EC [now Article 266 TFEU] to take all necessary steps to comply with the judgment annulling the decision was also rejected. The CFI held that given that the Commission would have had to pay interest on any fine paid pending the appeal, there was no loss suffered by the applicant for which the Commission should make recompense. The CFI noted that Article 233 EC requires the administration to make good further damage which may be caused by the unlawful act annulled only if the conditions laid down in the second paragraph of Article 288 EC are satisfied and they were not satisfied in this case.

Fn 1249. In the appeal Cases C-501/06 P, etc, *GlaxoSmithKline Services Unlimited v Commission*, judgment of 6 October 2009, the ECJ overturned part of the CFI's analysis though it ultimately upheld the outcome of the case. All parties were ordered to bear their own costs.

(c) Interim relief from the Court

13.246 Generally. Fn 1273. Where the main action is manifestly inadmissible, the claim for interim measures can be rejected on that ground: Case T-457/08 R *Intel Corp v Commission*, Order of 27 January 2009.

13.248 Interim relief to suspend fine. In Case T-113/04 *Atlantic Container Line v Commission* [2007] ECR II-171, [2008] 4 CMLR 1357 the CFI confirmed that because an undertaking has the option of paying the fine pending its appeal, there is an insufficient causal link between the annulled decision and the bank guarantee charges incurred to found a claim in damages. In Case T-398/02 R *Linea Gig v Commission* [2003] ECR II-1139 the CFI rejected a request for interim measures to suspend the fine even though Linea was in liquidation and the CFI found that the company had shown to the requisite legal standard that its situation made it objectively impossible for it to obtain the guarantee from a bank. The CFI balanced this point against the fact that suspension of the fine would prevent the Commission from bringing any action before the national court to recover the fine and to protect, as well as its own interests, the Community's financial interests. If the appeal was later dismissed, the applicant's assets might then no longer be adequate to pay the fine, in whole or in part. It was therefore necessary to maintain the enforceability of the decision in order not to preclude any measures which the Commission considers it necessary to take for the purposes of recovering the fine. An appeal against this rejection was dismissed: Case C-233/03 [2003] ECR I-7911. Contrast this with the decision of the CFI in Case T-11/06 R *Romana Tabacchi SpA v Commission* [2006] ECR II-2491 where the President of the

CFI found that the applicant (which had been fined €2.5 million for the Italian Raw Tobacco cartel) had established that it was impossible for it to acquire a bank guarantee and further found that the balance of interest lay in favour of ordering the applicant to provide a bank guarantee of €400,000, pay €200,000 to the Commission and pay the rest of the fine (with interest) in instalments.

Suspension of Commission order.   A negative administration order by the **13.249** Commission rejecting a request for interim measures cannot be suspended by the CFI because such a suspension could not affect the applicant's position: Case T-411/07 R *Aer Lingus v Commission* [2008] ECR II-411, [2008] 5 CMLR 53, para 47.

Fn 1285. But see Case T-411/08 R *Artijus Magyar v Commission* [2009] 4 CMLR 353 where the CFI rejected an application for interim measures to suspend parts of the Commission's order in the *CISAC* case. This judgment is under appeal: Case C-32/09 P(R), not yet decided.

Interim measures at complainant's behest.   Note however the comments of the **13.250** President of the CFI in Case T-411/07 R *Aer Lingus v Commission* [2008] ECR II-411, [2008] 5 CMLR 53 that a request that the CFI direct the Commission to take action under Article 8(4) or 8(5) of the Merger Regulation would constitute an interference with the exercise of the Commission's powers, incompatible with the distribution of powers between the various Community institutions. The President did not, however, rule out the grant of interim measures as against a third party to the appeal provided that procedural safeguards were put in place: para 56.

12. Appeals to the Court of Justice

Exercise of the jurisdiction.   In Case C-413/06 P *Bertelsmann AG and Sony* **13.254** *Corporation of America v Impala and Commission* [2008] ECR I-4951 the ECJ held that the extent of the obligation to state reasons is a question of law reviewable by the Court on appeal. Such a review must consider the facts on which the CFI based itself in reaching its conclusion as to the adequacy or inadequacy of the statement of reasons: para 30. The ECJ overturned the CFI's decision which had itself annulled the decision of the Commission approving a merger.

14

THE ENFORCEMENT OF THE COMPETITION RULES IN THE MEMBER STATES

2. Enforcement by National Competition Authorities

(c) Cooperation within the Network

Investigations on behalf of another NCA: Article 22(1).   The Austrian Supreme   **14.021**
Court has held that on receipt of a request under Article 22(1) from another
NCA, the Austrian NCA is entitled to determine whether the facts could give rise
to an infringement of EU competition law so as to justify the request, but that it
is irrelevant whether the Austrian NCA would have jurisdiction to take proceedings regarding the alleged infringement: *Deutsches Amtshilfeersuchen*, 16 Ok 7/09,
judgment of 15 July 2009.

(ii) Exchange of information and leniency programmes

Information exchange under Article 12.   Settlement submissions made under   **14.030**
the new cartel settlement procedure will only be transmitted pursuant to Article 12
provided that the conditions set out in the Network Notice are met: see Notice on
the Conduct of Settlement Procedures in cartel cases, OJ 2008 C167/1: Vol II,
App B17, para 37. For the settlement procedure generally see new paragraphss
13.113A–13.113D, above.

Disclosure of leniency programme information to national courts.   Similar   **14.032**
protection is conferred on settlement submissions under the new cartel settlement
procedure referred to above.

Note also *In re Rubber Chemicals Antitrust Litigation*, 486 F Supp 2d (ND Ca,
2007), where the US Court refused to order discovery of a defendant's leniency
statements to the Commission, holding that the EU is entitled to comity as a
sovereign entity and relying on the strong objection communicated by DG
Competition to such discovery as undermining its leniency programme.

(d) Enforcement of Community competition rules in the United Kingdom

(ii) Jurisdiction of sectoral regulators to apply Articles 81 and 82

14.040 **Case allocation in the United Kingdom.** In *R (oao Cityhook Ltd) v Office of Fair Trading* [2009] EWHC 57 (Admin) the High Court considered the application of the Concurrency Regulations in a case where a complainant was challenging the decision by the Office of Fair Trading not to investigate a complaint because the complaint was not an administrative priority. The Court held that the OFT ought to have considered whether to refer the case to OFCOM under the Regulations. The Court did not quash the OFT's decision but directed that proper consideration be given to the possible transfer of the case to OFCOM.

3. Enforcement by National Courts: Jurisdiction

(ii) Limitations on personal jurisdiction over defendants

14.051 **Declining jurisdiction.** **Fn 150.** See *Cooper Tire & Rubber Europe v Shell Chemicals* [2009] EWHC 1529 (Comm) (stay of proceedings to determine the Court's jurisdiction in the light of proceedings pending in Italy refused).

4. Convergence, Cooperation and Consistency in the Application of the Competition Rules

(a) Parallel application of Community and national competition law

14.058 **Raising competition law of the court's own motion.** The distinction is brought out by two contrasting Belgian judgments. See *Bima NV v Sodrepe NV*, Case 2002/AR/2580, judgment of 10 October 2008: on a claim under an agreement that expressly sought to share customers and exchange pricing information, the Brussels Court of Appeal of its own motion held that the agreement was void as a hard-core violation of Article 81 and the domestic Belgian equivalent. Cf *Brouwerij Haacht v BM*, Case C.08.0029.N, judgment of 15 May 2009: the Belgian Supreme Court held that where a party had relied only on a block exemption, the court was not required of its own motion, insofar as the agreement did not come within the block exemption, to consider the individual applicability of the conditions of Article 81(3) where this had not been raised by the parties to the dispute.

(c) Cooperation between the Commission and the national authorities

(i) Mutual assistance

14.070 **Submission of observations to the national court.** The Commission's power to intervene in national court proceedings under Article 15(3) is subject to the sole condition that the coherent application of Articles 81 and 82 [now Articles 101 and 102 TFEU] so requires. That condition may be fulfilled even if the proceedings concerned do not pertain to issues relating to the application of those articles. Thus, the ECJ held in Case C-429/07 *Inspecteur van de Belastingdienst v X BV*, judgment of 11 June 2009 that the Commission could intervene in proceedings in the German courts concerning whether fines imposed for cartel infringements were deductible from tax.

See also the questions referred under Article 234 [now Article 267 TFEU] concerning the rights of the national competition authority to make written submissions to the court under Article 15(1) of Regulation 1/2003: Case C-439/08 *VEBIC v Raad voor de Mededinging*, not yet decided.

Fn 198. The *Garage Gremeau* judgment is now reported at [2008] ECC 25.

(ii) Effect of national authority's action on the Commission

Effect of national decision on the Commission. In COMP/39.388 & 39.389 **14.072** *E.ON German electricity markets*, decn of 26 November 2008, para 23, the Commission referred to German decisional practice in OLG Düsseldorf, VI-2 KART 7/04 (V), *Stadtwerke Eschwege*, 6 June 2007 upheld by the Bundesgerichtshof on 11 November 2008, KVR 60/07 – *E.ON/Stadtwerke Eschwege* when leaving open whether the collective dominant position in the German wholesale electricity market involved two or three undertakings.

(iii) Effect of commencement of Commission investigation

Effect on proceedings in national courts. In *National Grid Electricity Trans-* **14.074** *mission plc v ABB Ltd* [2009] EWHC 1326 (Ch) the English High Court considered at what point in the preliminary stages of a follow-on action for damages arising from a cartel, the proceedings should be stayed pending an appeal from the Commission's decision to the CFI. The Chancellor noted that since a number of the defendants had made leniency applications during the Commission's investigation, the court was entitled to take into account the likelihood that the appeal to the CFI might not result in the cartel decision being annulled in its entirety. The Court ordered that the action should not be fixed for hearing until three months has elapsed from the end of the Luxembourg appeal process but that in the meantime pleadings should be served by the parties and the parties should meet to consider and if possible agree on the scope of disclosure of documents to be made pending the conclusion of the appeals.

(d) Duty to ensure consistency with decisions of European Commission

Subsequent infringement decisions. The principles in *Masterfoods* were applied **14.078** by the CFI in Case T-271/03 *Deutsche Telekom AG v Commission* [2008] ECR II-477, [2008] 5 CMLR 631 where the Court considered the relevance of price regulation in the telecoms sector on an allegation of margin squeezing by a dominant undertaking. The CFI rejected the argument that because the regulator approved the charges set by the applicant, that meant that they could not be contrary to Article 82 [now Article 102 TFEU]. The regulator was not a competition authority of the Member State and in any event, even if the regulator had decided that the charges were not contrary to Article 82, that finding did not bind the Commission: paras 113–124. The CFI's judgment is on appeal: Case C-280/08 P, not yet decided.

14.080 **Commission decisions in similar or related cases.** In its judgment on *Visa – MasterCard*, Case No. XVII AmA 109/07, judgment of 12 November 2008, the Polish Court for Competition and Consumer Protection held that the Polish NCA had not infringed Article 16(2) by adopting a market definition different from that applied by the Commission in its decision in *Visa International* (see paragraph 5.046 of the main work) since the Commission's decision concerned cross-border interchange fees whereas the Polish decision concerned only domestic fees and analysis of the national market. Paradoxically, in its pending appeal against this judgment, the Polish NCA contends that the Polish Court itself infringed Article 16(1) on the basis of inconsistency with the Commission's decision in *MasterCard* (ibid).

(e) Relationship between national courts and the Community courts

14.090 **Article 234 references.** Article 234 EC is now Article 267 TFEU. As to the obligation on a national administrative body to reopen a final decision which a later ruling of the ECJ (in another case) indicates was based on a misinterpretation of Community law see Case C-453/00 *Kühne & Heitz* [2004] ECR I-837, [2006] 2 CMLR 17; and Case C-2/06 *Kempter v Haupzollamt Hamburg-Jonas* [2008] ECR I-411, [2008] 2 CMLR 586.

Fn 266. Note that *inter partes* procedure is not a necessary condition: Case C-210/06 *Cartesio Okato*, judgment of 16 December 2008, [2009] All ER (EC) 296, paras 55–59.

5. Enforcement by National Courts: Remedies

(a) Declarations of invalidity

14.098 **Generally.** Fn 300. The appeal in *English, Welsh & Scottish Railway v E.ON UK plc* was withdrawn.

(ii) Severance

14.101A **Effect on resulting agreements.** The question of whether, and in what circumstances, Article 101(2) will apply to an agreement entered into separately but in consequence of the agreement or arrangement that infringes Article 101(1) has been little explored, despite its obvious significance. An unlawful horizontal agreement between competitors will often be implemented by a series of vertical agreements. As with other parts of the agreement to which Article 101(1) applies, it seems that the invalidity of resulting but distinct contracts is probably a matter of national law: Case 319/82 *Soc de Vente de Ciments et Betons v Kerpen & Kerpen* [1983] ECR 4173, [1985] 1 CMLR 511, paras 11–12. If, for example, competing suppliers of a product X entered into a cartel to raise prices, in consequence of which each supplier sold X at inflated prices, it seems clear that the individual contracts of sale would not be void under Article 101(2). Independent purchasers would have a remedy in damages but could not have the purchase declared void, or indeed fail to have acquired good title to the X that they had bought. In *Courage Ltd v Crehan* [1999] UKCLR 110, the English Court of Appeal articulated a test of whether the 'contract can be considered to be so closely connected with the breach of Article [101] that it should be regarded as springing from or founded on the agreement rendered illegal by Article [101]' (at para 60). On that basis, the Court there held that individual contracts for the supply of beer to tenants of a pub subject to an unlawful beer tie were not void. See also *BAGS v AMRAC* [2009] EWCA Civ 750, at paras 124–127, where the English Court of Appeal expressly reserved its position on the application of this test to the facts. The Swedish Supreme Court adopted a similar approach in applying domestic competition law in *Boliden Mineral AB v Birka Värme Stockholm AB*, Case NJA 2004 s. 804, judgment of 23 December 2004. In 1997, the arrangement between two trade associations whereby they promulgated a standard form agreement for the supply of electricity, incorporating a price adjustment clause, was found to violate competition law and they were ordered to cease their cooperation. The claimant argued that the price adjustment clause in its contract for the purchase of electricity which had been entered into on that standard form was accordingly void. The Supreme Court held that in general for such a 'follow-on' agreement to be void it must in itself constitute a restriction of competition; but that depending on the circumstances there may be such a close connection between that agreement and the original infringing agreement that the public interest in protecting competition might lead to the follow-on agreement also being declared void. In that case, the price adjustment clause in the claimant's contract could not in itself be considered incompatible with competition law and it was therefore valid and enforceable.

(b) Action for damages

The Ashurst Report and the Green Paper.   The Commission adopted a White **14.109** Paper on Damages Actions for Breach of the EC Antitrust Rules COM(2008) 165 (2 April 2008). See paragraphs below for discussion of particular issues covered by the Paper.

14.112 **Qualifying interest.** As to the last sentence of this paragraph, the German Federal Supreme Court upheld the decision that Cartel Damage Claims ('CDC') could pursue the cement cartel damages claims as assignee: *Cartel Damage Claims v Dyckerhoff AG*, Case KZR42/08, judgment of 7 April 2009. See Bundesgerichtshof Press Release No. 80/2009 of 17 April 2009. Subsequently, CDC commenced a follow-on claim in Germany on behalf of 32 customers against six producers arising from the Commission's decision in the hydrogen peroxides cartel.

14.113 **Indirect purchasers.** The Commission's White Paper on damages actions deals in some detail with possible collective redress, acknowledging that this is a sensitive issue in Member States because of its importance for access to justice. The Commission suggests two alternatives: 'opt-in collective actions' (which the Commission regards as more appropriate than opt-out actions); and representative actions brought by qualified entities such as consumer organisations or entities certified on an ad hoc basis by a Member State for the purpose of a particular antitrust infringement.

14.118 **Fault.** The Commission's White Paper on damages actions (COM(2008) 165 (2 April 2008)) suggests that the full application of a fault requirement whereby it must be shown that the infringer acted intentionally or negligently cannot be reconciled with the principle of effectiveness. However, there may be room for some defence of 'excusable error' in novel or complex situations where the infringer has taken every reasonable precaution but is still found to have infringed.

14.120 **Extent of damages recoverable.** In the White Paper on damages actions, the Commission stresses that national rules must not make it excessively difficult for victims to calculate the extent of the harm suffered and commits to producing non-binding guidance for courts on the calculation of damages.

14.121 **Damages cases.** The Hungarian Competition Act, by an amendment that came into force on 1 June 2009, provides that on a claim for damages resulting from a supply-side price cartel, there is a presumption that the prices charged by the participants in the cartel were increased by 10 per cent by reason of the infringement. The declared aim of the amendment is to assist victims of the cartel in recovering compensation but the claimants will still have to prove their loss, for example that they did not pass on any part of the increase to their customers. They can contend that in fact prices were raised by more than the presumed 10 per cent and equally a defendant can seek to rebut the statutory presumption.

Fn 385. In *Conduit Europe v Telefónica*, an appeal to the Madrid Provincial Court of Appeal was dismissed: judgment of 25 May 2006.

Fn 386. Cf the judgment of the Italian Corte di Cassazione, 3rd section, No. 2305 of 2 February 2007, quashing the decision of the Naples Court of Appeal that awarded damages to a consumer in a follow-on claim after the decision condemning the exchange of information among motor insurers: see fn 261 to paragraph 5.089 of the main work. It was held that the lower court should not have assumed that the increase in the premiums during the period of the infringement was caused by the infringement: causation had to be established on the evidence. Similarly, see judgment of the Corte di Cassazione, No. 3640, of 13 February 2009.

Access to evidence. In the White Paper the Commission notes that in many **14.121A** Member States the current systems of civil procedure offer no effective means for the victim to overcome the information asymmetry that is typical of antitrust cases. The Commission proposes a minimum standard of disclosure whereby obligations to disclose arise once a court has adopted a disclosure order and are subject to strict control by the court. The Paper also discusses the protection of confidential information and the need for effective sanctions to avoid refusal to hand over documents or destruction of evidence.

Exemplary damages. In *Devenish Nutrition v Sanofi-Aventis* [2007] EWHC **14.122** 2394 (Ch) the English High Court held that EU rules precluded the award of exemplary damages in a follow-on action for damages against participants in the vitamins cartels condemned by the European Commission (OJ 2003 L6/1). First the principle of *non bis in idem* applied where the defendants have already been fined (or had fines imposed and then reduced or commuted under the Leniency Notice) by the Commission: para 52. Secondly, to award exemplary damages would 'run counter' to the decision already adopted by the Commission and therefore contravene Article 16 of Regulation 1/2003. This was because if the national court were to award exemplary damages that could only be because the national court had concluded that the fines imposed by the Commission (including those fines that had been reduced or commuted) were insufficient to punish and deter: para 54. The point was not challenged on appeal: [2008] EWCA Civ 1086.

Restitution and prevention of unjust enrichment. In *Devenish Nutrition v* **14.123** *Sanofi-Aventis* [2008] EWCA Civ 1086, the English Court of Appeal held that Community law neither required nor precluded the availability of a restitutionary remedy but that under English law no such remedy was available on the facts of the case (follow-on claim for damages resulting from the vitamins cartels). Restitutionary remedies were only available in tortious claims where compensatory damages were an inadequate remedy. The judge at first instance had held that damages could not be regarded as an inadequate remedy if the difficulty facing the claimant was only one of evidential proof ([2007] EWHC 2394 (Ch), para 93). Arden LJ held that this went too far: it is at least arguable that the court should order an account of profits where the evidential difficulties were not the claimant's responsibility: para 105 of her judgment. However, in the instant case the claimants were not alleging that it was exceptionally difficult or impossible for them to prove their claim: para 106.

Fn 390. The *Consumers' Association v JJB Sports* case referred to in this footnote settled before judgment.

14.124 **'Passing-on' defence.** The Commission's White Paper on damages actions refers to the 'thorny issue' of passing on of overcharges. The Commission states that as regards the passing-on defence, purchasers of an overcharged product or service who had actually passed on that overcharge to their customers should not be entitled to compensation for that overcharge, though they may be entitled to loss of profits if that passing on has led to a reduction in sales. As a corollary of this, the customer to whom the overcharge has been passed should be able to claim compensation for the resulting harm. Recognising that these customers may be reluctant to bring actions, the Commission suggests that they be able to aggregate their claims via collective actions and that there should be a presumption operating in their favour that the overcharge has been passed on in its entirety to their level. That presumption can be rebutted by the infringer, for example by showing that he has already paid compensation for that same overcharge to someone higher up in the distribution chain.

14.125 **Examples of passing-on in the Member States.** In *Cement Cartel II*, Case 2 U 10/03 Kart., judgment of the Berlin Higher Regional Court (Kammergericht) of 1 October 2009, the court indicated that direct and indirect purchasers should constitute 'joint and several creditors' under German civil law, whereby each can sue the cartel participant directly for the damage it sustained. However, if only the direct purchaser sues it can recover for the full overcharge and then becomes liable to sub-purchasers to 'distribute' the damages to the extent that the overcharge was passed on. The claim there concerned only German competition law (as in force before the 7th Amendment referred to in the main text) but under the principle of equivalence the same reasoning would apply to a claim for violation of EU law. In that case, only the direct purchaser sued and the court awarded about a third of the damages claimed, illustrating the scrutiny applied to calculation of damages.

14.127 **Limitation.** In the White Paper on damages actions, the Commission suggests that the limitation period should not start to run before a continuous or repeated infringement ceases, or before the victim of the infringement can reasonably be expected to have knowledge of the infringement and of the harm it caused him. For follow-on actions, a limitation period of at least two years should apply starting with the date on which the infringement decision on which the claimant relies becomes final.

(c) Injunctive relief

14.133 **Mandatory relief.** In *Software Cellular Network Ltd v T-Mobile (UK) Limited* [2007] EWHC 1790 (Ch) the High Court granted an interim injunction to the applicant who alleged that T-Mobile's refusal to route calls from its subscribers to the applicant's phone numbers was a breach of Article 82 [now Article 102 TFEU].

The judge noted that the injunction sought was a mandatory order rather than a prohibitory order but held that the balance of convenience favoured the grant of the injunction pending trial.

(d) Reliance on Articles 81 and 82 as a defence

The nexus between infringement and abuse under Article 82: the Community **14.140**
Courts' approach.   See also Case T-119/09 *Protégé International v Commission*, not yet decided (appeal against rejection of complaint alleging abuse of dominant position by Pernod Ricard in filing legal proceedings against the applicant contesting the registration of trade marks. It is alleged that the proceedings were aimed not at protecting Pernod Ricard's intellectual property rights in its own marks ('Wild Turkey') but of eliminating the applicant as a competitor of Pernod Ricard in the Irish whiskey market). See also Case T-96/08 *Global Digital Disc v Commission*, not yet decided (appeal against rejection of complaint alleging breach of Article 82 [now Article 102 TFEU] in licensing practices in the CD-R field).

6. Practice and Procedure in the UK

Follow-on damages claims.   For further examples of follow-on actions brought **14.145**
in the High Court see *Cooper Tire & Rubber Europe v Shell Chemicals* [2009] EWHC 1529 (Comm) (stay of proceedings to determine the Court's jurisdiction in the light of proceedings pending in Italy refused); *National Grid Electricity Transmission plc v ABB Ltd* [2009] EWHC 1326 (Ch).

Note that the Commission's White Paper on damages actions proposes that a final decision by any national competition authority and a final judgment by a national court reviewing such a decision should be accepted in every Member State as irrebuttable proof of the infringement in subsequent civil damages claims.

It may sometimes be difficult to identify precisely what findings of infringement are contained in the regulator's decision: see, eg *Enron Coal Services Ltd v English Welsh and Scottish Railway* [2009] EWCA Civ 647 where the English Court of Appeal said 'The purpose of s.47A is to obviate the necessity for a trial of the question of infringement only where the regulator has in fact ruled on that very issue. We were not referred to any procedure for seeking clarification of any points of uncertainty from the decision-maker. The Tribunal ought therefore, ... to be astute to recognise and reject cases where there is no clearly identifiable finding of infringement and where they are in effect being asked to make their own judgment on that issue': para 31. The claim for damages was ultimately discussed by the Tribunal: [2009] CAT 36.

Limitation period.   Fn 485. Where an appeal to the CFI against a cartel deci- **14.149**
sion is limited to issues relating to the fine imposed and does not challenge the

finding of infringement, the limitation period is not suspended by the appeal and the follow-on action must be brought within two years of the expiry of the right to appeal: *BCL Old Company Ltd v BASF* [2009] EWCA Civ 434.

Fn 487. There have been three rulings of the CAT in the *Emerson Electric Co* claim. In *Emerson Electric v Morgan Crucible Company Plc and others* [2007] CAT 28 the Tribunal held that, where *any* of the addressees of a Commission decision had brought proceedings in the European Courts, the permission of the Tribunal was required for the bringing of a claim under section 47A even against an addressee which had not itself brought such proceedings. In ruling [2007] CAT 30 the Tribunal granted permission for a claim to be brought against an addressee which had *not* applied to annul the decision; and in ruling [2008] CAT 8 the Tribunal refused permission for claims to be brought against addressees which *had* applied to annul the decision. The case has been stayed pending the judgment of the ECJ on the appeals.

14.153 **Burden of proof.**   **Fn 497.** The correct citation for the *Attheraces* decision is [2006] ECC 24 and not [2006] ECC 12, [2006] EuLR 76.

14.158 **Disclosure of documents as between parties.**   For pre-action disclosure between potential parties to a claim for breach of Articles 81 and 82 [now Articles 101 and 102 TFEU] see *Hutchison 3G UK Ltd v O₂ (UK) Ltd* [2008] EWHC 55 (Comm) where Steel J held that under the relevant Civil Procedure Rules, the applicants 'have to show that it is more probable than not that the documents are within the scope of standard disclosure in regard to the issues that are likely to arise': para 44.

See also *British Sky Broadcasting v Virgin Media Communications* [2008] EWCA Civ 612. The applicant was involved in proceedings in the High Court, in the Competition Appeal Tribunal and in an investigation by OFCOM. A confidentiality ring was established in the High Court proceedings, limiting disclosure of commercially sensitive documents to external legal advisers. The question was whether the defendant should be able to use the same legal advisers (who were part of the ring) in the proceedings before the CAT and in the OFCOM investigation. The CA held that they could, indicating that it was hard to conceive of circumstances where disclosure in one set of proceedings would preclude lawyers from acting in other proceedings between the same parties.

14.160A **Stay of proceedings pending appeals in Luxembourg.**   In *National Grid Electricity Transmission plc v ABB Ltd* [2009] EWHC 1326 (Ch) the English High Court considered at what point in the preliminary stages of a follow-on action for damages arising from a cartel the proceedings should be stayed pending an appeal from the Commission's decision to the CFI. The Chancellor noted that since a number of the defendants had made leniency applications during the Commission's investigation, the appeal to the CFI might not result in the cartel decision being annulled in its entirety. The Court ordered that the action should not be fixed for hearing until three months has elapsed from the end of the Luxembourg appeal process but that in the meantime pleadings should be served by the parties and the parties should meet to consider and if possible agree on the scope of disclosure of documents to be made pending the conclusion of the appeals.

Class actions in cartel damages claims. In *Emerald Supplies v British Airways* **14.160B** [2009] EWHC 741 (Ch) the Chancellor considered an application to strike out part of an action according to which the claimants purported to be claiming 'on their own behalf and on behalf of all other direct or indirect purchasers of air freight services the prices for which were inflated by the agreements or concerted practices' alleged. Applying CPR Rule 19.6, the Chancellor noted that there were two conditions to be satisfied before a representative action could properly be brought. The first pre-condition is that there should be more than one person who satisfies the remaining pre-condition. The second is that those persons have the relevant interest at the time the claim is begun. There is no limit to the number of persons in the class to be represented and the mere fact that the relevant class is both numerous and geographically widely spread is not of itself an objection to a representative action. Nevertheless the more extensive the class the more clearly should the second pre-condition be satisfied. The Court held that the class referred to in the pleadings was inconsistent with the rule because it was impossible to say of any given person that he was a member of the class *at the time the claim form was issued*. The defect was not that the class consisted of a fluctuating body of persons but that the criteria for inclusion in the class could not be satisfied at the time the action is brought because they depend on the action succeeding.

Summary judgment. Summary judgment was refused in *Football Association* **14.161** *Premier League Limited v QC Leisure* [2008] EWHC 44 (Ch) (Article 81 [now Article 101 TFEU] defence was the legitimate subject for a trial). The judge also refused an alternative application that the trial of the Article 81 defence be stayed until the other issues in the case were resolved.

7. Arbitration Proceedings

Separability of the arbitration agreement. The decision of the Court of Appeal **14.164** in *Fiona Trust Corporation v Primalov* was upheld by the House of Lords: [2007] UKHL 40. Lord Hoffmann emphasised the importance of adopting a construction of an arbitration agreement consistent with what could be assumed to be the commercial rationale behind the parties' decision to enter into such an agreement. This meant that one should start from the assumption that the parties, as rational businessmen, are likely to have intended any dispute arising out of the relationship into which they have entered or purported to enter to be decided by the same tribunal. The clause should be construed in accordance with this presumption unless the language makes it clear that certain questions were intended to be excluded from the arbitrator's jurisdiction. The effect of section 7 of the Arbitration Act 1996 was that the arbitration agreement must be treated as separate from the main agreement and that the former can be invalidated only on a ground which relates to the arbitration agreement and is not merely a consequence of the invalidity of the main agreement. Where, therefore, the appellants argued that they were entitled to rescind the charterparties, including the arbitration agreements, because the charterparties were induced by bribery, this did not undermine the application of the arbitration agreement.

8. Table of National Enforcement Regimes

14.171 See the Appendix to this Supplement for an updated Table of National Enforcement Regimes.

15

STATE AIDS

1. Introduction

Generally. **Fn 1.** As to the application of the State aid rules to the sectors previously covered by the ECSC Treaty see Case T-25/04 *González y Díez v Commission*, judgment of 12 September 2007. The CFI held that the Commission had been correct to apply Article 88(2) EC [now Article 108(2) TFEU] and the Procedural Regulation in its decision adopted after the ECSC Treaty expired relating to an aid granted before that expiry. But the Commission erred in deciding that a State aid put into effect without its prior approval would be subject to the provisions of Regulation 1407/2002 which was adopted after the aid was put into effect. (Note that this conclusion may need to be reconsidered in the light of Case C-334/07 P *Commission v Freistaat Sachsen*, judgment of 11 December 2008). However, since the relevant provisions of Regulation 1407/2002 were identical to earlier provisions which were in force at the relevant time, the CFI in *González y Díez* found that the error did not affect the validity of the decision. **15.001**

As regards textbooks on State aids see now Bacon (ed), *European Community Law of State Aid* (2009); Vesterdorf and Nielsen, *State Aid Law of the European Union* (2008).

State aid reform. On progress with the Action Plan see the speech by Neelie Kroes at a conference on 'The new approach to state aids - Recent reforms under the State Aid Action Plan and next steps', Brussels, 21 November 2008 (Speech 08/634). **15.002**

Recent legislative developments. Since the 6th edition a number of significant legislative instruments have been adopted: **15.003**

- measures responding to the banking and financial crisis: see new paragraphs 15.003A–15.003C, below;
- the General Block Exemption Regulation: Regulation 800/2008, OJ 2008 L214/3: Vol II, App G16, see update to paragraph 15.067, below;

- new Community guidelines on State aid for environmental protection, OJ 2008 C82/1: Vol II, App G22A replacing the 2001 Guidelines (fn 18 refers), see update to paragraph 15.060, below;

- a new Notice on the application of Articles 87 and 88 to State aid in the form of guarantees, OJ 2008 C155/10: Vol II, App G26A, see update to paragraph 15.038, below;

- a Notice Towards an effective implementation of Commission decisions ordering Member States to recover unlawful and incompatible State aid, OJ 2007 C272/4: Vol II, App G8A, see update to paragraph 15.102, below.

- a new Notice on the enforcement of State aid law by national courts, OJ 2009 C85/1: Vol II, App G8B, see update to paragraph 15.111, below;

- a 'Simplification Package' comprising a Notice on a simplified procedure for treatment of certain types of State aid, OJ 2009 C136/3: Vol II, App G8C and a Code of Best Practice: Vol II, App G8D: see new paragraph 15.075A, below;

- amendments to Regulation 794/2004 in Regulation 271/2008, OJ 2008 L82/1 and Regulation 1147/2008, OJ 2008 L313/1, see update to paragraph 15.069, below.

15.003A **The global financial and economic crisis.** Since the second half of 2008, State aid rules and procedures have had to accommodate the measures taken by Member States to respond to the banking crisis which followed on from the collapse of Lehmann Bros bank. There have been two strands to this response so far as concerns State aid. The first strand is a series of Communications from the Commission dealing specifically with measures taken to rescue and support banking institutions. The second strand concerns aid measures which could be described as part of the 'stimulus' package adopted by Member States to mitigate the effects of the severe recession which followed the global crisis. The Commission published an Overview of national measures adopted as a response to the financial/economic crisis, MEMO/09/380 (9 September 2009) which contains links to the relevant documents. DG Competition also established an Economic Crisis Team as a first contact point for all State aid related measures for the real economy falling within DG Competition's area of responsibility.

15.003B **Banking aid measures.** In October 2008 the Commission issued a Communication 'The application of State aid rules to measures taken in relation to financial institutions in the context of the current global financial crisis', OJ 2008 C270/8: Vol II, App G26B. This provides guidance on the criteria relevant for the compatibility with the Treaty of general schemes to safeguard the stability of the financial system as well as the stabilisation of individual financial institutions of systemic relevance. While noting that assistance to undertakings in difficulty was usually assessed under Article 87(3)(c) [now Article 107(3)(c) TFEU], the Commission indicated that in the light of the level of seriousness that the current crisis in the financial markets had reached and of its possible impact on the overall economy of Member States, Article 87(3)(b) is available in limited circumstances as a legal basis for aid measures. The Communication then went on to explain how the rules would be applied to (i) guarantees covering the liabilities of financial institutions (particularly guarantees of deposits); (ii) recapitalisation of financial institutions; (iii) controlled winding up of financial institutions; and (iv) other forms of liquidity assistance. The Commission further assured Member States that it had taken appropriate steps to ensure the swift adoption of decisions upon complete notification, if necessary within 24 hours and over a weekend. On 5 December 2008 a further Communication giving more detail about banking recapitalisation was adopted (OJ 2009 C10/2: Vol II, App G26C) and in January 2009 further guidance was given on the treatment of impaired assets in the Community banking sector (OJ 2009 C 72/1: Vol II, App G26D). The Commission also adopted a large number of individual decisions approving particular aid schemes and aids to individual institutions: see MEMO/09/446 (13 October 2009) listing the decisions taken as at that date. A Communication explaining how the Commission will examine aid for the restructuring of banks was published in August 2009 (OJ 2009 C195/10: Vol II, App G26E). It sets out a model restructuring plan and applies to aids notified to the Commission on or before 31 December 2010.

'Recovery Plan' aids.   On 26 November 2008, the Commission adopted the   **15.003C** 'A European Economic Recovery Plan' (COM(2008) 800). This prompted the adoption of a Commission Communication 'Temporary Community framework for State aid measures to support access to finance in the current financial and economic crisis' which applies from 17 December 2008 (published OJ 2009 C16/1: Vol II, App G22B). The Communication noted that 'while State aid is no miracle cure to the current difficulties', well targeted public support for companies could help to unblock lending to companies and to encourage continued investment in a low-carbon future. The Communication described a number of measures that a Member State could take without falling within the State aid provisions, for example payment deadlines for social security and similar charges, or even taxes could be extended. The Communication referred to the existing State aid legislative measures which could be relied on by Member States. It goes on to state that the Commission will consider aids of various kinds as being compatible with the common market on the basis of Article 87(3)(b) of the Treaty. The kinds of aids covered are (a) limited aids above the existing *de minimis* threshold; (b) aids in the form of guarantees; (c) aid in the form of subsidised interest rates; (d) aid for the production of green products; and (e) risk capital measures. The Recovery Plan Communication also adapts the Communication relating to short-term export credit insurance (OJ 1997 C281/4: Vol II, App G24).

Some amendments to the detail of this Communication were made in February 2009 and a consolidated version of the Recovery Plan Communication was published in OJ 2009 C83/1.

15.004 **European Economic Area.** For a recent judgment of the EFTA Court concerning the application of the State aid provisions in the EEA Agreement see Case E-5/07 *Private Barnehagers Landsforbund v EFTA Surveillance Authority*, decn of the EFTA Court 8 February 2008, [2008] 2 CMLR 818 (municipal kindergartens not undertakings for the purpose of the State aid provisions).

2. The Concept of an Aid

(a) Generally

15.010 **An advantage.** In Case T-25/07 *Iride SpA v Commission*, judgment of 11 February 2009 the CFI rejected an argument that a payment did not confer an advantage because it only compensated the recipient for stranded costs arising from the liberalisation of the electricity market and so did no more than restore normal market conditions as compared with rival undertakings which did not have to bear the stranded costs. The CFI held that the alteration of the legislative framework in the electricity sector which occurred as a result of Directive liberalisation was part of normal market conditions and that, when the recipients of the aid made the investments that gave rise to the stranded costs in question, it was taking the normal risks related to possible legislative amendments.

See also Tosics and Gaál, 'Public procurement and State aid control – the issue of economic advantage' where the authors note that the Commission has received State aid notifications in which Member States ask the Commission to confirm in advance that the complex public procurement transactions that they are planning would not lead to a State aid. The article clarifies the Commission's practice in that regard: (2007) 3 Competition Policy Newsletter 17.

In Case C-431/07 P *Bouygues SA v Commission*, judgment of 2 April 2009 the ECJ upheld the finding of the CFI that the apparent advantage granted by France when it waived part of the fees to be paid by telecoms licensees did not constitute a State aid because the waiver was necessary to avoid unequal treatment of those licensees under the EU telecoms regulatory scheme then in force. The waiver brought their fees into line with the fees that Bouygues had agreed to pay in a later auction of the same licences. Since the CFI had been right to hold that the principle of non-discrimination required the French authorities to align the fees due with those charged to Bouygues, there was no State aid.

Fn 42. As regards the principle established in the Case C-237/04 *Enirisorse v Sotacarbo*, the CFI in Cases T-254/00, etc, *Hotel Cipriani v Commission*, judgment of 28 November 2008 rejected the argument that social security exemptions granted to undertakings in Venice and Chioggia were justified as compensation for the additional costs connected with the specific structural problems resulting from the fact that the towns are situated in a lagoon. There was no direct connection between the additional costs actually incurred and the amount of the aid received by the various operators. The case is on appeal: Cases C-71/09, 73/09 & 76/09, not yet decided.

Compensation for public service obligations.   As to the margin of discretion **15.011** conferred on the Member State in designating an activity as being a service of general economic interest see Cases T-309/04, etc, *TV 2/Danmark v Commission*, judgment of 22 October 2008 (public service broadcasting channel funded partly by licence fee and partly by advertising was such a service).

The *Altmark* criteria.   In Cases T-309/04, etc, *TV2/Danmark v Commission*, **15.012** judgment of 22 October 2008 the Commission had found that the licence fee arrangements for TV2 failed to meet the second and fourth *Altmark* criteria. The Commission found that the fee had resulted in a build-up of capital reserves and hence overcompensated TV2 for the public service broadcasting function. The Commission rejected the Danish Government's contention that these reserves were necessary to protect TV2 from fluctuations in advertising revenue by which it was also partly funded. The CFI annulled the decision for lack of reasoning. The Court held that the Commission had failed to examine the Danish Government's contentions seriously. The fact that TV2 did not have to draw on its reserves did not support the inference that those reserves had to be regarded as disproportionate to the funding needs of providing the public service. It is in the very nature of a reserve which is built up to deal with an uncertainty that it does not necessarily have to be used.

See also Case T-8/06 *FAB Fernsehen aus Berlin GmbH v Commission*, judgment of 6 October 2009 (first criterion of *Almark* not met).

See also Case T-266/02 *Deutsche Post v Commission* [2008] ECR II-1233 where the CFI annulled the prohibition of a State aid because the Commission had failed to check or determine whether the transfer payment alleged to constitute the aid in fact exceeded the applicant's net additional costs associated with the provision of a service of general economic interest for which, in accordance with the conditions laid down in the *Altmark* judgment, it had the right to claim compensation. The case is on appeal, Case C-399/08 P, not yet decided.

Note that the criteria can be applied when assessing the validity of a Commission decision which predates the *Altmark* judgment since the ECJ did not place any temporal limitation on the scope of its findings in that case: Case T-388/03 *Deutsche Post et DHL International v Commission*, judgment of 10 February 2009 (on appeal Case C-148/09 P, not yet decided).

See also Case C-206/06 *Essent Netwerk Noord v Aluminium Delfzijl* [2008] ECR I-5497, [2008] 3 CMLR 895 (it is for the national court to decide whether and to what extent a levy paid over to an electricity generating company to compensate it for investment in 'non-market-compatible costs' prior to market liberalisation should be regarded as compensating for the discharge of public service functions for the purposes of the *Altmark* criteria).

As regards the public service obligation, the CFI has confirmed that this concept has the same meaning here as the service of general economic interest for the purposes of Article 86(2) [now Article 106(2) TFEU] and that Member States have a wide discretion to define what they regard as SGEIs. The definition of such services by a Member State can be questioned by the Commission only in the event of manifest error: Case T-289/03 *BUPA v Commission* [2008] ECR II-81, para 166. The CFI went on to hold that a private medical insurance scheme adopted by Ireland did have an SGEI mission and that the other *Altmark* criteria were also satisfied.

15.013 **The 'market economy investor' principle.** In Case T-455/05 *Componenta v Commission*, judgment of 18 December 2008 the CFI annulled a Commission decision which had held that a transaction by which the Finnish town of Karkkila bought out the applicant's half share in a property company amounted to a State aid because the price exceeded the value of the interest. The CFI rejected the applicant's challenge to the way the Commission had valued the shares in the company but found that the Commission had not sufficiently explained how it had valued the land holdings of the company.

As to the application of this principle when the aid is granted by a State body allegedly exercising its a legislative or regulatory function see Case T-196/04 *Ryanair v Commission*, judgment of 17 December 2008, on appeal from the *Ryanair/Charleroi* decision cited in fn 53. There the CFI considered an arrangement under which the Walloon Region of Belgium which owns the Charleroi airport infrastructure agreed to grant Ryanair, first, a reduction in landing charges at the airport and, secondly, an indemnity in the event of losses which Ryanair might suffer following any change in the airport charges or opening hours of Charleroi airport. The CFI concluded that the Commission had been wrong to treat the Walloon Region and the airport operating company BSCA as separate entities; they were in fact a single undertaking. The CFI then considered whether the private investor principle could be applied to this single entity, given that the measures in question were said by the Commission to have been adopted by the Walloon Region in its legislative, regulatory role. The Court noted that for the purposes of determining whether a measure of State aid constitutes an 'advantage', a distinction must be drawn between the obligations which the State assumes when exercising an economic activity and its obligations as a public authority. It is necessary, when the

State acts as an undertaking to analyse its conduct by reference to the private investor principle. But application of that principle is excluded where the State acts as a public authority. In the latter case, the conduct of the State can never be compared to that of an operator or private investor in a market economy. However, the CFI disagreed with the Commission's characterisation of the relevant activities as part of the public function and held that they were economic activities. The Commission's refusal to apply the private investor principle to the measures adopted by the Walloon Region was, the CFI held, vitiated by an error in law.

For evaluation by a national court, see, eg *Svensson v Stockholm Municipality*, Case No. 4514-07, judgment of the Stockholm Administrative Court of Appeal of 25 May 2007, annulling the decision of the Municipality to approve a proposed investment by municipal housing companies for the purpose of extending the connection to broadband networks. Examining the commercial aims and financial calculations underlying the investment, the court held that it was unlikely that a private investor would have made an investment under those conditions. An application for permission to appeal to the Swedish Supreme Administrative Court is pending.

As to the last sentence regarding the private creditor comparator, see Case T-36/99 *Lenzing AG v Commission* [2004] ECR 3597, [2006] 1 CMLR 1213 (appeal dismissed: Case C-525/04 P *Spain v Lenzing* [2007] ECR I-9947, [2008] 1 CMLR 1068) (debt-rescheduling agreements and the non-enforcement of debts following the breach of those agreements).

For a discussion of the application of this principle by the Commission in a case concerning the roll out of a high speed broadband fibre access network in Amsterdam see Gaál, Papadias and Riedl, 'Citynet Amsterdam: an application of the market economy investor principle in the electronic communications sector' (2008) 1 Competition Policy Newsletter 82.

Fn 53. Following the CFI's annulment of the decision in Case T-296/97 *Alitalia v Commission* cited in the footnote, the Commission retook the decision, explaining in more detail why it considered that the minimum rate of return that had been used in the *Iberia* case was also appropriate for applying the private investor test to the Italian Government's investment in Alitalia. Alitalia's appeal against this decision was dismissed: Case T-301/01 *Alitalia v Commission* [2008] ECR II-1753. After noting that the Commission's assessment of whether an investment satisfies the private investor test is a complex economic matter so that judicial review of such a measure was limited, the CFI held that there were no manifest errors in the Commission's application of the test.

Absence of private investor comparator. The *Chronopost* saga has continued. **15.014**
The ECJ overturned the CFI's judgment in Case T-613/97 on the basis both that

the CFI had been wrong to say that the Commission decision was inadequately reasoned and because the CFI had erred in finding that there had been a State aid: Cases C-341 & 342/06 P *Chronopost and La Poste v UFEX* [2008] ECR I-4777, [2008] 3 CMLR 568. The CFI had held that the transfer of a client base by La Poste to Chronopost had taken place without any payment of consideration by Chronopost for this valuable intangible asset. The ECJ held that the CFI had ignored the legal and economic context of the transaction and had also failed to establish that the transfer had distorted or threatened to distort competition. The Court decided not to remit the matter a second time to the CFI but went on to determine the matter itself, setting aside the CFI's judgment and then dismissing the appeal against the Commission's decision to reject the complaint.

15.017 '**By a Member State or through State resources**'.   In Case T-233/04 *Netherlands v Commission (emission trading scheme)* [2008] ECR II-591 the CFI considered an emissions trading scheme for nitrogen oxides. The CFI held that although the Dutch Government did not directly grant emission allowances to the undertakings concerned, it authorised the undertakings subject to a binding emissions standard to trade between themselves the emission allowances which indirectly result from that standard, up to the limit of the ceiling applicable to each of them. Having examined the system, the Court concluded that the State had forgone State resources. The CFI however annulled the decision on the grounds that the aid was not selective. The judgment is on appeal: Case C-279/08 P, not yet decided.

15.019 State resources.   The distinction between *PreussenElecktra* and *France v Ladbroke Racing and Commission* was considered in Case T-25/07 *Iride SpA v Commission*, judgment of 11 February 2009 which concerned sums collected from electricity consumers and deposited in an account opened within the Equalisation Fund, before finally being transferred to a private undertaking. The Equalisation Fund was a public body appointed by the Italian State to arrange for the electricity distributors to receive compensation for stranded costs. The CFI held that the sums were properly characterised as State resources, not only because they were under constant State control, but also because they were State property. See also Case T-136/05 *EARL Salvat père & fils v Commission* [2007] ECR II-4063 (aid was not entirely funded by contributions levied but included State funds). See similarly, Case C-206/06 *Essent Netwerk Noord v Aluminium Delfzijl* [2008] ECR I-5497, [2008] 3 CMLR 895 (the company designated to collect the levy and transfer it to the beneficiary was not entitled to use the proceeds from the charge for purposes other than those provided for by the national law and was strictly monitored in carrying out its task: hence the case fell on the *Pearle* side on the line and was distinguished from *PreussenElecktra*).

In Cases T-309/04, etc, *TV2/Danmark v Commission*, judgment of 22 October 2008 the CFI held that a television licence fee was 'State resources' because the amount is determined by the Danish authorities; the obligation to pay the licence fee does not arise from a contractual relationship between TV2 and the person liable to pay, but simply from the ownership of a television or radio receiver; where necessary, the licence fee is collected in accordance with the rules on the collection of personal taxes; and, lastly, it is the Danish authorities who determine TV2's share of the income from licence fees (para 158). However the CFI held that the Commission had failed adequately to explain why it also treated the advertising revenue which partly funded TV2 as State resources.

No transfer of resources required.   See also Case C-431/07 P *Bouygues SA v*   **15.020** *Commission*, judgment of 2 April 2009 (waiver of fees for telecoms licence not an aid because it was required in order to avoid unequal treatment between licensees).

Imputability of the measure to the State.   The principles established in *Staurdust*   **15.021** *Marine* were applied in Case T-442/03 *SIC v Commission* [2008] ECR II-1161 where the CFI held that the applicant SIC had not succeeded in showing that the payment facility granted to the public service broadcaster which was late paying its network fee was imputable to the Portuguese Government: paras 93 *et seq*.

In *Skyways v Kristianstad Airport*, Case No. Ö 916-08, judgment of 7 May 2007 the Court of Appeal of Skåne and Blekinge upheld the grant of interim relief prohibiting the provision of various forms of financial assistance that the defendant airport had agreed to give to a competitor airline. The airport was 51 per cent owned by the Kristianstad municipality and 49 per cent by other public authorities and the Swedish courts considered that this probably constituted State aid. The proceedings were subsequently settled so no final judgment was given. But cf Case N791/2006 *Business case Norrköpping*, decn of 10 July 2007, where the European Commission held that assistance given by Norrköping airport was not attributable to the State as the municipality held only a 50 per cent interest in the airport operating company and the balance was held by private investors.

Fn 97. A claim for damages against the Commission by Stardust Marine was dismissed by the CFI on the grounds that there was insufficient causal link between the invalidity of the decision annulled and the loss alleged. The CFI did not consider whether the defects in the decision were sufficiently serious to give rise to a cause of action: Case T-344/04 *Bouychou v Commission*, judgment of 17 July 2007, [2007] ECR II-91*.

Favouring certain undertakings.   An advantage granted directly to certain natu-   **15.023** ral or legal persons who are not necessarily undertakings may constitute an indirect advantage, hence State aid, for other natural or legal persons who are undertakings: see Case C-156/98 *Germany v Commission* [2000] ECR I-6857, paras 22–35; Case C-382/99 *Netherlands v Commission* [2002] ECR I-5163, paras 38 and 60–66; Case T-445/05 *Associazione italiana del risparmio gestito v Commission*, judgment of 4 March 2009, paras 127 and 135 (tax reductions for investors in a certain kind of investment vehicle was an indirect benefit to those vehicles and was a selective benefit since it did not apply to the whole financial sector); similarly see Case T-424/05 *Italy v Commission*, judgment of 4 March 2009 'les mesures sélectives en faveur des petites et moyennes entreprises n'échappent pas non plus à la qualification d'aide d'État'; para 147.

In Case T-233/04 *Netherlands v Commission (emission trading scheme)* [2008] ECR II-591 the CFI annulled a decision relating to the trading of emission credits on the grounds that it was not selective. All large industrial facilities were subject to the emission ceiling laid down by the measure in question and could benefit from the advantage offered by the tradability of emission allowances for which it provided. The criterion for application of the measure in question was therefore an objective one, without any geographic or sectoral connotation. To the extent that the measure was aimed at the undertakings which are the biggest polluters, that objective criterion was consistent with the goal of the measure, that is the protection of the environment, and with the internal logic of the system: para 88. The judgment is on appeal: Case C-279/08, not yet decided.

15.024 **Difference in treatment not always favouring certain undertakings.** **Fn 116.** An appeal against the CFI's judgment in Case T-475/04 was dismissed: Case C-431/07 P *Bouygues SA v Commission*, judgment of 2 April 2009.

15.026 **The effect on trade between Member States.** In Case C-494/06 P *Commission v Italy and WAM*, judgment of 30 April 2009 the ECJ upheld the CFI's judgment in Cases T-304 & 316/04 (referred to in fn 135). The ECJ noted that the CFI had correctly stated that the Commission was not obliged to carry out an economic analysis of the actual situation on the relevant market or to examine the patterns of the trade in question between Member States or to show the real effect of the aid at issue. In this case the aid was not directly connected to the activity of the beneficiary on that market, but was intended to finance expenditure for a third country market penetration programme. In those circumstances where it involved aid, the grant equivalent of which was of relatively low value, the effect of the aid on trade and on intra-Community competition was less immediate and less discernible. The CFI had been right therefore to conclude that this required a greater effort to state reasons on the part of the Commission.

Cf Cases T-254/00, etc, *Hotel Cipriani v Commission*, judgment of 28 November 2008 where the CFI stated that a relatively small amount of aid may affect such trade where there is strong competition in the sector in which the beneficiary undertakings operate. Thus, where a sector has a large number of small companies, aid potentially available to all or a very large number of undertakings in that sector can, even if individual amounts are small, have an effect on trade between Member States. The Commission's decision had already excluded aids which were *de minimis* and the CFI upheld the finding that an aid may affect trade and distort competition even if the beneficiary undertakings which are in competition with producers in other Member States exercise their activities exclusively at local level. Where a Member State grants aid to an undertaking, domestic production may for that reason be maintained or increased with the result that undertakings established in other Member States have less chance of exporting their products to the market in that Member State: para 248. The case is on appeal: Cases C-71/09, 73/09 & 76/09, not yet decided.

See also Cases T-81/07, etc, *Jan Rudolf Maas v Commission*, judgment of 1 July 2009. The CFI confirmed that when State aid strengthens the position of an undertaking compared with other undertakings competing in intra-Community trade, that trade must be regarded as affected by the aid (para 76). See also Case T-189/03 *ASM Brescia SpA v Commission*, judgment of 11 June 2009, paras 66 *et seq* (there is no threshold or percentage below which trade between Member States can be said not to be affected and the fact that the companies eligible under a sectoral aid scheme did not operate outside their national territory did not preclude an effect on trade).

It is not necessary that the beneficiary undertaking itself be involved in intra-Community trade. Furthermore, the strengthening of an undertaking which, until then, was not involved in intra-Community trade may place that undertaking in a position which enables it to penetrate the market of another Member State: Case C-222/04 *Ministero dell'Economia e delle Finanze v Cassa di Risparmio di Firenze SpA* [2006] ECR I-289, [2008] 1 CMLR 705, para 143. See similarly, Case T-211/05 *Italy v Commission*, judgment of 4 September 2009, para 153; Case T-369/06 *Holland Malt BV v Commission*, judgment of 9 September 2009 (fact that the beneficiary of the aid sold its product 'almost exclusively' to third countries did not prevent the subsidy being an aid).

De minimis: the case law.   See also Cases T-227/01, etc, *Diputación Foral de* **15.027**
Álava and Comunidad autónoma del País Vasco – Gobierno Vasco v Commission, judgment of 9 September 2009, para 148: the fact that the tax advantages constituting the aid were temporary and that their influence was 'small and not decisive' did not prevent them from falling within Article 87 [now Article 107 TFEU] since there is no requirement in case law that the distortion of competition, or the threat of such distortion, and the effect on intra-Community trade, must be significant or substantial.

De minimis: **The Commission's approach and the adoption of block exemp-** **15.028**
tions.   See now the temporary measure that the Commission has adopted for cash grants of no more than €500,000 for companies that got into difficulties after 1 July 2008 because of the financial crisis: Commission Communication 'Temporary Community framework for State aid measures to support access to

finance in the current financial and economic crisis' (consolidated version published OJ 2009 C83/1), para 4.2.2.

15.029 **Calculating the amount of the advantage.** **Fn 152.** This Notice has been replaced by the Commission's Communication on the revision of the method for setting the reference and discount rates, OJ 2008 C14/2: Vol II, App G29.

(b) **Particular applications**

15.030 **Examples of State aids.** An aid which is intended to relieve an undertaking of the expenses which it would normally have had to bear in its day-to-day management or its usual activities in principle distorts competition: Cases T-81/07, etc, *Jan Rudolf Maas v Commission*, judgment of 1 July 2009, para 75 (aid intended to meet contractual commitments and cover the costs of a social plan by the recipient which was in liquidation).

Fn 158. The 2000 Notice referred to has been replaced by a new Commission Notice on the application of Articles 87 and 88 of the EC Treaty to State aid in the form of guarantees, OJ 2008 C155/10: Vol II, App G26A.

Fn 161. See also Case T-332/06 *Alcoa Trasformazioni v Commission*, judgment of 25 March 2009 on alleged Italian aid in the form of lower electricity tariffs.

Fn 169. As regards TV licence fees see Case T-354/05 *TF1 v Commission*, judgment of 11 March 2009 where the CFI upheld the Commission's conclusion that the French system satisfied the *Altmark* criteria and so did not constitute State aid. See also Cases T-309/04, etc, *TV2/Danmark v Commission*, judgment of 22 October 2008 (decision that the licence fee had overly compensated the public service broadcaster for its services was annulled). On the funding of public service broadcasting see Tosics, Van de Ven and Riedl, 'Funding of public service broadcasting and State aid rules – two recent cases in Belgium and Ireland' (2008) 3 Competition Policy Newsletter 81.

15.031 **Tax measures.** A tax advantage granted directly to natural or legal persons who are not necessarily undertakings may constitute an indirect advantage, and hence a State aid, for other natural or legal persons who are undertakings: Case T-445/05 *Associazione italiana del risparmio gestito v Commission*, judgment of 4 March 2009, para 127 (tax reduction for investors in a certain kind of investment vehicle was an indirect benefit to those vehicles).

Taxes do not fall within the scope of the provisions of the EC Treaty concerning State aid unless they constitute the method of financing an aid measure so that they form an integral part of that measure: Case C-206/06 *Essent Netwerk Noord v Aluminium Delfzijl* [2008] ECR I-5497, [2008] 3 CMLR 895, para 89. For a tax to be regarded as forming an integral part of an aid measure, it must be hypothecated to the aid measure under the relevant national rules, in the sense that the revenue from the tax is necessarily allocated for the financing of the aid and has a direct impact on the amount of that aid, *ibid*, para 90.

In Case T-442/03 *SIC v Commission* [2008] ECR II-1161 the CFI annulled a Commission decision which had held that legislative measures by which the Portuguese public broadcaster was (a) exempted from the payment of registration charges and fees relating to its transformation into a public limited company; and (b) benefited from an unlimited exemption from payment to all authorities of any charges and fees in respect of any act of inscription, registration or annotation did not amount to State aid. In order to be able to find that the exemption from notarial charges was justified by the nature and the general logic of the system of which it was a part, it was not sufficient to find, as the Commission did, that the recourse to legislation for the purpose of transforming public undertakings into public limited companies meant that the chargeable event for the notarial charges did not occur. The question which the Commission ought to have examined was whether it was compatible with the logic of the Portuguese legal system for the transformation of public undertakings into public limited companies to occur by legislation, or whether the recourse to legislation for such operations constituted a derogation which, in view of the consequences which resulted from that (namely rendering a notarial deed unnecessary so that no charges were incurred), was intended to confer an advantage on public undertakings in relation to other undertakings.

As to the selectivity of tax measures see Cases T-211 & T-215/04 *Gibraltar v Commission*, judgment of 18 December 2008 (Commission had not demon-strated that tax measures in Gibraltar constituted derogations from the common or 'normal' tax regime). The case is on appeal: Cases C-106 & 107/09, not yet decided.

Fn 176. See also Case C-222/04 *Ministero dell'Economia e delle Finanze v Cassa di Risparmio di Firenze SpA* [2006] ECR I-289, [2008] 1 CMLR 705, para 132.

Fn 177. See also Cases T-227/01, etc, *Diputación Foral de Álava and Comunidad autónoma del País Vasco – Gobierno Vasco v Commission*, judgment of 9 September 2009, para 126 (tax credits constituted an aid).

Tax measures: objective justification. The CFI's judgment in *British Aggregates* **15.033** was overturned by the ECJ on appeal: Case C-487/06 P *British Aggregates Association v Commission*, judgment of 22 December 2008. The ECJ held that the objective pursued by State measures is not sufficient to exclude those measures out-right from classification as 'aid' for the purposes of Article 87 EC [now Article 107 TFEU]. Article 87(1) does not distinguish between the causes or the objectives of State aid, but defines them in relation to their effects. The unavoidable conclusion was that the CFI erred in holding that Member States are free, in balancing the various interests involved, to set their priorities as regards the protection of the environment and, as a result, to determine which goods or services they decide to subject to an environmental levy. The ECJ confirmed that protection of the environment constitutes one of the essential objectives of the Community. However, that cannot justify the exclusion of selective measures, even specific ones such as environmental levies, from the scope of Article 87(1) EC. Account may in any event usefully be taken of the environmental objectives when the compatibility of the State aid measure with the common market is being assessed pursuant to Article 87(3) EC. The ECJ held that the CFI had erred in a number of other respects, including by applying only a limited standard of review to the Commission's decision. The ECJ referred the case back to the CFI for further consideration.

See also Case T-442/03 *SIC v Commission* [2008] ECR II-1161, discussed in the update to paragraph 15.031, above.

The principles in this paragraph were applied in Case T-211/05 *Italy v Commission*, judgment of 4 September 2009 where the CFI held that a tax exemption conferred on newly listed companies in Italy was selective and was inconsistent with the nature and overall scheme of the Italian tax system.

15.034 **Selectivity of regional taxation measures.**   The principles laid down in the *Azores* judgment were applied by the CFI in relation to a tax measure adopted by the Government of Gibraltar: Cases T-211 & T-215/04 *Gibraltar v Commission*, judgment of 18 December 2008. The CFT examined whether the tax reform satisfies the three conditions set out in para 67 of the *Azores* judgment namely (i) whether the tax reform has been devised by a regional or local authority which has, from a constitutional point of view, a political and administrative status separate from that of the central Government of the United Kingdom; (ii) whether the tax reform has been devised without the central Government of the United Kingdom being able to intervene directly as regards its content; and (iii) whether the financial consequences for Gibraltar of introducing the tax reform are offset by aid or subsidies from other regions or from the central Government of the United Kingdom. The Court rejected the argument that there was a fourth condition, namely the condition that the infra-State body must occupy a fundamental role in the definition of the political and economic environment in which the undertakings present on the territory within its competence operate. Nor was there a condition relating to the tax measure at issue being circumscribed by harmonisation criteria which are imposed by Community law on tax measures adopted by the Member State to which the infra-State body in question belongs. The CFI concluded that the reference framework corresponds exclusively to the geographical limits of the territory of Gibraltar, without there being any need to examine the applicants' arguments relating to Gibraltar not forming part of the United Kingdom and to Gibraltar and the United Kingdom lacking a common tax system. This meant that no comparison can be made between the tax regime applicable to companies established in Gibraltar and that applicable to companies established in the United Kingdom for the purpose of establishing a selective advantage favouring the former. As regards selectivity within the Gibraltar framework, the CFI held that the Commission had not demonstrated this to the requisite legal standard and the Commission's decision was therefore annulled. The case is on appeal: Cases C-106 & 107/09, not yet decided.

See also Cases C-428/06, etc, *UGT Rioja v Juntas Generales de Territorio Histórico de Vizcaya* [2008] ECR I-6747, [2008] 3 CMLR 1397 in relation to the regional introduction of lower tax rates and possible tax deductions that were not available in the rest of Spain. The ECJ confirmed that the only conditions which must be satisfied in order for the territory falling within the competence of an infra-State body to be the relevant framework for assessing whether the tax advantage is selective are the conditions of institutional autonomy, procedural autonomy and economic and financial autonomy as set out in para 67 of the *Azores* judgment. The ECJ, noting that the institutional system of Spain 'is particularly complex', found that the infra-State bodies had institutional autonomy but that it was for the national court to determine whether they also had procedural and economic and financial autonomy. The ECJ stated that an infra-State body cannot be said to lack autonomy solely on the ground that the acts that it adopts are subject to judicial review in the national courts.

Privatisation and the sale of public assets.   For the application of the principles **15.035** discussed here in three recent Commission decisions see von Buttlar et al, 'State aid issues in the privatisation of public undertakings – some recent decisions' (2008) 2 Competition Policy Newsletter 77.

State guarantees.   The 2000 Notice referred to has been replaced by a new **15.038** Commission Notice on the application of Articles 87 and 88 of the EC Treaty to State aid in the form of guarantees, OJ 2008 C 155/10 (corr. OJ 2008 C244/32): Vol II, App G26A. The Notice defines when a guarantee can be regarded as an advantage granted 'through State resources': the benefit of a State guarantee is that the risk associated with the guarantee is carried by the State. Where the State forgoes all or part of the premium which would normally be payable for taking on that risk, there is both a benefit for the undertaking and a drain on the resources of the State. Thus, even if it turns out that no payments are ever made by the State under a guarantee, there may nevertheless be State aid under Article 87(1) [now Article 107(1) TFEU]. The Notice clarifies that the market investor principle applies to determining whether a market premium is being charged for the guarantee and that this involves an assessment of the risk involved in guaranteeing the loan. Factors to be taken into account when assessing this risk include the amount and duration of the transaction; the security given by the borrower and other experience affecting the recovery rate evaluation; the probability of default of the borrower due to its financial position, its sector of activity and prospects; as well as other economic conditions. This analysis should allow the borrower to be classified by means of a risk rating, for example by an internationally recognised rating agency or, where available, by the internal rating used by the bank providing the underlying loan. However, the new Notice contains specific provisions for SMEs. If the borrower is an SME, the Commission can accept a simpler evaluation of whether or not a loan guarantee involves aid. In that case, and provided all the other conditions laid down in the Notice are met, a State guarantee would be deemed as not constituting aid if a minimum annual premium, as set out in a table in the Notice, is charged on the amount effectively guaranteed by the State, based on the rating of the borrower. The Commission has published a useful summary of the provisions of the Notice, highlighting where it differs from the earlier notice: MEMO/08/313 (20 May 2008). On the calculation of the aid element in guarantee schemes and the Commission's approval of notified methods for that calculation see also Tuchhardt, Tar and Galand, 'Approved guarantee methods for regional aid or de-minimis aid – the German and the Hungarian example' (2008) 3 Competition Policy Newsletter 41.

In Case T-442/03 *SIC v Commission* [2008] ECR II-1161 the CFI stated that in considering whether a State guarantee constituted a State aid, it was important not to confuse the question whether the State granted, expressly or implicitly, a guarantee with that of how the market reacted to the fact that the issuer of a bond was not just another private operator, but a wholly State-owned undertaking. The fact that the market agreed to subscribe to the 1994 bond issue – allegedly because the market considered that the State would guarantee *de facto* its repayment – does not mean that there was State aid, since it is not disputed that the State did not give its guarantee, either expressly or implicitly. Only objective findings leading to the conclusion that the State legally had to repay that issue in the event of default by the public undertaking would permit a finding of the existence of a State guarantee: see paras 121 *et seq.*

3. Aids that are Compatible with the Common Market

15.039 **Article 87(2).** Following the closure of US airspace immediately after the terrorist attacks of 11 September 2001, the Commission issued a Communication (COM(2001) 574 final of 10 October 2001) stating that Article 87(2)(b) EC [now Article 107(2)(b) TFEU] enabled certain problems facing the airlines because of those events to be dealt with. Having regard to the exceptional nature of the occurrences in question, the provisions of that article could authorise compensation for, first, the costs caused by the closure of American airspace for four days and, secondly, the extra cost of insurance. In Case T-268/06 *Olympiaki Aeroporia Ypiresies v Commission* [2008] ECR II-1091 the CFI considered the application of the criteria set out in the Communication to aid granted by the

Greek Government in respect of particular flights between Greece and the USA and Canada. The CFI held that in order to qualify for approval under Article 87(2)(b) there must be a direct link between the damage caused by the exceptional occurrence and the State aid and as precise an assessment as possible must be made of the damage suffered. But the requirement of a direct connection between the exceptional occurrence and the damage caused does not presuppose that they occur at the same time. On the contrary, there may be such a connection even where the loss arises shortly after the exceptional occurrence. The CFI disagreed with the Commission over the characterisation of some of the flights in contention so that the decision was annulled in part. Cf Case T-70/07 *Cantieri Navali Termoli v Commission*, judgment of 12 November 2008 where the CFI rejected an argument that the attacks of 11 September 2001 affected the relevant sector of the shipbuilding industry.

4. Aids that may be Compatible with the Common Market

(a) Generally

The exercise of the Commission's discretion. In Case T-162/06 *Kronoply v Commission*, judgment of 14 January 2009 the CFI upheld a decision by the Commission that 'the two fundamental elements of incentive and necessity' required for the aid to fall within Article 87(2) or (3) [now Article 107(2) or (3) TFEU] were not present. The CFI held that those two conditions governing the compatibility of aid each have their own specific meaning, so that the lack of incentive and the lack of necessity must each be regarded as autonomous reasons for finding that the aid was incompatible: para 60. **15.042**

The ECJ has stressed that the method by which aid is financed may render the entire aid scheme which it is intended to finance incompatible with the common market. Therefore, the aid cannot be considered separately from the effects of its method of financing and the Commission must take into account the method of financing the aid in a case where that method forms an integral part of the measure: see Case C-333/07 *Société Régie Networks v Direction de contrôle fiscal Rhône-Alpes Bourgogne*, judgment of 22 December 2008, para 89 and the cases cited there.

Operating aid. See, eg Case T-211/05 *Italy v Commission*, judgment of 4 September 2009 where the CFI held that a tax advantage available to newly listed companies in Italy was an operating aid and incompatible with the common market. Similarly, in Cases T-30/01, etc, *Territorio Histórico de Álava – Diputación Foral de Álava v Commission*, judgment of 9 September 2009 the CFI upheld the Commission's finding that corporate tax exemptions constituted operating aid: para 227. **15.043**

(b) Article 87(3)(a)

15.051 **Other aspects of entitlement to regional aid.**   See also the Communication from the Commission concerning the criteria for an in-depth assessment of regional aid to large investment projects, OJ 2009 C223/3: Vol II, App G22E.

15.052 **Block exemption for regional aid.**   Regulation 1628/2006 was repealed by the General Block Exemption Regulation; Regulation 800/2008, OJ 2008 L214/3: Vol II, App G18 (the GBER), see update to paragraph 15.067, below.

(c) Article 87(3)(b)

15.053 **Article 87(3)(b): aid for important projects or to remedy a serious distur-bance.**   The Commission has stated that in the light of the seriousness of the financial crisis which enveloped the global economy in the second half of 2008, certain State aids can be justified under Article 87(3)(b) [now Article 107(3)(b) TFEU]: see Commission Communication 'Temporary Community framework for State aid measures to support access to finance in the current financial and economic crisis' (consolidated version published OJ 2009 C83/1).

(d) Article 87(3)(c)

15.059 **Guidelines and rules on sectoral aid.**   The Commission has also issued guide-lines on the application of State aid rules in relation to rapid deployment of broad-band networks (17 September 2009) available on the Commission's website.

Fn 302. The 2001 Cinema Communication has been extended until such time as new rules on State aid to cinematographic and other audiovisual works come into effect, or, at the latest, until 31 December 2012: see Communication, OJ 2009 C31/1.

Fn 303. A Revised Draft Communication from the Commission on the applica-tion of State aid rules to public service broadcasting has been consulted upon: see Press Release IP/09/564 (8 April 2009).

Fn 307. The Framework on State aid to shipbuilding has been further extended until 31 December 2011: see OJ 2008 C173/3.

15.060 **Guidelines on horizontal aid.**   **Fn 315.** The 2001 Guidelines for environmental protection have been replaced by new Community guidelines on State aid for environmental protection, OJ 2008 C82/1: Vol II, App G22A. The Guidelines identify a series of measures for which State aid may, under specific conditions, be compatible with Article 87(3)(c) EC [now Article 107(3)(c) TFEU]. The main changes from the 2001 Guidelines are (i) a number of new kinds of aid are cov-ered, eg aid for early adaptation to standards, aid for environmental studies and aid for waste management; (ii) permissible aid intensities have increased; and

(iii) the Guidelines distinguish between a standard assessment and a detailed assessment. A detailed assessment method applies to large aid amounts to individual enterprises and involves greater scrutiny of individual cases which have the greatest potential to distort competition and trade. For comment on the new Guidelines see Winterstein and Tranholm Schwarz, 'Helping to combat climate change: new State aid guidelines for environmental protection' (2008) 2 Competition Policy Newsletter 12. See also the modifications made to the form for notifying environmental protection aids following the adoption of this Notice: Regulation 1147/2008, OJ 2008 L313/1.

Fn 315. An appeal against the CFI's judgment in Case T-176/01 was dismissed: Case C-49/05 P *Ferriere Nord v Commission*, judgment of 8 May 2008, [2008] ECR I-68*.

Fn 319. The 2000 Notice referred to has been replaced by a new Commission Notice on the application of Articles 87 and 88 of the EC Treaty to State aid in the form of guarantees, OJ 2008 C155/10: Vol II, App G26A, see further the update to paragraph 15.038, above.

Aid for rescuing and restructuring firms in difficulty.   The validity of the Rescue   **15.061**
Guidelines has been extended until 9 October 2012: OJ 2009 C156/3.

(e) Article 87(3)(d)

Aid to promote culture and heritage conservation.   Following the annulment   **15.064**
of the decision by the CFI in Case T-49/93, the Commission adopted a new decision approving the aid. This decision was also annulled by the CFI (Case T-155/98 [2002] ECR II-1179) on the grounds that the Commission had committed a manifest error of assessment as regards the definition of the relevant market. The Commission adopted a third decision approving the aid in 2004. This decision was annulled by the CFI in 2008: Case T-348/04 *SIDE v Commission* [2008] ECR II-625. In the most recent judgment the CFI held that the Commission had erred in law by applying Article 87(3)(d) [now Article 107(3)(d) TFEU] to the period before 1 November 1993 instead of applying the substantive rules in force during the period in question. (Note that this conclusion may need to be reconsidered in the light of Case C-334/07 P *Commission v Freistaat Sachsen*, judgment of 11 December 2008.) The Commission argued in the alternative before the CFI that the derogation relating to cultural objectives in Article 87(3)(d) was previously covered by subparagraph (c) of that provision and has simply been more clearly identified by the addition of subparagraph (3)(d). But the CFI held that since the decision relied only on Article 87(3)(d) as its legal base, the Court did not need to consider this alternative argument: para 69. The CFI went on to hold that the Commission had committed a manifest error of assessment in the way it calculated the costs of processing small orders of books and had therefore overestimated

the costs of processing small orders which were actually incurred by CELF and were supposed to be strictly and proportionately offset by the contested aid.

(f) Aid authorised by the Council

15.067 **Block exemptions pursuant to Regulation 994/98: SMEs, training and employment aids.**   The three block exemptions referred to in this paragraph, Regulation 68/2001 (training), Regulation 70/2001 (SMEs) and Regulation 2204/2002 (employment) all expired on 30 June 2008 and have been replaced by the General Block Exemption Regulation; Regulation 800/2008, OJ 2008 L214/3: Vol II, App G18 (the GBER). The GBER was adopted on 7 July 2008 and takes effect as from 29 August 2008 but it applies to individual aid granted before its entry into force, if the aid fulfils all the conditions laid down in the Regulation (Article 44). The GBER also repealed Regulation 1628/2006 (regional aid). As well as substantially increasing the aid intensities and notification ceilings of measures covered by the earlier exemptions, the GBER covers additional aid measures. The categories of aid to which the GBER applies are (a) regional aid; (b) SME investment and employment aid; (c) aid for the creation of enterprises by female entrepreneurs; (d) aid for environmental protection; (e) aid for consultancy in favour of SMEs and SME participation in fairs; (f) aid in the form of risk capital; (g) aid for research, development and innovation; (h) training aid; and (i) aid for disadvantaged or disabled workers. To qualify for exemption the aid must be 'transparent' as defined in Article 5 of the Regulation and must have an 'incentive effect' as defined by Article 8. Article 6 sets the individual notification thresholds for various kinds of aid. Chapter II of the GBER then sets out the criteria for exempting 26 different kinds of aid. The Member State granting the aid is required by the GBER to publish on the internet the full text of any exempted aid measure (Article 9). The text must set out the conditions laid down in national law which ensure that the relevant provisions of the GBER are complied with and must remain accessible on the internet as long as the aid measure concerned is in force. The GBER remains in force until 31 December 2013. Article 44 of the GBER sets out transitional provisions for agreements fulfilling the conditions set in the previous regulations. For general comment see Nyssens, 'The General Block Exemption Regulation (GBER): bigger, simpler and more economic' (2008) 3 EC Competition Policy Newsletter 12. Since the adoption of the GBER, the Commission has issued guidance on criteria for the compatibility analysis of training aid (OJ 2009 C188/1: Vol II, App G22D) and of aid for disadvantaged and disabled workers (OJ 2009 C188/6: Vol II, App G22C).

The State aid general block exemption was adopted by the EEA: OJ 2008 L339/111; EEA Supp No. 79, 18.12.2008, p. 20 Annex 15 State Aid.

Note that the rules that apply to the consideration of an aid which has been notified by a Member State are the rules in force at the date the Commission takes its decision, not as at the date of notification, provided the parties are given an oppor-tunity to comment on the application of any new rules: Case C-334/07 P *Commission v Freistaat Sachsen*, judgment of 11 December 2008, para 49.

(g) Article 86(2)

Individual exemptions for service of general economic interest: Article 15.068
86(2). Article 86(2) EC is now Article 106(2) TFEU. In Case T-442/03 *SIC v Commission* [2008] ECR II-1161, the CFI held that the application of the deroga-tion in Article 86(2) depended on the fulfilment of three conditions: first, the service in question must be a service of general economic interest and clearly defined as such by the Member State; secondly, the undertaking in question must have been explicitly entrusted by the Member State with the provision of that service; thirdly, the application of the competition rules of the Treaty – in this case, the ban on State aid – must obstruct the performance of the particular tasks assigned to the undertaking and the exemption from such rules must not affect the development of trade to an extent that would be contrary to the interests of the Community. There was **no** requirement to the effect that the Member State must have followed a competitive or any tendering procedure for the award of the service. The CFI went on to uphold the power of the Member States to designate the service provided by a public broadcasting undertaking as a service of general economic interest, even though the undertaking broadcast a wide range of pro-grammes and was able to carry on commercial activities, such as the sale of adver-tising space. The CFI further held that the Commission must satisfy itself that there is in place a mechanism for the State to monitor compliance by the under-taking with its public service remit: para 213. On the facts, the CFI found that the Commission had failed to place itself in a position in which it had sufficiently reliable information available to it to determine what public services were actually supplied and what costs were actually incurred in supplying them. In the absence of such information, the CFI held, the Commission was unable to proceed to a meaningful verification of whether the funding under challenge was proportion-ate to the public service costs and was unable to make a valid finding that there had been no overcompensation of the public service costs. The Commission's decision was therefore annulled.

As to the margin of discretion conferred on the Member State in designating an activity as being a service of general economic interest see Cases T-309/04, etc, *TV 2/Danmark v Commission*, judgment of 22 October 2008 (public service broadcasting channel funded partly by licence fee and partly by advertising was such a service).

Fn 369. The Commission has published a Staff Working Document answering frequently asked questions about Decision 2005/842: Vol II, App F8. See also the

Communication on services of general interest adopted on 20 November 2007 (COM(2007) 725): Vol II, App F7.

Fn 371. For further litigation regarding the aid to the Tirrenia Group see Cases T-265/04, etc, *Tirrenia di Navigazione v Commission*, judgment of 4 March 2009 (subsequent Commission decision annulled for inadequate reasoning as regards whether the aid was an existing or a new aid).

5. Supervision under Article 88

Note that Article 88 EC is now Article 108 TFEU

15.069 **Procedures under Article 88 and Regulation 659/1999.** **Fn 372.** Regulation 794/2004 has been amended: see update to paragraph 15.074, below.

(a) Review of existing aids

15.070 **Concept of an existing aid.** In Cases T-265/04, etc, *Tirrenia di Navigazione v Commission*, judgment of 4 March 2009 a Commission decision was annulled for inadequate reasoning as regards whether the aid was an existing or a new aid.

Fn 379. Once a general scheme of aid has been approved, the individual implementing measures do not need to be notified to the Commission, unless the Commission has issued certain reservations to that effect in the approval decision: Case T-20/03 *Kahla/Thüringen Porzellan v Commission*, judgment of 24 September 2008, para 92 (CFI upheld Commission's finding that the disputed aid was not in fact granted pursuant to a previously approved scheme and hence was properly analysed as new aid).

Fn 382. In Cases T-30/01, etc, *Territorio Histórico de Álava – Diputación Foral de Álava v Commission*, judgment of 9 September 2009 the CFI held that the Commission had never explicitly made a decision declaring that the schemes at issue did not constitute State aid schemes when they were put into effect so that the aids were not existing aids within Article 1(b)(v). It was not possible to construe the Commission's silence as a tacit decision that the scheme was not an aid. Further, the CFI held that the concept of 'evolution of the common market' can be understood as a change in the economic and legal framework of the sector concerned by the measure in question, for example as a result of the liberalisation of a market initially closed to competition. That concept does not cover the situation where the Commission alters its appraisal on the basis only of a more rigorous application of the Treaty rules on State aid. The mere finding that there has been an evolution of State aid policy is not in itself sufficient to constitute an 'evolution of the common market' within the meaning of Article (1)(b)(v) of

Regulation 659/1999, provided that the objective concept of State aid, as defined by Article 87 EC [now Article 107 TFEU], is not itself altered.

Review of existing aids. For the position of a complainant where the Commis- **15.071** sion refuses to investigate an alleged existing aid see Case T-152/06 *NDSHT v Commission*, judgment of 9 June 2009.

Existing aids no longer compatible with the common market. On the nature **15.073** of a recommendation which is accepted by the Member State see Case T-354/05 *TF1 v Commission*, judgment of 11 March 2009 where the CFI held that it was an act capable of legal challenge.

(b) Notification of new aids

Pre-notification of new aids. Regulation 794/2004 has been amended by the **15.074** following instruments:

- Regulation 271/2008, OJ 2008 L82/1 making use of certain web electronic applications compulsory for notification of aids and making amendments to the time limits for such notifications; adjusting the interest rate to be used for recovering State aid granted in breach of Article 88(3) [now Article 108(3) TFEU] and amending the Annexes which set out how the aid is to be notified;
- Regulation 1147/2008, OJ 2008 L313/1 amending the form for notification of environmental aids, following the adoption by the Commission of new guidelines on State aid for environmental protection; and
- Regulation 257/2009, OJ 2009 L81/15.

Fn 399. The extension of existing tax advantages enjoyed by municipal and special undertakings to a new class of beneficiaries which have different statutory characteristics constitutes an alteration that is severable from the initial scheme so that the aid granted to the new companies is a new aid and not an existing aid: Case T-189/03 *ASM Brescia SpA v Commission*, judgment of 11 June 2009, para 106. Similarly, see Case T-332/06 *Alcoa Trasformazioni v Commission*, judgment of 25 March 2009 (extension of preferential electricity tariff to cover subsequent years was a new aid not an existing aid: para 132). Further, the CFI held in that case that an earlier decision finding that the tariff as applied between 1996 and 2005 did not constitute aid did not create a legitimate expectation that an extension of the tariff from 2005 to 2010 would be approved: para 108.

Simplified procedure. As part of the reform of State aid regulation, the Com- **15.075A** mission has issued a Notice setting out a simplified procedure under which the Commission intends to examine within an accelerated timeframe certain types of State support measures which only require the Commission to verify that the measure is in accordance with existing rules and practices without exercising any discretionary powers: see Notice on a simplified procedure for treatment of certain types of State aid, OJ 2009 C136/3 (corr. OJ 2009 C157/20): Vol II, App G8C. The categories of measures to which the procedure in principle applies are (i) aid measures falling within the 'standard assessment' sections of existing frameworks or guidelines; (ii) measures corresponding to well-established Commission decision-making practice; and (iii) prolongation or extension of existing schemes. Member States wishing to take advantage of the procedure should provide the Commission with a draft notification form which may include a request to omit certain information. Within a specified timescale, the Commission will inform the Member State whether the simplified procedure is appropriate. The Member State must notify the aid within two months of being informed that the simplified procedure applies. There is no separate form for simplified notification; the ordinary form should be used. If the Commission is satisfied that the notified measure fulfils the criteria for the simplified procedure it will issue a short-form decision after the consultation process is complete. The second plank of the 'simplification package' is the publication of a Code of Best Practice: Vol II, App G8D. The Best Practice Code details how State aids procedures should be carried out in practice, in particular as regards regular pre-notification contact and the response by Member States to requests for information. It will apply to all cases which are not covered by the General Block Exemption Regulation and are not subject to the Notice on the Simplified Procedure. The Code also covers improvements to the procedure for dealing with complaints, including indicative deadlines and better information for complainants.

15.076 **Aids covered by a block exemption.** The block exemptions for aids for training and to SMEs and the block exemption for employment aids have been replaced by the General Block Exemption Regulation; Regulation 800/2008, OJ 2008 L214/3: Vol II, App G18, see update to paragraph 15.067, above.

15.078 **Time limit for review of new aid.** Article 4(1) of the Procedural Regulation, which provides that the Commission must examine a notification 'as soon as it is received', imposes merely an obligation of particular diligence on the Commission. It is therefore not a rule of application *ratione temporis* of the criteria for assessment of the compatibility of notified proposed aid with the common market. The rules that apply to the consideration of the notification are therefore the rules in force at the date the Commission takes its decision, not as at the date of notification, provided the parties are given an opportunity to comment on the application of any new rules: Case C-334/07 P *Commission v Freistaat Sachsen*, judgment of 11 December 2008, para 49.

15.080 **Preliminary examination of a notification.** In Case E-5/07 *Private Barnehagers Landsforbund v EFTA Surveillance Authority*, decn of the EFTA Court 8 February 2008, [2008] 2 CMLR 818, the Court described the notion of 'doubts' which trigger proceedings under the equivalent provisions in the EEA as being an objective notion: 'whether or not doubts exist with regard to the facts, points of law or economic or social assessments requires investigation of both the content of the contested aid scheme and the circumstances under which it was adopted or operated'. It follows from this that judicial review by the Court of the existence of 'doubts' under Article 4(4) in Part II of Protocol 3 SCA will go beyond simple consideration of whether or not there has been a manifest error of assessment by ESA in not initiating a formal investigation procedure.

(c) The formal investigation procedure under Article 88(2)

The operation of the formal investigation procedure. Fn 446. The 18-month **15.083** period is indicative only and a period of 22 months may, in the circumstances of the case, be acceptable: Case C-49/05 P *Ferriere Nord v Commission*, judgment of 8 May 2008, [2008] ECR I-68*, para 51.

Final decision under Article 88(2). In Case C-334/07 P *Commission v Freistaat* **15.085** *Sachsen*, judgment of 11 December 2008, Regulation 70/2001 came into force between the date when the planned aid scheme was notified to the Commission and the date on which the Commission took its decision under Article 88(2) [now Article 108(2) TFEU]. The Commission applied the new rules to the aid, holding that in order to be considered compatible with the common market, that aid must come within the scope of Regulation 70/2001 and not exceed the intensity thresholds laid down therein. The CFI annulled this decision on the basis that a contested decision infringed the principle of non-retroactivity (Case T-357/02). The ECJ overturned the CFI's judgment finding that there was no retrospectivity here. The notification by a Member State of aid or a proposed aid scheme does not give rise to a definitively-established legal situation which requires the Commission to rule on their compatibility with the common market by applying the rules in force at the date on which that notification took place. On the contrary, it is for the Commission to apply the rules in force at the time when it gives its decision, the only rules on the basis of which the lawfulness of the decision it takes in that regard falls to be assessed: para 59.

Conditional positive decisions. In Case T-25/07 *Iride SpA v Commission*, judg- **15.086** ment of 11 February 2009 the CFI applied the principle of *TWD Textilewerke Deggndorf* to a case where the unrecovered aid was not an individual aid granted to the undertaking but aid granted pursuant to an earlier sectoral scheme that had been held to be illegal and hence where there was no Commission order directing that the particular sum be recovered by the Member State from that undertaking. The principle applied where the unlawful aid received earlier was part of a tax exemptions scheme, the exact benefit of which for the recipient undertakings could not, because of the lack of cooperation from the Italian authorities, be determined and specified in the tax exemptions decision. Any other approach would be tantamount to rewarding Member States which, after granting unlawful aid, go on to disregard their duty to cooperate in good faith.

In Case T-301/01 *Alitalia v Commission* [2008] ECR II-1753 the CFI held that Alitalia had locus to challenge the conditions imposed by the Commission for clearing the State aid but the challenge was rejected on the facts.

7. Unlawful Aid and Misuse of Aid

15.092 **Unnotified aid not automatically incompatible with the common market.** As to the point discussed in the last sentence of this paragraph and in fn 483, see now the ECJ's judgments in Case C-199/06 *CELF v SIDE* [2008] ECR I-469, [2008] 2 CMLR 561; and Case C-384/07 *Wienstrom v Bundesminister für Wirtschaft und Arbeit*, judgment of 18 December 2008, discussed in the update to paragraph 15.109, below.

15.094 **Request for information and information injunction.** Fn 492. Even if the Commission is entitled to take a decision on the basis of information available to it, Article 13(1) of the Procedural Regulation does not allow the Commission to impose on a particular undertaking an obligation to repay, even jointly and severally, a fixed part of the amount of the aid declared to be incompatible, where it cannot be established on the facts that the undertaking benefited from the transfer of State resources: Case T-196/02 *MTU Friedrichshafen v Commission* [2007] ECR II-2889 (upheld on appeal Case C-520/07 P, judgment of 17 September 2009).

15.097 **Interrelationship between Article 88(3) and national courts.** See also the guidance given to national courts about enforcing recovery of illegal aid in the Commission notice on the enforcement of State aid law by national courts, OJ 2009 C85/1: Vol II, App G8B, discussed in the update to paragraph 15.111, below.

15.098 **Recovery decision.** Fn 508. For further proceedings regarding the recovery of the aid to Olympic Airways see Case C-369/07 *Commission v Greece (Olympic Airways)*, judgment of 7 July 2009.

15.099 **Recovery where recipient's assets have been sold.** See also Cases T-273 & 297/06 *ISD Polska v Commission*, judgment of 1 July 2009.

15.100 **Interest and tax.** Where the Commission sets a rate of interest for the recovery of a particular aid, that is a decision which can be challenged by any company which is required to reimburse aid increased at that rate of interest: Cases T-273 & 297/06 *ISD Polska v Commission*, judgment of 1 July 2009, para 73.

As to the imposition of compound interest, however, see Case T-369/00 *Département du Loiret v Commission* [2007] ECR II-851 where the CFI found that the imposition of compound interest was the first manifestation of a new and important policy of the Commission, which the Commission had wholly failed to explain. The Commission ought, first, to have indicated that it had decided to capitalise the interest and, secondly, to have justified its approach. That obligation to state reasons was all the greater since, in the light of the time which had elapsed between the grant of the aid and the contested decision, namely 13 years, the imposition of compound interest had had significant financial consequences on the amount of the aid to be recovered. The CFI indicated that the use of a compound rate would only be justified where the beneficiary still retains such an advantage at the date the aid is recovered. On appeal, the ECJ upheld the CFI's ruling on the interest rate but held that the inadequacy of reasoning as regards interest payable did not entitle the CFI to annul the Commission's decision as to the incompatibility of the aid: Case C-295/07 P *Commission v Département du Loiret,,* judgment of 11 December 2008.

The duty of a Member State to seek repayment. The Commission has issued a **15.102** Notice 'Towards an effective implementation of Commission decisions ordering Member States to recover unlawful and incompatible State aid', OJ 2007 C272/4: Vol II, App G8A, to explain the Commission's policy towards the implementation of recovery decisions. The Notice describes the Member States' obligation to recover unlawful and incompatible State aid and the exceptions to that obligation, stressing the duty of loyal cooperation and the importance of informing the Commission of unforeseen or unforeseeable difficulties which arise in executing the recovery decision within the required time limit. It describes how to identify the undertaking from whom aid must be recovered and how to calculate the amount to be recovered. In the final section of the Notice, the Commission sets out the steps that can be taken against a Member State which fails to fulfil these obligations.

Note that Article 260 TFEU which replaces Article 228 EC removes one of the steps that the Commission had to take before seeking a penalty for non-compliance by a Member State with a judgment of the Court of Justice. Under Article 228 EC, the Commission had to issue a reasoned opinion specifying the points on which the Member State had failed to comply and set a deadline for the Member State to comply. Only if the Member State failed to comply with that deadline could the Commission bring an action before the Court seeking a penalty. Under Article 260 TFEU, the Commission may, if it considers the Member State has not complied with the judgment, bring a case before the Court of Justice seeking a penalty, provided that it has given the State the opportunity to submit observations.

On recovery of State aid by a Member State see Case C-369/07 *Commission v Greece (Olympic Airways)*, judgment of 7 July 2009. That case related to a decision by the Commission in December 2002 that certain aids granted by Greece to

Olympic Airways were incompatible with the common market. The Commission subsequently brought infringement proceedings in which the ECJ found that Greece had failed to recover the aid (Case C-415/03 *Commission v Greece* [2005] ECR I-3875). The Commission then brought a further action against Greece alleging that it had failed to comply with the judgment in Case C-415/03 and seeking daily penalties for non-compliance. The ECJ held that the question whether Greece had failed to comply had to be assessed as at the expiry of the time allowed for compliance in a reasoned opinion issued by the Commission after the judgment in Case C-415/03 (para 50). When it came to assessing the penalties to be imposed, Greece argued that the amount of the aid had effectively been set off against damages that had been awarded to Olympic Airways by a Greek court in an unconnected action brought by the airline against the Greek Government. The ECJ held that in principle, so long as it is provided for under the national legal system as a mechanism for extinguishing debts, a set-off operation can constitute an appropriate means by which State aid may be recovered (para 68). The ECJ further held that it was for the Greek Government to prove that the set off had in fact taken place. After examining the relevant documentation provided by Greece, the ECJ found that some, but not all, of the incompatible aid had been duly recovered. As to the amount of the penalty to be imposed, the ECJ held that it had power to impose both a lump sum penalty for non-compliance and a daily penalty payable until full compliance took place (para 143). The ECJ held penalties imposed for non-compliance therefore related only to the parts of the aid that had not been recovered. The ECJ imposed a lump sum penalty of €2 million and a daily penalty of €16,000.

15.103 **Defences open to the Member State: absolute impossibility.** Where the recipient of the aid has gone into liquidation before the Commission adopts its decision requiring the recovery of the aid, restoration of the previous situation and removal of the distortion of competition resulting from aid unlawfully paid may, in principle, be achieved by registration as one of the liabilities of the undertaking in liquidation of an obligation relating to repayment of the aid concerned, except insofar as that aid has benefited another undertaking: see Cases T-81/07, etc, *Jan Rudolf Maas v Commission*, judgment of 1 July 2009, paras 192 *et seq* and the cases there cited.

15.104 **The position of the recipient of the aid.** Note too that the General Block Exemption Regulation, Regulation 800/2008 does not benefit ad hoc aid in favour of an undertaking which is subject to an outstanding recovery order following a previous Commission decision declaring an aid incompatible with the common market or to aid schemes which do not explicitly exclude the payment of individual aid in favour of an undertaking which is subject to such an order.

15.105 **Legitimate expectation as a defence.** In Case C-199/06 *CELF v SIDE* [2008] ECR I-469, [2008] 2 CMLR 561, the ECJ considered a question referred by the

French court as to the application of Article 88(3) [now Article 108(3) TFEU] to the period between the Commission adopting a decision approving an aid, and the annulment of that decision by the CFI. The ECJ noted that this question juxtaposed, on the one hand, the principle that acts of the Community institutions are presumed to be lawful and, on the other, the rule laid down by the first paragraph of Article 231 [now Article 264 TFEU], namely that annulment of a decision leads to the disappearance retroactively of the contested act with regard to all persons. The Court held that although a recipient of unlawfully implemented aid is not precluded from relying on exceptional circumstances on the basis of which it had legitimately assumed the aid to be lawful, where an appeal is brought against the approval decision and that appeal is pending, the recipient 'is not entitled to harbour such assurance so long as the Community court has not delivered a definitive ruling': para 68.

Legitimate expectation: existing aids. See also the discussion of the *Belgian* **15.106** *Coordination Centre* judgment in Case C-519/07 P *Commission v Koninklijke FrieslandCampina NV*, judgment of 17 September 2009. The ECJ overturned the earlier judgment of the CFI (Case T-348/03) and distinguished between undertakings which were already beneficiaries of the scheme now declared incompatible and undertakings who had merely submitted a request for authorisation under the scheme. The latter did not have a legitimate expectation which entitled them to transitional measures.

Right to repayment of unlawfully levied charges. Fn 548. See also Case **15.107** C-333/07 *Société Régie Networks v Direction de contrôle fiscal Rhône-Alpes Bourgogne*, judgment of 22 December 2008 where the ECJ held that the net revenue from the charge on advertising companies was used wholly and exclusively to finance the challenged radio broadcasting aid and therefore had a direct impact on the amount of that aid. However, the French Government had asked the Court, in the event that the Commission's decision approving the aid was declared invalid, to limit the temporal effects of its judgment, so that neither the levying of the charges nor the allocation of the aid would be affected. The ECJ noted that the aid scheme had applied for five years and that a great deal of aid was paid under the scheme, affecting a large number of operators. Secondly, the overriding considerations of legal certainty were capable of justifying the imposition of a limitation on the temporal effects of the invalidity of the decision. The effects of the Court's declaration that the decision was invalid were therefore suspended for a period not exceeding two months from the date of delivery of the judgment if the Commission decided to adopt such a new decision under Article 88(3) EC [now Article 108 TFEU], and for a reasonable further period if the Commission decided to initiate the procedure under Article 88(2). Only undertakings which, prior to the date of delivery of the judgment, brought legal proceedings or made an equivalent complaint regarding the levying of the charge on advertising companies established by the aid in question were excluded from the temporal limitation of the effects of this judgment.

8. Judicial Remedies

(a) National courts

15.109 **New aids (including alterations to existing aids).** In Case C-333/07 *Société Régie Networks v Direction de contrôle fiscal Rhône-Alpes Bourgogne*, judgment of 22 December 2008 the ECJ considered a reference under Article 234 EC [now Article 267 TFEU] from a court before which the applicant was seeking reimbursement of a tax levied to pay for an aid scheme which the Commission had approved. The applicant argued that the Commission's approval decision was inadequately reasoned. The ECJ held that the claim was admissible given that, if the decision were annulled for lack of reasoning, there was a possibility, though not a certainty, that the Commission would in the end find that the aid was incompatible so that the tax levied would have to be reimbursed. The reference under Article 234 was therefore admissible.

As regards the obligations on the national court under the final sentence of Article 88(3) [now Article 108(3) TFEU] when an aid is subsequently found to be compatible with the common market, see Case C-199/06 *CELF v SIDE* [2008] ECR I-469, [2008] 2 CMLR 561; and Case C-384/07 *Wienstrom v Bundesminister für Wirtschaft und Arbeit*, judgment of 18 December 2008. The position now appears to be as follows. The ECJ noted (i) that a positive Commission decision puts an end to the prohibition on putting advance aid into effect; (ii) where planned aid was properly notified to the Commission and was not put into effect prior to that decision, it can be put into effect as from the moment at which the decision is adopted, including, where relevant, in respect of a period predating the decision which is covered by the measure that has been declared compatible; (iii) where aid has been granted to a recipient in disregard of the last sentence of Article 88(3) EC, the national court may be required, upon application by another operator and even after the Commission has adopted a positive decision, to rule on the validity of the implementing measures and the recovery of the financial support granted. In this last situation Community law requires the national court to order the measures 'appropriate effectively to remedy the consequences of the unlawfulness'. However, even in the absence of exceptional circumstances, EU law does not impose an obligation of full recovery of the unlawful aid. EU law does require that the national court order the aid recipient to pay interest in respect of the period of unlawfulness. Within the framework of its domestic law, it may, if appropriate, also order the recovery of the unlawful aid, without prejudice to the Member State's right to re-implement it, subsequently. It may also be required to uphold claims for compensation for damage caused by reason of the unlawful nature of the aid. Therefore, in a situation where the unlawful putting into effect of aid is followed by a positive Commission decision, EU law does not appear to preclude the recipient from, on the one hand, demanding the disbursement of aid payable for the future and, on the other hand, keeping aid received that was granted prior to the positive decision, subject always to the consequences arising from unlawfulness of aid disbursed prematurely. The criterion that determines whether aid can be disbursed to a recipient in relation to a period predating a positive decision, or whether that recipient can keep aid already disbursed is therefore the finding, by the Commission, that the aid is compatible with the common market. In the *CELF v SIDE* case, the ECJ also dealt with a question referred by the French court as to the application of Article 88(3) to the period between the Commission adopting a decision approving an aid, and the annulment of that decision by the CFI. The ECJ noted that the question referred juxtaposed, on the one hand, the principle that acts of the EU institutions are presumed to be lawful and, on the other, the rule laid down by the first paragraph of Article 231 [now Article 264 TFEU], namely that annulment of a decision leads to the disappearance retroactively of the contested act with regard to all persons. The Court held that although a recipient of unlawfully implemented aid is not precluded from relying on exceptional circumstances on the basis of which it had legitimately assumed the aid to be lawful, where an appeal is brought against the approval decision and that appeal is pending, the recipient 'is not entitled to harbour such assurance so long as the Community court has not delivered a definitive ruling': para 68. Note that in the French national proceedings, the Conseil d'État annulled the earlier decision of the Administrative Court which had ordered the recovery of the aid: decn of 19 December 2008 *CELF v Ministre de la culture et de la communication*. The Conseil ordered that further questions be referred to the ECJ concerning first, whether the national judge could stay the proceedings brought for the recovery of the aid until the issue of compatibility of the aid was final; and secondly, whether the fact that the aid had been found by the Commission, on three occasions, to be compatible with the common market could (even though each of those decisions had been annulled by the CFI) constitute exceptional circumstances likely to enable the national judge to limit the obligation to recover the aid. In the meantime the Conseil d'État ordered the French Ministry of Culture to recover the interest on the sums illegally granted to CELF from 1980 including during the periods between the European Commission adopting the decision declaring the aid to be compatible and the annulment of those decisions by the CFI.

Fn 563. Accordingly, as the French Conseil d'État has observed, national courts have to determine whether or not a national decision constitutes a State aid within Article 87(1) [now Article 107(1) TFEU]. See *Chambre de commerce et d'industrie* *de Strasbourg v Brit Air*, judgment of 27 February 2006, upholding the lower courts' decisions that the agreements made by the Strasbourg Chamber of Commerce with Ryanair in connection with the opening of its new Strasbourg-London route constituted State aid since the financial commitments undertaken in favour of Ryanair greatly exceeded the cost of tourist promotion promised by Ryanair, and no private investor would have granted such advantages in view of the limited services offered in return. But cf Case T-196/04 *Ryanair v Commission*, judgment of 17 December 2008, discussed in the update to paragraph 15.013, above.

Fn 568. See, eg *Skyways v Kristianstad Airport* Case No. Ö 916-08, judgment of the Court of Appeal of Skåne and Blekinge, 7 May 2007, where a Swedish airline claimed damages against a publicly owned airport for aid granted to a competitor that had not been notified to the Commission and the Swedish courts granted interim relief prohibiting the application of the relevant agreement. The damages claim was subsequently settled.

15.110 **Enforcement of Commission decisions.**   The risk of inconsistent decisions between national courts and the Community institutions is illustrated by the proceedings concerning the sale of land for construction of a supermarket by the Municipality of Åre in Sweden. The decision by the Municipality to sell the site to a cooperative society selling consumer goods, at a price significantly below a rival bid by a competing, large retailer, was challenged as constituting unlawful State aid that had not been notified to the EU Commission. The first instance administrative court held on the facts that the sale would not involve State aid, but subsequently the EU Commission adopted a decision that the sale was State aid: Case C35/06 (ex NN 37/06) *Konsum Jämtland Ekonomisk Förening*, OJ 2008 L126/3. On that basis, the Sundsvall Administrative Court of Appeal reversed the lower court and annulled the Municipality's decision on the ground that it involved a State aid that had not been notified in breach of Article 88(3) EC [now Article 108(3) TFEU]: Case No. 1715-06 *Andersson v Åre Municipality*, judgment of 9 April 2008. However, the Commission's decision has in turn been appealed to the CFI: Case T-244/08 *Konsum Nord v Commission*, not yet decided.

The Commission has issued a Notice towards an effective implementation of Commission decisions ordering Member States to recover unlawful and incompatible State aid, OJ 2007 C272/4: Vol II, App G8A, to explain the Commission's policy towards the implementation of recovery decisions, see update to paragraph 15.102, above.

15.111 **Notice on cooperation between national courts and the Commission in the State aid field.**   The 1995 Notice referred to in this paragraph has now been replaced by the Commission notice on the enforcement of State aid law by national courts, OJ 2009 C85/1: Vol II, App G8B. The new Notice gives guidance on general issues such as identifying State aids; the 'standstill obligation'; the role of the national court in stopping the payment of illegal aid and in ensuring the recovery of illegal aid and interest. The Notice contains guidance on damages claims by competitors of the beneficiary brought either against the State or against the beneficiary itself. It provides guidance on procedural issues such as standing to bring an action and contains a section on what support the court can request from the Commission in terms of transmission of information or the giving of an opinion on aspects of the State aid rules. As with the earlier Notice, the Commission will publish a summary concerning its cooperation with national courts in its annual Report on Competition Policy. It may also make its opinions and observations available on its website. The Commission has also issued a Notice towards an effective implementation of Commission decisions ordering Member States to recover unlawful and incompatible State aid, OJ 2007 C272/4: Vol II, App G8A, to explain the Commission's policy towards the implementation of recovery decisions. This Notice contains a section concerning litigation before national courts relating to the recovery of aid: see paras 55 *et seq.*

(b) The Community Courts

(i) *Reviewable acts*

Generally. In Case T-152/06 *NDSHT v Commission*, judgment of 9 June 2009   **15.112** the CFI examined in detail the text of a letter sent by a Commission official to the complainant in which the official stated that DG Comp had decided not to pursue the complaint because an initial investigation indicated that the aid challenged was an existing aid. The CFI considered whether it was apparent from the substance of the contested letters that 'they may be deemed to constitute a decision under Article 4 of Reg No 659/1999, whose true addressee is the Member State concerned and which affects the interests of the applicant by bringing about a distinct change in its legal position'. The CFI concluded that they were not, and that there was no reviewable act. Cf Case C-521/06 P *Athinaïki Teckniki v Commission* [2008] ECR I-5829, [2008] 3 CMLR 979 where the ECJ held that a letter in which the Commission informed the complainant that it was closing the file because on the basis of information available there were no grounds to justify an investigation, was in fact a statement by the Commission that the review initiated had not enabled it to establish the existence of State aid within the meaning of Article 87 [now Article 107 TFEU] and it implicitly refused to initiate the formal investigation procedure provided for in Article 88(2) [now Article 108(2) TFEU]. The informal nature of the decision and the fact that it left it open for the complainant to provide more information did not change its nature and it was a reviewable act.

A letter setting out the opinion of the Commission on the proper interpretation of a exemption from the State aid rules contained in the Act of Accession of

10 Member States who joined the EU in 2004 is not a reviewable act: Case T-22/07 *US Steel Košice s.r.o. v Commission*, judgment of 14 May 2009.

A recommendation in relation to an existing aid made by the Commission under Article 18 of the Procedural Regulation and accepted by the Member State is an act capable of legal challenge: Case T-354/05 *TF1 v Commission*, judgment of 11 March 2009.

Fn 581. See also Case T-332/06 *Alcoa Trasformazioni v Commission*, judgment of 25 March 2009, paras 38 *et seq.* In that case the CFI went on to point out that since the classification of a measure as State aid in a decision to initiate the formal investigation procedure is merely provisional, review by the European Courts when such a decision is challenged is limited to ascertaining whether or not the Commission has made a manifest error of assessment in forming the view that it was unable to resolve all the difficulties on that point during its initial examination of the measure concerned. To avoid confusion between the administrative and judicial proceedings, and to preserve the division of powers between the Commission and the Courts, the Courts must avoid giving a final ruling on questions on which the Commission has merely formed a provisional view: para 61.

(ii) Applicants before the Community Courts

15.113 **Actions by the Commission.** See, eg the actions brought by the Commission in respect of Greece's non-compliance with its obligation to recover illegal State aid granted to Olympic Airways: Case C-369/07 *Commission v Greece (Olympic Airways)*, judgment of 7 July 2009.

The Member State cannot challenge the correctness of the Commission's decision as a defence to an action enforcing that decision under Article 226 [now Article 258 TFEU], unless it alleges that the decision was so defective as to be non-existent: Case C-177/06 *Commission v Spain* [2007] ECR I-7689.

15.114 **Actions by Member States and regional bodies.** A Member State can challenge a decision approving an aid if it argues that the measure does not constitute State aid at all: Case T-233/04 *Netherlands v Commission (emission trading scheme)* [2008] ECR II-591. The judgment is on appeal: Case C-279/08, not yet decided.

15.115 **Actions by private parties against decisions prohibiting aid.** Note that the wording of Article 263 TFEU is different from that of Article 230 EC which it replaces. Article 230 EC provided that a third party could challenge a decision 'which, although in the form of a regulation or a decision addressed to another person, is of direct and individual concern to the former'. Article 263 TFEU provides that individuals may institute proceedings against an act which is of direct and individual concern to them and 'against a regulatory act which is of direct concern to them and does not entail implementing measures'. It appears therefore that, as regards regulatory acts which do not entail implementing measures, the test for standing has been relaxed by the removal of the requirement that the act be of individual concern. However, since the term 'regulatory acts' is not defined, it is not clear whether this will affect the issue of standing discussed in this paragraph.

A company mentioned in the Commission's decision as being under an obligation to reimburse the aid in question is individually affected and hence the parent company of that company is also individually affected: Case T-112/97 *Monsanto v Commission* [1999] ECR II-1277, para 58; Cases T-273 & 297/06 *ISD Polska v Commission*, judgment of 1 July 2009, para 43. A company which was not only active in the sector covered by a sectoral aid scheme which has been declared illegal but was also the actual recipient of aid which the Commission has ordered the Member State to recover does have standing to challenge the prohibition decision: Case T-189/03 *ASM Brescia SpA v Commission*, judgment of 11 June 2009, paras 41 and 42; see similarly Case T-445/05 *Associazione italiana del risparmio gestito v Commission*, judgment of 4 March 2009, para 51. In Cases T-254/00, etc, *Hotel Cipriani v Commission*, judgment of 28 November 2008 the CFI reviewed the authorities on the standing of individual recipients of an aid where the scheme had been prohibited, in the context of a scheme allowing reductions in social security contributions. Although the prohibition decision ordered Italy to recover the aid, the Commission argued that it did not know who the beneficiaries of the aid were and hence did not order recovery of the aid from specific undertakings. The CFI agreed that the decision prohibiting the aid could not be regarded as a bundle of individual decisions relating to each individual beneficiary (para 73) but it distinguished *Van Der Koy* on the basis that the decision there did not impose any recovery obligation (para 76). Analysing the ECJ's judgment in *Italy and Sardegna Lines* the CFI concluded that the fact of belonging to a closed class of actual beneficiaries of an aid which the Commission has ordered the Member State to recover, is sufficient to differentiate those beneficiaries from all other persons. It was not necessary for the Commission to have examined the case of the particular individual in the course of its investigation. It was also not necessary to show that the aid scheme would need to be implemented by a series of individual decisions by the Member State. The case is on appeal: Cases C-71/09, 73/09 & 76/09, not yet decided.

If an aid is declared compatible with the common market then a challenge by the recipient (eg to the fact that it was classified as an aid) is inadmissible: Case T-212/00 *Nuove Industrie Molisane v Commission* [2002] ECR II-347, [2003] 1 CMLR 257; and Case T-141/03 *Sniace v Commission* [2005] ECR II-1197, [2006] 2 CMLR 621. But where the Commission finds that an aid is partly compatible and partly incompatible with the common market (without clearly distinguishing between the different elements) the recipient has locus to challenge the whole decision even if it could be said that the decision was, overall, favourable to the applicant: Cases T-309/04, etc, *TV2/Danmark v Commission*, judgment of 22 October 2008, para 72. Further, the CFI found in that case that TV2 had sufficiently demonstrated that the risk of legal proceedings at national level at the date on which TV2 initiated its challenge 'was vested and present' since, far from remaining hypothetical, that risk actually materialised in the form of the legal proceedings brought by Viasat after TV2 lodged its challenge and those proceedings were pending before the national court and had been stayed specifically to await the CFI's judgment. Accordingly, TV2 had sufficient legal interest in bringing an action for annulment of the contested decision in its entirety, even insofar as that decision classified the contested measures as State aid which is partly compatible with the common market.

Note that in Case T-136/05 *EARL Salvat père & fils v Commission* [2007] ECR II-4063 the CFI held that the appellants had standing to challenge those parts of the Commission's decision which prohibit aspects of the aid scheme as incompatible but did not have standing to challenge the part of the decision approving an aspect of the aid scheme.

As to the standing of a trade association to bring an appeal, see Cases T-254/05 & T-375/03 *Fachvereinigung Mineralfaserindustrie v Commission*, judgment of 20 September 2007, [2007] ECR II-124*, where the CFI reviewed the case law and found that the claim was inadmissible. See also Case C-319/07 P *3F v Commission*, judgment of 9 July 2009 (ECJ overturned judgment of the CFI and held that trade union's challenge to the Commission's rejection of a complaint was admissible).

15.116 **Challenge by complainants to refusal to open formal procedure.**   In an appeal to the ECJ against the CFI's judgment in *British Aggregates* the ECJ upheld the finding of admissibility: Case C-487/06 P *British Aggregates Association v Commission*, judgment of 22 December 2008. The ECJ held that an action brought by an association acting in place of one or more of its members who could themselves have brought an admissible action will itself be admissible (para 39). The ECJ rejected the Commission's arguments that in order for a competitor to show that it is individually concerned by a decision approving a general aid scheme it was necessary to show factors such as a significant decline in turnover, appreciable financial losses or a significant reduction in market share following the grant of the aid in question. In this case the aid challenged was specifically designed to have an effect on the structure of the market in question by transferring some of the demand for aggregates from virgin aggregates to alternative products, with the result that that levy was specifically intended to affect the competitive position of undertakings active on the market.

In Case T-289/03 *BUPA v Commission* [2008] ECR II-81 the CFI found first that BUPA had standing to challenge the Commission's refusal to open a formal investigation into the alleged aid under Article 88(2) [now Article 108(2) TFEU] (para 73) and then went on to consider whether BUPA also had standing to challenge the Commission's substantive conclusion that the aid was compatible. The CFI held that it did because its competitive position in the market was substantially affected and it was in fact the only net contributor to the fund which was under challenge. See also Case C-176/06 P *Stadtwerke Schwäbisch Hall v Commission*, judgment of 29 November 2007, [2007] ECR I-170*; Case T-388/02 *Kronoply and Kronotex v Commission*, judgment of 10 December 2008 (applicants failed to establish that they were individually affected for the purpose of challenging the substance of the Commission's decision but did have standing to challenge the failure to open the formal procedure).

In Case E-5/07 *Private Barnehagers Landsforbund v EFTA Surveillance Authority*, decn of the EFTA Court 8 February 2008, [2008] 2 CMLR 818, the EFTA Court held that the test for locus was the same whether the alleged aid concerned was a new or an existing aid: para 64.

In Case C-319/07 P *3F v Commission*, judgment of 9 July 2009 the ECJ, applying the test set out in *Sytraval* and *ARE*, noted that a trade union may be regarded as 'concerned' within the meaning of Article 88(2) EC [now Article 108(2) TFEU] if it shows that its interests or those of its members might be affected by the granting of aid. The trade union must, however, show to the requisite legal standard that the aid is likely to have a real effect on its situation or that of the workers it represents: para 33. The ECJ held that the CFI had been wrong to interpret Case C-67/96 *Albany* [1999] ECR I-5751, [2000] 4 CMLR 446 (which held that Article 81(1) [now Article 101(1) TFEU] does not apply to collective labour agreements: see paragraph 2.034 in the main work) as meaning that the union could not rely on its interest in competing with other unions as the basis for its locus. It cannot be deduced from the fact that an agreement could be excluded, by reason of its nature and purpose and the social policy objectives pursued by it, from the scope of the provisions of Article 81(1) EC that collective negotiations or the parties involved in them are likewise, entirely and automatically, excluded from the Treaty rules on State aid, or that an action for annulment which might be brought by those parties would, almost automatically, be regarded as inadmissible because of their involvement in those negotiations.

The proceedings brought by a complainant may be protracted: see the procedural history recounted in Case T-442/03 *SIC v Commission* [2008] ECR II-1161, paras 6 *et seq*.

Challenge by complainants to decision following formal investigation.   See   **15.117** also Case T-388/03 *Deutsche Post et DHL International v Commission*, judgment of 10 February 2009 where the CFI held that the applicants did not have sufficient standing to challenge the substance of the Commission's decision that the notified measure was not State aid, but that they did have standing to challenge the Commission's decision not to open the formal procedure. The role of the Court's review in such a case was to consider any grounds which are directed at the annulment of the contested decision and, in any event, the initiation by the Commission of the procedure referred to in Article 88(2) EC [now Article 108(2) TFEU]; it is not for the Court of First Instance to rule at that stage on whether aid exists or whether it is compatible with the common market. Only pleas which seek to establish that the examination by the Commission during the pre-liminary examination stage was insufficient or incomplete, may be examined by the Court. These included in this case a plea that the examination carried out by the Commission was insufficient in the light of the criteria laid down in *Altmark*. The Court found that there was a body of objective and consistent evidence – deriving from the excessive length of the preliminary examination procedure, from the documents which reveal the scope and complexity of the examination to be carried out and from the partially incomplete and insufficient content of the contested decision – which shows that the Commission adopted the contested decision in spite of the existence of serious difficulties. The CFI held that there were serious difficulties which should have led the Commission to initiate the procedure referred to in Article 88(2) EC. The case is on appeal Case C-148/09, not yet decided.

In Case C-260/05 P *Sniace v Commission* [2007] ECR I-10005, [2008] 1 CMLR 1035, the ECJ dismissed the appeal from the CFI judgment referred to in fn 621. The ECJ confirmed the *COFAZ* test but said that the CFI was wrong if, in its *Sniace* judgment, it had treated active participation by the applicant in the formal examination procedure as a necessary condition for it to be regarded as individually concerned by the contested decision: para 59. But the CFI had found as a fact that Sniace had failed to show that the decision was likely to harm its legitimate interests by substantially affecting its position on the market and that finding could not be challenged before the ECJ. The appeal was dismissed. See also Case C-525/04 P *Spain v Lenzing* [2007] ECR I-9947, [2008] 1 CMLR 1068 where the ECJ confirmed that it is not sufficient for the challenger simply to show that it competes with the recipient of the aid. But in that case the ECJ noted that the CFI had stressed the distinctiveness of the competitive situation of the viscose fibres market, which was characterised by a very small number of producers and by serious pro-duction overcapacity, the significance of the distortion created by the grant of aid to an undertaking operating in such a market, and the effect of that aid on the prices applied by a competitor. The case was therefore distinguishable from *ARE*.

The stricter test for individual concern set out in *ARE* and *Sniace* was applied by the EFTA Court in Case E-5/07 *Private Barnehagers Landsforbund v EFTA Surveillance Authority*, decn of the EFTA Court 8 February 2008, [2008] 2 CMLR 818 (association of privately run kindergartens did not have locus to challenge a finding that public funding in Norway of municipal kindergartens was not a

State aid). However, the Court went on to hold that the applicant did have locus to challenge the ESA's failure to open a formal investigation.

Fn 621. An appeal against the CFI's ruling on admissibility in Case T-88/01 was dismissed by the ECJ: Case C-260/05 P *Sniace v Commission* [2007] ECR I-10005, [2008] 1 CMLR 1035. The ECJ held that participation in the Commission's formal procedure is not a necessary condition for the finding that a decision is of individual concern. But on the facts, the CFI's decision was upheld.

(iii) The grounds of annulment

Lack of reasoning.   For a robust judgment of the CFI annulling a decision on   **15.120** this ground see Cases T-309/04, etc, *TV2/Danmark v Commission*, judgment of 22 October 2008 where the CFI found that 'the lack of a serious and detailed examination, in the contested decision, of the conditions under which TV2 was financed during the period under investigation is in turn reflected in the peremptory tone of the Commission's assertions in recital 71 of the contested decision'.

In Case C-333/07 *Société Régie Networks v Direction de contrôle fiscal Rhône-Alpes Bourgogne*, judgment of 22 December 2008 the ECJ held (in an Article 267 TFEU reference) that while it would have been preferable for the Commission in the contested decision expressly to have identified which of the categories of exception set out in Article 88(3) [now Article 108(3) TFEU] applied, the contested decision was not unlawful simply on the ground that no specific reasons were given which addressed those points: para 72. In Case T-268/06 *Olympiaki Aeroporia Ypiresies v Commission* [2008] ECR II-1091, part of the Commission's decision, concerning aid granted to an airline for losses incurred in the immediate aftermath of the terrorist attacks of 11 September 2001, was annulled for lack of reasoning. A challenge based on lack of reasoning was rejected by the CFI in Case T-301/01 *Alitalia v Commission* [2008] ECR II-1753.

In Cases T-265/04, etc, *Tirrenia di Navigazione v Commission*, judgment of 4 March 2009 a Commission decision was annulled for inadequate reasoning as regards whether the aid was an existing or a new aid.

Fn 638. The appeal in Cases T-304 & 316/04 was dismissed: Case C-494/06 P *Commission v Italy and WAM*, judgment of 30 April 2009.

Fn 639. In Cases T-50/06, etc, *Ireland v Commission*, judgment of 12 December 2007, [2007] ECR II-172*, the CFI noted that the appellants had raised a total of 23 pleas challenging an approval decision but decided the case on the ground of lack of adequate reasoning which it raised of its own motion. The case is on appeal: Case C-89/08 P, not yet decided.

Fn 640. In Cases C-341 & 342/06 P *Chronopost and La Poste v UFEX* [2008] ECR I-4777, [2008] 3 CMLR 568 the ECJ overturned the CFI's judgment in

Case T-613/97 *UFEX v Commission*, holding that since the contested decision clearly disclosed the Commission's reasoning, enabling the substance of that decision to be challenged subsequently before the competent court, it would be excessive to require a specific statement of reasons for each of the technical choices or each of the figures on which that reasoning is based. Neither the fact that this was the first decision dealing with the complex issue of how to calculate the aid in particular circumstances nor the fact that the Commission's decision was taken after it had withdrawn an earlier decision rejecting the complaint, increased the obligation on the Commission to state reasons.

15.122 **Review of the exercise of the Commission's discretion.** In adopting rules of conduct such as guidelines and notices, and announcing by publishing them that they will henceforth apply to the cases to which they relate, the Commission imposes a limit on the exercise of its discretion inasmuch as the guidelines and notices do not depart from the rules in the Treaty and are accepted by the Member States: see Cases C-75 & 80/05 P *Germany and Glunz v Kronofrance SA* [2008] ECR I-6619, para 61.

In Case C-525/04 P *Spain v Lenzing* [2007] ECR I-9947, [2008] 1 CMLR 1068 the ECJ rejected an argument that the CFI had gone beyond the scope of proper review of the Commission's decision.

In Case T-301/01 *Alitalia v Commission* [2008] ECR II-1753, the CFI noted that the Commission's assessment of whether an investment satisfies the private investor test is a complex economic matter so that judicial review of such a measure was limited.

Fn 653. In Case C-487/06 P *British Aggregates Association v Commission*, judgment of 22 December 2008, the ECJ held that the CFI erred in conducting only a limited review of the Commission's decision that the levy challenged was not a State aid.

Fn 654. In Case T-68/05 *Aker Warnow Werft GmbH, & Kvaerner ASA v Commission*, judgment of 10 March 2009 the CFI annulled the Commission's decision on the ground that there had been a manifest error of assessment.

Fn 659. See also Case T-332/06 *Alcoa Trasformazioni v Commission*, judgment of 25 March 2009 (extension of preferential electricity tariff to cover subsequent years was a new aid not an existing aid) where the CFI stressed that to avoid confusion between the administrative and judicial proceedings, and to preserve the division of powers between the Commission and the European Courts, the Courts must avoid giving a final ruling on questions on which the Commission has merely formed a provisional view: para 61.

15.123 **Infringement of the Treaty or of any rule of law.** Fn 664. See also Case T-332/06 *Alcoa Trasformazioni v Commission*, judgment of 25 March 2009 (extension of preferential electricity tariff to cover subsequent years was a new aid not an existing aid).

9. The Relationship between Articles 87–89 and other Provisions of the Treaty

Article 90.   Article 90 EC is now Article 110 TFEU. In Case C-206/06 *Essent*   **15.135**
Netwerk Noord v Aluminium Delfzijl [2008] ECR I-5497, [2008] 3 CMLR 895
the ECJ held that a levy imposed on suppliers of domestic and imported electricity
could be both contrary to Article 90 EC and a State aid because the levy was used
to benefit domestic producers of electricity: 'A measure carried out by means of a
discriminatory taxation and which is liable at the same time to be considered as
forming part of an aid within the meaning of Article 87 EC, is governed both by
the provisions of Articles 25 EC or 90 EC and by those applicable to State aid':
para 59.

Appendix: Table of National Enforcement Regimes

	National authority(ies)	Maximum financial penalty	Criminal sanctions	Leniency policy	Appeal from national competition authority (NCA)	Status of the NCA decision in subsequent private action	Status of another MS's NCA decision in subsequent private action
Austria	Prosecuting authorities: – Bundeswettbewerbsbehörde (Federal Competition Authority) – Budeskartellanwalt (Federal Cartel Prosecutor) Judicial authority: Kartellgericht (Cartel Court)	10% of annual worldwide turnover	No (except for bid-rigging in procurement proceedings: up to 3 years' imprisonment)	Yes, but not for criminal sanctions	Appeal against Kartellgericht decisions to the Kartellobergericht (Supreme Court)	Kartellgericht decisions probably binding in subsequent court proceedings	Not binding
Belgium	Investigating authorities: Dienst voor de Mededinging/Service de la concurrence (Competition Service)[1] Auditoraat/Auditorat[2] Administrative adjudicating authority: Raad voor de Mededinging / Conseil de la concurrence (Competition Council)	10% of annual turnover on the national market and by way of exports from Belgium	No (except for bid-rigging in public procurement proceedings: up to 6 months' imprisonment)	Yes	1st Instance: Court of Appeal of Brussels 2nd instance: Supreme Court (on points of law only)	Take into account as evidence	Taken into account as evidence

[1] Part of the Federal Public Service Economy, SMEs, Self-employed and Energy.

[2] Guides and organises the investigation, and monitors the implementation of the decisions of the Competition Council of which it is formally a part.

	National authority(ies)	Maximum financial penalty	Criminal sanctions	Leniency policy	Appeal from national competition authority (NCA)	Status of the NCA decision in subsequent private action	Status of another MS's NCA decision in subsequent private action
Bulgaria	Комисия за защита на конкуренцията (Commission on Protection of Competition)	10% of total turnover in the preceding financial year	No	Yes	Supreme Administrative Court	Binding	As yet undetermined
Cyprus	Επιτροπή Προστασίας του Ανταγωνισμού (Commission for the Protection of Competition (CPC))	10% of annual turnover[3]	No (except for continuing to give effect to an agreement or engage in abusive conduct in contravention of a decision by the CPC)	Yes[4]	Cyprus Supreme Court	Binding	No special provision in that regard
Czech Republic	Úřad pro ochranu hospodářské soutěže (Office for the Protection of Competition)	CZK 10 million or 10% of annual net worldwide turnover	Yes: for bid-rigging and anti-competitive agreements: up to 5 years' imprisonment	Yes	1st instance: Regional Court Brno; 2nd instance: Supreme Administrative Court	Binding	Taken into account as evidence

[3] The legislation does not specify whether this is national or worldwide turnover.

[4] At the time of writing, a leniency policy is being drafted and its introduction is expected.

Country	Authority						
Denmark	Konkurrencerådet (Competition Council) decides on major cases and test cases on the basis of submissions from the Konkurrencestyrelsen (Competition Authority). The Konkurrencestyrelsen is responsible for day-to-day management on behalf of the Council	No legal maximum: gravity, duration and annual turnover taken into account	Yes (all sanctions are criminal: fines imposed by Criminal Courts both on undertakings and individuals–no imprisonment)	Yes	1st instance: Competition Appeal Tribunal; 2nd instance: Ordinary courts	Binding	Taken into account as evidence
Estonia	Konkurentsiamet (Competition Board)	Maximum varies according to nature of violation: lesser violations attract civil penalties imposed by Competition Board; more serious violations are criminal. Figures below are for serious violations, ie: infringement of Art 81 (or equivalent); or repeated abuse of dominant position, violation by undertaking with special or exclusive rights or in control of essential facilities, in respect of the same act.	Yes – serious violations are crimes under the Penal Code, for which penalties are imposed by the criminal courts: see previous column. Fines both on undertakings and individuals; up to 3 years' imprisonment for individuals	Yes – under the general rules of criminal procedure	Ordinary courts	Taken into account as evidence	Taken into account as evidence

(Continued)

	National authority(ies)	Maximum financial penalty	Criminal sanctions	Leniency policy	Appeal from national competition authority (NCA)	Status of the NCA decision in subsequent private action	Status of another MS's NCA decision in subsequent private action
		For a legal person: 250 million EEK For an individual: 500 'daily rates' (calculated on the basis of the individual's average daily income)					
Finland	Kilpailuvirasto (Competition Authority): takes decisions on infringement and acts as prosecuting authority for penalties Market Court: judicial authority for penalties	10% of worldwide turnover in the preceding year	No	Yes	(a) Market Court – from decisions of the Kilpailuvirasto (b) Supreme Administrative Court – from decisions of the Market Court	Taken into account as evidence	Taken into account as evidence
France	Autorité de la Concurrence (Competition Authority) And in a residual way, Ministre de l'Economie – Direction Generale de la Concurrence, Consommation et Repression des Fraudes (Minister of Economy – DGCCRF)	10% of highest worldwide turnover (net of tax) in any financial year in which the infringement was carried out, preceding the year in which it was terminated– save that where the undertaking is not a company, maximum penalty of €3 million.	Yes (up to 4 years imprisonment and criminal fines for individuals)	Yes, but in theory not for criminal sanctions	Paris Court of Appeal	Competition Authority decision taken into account as evidence	Taken into account as evidence

Germany	Bundeskartellamt (Federal Cartel Office) and Landeskartellbehörden (State Cartel Offices)	10% of annual worldwide turnover + disgorgement of illicit profits if they exceed the fine; penalties on individuals up to €1 million	No (except for bid-rigging in public tenders: criminal fines on individuals and up to 5 years imprisonment)	Yes, but not for criminal sanctions	1st instance: Court of Appeal Düsseldorf (or the respective Higher Regional Court of Appeal); 2nd instance: Federal Supreme Court	Binding	Binding
Greece	Επιτροπή Ανταγωνισμού (Hellenic Competition Commission)	15% of annual turnover	Yes, where the individual is the undertaking (whether as sole owner or partner) or a representative of the undertaking that committed the infringement (criminal fines up to €150,000; doubled for repeat offence). For cartels: *minimum 6 months'* imprisonment	Yes	1st instance: Athens Administrative Court of Appeals; 2nd instance: Supreme Administrative Court	Persuasive authority	Taken into account as evidence

(Continued)

	National authority(ies)	Maximum financial penalty	Criminal sanctions	Leniency policy	Appeal from national competition authority (NCA)	Status of the NCA decision in subsequent private action	Status of another MS's NCA decision in subsequent private action
Hungary	Gazdasági Versenyhivatal (GVH) (Competition Authority)	10% of annual worldwide turnover	No (except for bid-rigging in public procurement and concession proceedings – up to 5 years' imprisonment for individuals and criminal sanctions on undertakings)	Yes – both for administrative and criminal sanctions	1st instance: Metropolitan Court, Budapest; 2nd instance: Court of Appeal, Budapest	Binding	Taken into account as evidence
Ireland	Prosecuting authorities: – Competition Authority (summary offence) – Director of Public Prosecutions (prosecution on indictment) Judicial authority: every Court in Ireland	€4 million or 10% of annual turnover, whichever is the higher[5]	Yes: all sanctions are criminal. For an individual, up to 5 years' imprisonment	Yes	Ordinary courts	Taken into account as evidence	Taken into account as evidence

[5] Probably refers to the turnover of the legal person subject to penalty and not the group of which it is part.

Italy	Autorità Garante della Concorrenza e del Mercato (Italian Competition Authority)	10% of annual worldwide turnover	No	Yes	First instance: Latium Regional Administrative Tribunal Second instance: Consiglio di Stato (Council of State)	Taken into account as evidence	Persuasive authority
Latvia	Konkurences padome (Competition Council of Latvia)	10% of annual net worldwide turnover	No	Yes	Administrative Courts	Taken into account as evidence	Taken into account as evidence
Lithuania	Lietuvos Respublikos konkurencijos taryba (Competition Council of the Republic of Lithuania)	10% of gross annual worldwide income (ie before tax) in the preceding financial year	No	Yes	1st instance: Vilnius Regional Administrative Court; 2nd instance: Supreme Administrative Court	Taken into account as evidence	Taken into account as evidence
Luxembourg	Prosecuting authority: Inspection de la concurrence (Competition Inspectorate) Administrative adjudicating authority: Conseil de la concurrence (Competition Council)	10% of annual net worldwide turnover	No	Yes	1st instance: Administrative Court; 2nd instance: Administrative Court of Appeal	Taken into account as evidence	Taken into account as evidence

(Continued)

	National authority(ies)	Maximum financial penalty	Criminal sanctions	Leniency policy	Appeal from national competition authority (NCA)	Status of the NCA decision in subsequent private action	Status of another MS's NCA decision in subsequent private action
Malta	1-Ufficċju tal-Kompetizzjoni Ġusta (Office for Fair Competition)	10% of annual turnover on the market affected by the infringement	Yes (all fines are of criminal nature and are imposed by criminal courts)	No	Commission for Fair Trading. Thereafter, no further appeal but judicial review under administrative law	Taken into account as evidence	Taken into account as evidence
Netherlands	Nederlandse Mededingingsautoriteit (NMa) (Netherlands Competition Authority)	€450,000 or 10% of annual worldwide turnover, whichever is the higher	Yes: fines up to €450,000 for the executives of the undertaking which committed the infringement	Yes	Initially an internal administrative review by the NMa and thereafter (or directly with the NMa's consent) appeal to: 1st instance: Rotterdam District Court; 2nd instance: Trade and Industry Appeals Tribunal	Taken into account as evidence	Taken into account as evidence

Norway	Konkurransetilsynet (Competition Authority) – responsible for enforcement and able to impose administrative fines Fornyings, administrasjons- og kirkedepartementet (Ministry of Reform and Church Affairs) – responsible for determining competition policy and priorities for the Competition Authority	10% of annual net worldwide turnover	Yes, but not for abuse of dominance Criminal fines and imprisonment of up to 3 years (or 6 years in 'severely aggravating circumstances')	Yes – both for administrative and criminal sanctions[6]	Ordinary courts, save that a decision ordering the termination of an infringement (but not the imposition of an administrative fine) may be appealed to the Ministry of Reform and Church Affairs	Taken into account as evidence	Taken into account as evidence
Poland	Prezes Urzedu Ochrony Konkurencji i Konsumentow (President of the Office for Competition and Consumer Protection)	10% of annual worldwide turnover	No (except for bid-rigging for public procurement: up to 3 years' imprisonment for individuals and criminal fines for undertakings)	Yes	1st instance: Court for Competition and Consumer Protection (a division of the Warsaw District Court); 2nd instance: Court of Appeal in Warsaw.	Binding	Probably taken into account as evidence

[6] Leniency for individuals from criminal sanctions has not yet been enacted at the time of writing but is the subject of proposed legislation.

(*Continued*)

	National authority(ies)	Maximum financial penalty	Criminal sanctions	Leniency policy	Appeal from national competition authority (NCA)	Status of the NCA decision in subsequent private action	Status of another MS's NCA decision in subsequent private action
Portugal	Autoridade da Concorrência (Competition Authority)	10% of annual turnover[7]	No special criminal offence, except for bid-rigging	Yes, but not for criminal sanctions	Lisbon Court of Commerce	Creates a rebuttable presumption	Taken into account as evidence
Romania	Consiliul Concurentei (Competition Council)	10% of annual worldwide turnover	Yes (criminal fines and up to 4 years' imprisonment)	Yes, but not for criminal sanctions	Court of Appeal Bucharest, Administrative Section	Taken into account as evidence	Taken into account as evidence
Slovak Republic	Protimonopolný úrad Slovenskej republiky (Antimonopoly Office of the Slovak Republic AMO)	10% of annual worldwide turnover	Yes (criminal fines and up to 6 years' imprisonment)	Yes, but not for criminal sanctions	First instance: Council of the AMO Second instance: Judicial review in Regional court in Bratislava (administrative section)	Binding	Probably binding
Slovenia	Urad RS za varstvo konkurence (Competition Protection Office)	Legal persons: up to 10% of annual sales; Individuals: up to €30,000	Yes: for individuals up to 5 years' imprisonment	Yes	Supreme Court for substantive orders and decisions of the CPO; District Court for pecuniary sanctions	Binding	Taken into account as evidence

[7] It is unclear whether this applies to national or worldwide turnover, but to date it has been applied in respect of national turnover.